The Funnies

The Funnies

100 Years of American Comic Strips

Ron Goulart

Adams Publishing
Holbrook, Massachusetts

Published by Adams Media Corporation
260 Center Street, Holbrook, MA 02343

ISBN: 1-55850-539-3

Printed in the United States of America.

J I H G F E D C B A

Library of Congress Cataloging-in-Publication Data
Goulart, Ron. 1933–
The funnies : 100 years of American comic strips / Ron Goulart.
p.   cm.
Includes bibliographical references.
ISBN 1-55850-539-3 (pb)
1. Comic books, strips, etc. —United States—History and criticism. I. Title
PN6725.G634   1995
741.5'0973—dc20   95-21029
CIP

Book design by Janet M. Clesse

This book is available at quantity discounts for bulk purchases.
For information, call 1-800-872-5627.

Contents

Acknowledgments

I am indebted to the following people for providing information, research material, and a limited amount of moral support: Bob Bindig, Bill Blackbeard, Orlando Busino, Gordon Campbell, R. C. Harvey, Stephen L. Harris, Margaret A. Howell, Doug Kendig, Mark Johnson, Amy Lago, Jeffrey Lindenblatt, Jay Maeder, Richard Marschall, Tom Roberts, Rob Stolzer, and Brian Walker.

I am also grateful to the many cartoonists who took the time over the years to talk to me about the funnies.

Chapter 1

Dawn in Hogan's Alley

The people who invented the funnies, like Columbus, had an entirely different objective in mind when they started out. What they originally intended to do was create weekly humor sections for their Sunday editions. Comic supplements, imitating such popular newsstand magazines of the day as *Judge, Puck,* and *Life,* would hopefully lure more newspaper readers. The words "comic" and "funny" as applied to these efforts referred to the content and not the format and the first comic supplements were mixtures of typeset text and panel cartoons. Comic strip layouts, dialogue balloons, and even recurrent characters came a while later. That the Sunday funnies developed at all was the result of the confluence of several technological advances, plus a circulation war between an established New York press lord and an aspiring newspaper mogul from out of the West.

Joseph Pulitzer was a classic example of the self-made man. A Hungarian immigrant, he arrived in America penniless at the age of seventeen. After serving as a very unexceptional, unheroic soldier in the Union Army during the Civil War, the tall, skinny Pulitzer settled in St. Louis. By the time he was in his early thirties, through a combination of pluck and luck and political maneuvering, he was the publisher of the *St. Louis Post-Dispatch.* With a mixture of sensationalism, reform crusading, and hard news,

he made the paper a success. "In three and a half years," reports biographer W. A. Swanberg, "he had built a ruin into a thriving newspaper, the most independent and constructive in town as well as the raciest." When the paper began to slip, Pulitzer looked around for another and in 1883 he moved to Manhattan and bought the moribund *New York World* from the notorious financial robber baron Jay Gould. What Pulitzer had in mind, as Swanberg puts it, "was a newspaper so astonishingly liberal, reformist and newsy that it would charm the workmen and still appeal to a segment of the white-collar class." Using the mixture as before, Pulitzer transformed the failing *World* into a success with a continually growing circulation.

William Randolph Hearst, in contrast to Pulitzer, was a rich man's son and the first newspaper he ran was given to him by his father. Thrown out of Harvard, where he had been the business manager of the *Lampoon,* Hearst took over control of the faltering *San Francisco Examiner* in 1887. He was twenty-four years old. "The *Examiner* was then an imitation of the *New York World,*" observed the far from impartial Ferdinand Lundberg in his book *Imperial Hearst.* "Hearst has never been diffident about appropriating another man's ideas. One of his first innovations was to subscribe to the *World*'s news service, which brought a cosmopolitan note into San Francisco journalism." By imitating Pulitzer, and adding some touches of his own, especially in the area of graphics, Hearst turned the *Examiner* into a prosperous enterprise. He then decided to challenge Pulitzer on his own turf. In 1895 the young publisher journeyed eastward, where he purchased the *New York Morning Journal*, a failing newspaper with, in Lundberg's phrase, "a faintly unsavory reputation." Until the previous year the *Journal* had belonged to Albert Pulitzer, Joseph's brother. He'd sold it for $1,000,000 but Hearst, using money advanced by his supportive mother, got it for just $180,000 from the current owner. He then proceeded to apply all he'd learned in San Francisco to building up the circulation of his newly acquired *Journal*. "Though reckless with money, Hearst bet on what seemed a sure thing by imitating every Pulitzer policy and carrying it a mile or two further," observes Swanberg. "His *Journal* appealed

frankly to the working class, used the simplest language, lured the reader with entertainment, sensationalism and crusades and indulged in self-advertisement so blatant as to make the World seem self-effacing."

Author and editor Roy L. McCardell is one of the many forgotten men in the history of the comics. In the early 1930s, when he was in his sixties, McCardell casually mentioned in his *Who's Who* entry that he was the "originator of newspaper colored comic sections." Back in the June, 1905 issue of *Everybody's Magazine*, he'd put his claim in somewhat more modest terms. His article, titled "Opper, Outcault and Company," is one of the earliest accounts of the beginnings of the funnies and one of the few written by someone who was actually in at the creation. What McCardell said then was, "In 1891, the present writer, then on the *World*'s staff, suggested to Ballard Smith, the managing editor, that as the American public worried mostly about being amused, it might be well to try the effect on them of a comic colored supplement to the Sunday paper; but it was not until three years later that a

The Yellow Kid, *R. F. Outcault. Titled "The Racing Season Opens in Hogan's Alley," it appeared in the* New York World *on Sunday, May 24, 1896.*

color press was produced that would print and 'register' properly—print the different colors in the places where they should be printed."

When the *World* finally got around to trying a comic supplement, toward the end of 1894, McCardell was working at the humor magazine *Puck*. But he was still in touch with people at the newspaper, in particular with Morrill Goddard, who'd recently been put in charge of the Sunday edition. Goddard came from a prestigious old Maine family; his maternal grandfather had been governor of the state. He was expelled from Bowdoin College, but graduated from Dartmouth. A diligent reporter with an affinity for sensationalism, he got himself hired by Ballard Smith while still in his teens. "Goddard had a visual imagination," notes the *Dictionary of American Biography*, "and he had Pulitzer's astute understanding of popular psychology, a subject that he never ceased to explore. Hiring his own staff—itself a departure in Sunday journalism—he furnished them with striking ideas and displayed their wares in layouts that startled his readers: blazing headlines and zinc etchings that sometimes filled entire pages. Circulation soared."

The *World* had acquired a color press early in 1893. The first newspaper color press in America, inspired by one seen in operation in Paris, had been built by Walter Scott & Co. for the *Chicago Inter-Ocean* just the year before. The second, built by R. Hoe & Co., went into the *New York Recorder* plant a few days before Pulitzer's was installed. The *World*'s had been built by Scott. It was Pulitzer's intention to win hordes of new readers by offering them color reproductions of fine paintings as well as colored fashion plates. Goddard felt otherwise. It was "his

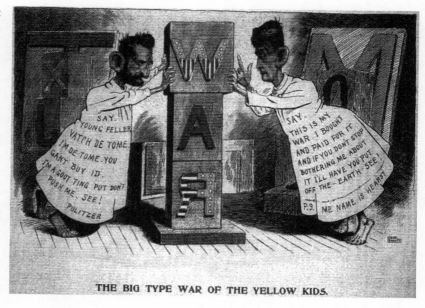

THE BIG TYPE WAR OF THE YELLOW KIDS.

An 1898 caricature from the magazine Vim *by Leon Barritt, showing Hearst and Pulitzer as rival Yellow Kids squabbling over the right to exploit the Spanish American War.*

professional opinion," recalled McCardell, "that American humor, not fashion, ought to have a colored pictorial outlet. He told me ... he intended to try the comic-weekly idea as a Sunday supplement, and asked if I knew of any disengaged artists who could do comic work." The young man McCardell recommended was Richard F. Outcault.

Outcault was a Midwesterner whose interest in drawing led him into a career in commercial art. A protégé of Thomas Edison, he was living in New York and doing technical illustrations for *Electrical World* magazine and freelancing some cartoons to *Life* and *Judge*, when the opportunity with Goddard opened up. Outcault was in his early thirties. Other artists had preceded him on the *World* itself and Walt McDougall had done a large full-color drawing for the paper back in May 1893. But it was Outcault who came up with a continuing series for the comic weekly that led to the establishment of the funnies. On February 17, 1895, he did a small one-panel cartoon for the weekly—which was, keep in mind, still a blend of printed texts, jokes, and humorous drawings. Standing on the sidelines in a group of urchins was a bald little kid—Outcault eventually named him Mickey Dugan—who wore a dirty nightshirt. The artist had used him before in his magazine cartoons, and he now threw him into the *World*. In May came a much larger and more complicated cartoon dealing with tenement kids again and set in a locale called Hogan's Alley. The title of the drawing was *At the Circus in Hogan's Alley*, and it showed a bunch of street kids putting on a ragtag version of a real circus. The urchin in the nightgown was among them. He appeared several more times, taking a more prominent part, over the year. Eventually his garment got colored yellow. He and his tenement colleagues often amused themselves by staging lower-class burlesques of upper-class activities such as dog shows and horse races. Although works such as reporter Jacob Riis' *How the Other Half Lives* had already pointed out the dire conditions of life in the slums of Manhattan, urchins and tenement children—Outcault called them gamins—continued to be used by many humorists and cartoonists, often in burlesques of high-society life.

Although Outcault would probably have preferred to call the panel *Hogan's Alley*, the public took to calling it *The Yellow Kid*. The paper's audience, made up in large part of working class people and immigrants, enjoyed the broad satire and frantic action of the feature and it became enormously popular. By the spring of 1896 Mickey Dugan was appearing every Sunday in the humor supplement, usually in one big crowded and frenetic panel. The Kid began talking directly to the readers, but usually by way of dialogue lettered on the front of his gown.

One of the unanswered questions about the Kid's raiment remains: Why was it yellow? The standard answer for many years had to do with the testing of yellow ink. Stephen Becker's *Comic Art in America* (1959) gave a typical version of the accepted legend. "By 1896 all the kinks had been ironed out of the color press save one: the yellow ink, on which depended greens and oranges, persisted in its refusal to dry properly," he wrote. "It ran and smudged incorrigibly.... The story goes that Charles Saalburgh, foreman of the color-press room, needed an open white space which the presses could print yellow.... Saalburgh chose the nightgown as the test area for his tallow-drying yellow." Like a certain portion of all history, this turns out not to be true. "Why yellow?" writes Richard Marschall in his chapter on Outcault in his *America's Great Comic-Strip Artists*. "It was not because yellow printing inks were drying improperly and a large blank area was needed on which to test a new formula. Comics histories have nurtured this pleasant and convenient canard for years, but in fact newspapers—the *World* certainly included—had been printing beautiful color work since 1893, with yellows bright, attractive, and well behaved." Outcault himself had no notion why the Yellow Kid's outfit was yellow. Writing in a newspaper in 1898, he said, "One day my editors decided to produce a colored supplement with the Sunday edition, and I was directed to make a half-page picture. The scene was Hogan's Alley, which you may remember was the scene of most of the Yellow Kid's adventures. The picture was made and colored. I don't remember who did the coloring—I know I didn't—but whoever it was colored Mickey Dugan's dress yellow, a bright, glaring, golden, gleaming, gorgeous yellow! And that dress has never changed color from that day to this."

Running true to form, Hearst began hiring staff members away from Pulitzer. Early in 1896 he succeeded in luring Goddard and a goodly portion of the Sunday staff over to his newspaper. In the autumn of the year he launched a Sunday *Comic Supplement*. Hearst finally succeeded in getting Outcault, and the Yellow Kid was now the star of the *Journal* humor section. The Sunday *World*, with Arthur Brisbane in charge, continued with a Yellow Kid of their own, now drawn by George Luks. The

Pulitzer-Hearst rivalry continued with both sides touting their Yellow Kids in gaudy rival advertising campaigns.

One of the major side effects of the Kid's impressive popularity was the birth of a whole new industry. That was the merchandising of comic characters, which over the years would make quite a few cartoonists very wealthy and well-known men. The Yellow Kid began to appear on all sorts of products and promotions and also on the stage. In the 1898 article Outcault kidded the whole idea, but he was obviously hugely gratified by all that had happened to him in the few years since he'd abandoned technical illustration. "People called me 'Yellow Kid

Outcault,'" he complained. "Then there came the Yellow Kid buttons, crackers, cigarettes and such things, and I cursed the day they ever came into existence. I wanted to do some other work, but no; nobody seemed to want it, and I finally settled down with a sigh of resignation to draw Yellow Kids all the rest of my days." He estimated that he'd by that time drawn "twenty thousand Yellow Kids, and when the million buttons, the innumerable toys and cigarette boxes and labels and what not are taken into consideration, some idea can be gleaned of how tired I

The Katzenjammer Kids, *Rudolph Dirks. The final panels from a 1907 Sunday page.*

Happy Hooligan, *Frederick B. Opper. Alphonse, Gaston and Maude the Mule join Happy in this panel from a 1907 Sunday.*

am of him." Indeed, Outcault did give up Mickey Dugan that year, but bigger and better things, as we'll see, lay ahead, along with some of the most lucrative merchandising of the twentieth century.

The next major comic feature to emerge after the Yellow Kid originated not with Pulitzer but with Hearst and also dealt with mischievous children. *The Katzenjammer Kids* started in the *Journal* on Sunday, December 12, 1987. Not that much older than his quintessential brats, Rudolph Dirks was just twenty when he went to work for Hearst and editor Rudolph Block. Born in Germany and raised in Chicago, both Rudy and his brother Gus had come to New York to conquer the cartoon markets. Contemplating the tremendous success of little Mickey Dugan, Hearst rightly assumed that the public would go for more of the same. He instructed Block to have Dirks come up with an imitation of his childhood favorites, Max and Moritz. These two

diabolic brats had been invented by the German comic artist Wilhelm Busch for the magazine *Fliegende Blatter* in 1865, and books reprinting their text and illustration escapades were still being printed around the world. And, in fact, the two little rascals, under the names Tootle and Bootle, had begun being reprinted in the British periodical *Comic Cuts* in 1896. When Block suggested Dirks go look up Max and Moritz and come up with something along that line, the young cartoonist replied that he was already familiar with Busch's work and the inventive, sometimes lethal, pranks of Max and Moritz.

Over the next few years, Dirks was one of those who developed the basic comics format. He went from pantomime and typeset captions to pages that involved dialogue balloons, speed lines, clouds of dust, and the other devices that became the standard vocabulary of the funnies. He developed, too, a simple, direct cartoon style, one that fit the direct and fast-moving action he depicted. Outcault was definitely a nineteenth century artist and his work always maintained some of the stiffness and formality of a woodcut or a steel engraving. But Dirks understood that the comics were a new medium and required a new, informal style.

Hans Katzenjammer, the dark-haired one, and his brother Fritz, the blond, were part of a long-established graphic comedy tradition. Yet they also owed quite a bit to the slapstick and dialect humor of the vaudeville stage, especially to such extremely popular teams as Weber & Fields, who affected thick Dutch accents and listed among their sure-fire bits of business poking a man in the eye, kicking him in the backside, and poking two fingers in his eyes. As the immigrant populations, especially in the expanding urban areas, increased, ethnic and racial humor became increasingly popular in America. *The Katzenjammer Kids* was meant not only to make fun of German-Americans but to appeal to them. "In fact, the prime motivator was probably commercial," suggests Marschall. "A German-born cartoonist drawing a feature about Germans reminiscent of a German children's book classic was obviously meant not to lampoon but to attract German readers. Immigrants still composed a large percentage of urban audience and publishers aimed, by simplified dialogue, clearly delineated drawings, and sympathetic character types, to cater to these readers."

Young Dirks worked with a small core of performers at first. There was plump forgiving Mama; the two hyperactive boys and then the Captain, the

Dirks, Opper and Schultze teamed up on the 1902 Sunday page from which this panel is taken. Such jam sessions were fairly common in the early years of the century. Happy and Mama Katzenjammer chastise the Kids while Foxy Grandpa floats and Alphonse and Gaston attempt to decide who should go up the ladder first.

bewhiskered seadog who became not only a perennial houseguest but the kids' favorite and most frequent target; and the short white-bearded Inspector, once a School Inspector, who also became a permanent part of the ménage and the number two foil for Hans and Fritz. The brothers were not above, especially in their younger days, playing violent pranks on each other. As the Captain once observed, while spanking the pair, "One iss just as bad as both der other ones!" Although a spanking or a thrashing was their fate in the final panel of the majority of Katzie pages, corporeal punishment never deterred the boys. They remained inventive and unflagging anarchists, intent on bedeviling and deflating established authority as personified by the Captain, the Inspector, and assorted pompous and self-important types who crossed their path.

Hearst continued to collect people and in 1899 tried a bit of big game hunting. Frederick Burr Opper was already in his early forties and was being referred to as the Dean of American Cartoonists when Hearst offered him the impressive salary of $20,000 a year to come to work for the *Journal*. A Midwesterner originally, Opper had come East in the middle 1870s. At the start of the next decade he was hired by Joseph Keppler to work for *Puck*. He became, as Richard Marschall has pointed out, a specialist in the social cartoon. "With a sympathetic eye," Marschall writes,

"Opper examined the minutiae of everyday life—raising children, meeting bills, keeping servants, catching trains, growing gardens—and he explored the fancies of late Victorian America, such as cigarette smoking, parlor games, and bicycle riding. He continued to draw political and ethnic cartoons, but in the social cartoons he displayed a brilliant talent for observation." By the 1890s, Opper had become *Puck*'s most popular cartoonist. Hearst was interested in him not only for his drawing ability but for his reputation. He would provide the already maligned and criticized comic sections a needed touch of respectability. "Not only the most revered," points out Marschall, "he was perhaps the most dignified of illustrator/cartoonists."

The tramp had a long tradition as a humor stereotype in print and on the stage. The notable British cartoonist Tom Browne had introduced his popular *Weary Willie and Tired Tim* tramp page in the English comic weekly *Illustrated Chips* in 1896. When Opper moved into the funny papers, he chose a hobo for his first regular character. *Happy Hooligan* started in the *New York Journal* on March 11, 1900. Happy, as his first name implied, was a good-natured fellow with the somewhat monkey-like features of the traditional cartoon Irishman. He wore patched, tattered, and mismatched clothes, and for a hat he had an empty tomato can. As Marschall has pointed out, Hooligan was "the essence of the well-intended little guy whose goodness went awry, went unnoticed, and, in fact, invariably went kaflooey." Opper used this simple formula for years. Happy would set out, say, to stop a mean-minded delivery man from beating his mule

and proceed to cause, inadvertently, a train wreck. He'd end up getting whacked by a cop's nightstick and dragged off to jail. The hoosegow was seen frequently in the final panel of the *Happy Hooligan* Sundays, as were the doorways and windows the well-meaning tramp was repeatedly being tossed out of. Opper eventually added other characters, including Happy's brother, Gloomy Gus, and his three tiny can-wearing nephews, who spoke in the sequential style picked up much later by Donald Duck's trio of nephews. Opper's other major creations for Hearst were *Alphonse and Gaston* (1902), a one-note page about two Frenchmen who were so excessively polite—"After you, Alphonse," "Oh, no, after you, my dear Gaston."—as to impede the progress of just about everything they came in contact with, and *And Her Name Was Maud!* (1904), which dealt with white-whiskered farmer Si Slocum and his monumentally stubborn mule. Each week the almost equally stubborn Si would try to coax, cajole, con, or convince Maud with a stick to undertake some simple task. This inevitably resulted in the mule's rearing up her hind legs and kicking the eternally unsuspecting rustic in his broad backside. On some occasions Si would sail several yards and smack into the side of a barn, on others, when

Little Jimmy, *James Swinnerton. The hapless tyke is still being sidetracked in this portion of a 1921 Sunday page.*

Buster Brown, *R. F. Outcault. The resolution panel from a 1906 Sunday.*

Maud was in especially good form, Si would fly over the tree tops for a goodly distance before landing. No one was immune from the mule's powerful hooves and she launched others besides Si.

Despite the primitive and uncomplicated nature of his humor, Opper was important to the codifying of some of the basic comic strip conventions, particularly the speech balloon. "Opper's balloons," points out Marschall, "were more than superfluous accompaniment to visual action. With his strips, readers were just as dependent upon words as pictures; the comic strip had finally become a synthesis of artwork and text."

Jimmy Swinnerton was another important early comic artist, but some of the things he often gets credit for he never actually did. Several books over the years have lauded him for a comic strip titled *Little Bears and Tigers.* What Swinnerton really drew for Hearst's *San Francisco Examiner* in the 1890s was little bears and tykes—meaning little kids—and there was never a comic strip. A native Californian, Swinnerton obtained a job as a staff artist with the

paper in 1892, while still a teenager. The young cartoonist commenced a lifelong friendship with the young publisher and, according to his biographer Harold G. Davidson, "Hearst always considered Swinnerton his personal protégé." During his first years with the *Examiner*, Swinnerton was a sketch artist as well as a cartoonist, covering, in those years before the use of photographs was practicable, murders, parades, trials, ball games, and fires. Eventually his little bears, inspired by the big bear on the California state flag, started showing up in the paper. At first they decorated the weather report box and then branched out into panels and full pages. Swinnerton was also fond of drawing very small kids and, inevitably, the tykes and the bears arranged a merger and took to appearing together. Swinnerton, however, didn't draw any tigers until he went to New York.

He made the move east, at Hearst's request, in 1899. A fan of the little bears, Hearst suggested something similar for the *Journal*. This time Swinnerton used the Tammany Hall symbol of a tiger for his inspiration. Little tigers, humanized and fashionably dressed, began to figure in his Sunday pages. After awhile the cartoonist turned the page over to Mr. Jack, a married, white collar tiger who was something of a womanizer. Some have suggested that the carousing, philandering Swinnerton was being autobiographical with his first important feature. Like his colleague Dirks, he drew in a simple, direct style, avoiding shading, fancy frills, and clutter. He adjusted easily to the comic page format that was developing and by the early years of the new century he had mastered the form. He had the habit of putting quotation marks around the dialogue in his balloons and he continued to do that throughout his long career.

He created a number of other features, including *Mount Ararat, Weary Willis,* and *Mister Batch.* His most successful creation, however, was *Jimmy,* later called *Little Jimmy.* It began in 1904 and was to continue, with interruptions, until 1958. Swinnerton's only serious flaw as a comic artist was his prosaic sense of humor. His *Little Jimmy* was one of the many examples of what have been called one-note comics. It was based on a simple and obvious humorous concept and for years the formula was rarely abandoned. The page began Sunday after Sunday with the hapless little Jimmy Thompson, one of the tiniest tykes in the funnies, innocently starting an errand for his father or mother. He would never arrive at his destination on time and he rarely achieved his goal. Jimmy, a very easily distracted little boy, would be lured into playing ball or going to the beach or watching some event that fascinated his peers. The Thompson family, like the majority of funny paper parents of the period, didn't believe in sparing the rod. Most of the pages ended with the hapless Jimmy getting, or about to get, a sound thrashing from his father. Unlike Hans and Fritz and the other anarchist brats, Jimmy got into trouble inadvertently and rarely tried to play a prank on anyone. He came across as a bland, amiable, and easily swayed tyke. It says something about both Swinnerton and his audience that they found the sight of a small boy being beaten for an unintentional failure to be amusing.

The Fineheimer Twins, *H. H. Knerr. These panels from a 1907 Sunday show why Knerr was later picked to succeed the defecting Dirks.*

Swinnerton's oddest creation of these years was a short-lived half-page devoted to a character named Sam. In the early years of the funnies, a feature's name might vary from week to week and just describe what was happening that day—*And Sam Jes' Roared!*, *The Whole Sam Family!*, *And Sam Laughed!*, etc. Seen only in 1905, its central character was a plump black man whose quest for permanent employment was hampered by his uncontrollable sense of the ridiculous. Sam couldn't help finding the hypocritical social attitudes and customs of his white employers to be amusing. He was also greatly tickled by the appearance of some of the less handsome among them. Sam would struggle valiantly to control his laughter—making stifling sounds like "mp mp mp." But then he'd burst out with a powerful "Wow!" and a hearty "Har! Har!" He would thereafter be tossed out the door, bonked on the noggin with a blunt instrument, or otherwise severed from his position. On one occasion he was even fired by Rudolph Dirks for an outburst of unseemly laughter that followed his spilling a pot of hot coffee over the cartoonist. Racial and ethnic stereotypes, as will become evident, abounded in the early funnies. But, of course, other stereotypes also flourished in the early years, from the prim spinster to the dimwitted country bumpkin. And while Swinnerton did not flatter blacks in his draw-

ings, he did not draw whites as gods and goddesses either. History, by the way, is an account of the way it was and not of the way it should have been. We will, obviously, take note of the various racial, ethnic, and cultural stereotypes and prejudices that were to be found in the comics during their century-long run. But, except in the most flagrant or unusual instances, there won't be any strenuous attempts either to condemn or to explain them away. The cartoonist's art depends on exaggeration and caricature, and in an ideal world, perhaps, it would not be necessary to defend or attack the use of those tools no matter what their target.

The number of Sunday papers in the United States had been steadily increasing in the years after the Civil War. In 1870, according to Frank Luther Mott in *American Journalism*, "less than fifty dailies (about 7 percent of the total) published Sunday editions." By 1890 more than 250 daily newspapers were publishing on Sunday. The circulations of the Sunday editions in the largest cities grew to well over a half-million copies. The price of newsprint had been continually dropping and that made editions of fifty and sixty pages feasible, as did the increasing amount of advertising. Other papers that added Sunday comic supplements included the *New York Herald*, the *Boston Globe*, and the *Chicago Tribune*. And fairly soon, as McCardell pointed out in 1905, the newspapers "realized that their patrons were spectators rather than readers—that is, that they cared little or nothing for humorous writing, however good it might be, but they did care for pictures; so the jokes, verses, and sketches were stricken out, and the comic supplements became what they are now, merely collections of pictures." The major comic supplements were syndicated to other papers and

It becomes a regular blizzard, much to Muffaroo's alarm. "We must get out of this!" cries he.

The Upside-Downs, *Gustave Verbeeck. Two panels in one from a 1904 Sunday.*

the funnies fairly quickly became an accepted, and expected, part of the Sunday paper. From the advent of the Yellow Kid to the turn of the century several hundred new features, many of them extremely ephemeral, appeared. In the first years of the twentieth century, several hundred more arrived to vie for spots in the brightly colored comic supplements. Before the nineteenth century ended, the *World* had tried out several dozen Sunday features, most of which ran only a few times. These included *Lariat Pete* by Daniel McCarthy, *Darktown* by Thomas Worth, *Merry-Go-Rounders* by William Glackens, *The Captain Kidd Kids* by J. B. Lowitz, *Dummydom* by Clarence Rigby, *The Four Comical Coons* by Sydney Griffin, and *Father Goose* by W. W. Denslow.

William Randolph Hearst's most significant accomplishment in the 1890s, in the opinion of many historians was the Spanish-American War.

The Cuban struggle for independence from Spain was taken up by Hearst, who championed American intervention on the rebel side. "His newspaper ... was in the middle of a battle with Joseph Pulitzer's *World*," wrote Philip Knightley in *The First Casualty*, "and war was good circulation-building material. If, of course, America could be involved in the war, then circulation prospects would be even better." The familiar anecdote about the exchange of telegrams between artist Frederic Remington in Cuba and his publisher back home, while untrue, illustrates what Hearst's attitude toward the war was thought to be. "Everything is quiet. There is no trouble here," telegraphed Remington. "There will be no war. I wish to return." Hearst supposedly replied, "Please remain. You furnish pictures. I will furnish war."

Little Nemo, Winsor McCay. Impy and Nemo become giants in this 1907 Sunday.

Pulitzer's *World* was also eager for a war and after the never-explained explosion of the U.S. battleship *Maine* in Havana harbor on February 15, 1898, finally lead to a declaration of war by America in April of the year, both papers, in the words of Lundberg, "were in ecstasy." Edwin Godkin wrote in *The Nation*, "The fomenting of war and the publication of mendacious accounts of war have, in fact, become almost a special function of that portion of the press which is known as 'yellow journals.' The war increases their circulation immensely. They profit enormously by what inflicts sorrow and loss on the rest of the community." The designations "yellow journals" and "yellow journalism" were inspired by the color of Mickey Dugan's nightshirt. The sales wars between Hearst and Pulitzer, symbolized by the existence of two separate Yellow Kids, first inspired the phrases. Soon any and all of the vulgar and mercenary techniques used by both newspapers were labeled "yellow." Some of that

spilled over onto the newborn funnies, and, for critics, these too became a symptom of what was
wrong with crass metropolitan newspapers.

Another frequently maligned popular entertainment medium was born at just about the same time
as the funnies and they grew up side by side, appealing often in their early days to very similar audiences. Movies, initially only a minute or two in
length, began appearing in the middle 1890s. "And
in 1896 [came] large-screen motion-picture projec-
tion," writes Robert Sklar in *Movie-Made America*.
"The movies moved into vaudeville houses and
penny arcades, and within a decade had found a
secure and profitable home in working-class neighborhood storefront theaters. The urban workers,
the immigrants and the poor had discovered a new
medium of entertainment without the aid, and
indeed beneath the notice, of the custodians and
arbiters of middle-class culture." The funnies and
the movies shared similar growing pains in their
developing years. Tom Gunning, in his essay *The
Development of the American Film Comedy*, talks about
how the comic strips of this period, like the comedy
short, moved "away from the satirical caricature
heavily dependent on written captions" and "began
to unfold a successive action over a number of panels." Comic strip artists and movie makers would, as
we'll see, influence each other considerably. And the
early movies and the funnies would inspire similar
criticisms and attacks on moral grounds.

The comics continued to proliferate. The *New
York Herald*, whose comics were a bit more sedate,
tried out over sixty separate features from 1899 to
1905. Their earliest success was another one-note
strip about a pair of indistinguishable boys and
their attempts to play tricks on a plump jolly gentleman who was presumably their grandfather. The
switch in *Foxy Grandpa* was that the target of their
plots and assaults always outfoxed the lads.
Grandpa was unlike the Captain, Little Jimmy's dad,
or countless other vindictive parents and guardians
in the funnies. He always outwitted the boys but the
final punishments were rarely of a physical sort. The

artist was Carl E. Schultze, who signed his work with
the name Bunny and a little drawing of a rabbit.
Schultze's work was simple, direct, and dull and he
preferred typeset captions under his panels to dialogue balloons. Quite popular in its early years, in
spite of its quiet and repetitious nature, *Foxy Grandpa*
was acquired by Hearst and began appearing in his
growing chain of newspapers in 1902.

Richard Outcault, meanwhile, had returned to
the *World*, having abandoned Hearst, the *Journal*,
and *The Yellow Kid* early in 1898. Among the features
he drew while back in the Pulitzer fold were *Kelly's
Kids* and *The Gallus Coon*. "The use of such racist ter-
minology was common at the time," points out
comics historian Kenneth Barker, "and did not
reflect any *unique* racism on Outcault's part." In
January 1900, he moved to the *Herald*. He drew
another black kid page for them, intermittently from
December 1900 to August 1902. It was a half-page
titled *Pore Lil Mose* and consisted of a large block of
hand-lettered text surrounded by four or five drawings. The copy was devoted to either anecdotes told
by Mose or to letters he wrote to his Mammy while
away from his hometown of Cottonville, Georgia,
on a trip to New York City. There were fantasy elements in *Mose*. For one thing, the little boy had the
ability to talk to animals, and he traveled with an
entourage that included a cat, a monkey, a bear
named Billie, and a dog named Tige. Outcault
wrote in dialect—(e.g., "A coon came runnin' into
town one night, all out ob bref.")—and sometimes
went in for verse as well.

On May 4, 1902, Outcault began another page,
one that was to be his most successful feature.
Buster Brown starred not an Irish guttersnipe or a
rural black child, but a comfortably middle-class
white kid. Buster wore a Little Lord Fauntleroy suit
and had long golden hair. His dog, too, was named
Tige (short for Tiger) and his girlfriend was named
Mary Jane. The page was rich in the trappings of
turn-of-the-century gentility, but, as Richard
Marschall has noted, "Mickey Dugan and Buster
Brown were brothers under the skin. Buster was

more than mischievous; he was a congenital prankster.... Buster wrecked his parents' ballroom, terrorized the help, sabotaged dinners, frightened elderly relatives, and reveled in every moment of scheming and execution. So did the public, which took Buster Brown to heart as enthusiastically as they had the Yellow Kid."

On his Buster page, Outcault worked in the now-established comic strip format. The action was enclosed in ruled panels, the dialogue was in balloons, and the action was sequential. Instead of capturing a single moment in Hogan's Alley or recounting one of Lil Mose's excursions with illustrated text, *Buster Brown* showed pranks that took place across a stretch of time. The artist did use a sizable chunk of prose in his final panel each Sunday. There appeared a large sign that Buster had lettered and posted on the wall. It was headed *Resolved* and gave the moral of the day's episode along with the boy's promise to sin no more. The resolution, for example, that followed a chaotic visit to his father's brokerage firm by Buster, Mary Jane, and Tige read, "Resolved that people who go around making social calls in business hours are a big nuisance and shouldn't be surprised when they are kicked out. Children have no right in business which is a blessed thing for them. They'll get to the cares and worries of business soon enough. Oh business *business*, what a lot of trickery is done in thy name. How many so

called Christians excuse their meanness by saying 'Business is business.' There's lots better ways of being good a Christian than going to church—One is being honest and generous in business."

Like Mose before him, Buster possessed the ability to talk to animals, and they could communicate with him. Tige spoke, too, and would give advice to his young master, comment on the action and deliver an aside now and then. Buster's pranks were rarely as violent as those of Hans and Fritz and their disciples and he never went in for dynamite or wildcats. But, like the more inventive Katzenjammer boys, Buster frequently wound up getting spanked. In his middle-class environment, however, it was most often his pretty Gibson girl mother who handed out the punishment. Sometimes Outcault

Hairbreadth Harry, C. W. Kahles. Belinda, Rudolph and a youthful Harry in a panel from a 1908 page.

showed Buster being beaten, in others the thrashing took place off stage. On these occasions, readers would see him being dragged away by his angry mother while he protested, "Ma, have mercy on a little child."

As a property Buster Brown proved even more lucrative than the Yellow Kid. There were stage shows and books, and Buster's image was used to sell clothes, including the "rich, stylish" Buster Brown Suit, candy, bread, postcards, coffee, games, rings, and Christmas cards. The longest lasting licensing enterprise was the Buster Brown Shoe Co. A type of little girls' shoes is still called Mary Janes because of Buster's girlfriend.

Outcault made another move early in 1906, returning to Hearst and taking Buster with him. The *Herald* continued with their own version of *Buster Brown*, drawn by a succession of artists that included William Lawler, Wallace Morgan, and Winsor McCay. There was legal action after Outcault defected and the final court ruling was that, as Marschall puts it, "Outcault could draw Buster's adventures for whomsoever he pleased but could not use the title, which belonged to the *Herald*, and the *Herald* could freely continue *Buster Brown* with a cartoonist of its choosing."

Hairbreadth Harry, C. W. Kahles. Belinda is prettier, Harry is full-grown and blond, Rudolph is much the same rascal in this 1930 sequence.

The perception of people who did not follow the early comic sections was that the funnies were primarily for children. But, as McCardell noted in 1905, using what was already a cliché, they were "read by children of all ages." Still, a great many features had kids as their central characters. After Mrs. Katzenjammer's boys proved so popular, the brat strip, often with a pair of demonic Dutch boys, became a thriving genre of its own. Covering all bets, Gene Carr turned out a page called *Stepbrothers* in which one kid was German and the other Irish.

Harold H. Knerr was a talented and inventive young cartoonist who was especially good at drawing funny animals. The son of a physician, he lived in the Philadelphia area and started doing Sunday pages in 1901. His most successful feature during the century's first decade was *Die Fineheimer Twins*, which was by far the best of the several *Katzenjammer* imitations then flourishing. The Knerr version, drawn for the *Philadelphia Inquirer*, offered a pair of destructive lads named Johann and Jakey who were, except for Dutch boy hairdos, exact twins of Hans and Fritz. Their Ma bore a striking resemblance to Mama Katzenjammer, and Uncle Otto, who resided in the same household, could have doubled for the Captain. In later years—Knerr drew the twins from 1903 to 1914—Otto and Ma changed in appearance, but the boys remained Hans and Fritz simulacra.

H. H. Knerr was an impressively prolific artist. As Knerr authority James Lowe has discovered, "between 1901 and 1914, he turned out more than 1,500 Sunday comic pages spread among a half dozen continuing features and numerous one-shots."

Among his other features were *Mr. George and Wifey*, about a would-be philanderer; *Scary William*, chronicling the one-note adventures of a little boy who was easily frightened by just about everything; and *Zoo-Illogical Snapshots*, which dealt entirely with humanized animals. A more unusual page was *The Irresistible Rag*. This starred a black man, built along the lines of Swinnerton's Sam, who had concocted a little jazz tune that had almost magical power. Whenever he played it on his flute, anyone who heard it could not help starting to dance: "Wee!" exclaimed a plump housewife under the spell of the rag, "I hain't danced fer twenty years!" While his victims were jigging, the piper would slip in and swipe a pie, a couple of fat porkers, or something else that would contribute to his well-being. Knerr gave up all his creations late in 1914 when he was tapped by Hearst to draw the original Katzenjammers.

An assortment of other boys, of varying temperaments and dialects, swarmed over the comic sections in the early years. Among them were C. W. Kahles' *Pretending Percy*, Dink Shannon's *Sammy Small*, Frank Crane's *Muggsy*, and Jack Farr's *Cousin Bill*. Bill was a kid who was visiting his country cousins. Each week they tried to play a prank on him, such as dressing up as bandits to scare him, and each week the resilient city lad got wind of the planned assault in advance and turned the tables. He operated as a sort of miniature Foxy Grandpa. Little girls, too, filled the funnies—brats, angels, and brats who posed as angels. *The Angel Child*, begun in April 1902 by Kate Carew, was about a sweet-seeming blond little girl who was continually plotting and carrying out mischievous schemes. A similar page was *Mama's Angel Child*, which came along a few years later. Drawn in an eccentric art nouveau style by a gentleman named Penny Ross, this one featured a misbehaving little blond girl named Esther. It was a depressing page, since everybody knew what a brat little Esther was. Her peers shunned her. Most parents didn't want anything to do with her either, and even her mother wasn't that fond of her. The young lady who gave

The Explorigator, *Harry Grant Dart. The opening panels from a 1908 Sunday page.*

her name to *Angelic Angelina* had some affinities to the later vamps of silent films and the shady ladies of forties *film noir* movies. She was a brunette of about eleven or twelve, and her specialty was persuading her boy friends to commit acts of mischief that would usually benefit her and leave them taking the entire blame. The artist was Munson Paddock. He drew in a unique style with some Art Nouveau touches and in the 1930s was a contributor to the original material comic books. There were also a number of little girls who truly were angelic, and numbingly cute on top of that. The predominate creator of this sort of thing was Grace Drayton. Born Grace Gebbie, she did her early work under her first husband's name and signed herself Grace Weiderseim. Best remembered today for inventing the Campbell Soup Kids, Drayton drew children who were almost always about five years old, dimpled, encased in baby fat, and given to lisping and baby talk. They were the sort of kids who'd automatically evoke reactions like "Just adorable" from maiden aunts. Among her early comic section entries were *Naughty Toodles*, *Dottie Dimple*, *Dimples*, and *The Turr'ble Tales of Kaptain Kidd*. Her sister

Margaret G. Hays did a feature similar in tone and appearance called *Jennifer and Jack, and the Dog Jap*.

Fantasy features about kids were also frequent. Among the early ones were *The Wish Twins and Aladdin's Lamp* by W. O. Wilson, *Madge the Magician's Daughter* also by Wilson, and *The Terrors of the Tiny Tads* by Gustave Verbeeck. This latter effort was an extremely odd one, even in those experimental and eclectic days. It began in the *Herald* on May 28, 1905 and occupied a half-page. In the first episode readers met the four shaggy haired little boys who made up the Tiny Tads band. Traveling by way of a creature that was part hippopotamus and part car— what Verbeeck calls a Hippopautomobile—they took off for "some far off, magical land." There are those who might feel that a land that could produce a Hippopautomobile was magical enough, but not the quartet of Tads. In the course of a lengthy odyssey, covered by Verbeeck at the rate of six panels per week, they encountered such freaks of nature as the Pianimal, Pantaloonatics, Canniballoons, a Buffalocomotive, a Hotelephant, a Vampirate, and hundreds of other uncannymals. The dark-haired Tiny Tads sometimes shared adventures with four identical little blond girls known as Tots. Verbeek drew all this in a simple, appealing style and used few dialogue balloons. He favored running typeset text beneath his panels and his copy was always in verse— "'And here's my garden,' says the Tot, 'step out and walk with me; We'll pick sweet apricottages that grow upon my tree.'" Though most of the Tads' adventures involved their being pursued or attacked by some bizarre composite creature, they always, sometimes aided by their trusty Hippopautomobile, escaped the terror of the week. They seemed to thrive upon their unusual life style and *The Terrors of the Tiny Tads* lasted into the second decade.

Verbeeck had earlier drawn a feature called *Easy Papa* for the *New York World*. It's been described as "a weak carbon-copy of *Foxy Grandpa*." When he moved to the *Herald* in 1903, it seemed to liberate his imagination. There he created one of the most unusual pages ever done. Its full title was *The Incredible*

Yens Yensen, Yanitor, *R. W. Taylor. A typical conclusion, from a 1908 page.*

Upside-Downs of Little Lady Lovekins and Old Man Muffaroo. Each half page consisted of six panels and after you read your way through them, you turned the paper upside down and found that panels 1–6 had become panels 7–12, continuing that Sunday's adventure in a fantasy world quite a bit like the one that would later be inhabited by the Tiny Tads. Verbeek's two leading characters became each other when rotated 180 degrees. His beard became her hair, her dress became his hat, and so on. Everything else in each panel had to have a double function as well, with little boys turning into old men, birds becoming fish. And, of course, the first panel had to work as the last panel as well, providing both the setup and the payoff. After inventing *Upside-Downs* pages for well over a year, Verbeeck retired Little Lady Lovekins and Old Man Muffaroo. He then occupied himself with the easier challenges required in coming up with new and better monsters each week to pursue his Tiny Tads.

A little fellow who lived a borderline fantasy life was Willie Westinghouse Edison Smith, another creation of Frank Crane. First seen in the *New York Herald* early in the century, Willie was, as his name implies, an inventive lad. He concocted such things

as a mechanical watch dog, an automatic baby carriage pusher, a robot kangaroo, a mechanical monkey, a windcycle, and a snowmobile. Needless to say, Willie's inventions always malfunctioned by the final panel. Crane often included blueprints for Willie's inventions, but no statistics survive as to how many youthful readers actually built their own mechanical kangaroo.

Dreamland became a popular kid hangout during the first decade of the century. The leading authority on the place was an erstwhile sign painter named Winsor McCay. McCay was preoccupied in his strips and pages with dreams and what went on beyond the wall of sleep. McCay spent more time than Freud thinking about dreams and he drew an assortment of early features dealing with dreams, and, more frequently, nightmares. Among his many creations dealing with these topics were *Dream of the Rarebit Fiend*, *Day Dreams*, and *It Was Only A Dream*. His most successful exploration took place in a bright, handsome Sunday page entitled *Little Nemo in Slumberland*, which began in the *Herald* in 1905. In addition to being a dream fantasy, the masterfully drawn and colored page was also an inspired amalgam of psychology, Carollian logic, vaudeville, minstrel show, and science fiction. Although Nemo awakened at the end of each Sunday page, nightshirted again and back in or about his own little bed, a continuity was always maintained and each subsequent segment of a dream began were the last one left off. McCay involved his youthful hero, named perhaps after Jules Verne's adventurous captain, with all sorts of science fantasy elements, including undersea races, space travel, giants, dragons, lost empires, and monsters. Fluctuations in size always fascinated McCay, and Nemo and his nightside cronies were frequently encountering incredible shrinking people, amazing colossal people, and similarly afflicted plants, animals, and buildings. In a memorable 1907 sequence Nemo and his black pal Impy become giants themselves and climb the multistoried buildings of New York City, long before either King Kong or the Empire State Building existed. The year 1910 found Nemo and company undertaking a trip around the universe aboard a very Art Nouveau zeppelin. The journey, which lasted several months, included stops on the Moon and Mars.

McCay's inventiveness and technical capabilities were such that he does not quite fit into his time period. "He was so far ahead of his time that many of his innovations were beyond the abilities of his contemporaries," observes Robert C. Harvey in *The Art of The Funnies*. "What he had discovered and demonstrated... had to be rediscovered decades later by the next generation of cartoonists." In addi-

tion to his exceptional drawing skills, McCay was, as Harvey notes,

> *acutely aware of the sequential art's inherent propensity for timing the action of a narrative. Sometimes he emphasized the progression of events through his panel compositions for several panels running, varying the visuals by changing only his characters' poses slightly from panel to panel in order to indicate the key developments in an emerging fiasco ... or he might indicate the pace of events with a series of panels all exactly the same size and shape.*

Motion pictures, especially in the way they captured time, had an important effect on McCay's work, and he in turn influenced the developing cinema. As one example, McCay drew bumbling policemen in *Nemo* long before the Keystone Cops of the Sennett comedies had thrown a single pie.

McCay's fascination with the sequential presentation of action led him into animation. In fact, he was one of the pioneers of the development of animated cartoons in America. He later said he was inspired by some flip-books his son Robert, the original inspiration for the Little Nemo character,

Dictionary Jacques, *Ed Carey. An excerpt from a 1913 Sunday.*

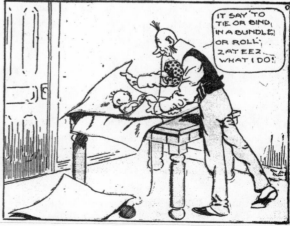

Dimples. *Grace Drayton. The epitome of cuteness, as displayed in a 1917 page.*

showed him. McCay's initial effort was a short, plotless cartoon about Nemo and some of his Slumberland cronies. "He worked for as much as four years on *Little Nemo*, which finally debuted in April 1911," writes Leonard Maltin in *Of Mice and Magic*. "After laboriously animating four thousand drawings, McCay hand-colored the 35mm frames." McCay, an outgoing and gregarious man, appeared with his cartoon in vaudeville houses. In 1914, having abandoned the *Little Nemo* page in order to concentrate on editorial cartoons for the Hearst papers, McCay single-handedly turned out an animated short about Gertie the Dinosaur. He toured with this film, too, and interacted with the screen image of Gertie.

William J. Steinigans, a native New Yorker on the art staff of the *World*, was in his early twenties when he made his initial excursion into the land of dreams. His *The Dream That Made Bill a Better Boy* started in August 1905 and lasted into the spring of 1911. He combined elements of *Little Nemo* and *Rarebit Fiend*, and the experiences Bill had after dozing off would be classified as nightmares. In a typical episode Bill sneaks a smoke on his dad's pipe and that night dreams he's down in Hades being stuffed into a huge pipe and smoked by the Devil. He awakes and swears he'll never do it again. Though drawn in a light cartoon style, Steinigans' feature usually had the moral tone of a didactic nineteenth-century children's book.

George McManus was another enterprising young cartoonist who came to New York, in his case from St. Louis, to earn fame and fortune with his pen. A professional since he was fifteen, McManus was drawing for the *New York World* by the time he was twenty-one. Though he dealt with rowdy and lowlife topics in many of his Sunday pages, he drew with a very delicate line and filled his work with intricate Art Nouveau touches and flourishes. He alternated domestic comedies, such as *The Newlyweds*, with rowdier efforts such as *Panhandle Pete*. Briefly in

the spring and summer of 1906, McManus flirted with fantasy in a page titled *Nibbsy the Newsboy in Funny Fairyland*. This was an ambitiously staged burlesque of *Little Nemo*, with a tough kid who sold the *World* on a street corner as its focal. Unlike McCay's little hero, Nibbsy actually went on visits to McManus' somewhat rough fairyland. He was a reluctant visitor most times: "Cut dat out!" he complained when first transported there, "Dis town's good enough for me!" Most of the characters he encountered were nitwits or worse, such as the bulky Princess Fatissima and the King of Fairyland, whose favorite expression was "Skidoo!" After deserting the fairy realms, McManus returned to domestic situations, reviving his newlywed couple in 1907 and added a baby named Snookums. Married life of a less idyllic sort would soon prove to be his forte.

An unusual and influential funny paper youth was Hairbreadth Harry, one of the many characters created by the prolific Charles W. Kahles. When Harry Hollingsworth first appeared in the comic supplements, syndicated by the *Philadelphia Press*, he was a mere lad in his early teens. Kahles, whose spelling was sometimes deficient, originally called his page *Our Hero's Hairbreath Escapes*. He was soon informed that there was a "d" in there and later Kahles rechristened his feature *Hairbreadth Harry*. What he was doing was parodying Horatio Alger, Jr.'s numerous uplifting books as well as innumerable tales of youthful bravado that appeared in dime novels and, more importantly, in the serials in boys' fiction weeklies. "A wealth of bizarre heroics was Harry's stock-in-trade," notes comics historian Cole Johnson. "Such exploits as capturing wild monsters, stopping burst damns, exploring strange lands, making fortunes, eluding pirates, foiling anarchists, and other acts of derring-do filled this early period." Kahles borrowed the cliffhanging element from the magazine serials and applied it to his strip. That makes him, even though he was kidding, one of the pioneers of suspense continuity in comics.

While *Hairbreadth Harry* also sounds like a movie serial, there were not any motion picture chapter plays until the next decade. Early in the saga, Relentless Rudolph Rassendale stepped into the role of recurring villain. Tophatted, mustached, and always clad in black tie and tails, Rudy was a parody of the villains of stage melodrama, not only of the wicked squire who was perennially about to foreclose the mortgage but also of the rich ne'er-do-well who was intent on ruining the innocent heroine in one way or another. His name is a misspelling of that of the hero of Anthony Hope's popular Ruritanian novel, *The Prisoner of Zenda*. In the autumn of 1907, Belinda Blinks, some ten or so years Harry's senior, entered the page. A plain young woman at the offset, she was described by Kahles as "a ravishing creature of dazzling loveliness." She eventually turned into a pretty blond young woman and Harry, adding at least ten years to his age, turned into a handsome, broad-shouldered young man with wavy blond hair and a strong chin. Belinda remained the love of his life throughout the long run of *Hairbreadth Harry* and was also *the* woman for Rudolph. Many plots revolved around his trying to get her into his clutches and even to the altar.

Kahles, a New Yorker, was one of the most productive cartoonists of his day. In the first decade of the twentieth century, he turned out a score of different features and for several years produced eight separate pages at the same time for an assortment of newspapers and syndicates. His *Sandy Highflyer* was about an aviator who took to the air well over a year before the Wright Brothers. In a 1928 magazine interview, Kahles talked about his early work, saying,

> I went on the World *when I was 20 as a regular assignment artist. One day they wanted a comic and I was the only man in the office. They told me to get to work and start one. So I started* Clarence the Cop.... *In 1906 I heard that the* Philadelphia Press *wanted a comic serial. I was*

then drawing Clarence the Cop, The Teasers, Mr. Butt-in *and* Billy Bounce, *but I was willing to take on another, so I went to Philadelphia and saw the managing editor. Then was born that character which is still alive today, Hairbreadth Harry.*

All sorts of other funnies came into being in these early years. Racial and ethnic pages such as Billy Marriner's *Sambo and His Funny Noises*, about a little black kid who outwitted his white contemporaries with his ability to mimic various sounds, and C. W. Taylor's *Yens Yensen, Yanitor*, which dealt with a lean and hapless Scandinavian custodian who was incapable of doing anything right; and Clarence Rigby's *Ah Sid, the Chinese Kid*, about a trouble-prone Oriental boy. There were adult pranksters to be found in Ed Carey's *Simon Simple* and Norman E. Jennett's *Monkey Shines of Marseleen*. The protagonists in both of these efforts dressed in clown outfits and also had some of the characteristics of the traditional fool. Carey was fond of characters who took things literally and also drew a page called *The Troubles of Dictionary Jaques*, whose hero was a Frenchman who did not quite understand English and relied on his dictionary. When instructed to bundle up the baby, for instance, he looked up bundle and proceeded to wrap the tyke up as a parcel.

The Kin-Der-Kids

Copyright 1906 by Tribune Company

There were other dream strips, such as illustrator Peter Newell's *The Naps of Polly Sleepyhead*. There was a short-lived and beautifully drawn page about a group of boys who travel through space, Harry Grant Dart's *The Explorigator*.

The *Chicago Tribune* introduced a comic supplement of their own in 1906. They hired Lyonel Feininger, an American-born artist living in Germany and well-known for his humorous illustrations in European periodicals, to create a Sunday page for the new section. "The Chicago of that time, and its hinterland, held a large German population, a generally literate group with a strong awareness of the current literature and arts of the homeland, part of which was a proud recognition of the generally acclaimed status of the German humor magazine cartoonists as the world's best," speculates comics historian Bill Blackbeard. "The *Tribune* decided it would be a great stroke of editorial pizzazz to sign up a number of these cartoonists to draw comic art for the *Tribune*'s Sunday paper." Feininger was the major artist hired and he designed a page called *The Kin-Der-Kids*. Drawn in a quirky, angular style and inventively staged and colored, it was a surreal sort of thing built around a world tour undertaken by a bunch of tykes that included Pie-Mouth, Daniel Webster, and Strenuous Teddy. Fascinating to look at but more cryptic than funny, *The Kin-Der-Kids* last-

The Kin-Der-Kids, *Lyonel Feininger. Two imaginative and cryptic panels from a 1906 page.*

ed but twenty-nine weeks. The artist then replaced it with *Wee Willie Winkie's World*, another attractive and not especially comprehensible page. That held on for twenty weeks and then Feininger was gone from the funny papers forever.

One more prolific artist of this period was George Herriman, a young New Orleans-born car-toonist. In this period he drew several Sunday pages, including *Musical Mose*, *Two Jolly Jackies*, *Acrobatic Archie*, *Lariat Pete*, *Major Ozone*, *Bud Smith*, and *Rosy Posy*. Herriman, however, didn't find the true vehicle for his talents until the following decade and we'll consider him again in the next chapter.

Chapter 2

Every Day of the Week

As might be expected, the increasing popularity of the funnies was not met with unanimous enthusiasm throughout the land. The comics had their critics, especially among those who believed that the Sunday supplements were meant for children only. Various persons and groups who took it upon themselves to safeguard the morals of American youth attacked the upstart new medium with increasing vigor in the first decade of this century. There had been criticisms from the start, to be sure, almost before the ink on the Yellow Kid's nightshirt was dry. But it grew worse and multiplied as more and more newspapers added comic supplements to their Sabbath editions. The funnies managed to survive, to attract a larger adult audience, and to become not only a Sunday but a daily reading habit. For quite a while, however, they had to suffer some pretty formidable slings and arrows.

In 1908, the *Herald*, a leading paper in traditionally conservative Boston, decided to drop its comic supplement. In an explanatory editorial, the newspaper stated that the comic section "has had its day." They also explained that the funnies were not funny anymore and "they have become vulgar in design as they are tawdry in color." Furthermore, "many protests come from the public against the continuance of the comic supplements. Parents and teachers object to them. Most discerning persons

throw them aside without inspection, experience having taught them that there is no hope for improvement in these gaudy sheets." An article in the December 1908 issue of *Current Literature* speculated that

> it begins to look as if the death knell ... of the comic supplements had struck. A tide of protest is rising all over the land.... Mothers' meetings have declaimed, and educational conferences had resolved, against them. One lady speaker before the recent American Playgrounds Congress in New York registered her conviction that the comic supplement is "debasing the morals of the children" by emphasizing and apparently condoning "deceit, cunning, and disrespect for gray hairs."

An unsigned piece in the March 6, 1909, issue of *The Outlook* lauded the *Boston Herald*'s decision. It went on to state that the funnies had always been trash, "conceived in vulgarity and born in tawdriness. They never amused an intelligent public." Warming up to the topic, the piece called for a nationwide campaign against comics. "There is probably at present no single influence that is poisoning America at the fountain sources more than the so-called comic supplement," insisted *The Outlook*. "Not long ago a man interested in this subject secured examples of the Sunday supplement from all parts, from Boston to San Francisco, spread them out on the floor of a room, hoping to find in them some reason for their being, and was appalled at the inanity and vulgarity of illustration, text, and color which stamped them from the Atlantic to the Pacific." The magazine regarded "this outrage on children as one of the greatest perils in the life of the country today" and advised its readers to bolt the door "against the intrusion of the comic supplement. No copy of these supplements ought to lie on the table in a decent American home. Every man and woman can register an individual protest in the office of the newspaper which sends this supplement to the house."

A similar campaign was being waged against the burgeoning motion picture industry. While the nickelodeons multiplied, so did the attempts to censor, control, or simply stop the movies. There was, as in the war against the funnies, a class element to all this. "As the Progressive movement began to take form early in the century," observes Robert Sklar in *Movie-Made America*, "it drew much of its energy from the middle classes' discovery that they had lost control over—and even knowledge of—the behavior and values of the lower orders; and the movies became prime targets of their efforts to reformulate and reassert their power." The flickers were also attacked because many of them were, like the comic supplements, irreverent

What gits us is how a feller kin git by with big tortoise shell spectacles an' do-dad mustache. President Coolidge don't have t' milk these days, but he still gits up at 5 a. m.

Abe Martin, *Kin Hubbard. Abe was still loafing and observing in the early 1920s, when this panel appeared.*

and given to broad humor. "If American civilization had been founded on seriousness of purpose, rooted in idealism and committed to achievement," notes film historian Henry Jenkins in commenting on the attitudes of many middle-class citizens, "then a new 'flippancy,' with its mixture of cynicism and immediate gratification, would destroy it.... America had become a laughing nation, a country of frivolists.... Only a return to self-restraint and discipline, only a resurrection of the nineteenth-century comic aesthetic could divert America from its course toward anarchy and immorality."

Despite being denounced and preached against, the movies and the funnies managed to survive and prosper. In both cases a major factor in their continuation had to do with their gaining increasing acceptance among the middle class. The comics did this in various ways, including toning down their lowbrow slapstick tendencies and expanding their emphasis on family life and values. Also important was their moving, albeit slowly, into the daily newspapers. There were well over two thousand daily papers by this time and the weekday audience was almost entirely adult. Comics had appeared sporadically in the dailies almost from the beginning. In 1898, for instance, Richard Outcault had drawn a brief *Yellow Kid* daily series in the *New York Journal* dealing with the Spanish-American War. In the first years of the twentieth century various artists had drawn an occasional daily strip, and one-column panels that mixed a cartoon with typeset copy also showed up. The earliest, and by far the most successful, of this latter type was Kin Hubbard's *Abe Martin*. It started at the end of 1904 and for the first few years ran only in the *Indianapolis News*. Each day Hubbard would draw Martin, a lanky, bearded small town idler and social commentator, in some lazybones pose with a scrap of the town in the background. Abe would offer comments on just about anything: "Women are jest like elephants t' me. I like t'look at 'em, but I wouldn't want one," or, "Some fellers git credit fer bein' conservative when there only stupid." The panel went into syndication in 1910 and many similar ones followed in its wake. Will Rogers didn't do badly delivering comparable material from the stage.

In 1903 Clare Briggs started a daily strip called *A. Piker Clerk* for Hearst's *Chicago American*. Clerk, a chinless fellow with a mustache, was addicted to betting on the races and was "linked to the paddock and the track," as Moses Koenigsberg, editor of the *American* at the time, later explained. It was Koenigsberg's notion that a strip about the paddock and the track would pull in readers. Like many of the pioneering daily strips that followed, *A. Piker Clerk* ran in the sports section and was aimed not at little kids but full-grown men. Unsuccessful, it was dropped in June of the following year after a sporadic run. Koenigsberg would later, by the way, head King Features Syndicate. The name derived from his own since Koenig is the German word for king.

The Newspaper Enterprise Association started syndicating A. D. Condo's *The Outbursts of Everett True* in 1905, but the strip didn't run every day. It usually appeared in a two-column wide format, with its panels stacked one above the other. "A single-minded and direct character, the bald, middle-aged Everett True was incapable of suffering fools," observes *The Encyclopedia of American Comics*. "He couldn't put up with cant, hypocrisy and rudeness, and he lashed out at them with words or, more often, his cane, his rolled-up umbrella or just about any other weapon that came to hand." Despite the fact that he usually had a valid point to make, the thickset dark-coated Everett was pretty much a bully. But, as comics historian Mark Johnson has pointed out, he often would "fight for the underdog. He'd let the office boy go to the ball game, or violently persuade a manager to talk to his striking employees; he'd punch a man that mocks cripples." For all its predictability and adherence to the one-note approach to humor, the strip survived until January 13, 1927.

The Outbursts of Everett True, A. D. Condo. Everett has a Thanksgiving outburst at home in this 1905 panel.

Harry C. Fisher, nicknamed Bud, was an audacious, wisecracking young man with a great deal of confidence in himself and his drawing ability. Never much of a cartoonist, he nevertheless assured his cronies in turn of the century San Francisco that he'd become rich and famous with his pen. A certain percentage of braggarts actually make good on their boasts and Bud Fisher was one of them. He parlayed a crudely drawn strip about another chinless race track devotee into an enormously successful property and was the first man to earn a million dollars as a cartoonist. Fisher was in his early twenties and on the art staff of the *San Francisco Chronicle* when he began doing a strip called originally *A. Mutt*. The strip was one of the first to stretch all the way across

Mutt & Jeff, *Bud Fisher. Part of an early daily, with a race track setting. ©1995, estate of Aedita S. deBeaumont.*

the page, instead of stacking its panels. "I thought I would get a prominent position across the top of the sporting page, which I did, and that pleased my vanity," Fisher later confessed. "I also thought the cartoon would be easy to read in this form. It was." In the beginning he concentrated on following the hapless Augustus Mutt's betting on the ponies. Since the names of real horses were used, many of the track followers who read the new strip assumed Fisher was

Silk Hat Harry, *Tad Dorgan. A 1911 portrait of Harry and a couple of his disreputable cronies.*

passing out tips. That added to the popularity of his work. Fisher soon branched out into other areas, and in March 1908, while Mutt was enjoying a stay in the bughouse, Jeff was introduced. The short half of the team was suffering at that time under the illusion that he was James Jeffries, the heavyweight boxing champion from 1899 to 1905, and that is why he was called Jeff. He and the tall, lean Mutt joined forces soon after and eventually the strip assumed the title *Mutt and Jeff.*

It continued to grow in popularity in the Bay Area, eventually coming to the attention of Hearst. He hired Fisher to draw his strip for the *San Francisco Examiner.* Somewhat shrewder than most of his colleagues, the cocky Fisher had copyrighted his strip early on. *The Chronicle* attempted a rival version, drawn by Russ Westover, but Fisher was soon able to persuade his former bosses to cease and desist. Hearst started syndicating *Mutt and Jeff* around the country, and by the second decade young Fisher's weekly income had risen to $300. In 1913 the enterprising John Wheeler offered Fisher a guarantee of $1,000 per week plus 60 percent of the take. Fisher moved over to what would become the Bell Syndicate. During the legal squabbling that followed, Hearst contemplated a rival version and assigned the task to Ed Mack from the *Journal* bullpen. Fisher eventually established his right to draw *Mutt and Jeff* for whomever he pleased and not to be bothered by imitations. But he did not forget Eddie Mack and eventually hired him to be the ghost artist for the *Mutt and Jeff* feature. Long too busy to draw his own strip, what with his activities as a man about town, companion of chorus girls, and owner of race horses, Fisher had been farming out the work to ghosts. The chief ones were Ken Kling, followed by Mack in the twenties and Al Smith from the early thirties onward. Each man in turn improved the looks of the strip.

Fisher used continuity in the strip sometimes, but made sure there was a joke each day. He relied on all sorts of ethnic and racial stereotypes and even made fun of the Bolshevik movement. Gradually his strip and the Sunday page that was added in the summer of 1918 became a major source of recycled vaudeville jokes. Since neither partner had a fixed job, they could turn up working at an assortment of occupations, ranging from office work to peddling on the street. Jeff in particular often found employment in a restaurant and in the course of its long life *Mutt and Jeff* made use of every variation of the classic "Waiter, there's a fly in my soup" joke known to man. There was considerable merchandising of the Fisher characters; reprint books and toys added to his income. In 1915 Fisher went into partnership with an animator named Charles Bowers, forming

an outfit called Celebrated Players to turn out short *Mutt and Jeff* movie cartoons. By 1917 the studio name had been changed to the Bud Fisher Films Corporation and they were turning out fifty-some short animated cartoons per year. In full page trade ads ran the promise that "Bud Fisher places his reputation and personal guarantee behind every transaction." Never one for modesty, Fisher, who rarely even set foot in the animation studio, took full credit in interviews for coming up with all the scenarios and even hinted that he did most of the drawing. "In 1921 the Bud Fisher Films Corporation and Bud Fisher's Mutt and Jeff Cartoon Corporation were both dissolved, apparent victims of the cartoonist's extravagant spending," reports Donald Crafton in *Before Mickey*. "When Fisher's lawyers were going over the books, they discovered that Bowers had been padding the payroll."

George Herriman was working for Hearst's *Los Angeles Examiner* in 1907. Early in December of the year he introduced a race track daily to the sporting section. Titled *Mr. Proones, the Plunger*, it ran intermittently and was last seen on the day after Christmas. As Bill Blackbeard has noted, there is a "striking similarity between Herriman's bald, rotund, heavily-mustached top-hated Proones and

The Dingbat Family, George Herriman. The Dingbats upstairs, Krazy and Ignatz downstairs. ©1913, International News Service.

*Dauntless Durham of the U.S.A., Harry Hershfield.
All three members of the triangle in this sample.*

Fisher's later Little Jeff. They are simply ringers for one another." Herriman, who'd been a newspaper cartoonist since early in the century, now began turning some of his attention to the daily strip format. His next regular effort was *Baron Mooch*, about a rather Dickensian freeloader. That one lasted a little over two months at the end of 1909. Among his other short-lived weekday efforts were *Mary's Home From College*, a middle-class family strip that lasted only four days, and *Gooseberry Sprig*, a strip populated by humanized birds. Sprig was a duck about town and the feature, though nowhere near as raucous and slangy, was probably inspired by Tad Dorgan's earlier daily *Silk Hat Harry*, which was populated by disreputable dogs in human garb.

In the spring of 1910 Herriman, then approaching thirty, made what was to prove an important move. At Hearst's invitation, he went to New York to work in the art bullpen of the *Evening Journal*. He'd been doing sports cartoons as well as strips out West and he continued to do both once established in Manhattan. His colleagues at the *Journal* included Winsor McCay, Swinnerton, Opper, Tom McNamara, and Tad Dorgan. A lanky, cynical man, Dorgan had made the journey eastward from California in 1904. He became a good friend of

Sherlocko the Monk, Gus Mager. This 1911 strip was entitled "The Strange Case of the Battered Clock" and costarred Groucho.

Herriman's and was responsible for introducing him to New York saloon life and often led the newcomer astray in other ways. The best known sports cartoonist in America, Thomas Aloysius Dorgan had lost most of the fingers of his right hand in a boyhood accident in San Francisco and taught himself to draw with his left. He was a clear-eyed observer of not only the sports scene but of American life in general. Through his strips and panels Tad coined or popularized an enormous amount of slang. Tad was especially good at spotting fakes and frauds and many of the standard phrases for them—windbag, four-flusher, drugstore cowboy—were invented and applied by him. To be a

friend of his, as Herriman was, meant you were not any of the above.

Herriman started a new daily comic strip for the *Journal* and other Hearst papers in June 1910. It was initially titled *The Dingbat Family* and dealt with a mid-

S'Matter, Pop?, *C. M. Payne. The strip was actually using the alternate title* Say Pop *during this Hearst stint.* ©1920, *King Features Syndicate.*

dle-class family that consisted of E. Pluribus Dingbat, a short, mustached man who worked in an office, and his plump wife, college-age daughter, young son, and baby. There was also, from the first day, a scraggly black cat who wore a ribbon around her/his neck. The feline was addressed as "Kat" by the family dog on the strip's second day. A similar cat had popped up occasionally in some of Herriman's earlier efforts. Although his new strip could have become one of the first to chronicle the funny side of everyday middle-class family life, Herriman was simply not the man for anything so tame. Early in the strip's life, for instance, he took to drawing a secondary narrative along the bottom. This involved the interactions between a belligerent little mouse and the cat. On one memorable day, July 26th, acting against stereotype, the feisty rodent tossed a small rock and conked the cat with it. Conversations and similar acts of aggression continued over the ensuing weeks. In the main storyline, the Dingbats had become obsessed with the people living in the flat above them. On August 1 the title was changed to *The Family Upstairs*. This second family was never seen, but they managed to perpetrate an indignity against the Dingbats six days a week. They frequently played loud music, they had plumbing problems that flooded the Dingbat apartment, they did much more bizarre things such as inviting in a small elephant that was apparently learning to tap dance. E. Pluribus and his wife could never get the better of their upstairs neighbors, nor could they, no matter how they contrived, even get a look at them. With the thirty-third episode, Herriman started ruling off the bottom section and giving the cat and mouse a tiny strip of

their own. The very first began with the legend *And This Another Romance Tells*. Now and then the cat and mouse saga would take over the main section of the strip and the Dingbats would occupy the cramped lower space. Herriman was soon adding other animals and birds, including Gooseberry Sprig. Fairly soon the mouse developed his full maverick nature and was christened "Ignatz." The cat had become "Krazy Kat" even earlier, acquiring the name from the phrase the mouse used to describe her behavior and outlook on life. Judging by the occasional references to reader response that Herriman interpolated, the public liked Ignatz and Krazy, even in minute form. At the end of 1911, due to the apartment's being torn down, *The Family Upstairs* concluded. The strip again became *The Dingbat Family*. In October 1913, *Krazy Kat* severed its connection to become a daily on its own. The later career of the Herriman menagerie will be considered up ahead.

Born in Iowa of Jewish immigrant parents, Harry Hershfield became a full-time cartoonist for the *Chicago Daily News* in 1899 while he was still in his teens. After working on the *Chronicle* in San Francisco, he switched to the *New York Journal* in 1909. One of the great raconteurs of the first half of the century and a man with an immense drive toward self-promotion, Hershfield was not popular with all of his New York colleagues. Tad, for instance, disliked him and he brought out an unpleasant streak of anti-Semitism in the sometimes far from amiable cartoonist. Hershfield drew in a much-noodled and shaded style that was long on intensity if lacking in technical skill. An obsession of his was Kahles's *Hairbreadth Harry*, and in 1910 he started drawing a daily strip called *Desperate Desmond* for Hearst. His alliterative villain was very similar to Kahles's Relentless Rudolph and his hero, Claude Eclair, except for dark hair, could have passed for a close kin of Harry. Both villain and hero were enamored of the blond heroine Rosamond. Like Kahles, Hershfield parodied melodramas and worked up impossible cliffhangers in his continuities. Text was as important as art to him, and his dailies were rich with copy. He converted the strip to

Dauntless Durham of the U.S.A. in 1912. His new hero was, as one historian puts it, "a handsome, pipe-smoking combination of Sherlock Holmes, Nick Carter and Frank Merriwell." The imperiled heroine was now a lady named Katrina, but Desmond continued as the desperate villain of the piece. Temporarily tiring of mock heroics, Hershfield turned to his roots and in 1914 created *Abie the Agent*. This was the first newspaper strip to treat Jewish life in a humorous but sympathetic way.

Gus Mager (pronounced maw-grrr) was a New Jersey boy who went to work for Hearst early in the century. He contributed various gag panels, often about animals, and in 1904 he commenced doing a daily strip about monkeys who dressed like and acted like humans. Mager, who drew somewhat in the manner of his friend Rudy Dirks, had the habit of naming his characters after their primary characteristic and the strip sported such titles as *Tightwaddo, the Monk*, *Knocko, the Monk*, and *Groucho, the Monk*. Mager's monks gradually morphed into humans as the strip progressed. In 1910 he started a new strip devoted to human characters and starring Sherlocko the Monk and Dr. Watso. This was a burlesque of Arthur Conan Doyle's immensely popular sleuth, but unlike most other spoofs of Sherlock Holmes its detective was a clever fellow who always solved his cases. There was a new case each day and they ran under such titles as *The Mystery of the Purloined Pants*, *The Strange Episode of the Horse That Didn't Come Back*, and *The Mystery of the Stolen Park Bench*. Sherlocko's recurring clientele included many of Mager's

Dolby's Double, *Ed Carey. This three-tier format was common in 1909, when the strip appeared.*

favorite monks, now in human form, among them Tightwaddo, Groucho, and Coldfeeto. It was Mager's manner of concocting names that led to the first names of the Marx Brothers, who were fans of his.

An earlier and short-lived daily that parodied Sherlock Holmes was H. A. MacGill's *Padlock Bones, the Dead Sure Detective*. MacGill fared better with *The Hall-Room Boys*, begun in 1906 for the Hearst papers. This stiffly drawn daily concerned the life and times of Percy and Ferdie, two opportunistic fellows who shared a boarding house room. Among other early dailies were *Mr. E. Z. Mark*, a one-note strip drawn in a grotesque and unappealing style by F. M. Howarth; *Mr. Jack* by Swinnerton and *S'Matter, Pop?*, a middle-class family comedy begun in 1910 by C. M. Payne. In 1908 Sidney Smith, destined to be one of the most successful cartoonists in America, introduced an animal strip called *Buck Nix* and starring a humanized goat. Appearing on the sports page of the *Chicago Examiner* and other papers, it was an eccentric parody of melodramas. There was breathless continuity, and Smith frequently ended a strip with such queries as "Who is this old man of mystery? What will tomorrow bring??"

A variety of other dailies showed up in the first decade, often appearing alone on a page of news. Some ran every day, some only every few days. In 1909 the prolific and ubiquitous Ed Carey drew *The Adventures of a Bad Half Dollar*, which followed a coin as it traveled from hand to hand. He alternated that with *Dolby's Double*, an odd urban strip about the tribulations brought into the life of a plump, pompous business man by his prankish exact double. Pop Momand's *Pazaza* was another one-note strip that showed the effects of a super

Foolish Questions, *Rube Goldberg. This was designated question #2719.*

patent elixir on the lives of assorted folks. Clarence Rigby did *Book Taught Bilkins*, dealing with a trouble-prone head-of-household. Munson Paddock's *Wisdom of Wiseheimer* had as its central character a fellow who was gifted at working out self-benefiting schemes, and his *Little Mrs. Thoughtful* concentrated on a pretty young wife who was an expert at getting her way with her stodgy businessman husband. These strips, and many like them, were either too narrow in scope or too scattered in focus to attract lasting audiences.

A native Californian, Rube Goldberg attended the University of California and worked on its humor magazine, *The Pelican*. Instead of pursuing a career as a mining engineer, which his wealthy father intended, Goldberg went to work as a cartoonist. Starting in 1904, he drew for a succession of San Francisco papers as both a sports and general cartoonist. In 1907, at age twenty-three, he headed for New York and obtained a position with the *Evening Mail*. In a corner of his sports cartoon, he introduced a panel he called *Foolish Questions*. The very first one, as Goldberg explained years later, "showed a man who had fallen from the top of the Flatiron Building, at that time the best-known skyscraper in New York, and saying to the goofy one who asks if he's hurt, 'No, you idiot. I jump off this building every day to limber up for business.'" The feature became popular, soon appearing in a panel of its own. Another early panel was *Mike and Ike, They Look Alike*. This was a somewhat surreal feature about the two short, bewhiskered twins of the title. Each day they appeared in unusual settings and told jokes or riddles. Mike: "What is the one thing that inspires a young man to go forth into the world and battle with the great problems of life?" Ike: "An alarm clock." Goldberg drew a strip involving puns and that one was called *I'm The Guy*. The pay-off line would involve a play on words, such as "I'm the guy who put the end in endurance" and "I'm the guy who put the bard in bombardment." Goldberg also drew a daily strip that consisted of several odd-size panels in which he commented on various social foibles. Its title was *Lunatics I Have Met*. A few years later, Goldberg started drawing strips devoted to the intricate inventions for doing simple tasks that put the phrase "Rube Goldberg invention" into many dictionaries. It still shows up regularly in editorials and op-ed pieces, often in reference to some governmental circumlocution.

Daily strips continued to spread as the second decade of the century got under way. For a time a newspaper would only have a single strip and then perhaps two, but not necessarily on the same page. From 1912 onward, following the lead of Hearst's *New York Evening Journal*, an increasing number of papers introduced a full page of daily black and white strips. "Initially made up of four daily strips," notes Bill Blackbeard, "the Hearst page expanded to five, then six, and finally nine daily strips through the teens and twenties."

The syndication of newspaper features began in America long before there were any funnies. In fact, Frank Luther Mott has pointed out that syndication began while the United States was still a colony of England. In Mott's opinion, "the 'Journal of Occurrences,' which was edited by Boston patriots for distribution throughout the colonies and in England ... constitutes the first syndicated 'column' in the history of American journalism. Its purpose was propaganda, but it was definitely a news feature." Something closer to a modern syndicate was put together by Ansel N. Kellogg, a Wisconsin news-

Mike & Ike, *Rube Goldberg*.

paper publisher, during the Civil War. As Robert C. Harvey notes, Kellogg began "supplying small town newspaper editors with newsprint already printed on one side with 'evergreen' material (feature stories and illustrations that were time-less, without topical or local reference). Country editors who bought the service then printed local news and advertising on the blank sides of the sheets."

S. S. McClure, whose *McClure's* magazine would be the chief muckraking journal of the next century, began a syndicate in the 1880s. It provided fiction by such eminent authors as Rudyard Kipling, Arthur Conan Doyle, H. Rider Haggard, and Robert Louis Stevenson as well as humor from the likes of Bill Nye. Irving Bacheller, a noted novelist of the day, founded the New York Press Syndicate in 1892 and also offered prestigious authors to large city newspapers. Beginning in 1895, Hearst started several syndicates to distribute material that originated in his papers. The rival *New York World* began in 1898 to syndicate its features, including the colored Sunday funny paper sections, and by 1905 was a large, thriving operation. The *New York Herald* also established a syndicate that eventually sold *Little Nemo* and other strips and pages. "Other metropolitan papers in New York, Philadelphia, Chicago, Boston, San Francisco and St. Louis did the same over the next ten years," notes Harvey. Syndicates that were independent of newspaper chains also grew up, including the George Matthew Adams Syndicate and the McNaught Syndicate. The World Color Printing Company of St. Louis syndicated a complete colored Sunday comic section to rural newspapers from early in the century. In addition to all the syndicated material available, a great many newspapers, large and small, had staff cartoonists of their own and there were hundreds of strips and panels that were to be found in only one newspaper. It would be decades before local material faded away and the comics pages became homogenized.

Meantime, syndication turned the funnies into a big business and made it possible for the most popular comic strip artists to become some of the wealthiest men in America.

Chapter 3

Family Values

During the second decade of the century more and more middle-class families began to homestead the comic sections. The funnies were reaching larger and larger audiences and some of the earlier rawness and rowdiness was fading. There was less kidding of aliens, eccentrics, and outsiders, more joking about everyday domestic life. The homogenizing of America accelerated during this period, and, at an increasing rate, people were becoming more similar in what they liked and what they knew.

One major factor in the process was the Ford Model T. The first cheap and fairly dependable mass produced auto, it was introduced in 1909. As the car caught on, Henry Ford kept dropping the price and the sales climbed from around twenty thousand a year to well over one million in 1920. What's been termed the automobile revolution would bring about even more profound changes in the twenties, but it was already irrevocably changing the country in this more innocent period. The family car served as a means of communication, helping, for instance, to end the isolation of rural residents. It gave the average citizen an affordable means of seeing more of the country. The big cities ceased to be distant, unreachable places and the countryside was no longer an unknown land. The automobile made suburban living much easier and it also encouraged a national restlessness. As histo-

rian Frederick Lewis Allen points out in *The Big Change*, "Americans felt that a rolling stone gathers experience, adventure, sophistication, and—with luck—new and possibly fruitful opportunities." This new mobility also contributed to the spread of syndicated comic strips. Tourists who became interested in a comic they'd discovered in, say, a Chicago newspaper, would often suggest that their hometown paper pick it up so that they could continue to follow it.

Another product that provoked change was the mass circulation magazine. At the turn of the century a family-oriented weekly like the *Saturday Evening Post* had a circulation of a little over three hundred thousand copies per issue. By 1920, due chiefly to the efforts of editor George Horace Lorimer, the *Post* was selling over two million copies each and every week. Rival magazines, notably *Collier's*, were doing equally well. As Allen notes there were two important effects of the success of such magazines:

> *First ... millions of Americans were getting a weekly or monthly inoculation in ways of living and thinking that were middle-class, or classless America (as opposed to plutocratic or aristocratic or proletarian).... Second, through the same media they were being introduced to the promised delights of the automobiles, spark plugs, tires,*

typewriters, talking machines, collars, corsets, and breakfast foods that American industry was producing, not for the few, but for the many.

The movies, another great disseminator of social values and fashions, conquered the middle class during this decade and added it to its already loyal working class audience. "The first American theater built especially for motion pictures, the Regent at 116th Street and Seventh Avenues in New York, opened in February 1913," states Robert Sklar. Theaters, from small neighborhood ones to downtown movie palaces, were soon being built all across the country. By the time America entered the First World War, the motion picture industry could claim to be one of the largest in America.

While *Polly and Her Pals* can be classified as one of the first of the many pretty girl strips that followed, it was also one of the earliest to concentrate on the daily doings of a middle class urban family. Cliff Sterrett had been doing a similar strip, *For This We Have Daughters*, when Hearst hired him to work for the *New York Evening Journal*. The result was *Polly*. It was distributed originally by the Newspaper Feature Service and later by King Features, which was a merging of several early Hearst syndicates. When first met, the Perkins family dwelt in a big city apartment, though they later moved to a large house. The central figure was not Polly, but Paw, a short, bald man with white whiskers and a quick temper. Maw was equally short and had quite a temper of her own. She and her elderly-looking husband were frequently observed squabbling. Polly was a rather vacant young woman, interested in clothes, young men, and the fads of the day. Sterrett developed into a very impressive cartoonist, but attractive women were never his forte. He always drew his heroine in profile and her face looked like the pretty girl doodles found in the margins of school notebooks. The Perkinses had a Japanese servant named Neewah and were plagued throughout the long life of the strip by visiting and squatting relatives of one sort or another. Paw, who appeared

old enough to be pretty Polly's grandpa, spent considerable time overreacting to her extravagant spending, her latest dress—too gaudy, too short, too flimsy, depending on the year—or her latest beau. Never a great humorist, Sterrett excelled as a cartoonist. His dailies became striking examples of the inventive use of black and white. It was in the Sunday Polly pages that he was at his very best, particularly in the twenties and early thirties, when there was an enormous energy and inventiveness on display, all in dazzling color. The pages of this period have been called Cubist and Expressionistic. They are certainly among the most visually appealing of the period. Sterrett transformed everything he drew and his buildings, furniture, and bric-a-brac all have the unmistakable mark of his vision. Even the flowers, growing everywhere and spilling out of vases, were completely his.

C. A. Voight's *Petey* was close to *Polly* in several ways. It was a family strip that was only moderately amusing but beautifully drawn. It had begun in the *Boston Traveler* in 1908 as *Petey Dink* and later went into syndication. As just plain *Petey* the daily strip was about short, mustached, and middle-aged Petey and his large, plump wife. Their pretty young niece lived with them and fulfilled the Polly function by being vapid and interested chiefly in her clothes and her social life. Voight was basically a gifted illustrator. He carefully penciled his strips, but his ink line always looked lively and spontaneous.

As noted earlier, *Abie the Agent* began in 1914. It, too, was about middle-class family life. Harry Hershfield's strip differed from the others in that its characters were all Jewish. Abe Kabibble was a small, chubby bachelor in the early years of the strip, living in Manhattan and working as an agent—meaning a dealer—for the Complex motor car. As one comics historian has pointed out, the artist "didn't usually go in for jokes with socko punchlines. Hershfield was more interested in kidding the ambitions and pretensions of his upwardly mobile characters." A short-tempered man and one ever on the lookout for social slights and injustices done to him, Abie was nevertheless an appealing character. His life revolved around demonstrating the Complex car to prospective customers or trying to sell it to anybody who'd listen to his spiel, meeting his social and familial demands, and squiring his longtime, pretty fiancee Reba. A well-educated and cultured young woman, Reba spoke perfect English and devoted considerable time to reforming and polishing the aggressive and roughcut Abe. Eventually she married him. But in spite of all her efforts, he retained his strong first generation accent. To an office boy he suspected of lying he said, "Remember, I ain't calling *you* no names—You're only a chip off from the old block. Your *father* is a crook, a bendit, a grefter and a lazy faker." When a salesman for a rival car ran into Abe at lunch and interrupted his ordering to ask his opinions on World War I, he said, "I'll have a corn beef sandwich, have it should be fatless. Don't bother me, Sparkman—the war don't interests me at all!" When the nephew he was escorting momentarily ran off, some passersby suggested that it was Abie's treatment of him that was the cause of the trouble. Abe replied, "Say, please don't gimme no arguments! Running away don't come from treatment! If thets would be the case I would be in China now myself." Writing about *Abie the Agent* in *Nemo* magazine John J. Appel observed, "The strip kidded rather than satirized aspects of American Jewish life: Abie's ... eagerness to purchase at discount; his tortuous attempts to make a better living and be a responsible family man."

The most successful and influential family strip to come along in these years was *The Gumps*. After Sidney Smith had been hired away from Hearst's *Chicago American* by the rival *Chicago Tribune*, he converted his dapper goat character Buck Nix into Old Doc Yak. In addition, he produced other features for the *Trib*, among them a mock detective called *Sherlock, Jr.* In 1917 Smith was selected to develop an idea of Captain Joseph Medill Patterson. Patterson was a cousin of the paper's publisher, Colonel Robert McCormick. He would go on to found the *New York Daily News*, the country's first tabloid, in 1919 and become the head of the N.Y. News-Chicago Tribune Syndicate. A onetime socialist, Patterson took a strong interest in the funnies and was to have a hand in the creation of several other long-running strips. What he wanted from Smith was a strip that would be "true to American life." He suggested that it be called *The Gumps*. "Gump" was a Patterson family word for nitwit, which indicates what the captain thought of the average man. Smith's human characters were better looking than his goats, but not by much. Andy Gump, the man of the house, was a long-nosed, chinless fellow with a squiggly mustache. His wife Min was a thin, plain woman, whom Smith described as being "the brains of the family. Gentle, loving and enduring, with a strong mother's instinct. But a terror when aroused." Minerva was rather easily aroused and theirs was not the most placid of relationships. Yet she was truly fond of Andy and whenever he was in trouble and called out plaintively, "Oh, Min!," she hurried to his side. The little son was named Chester, and the other important character was

Polly and Her Pals, *Cliff Sterrett. ©1914, Newspaper Feature Service, Inc.*

Andy's extremely rich Uncle Bim. The daily *Gumps* strip was usually extremely static, with Andy, Min, and Bim sitting around and talking. They could talk for days on end about domestic problems, social aspirations, and, most frequently, money. Smith was fond of the soliloquy, too, and in panels which were sometimes two-thirds dialogue balloons, Andy would often search his soul:

> How will I ever face the world after this? To be pointed out as a failure. The very ones who fawned on me for favors will be the first to mock and jeer. It seems unjust that one false step should blacken a man's good reputation forever. I'm a strong man. I can begin life anew but my heart aches when I think of Min and little Chester. Instead of riches and luxury I offer them disgrace and poverty. If I had only listened to Min's wise words. She warned me against trusting that swindler, J. Ambrose Hepwing.

What Sidney Smith developed with *The Gumps* was a primitive soap opera. Soon abandoning jokes, he concentrated on continuity and suspense.

The public responded to these simply drawn tales and there was a demand for the strip all over the country. The Tribune-News Syndicate was built on the strip. In the 1920s, such suspenseful stories as the one in which Uncle Bim almost married the Widow Zander were matters of national concern. Smith became rich from drawing Gumps. He signed the first million dollar contract ever given for a comic strip, getting the money in a yearly chunk of $100,000. He bought himself a Rolls Royce and an estate or two. Since his social life now occupied quite a bit of time, he hired assistants. Stanley Link took on much of the drawing and both Sol Hess and Brandon Walsh worked on the writing.

During Walsh's stint with the Gump clan, the Sunday page was often taken up with the adventures of young Chester. The theory still held at the time was that the daily strips were for adults and the Sundays were for children. The things that

Abie the Agent, *Harry Hershfield. Excerpt from a daily strip.* ©1915, International News Service.

befell the boy had a strange daydream quality. Rich Uncle Bim would summon him to some remote and exotic spot and the fun would begin. Unlike many funny paper moppets, Chester was a well-behaved and polite kid. What is more, almost everybody he met liked him. "Wouldn't you like to be little Chester traveling on such a wonderful train to visit his rich Uncle Bim?" asked a typical caption. "When he reaches Australia he will have the most marvelous toys and he will live in a great big beautiful castle like a little prince." On a later jaunt to Australia, this one by blimp, Chester was marooned on a Pacific island with Bim's servant, Ching Chow. He was the first of the many epigrammatic Chinese who would inhabit later adventure strips. He was fond of saying such things as "It is written that every rope has two ends," "It is written when heaven has endowed a fool at his birth it is a waste of instruction to teach" and "It is written that patience and a mulberry leaf will make a silk gown." So popular was Ching Chow that he was rewarded with a small panel of his own wherein he could dispense a

daily dose of fortune cookie wisdom. The panel is still going, having outlived *The Gumps* by almost two score years.

A domestic strip much simpler than *The Gumps*, and one that was content to special-ize in gags, was *Married Life*. It was the work of an ambitious young car-toonist named Billy DeBeck and began in the *Chicago Herald* in 1916. A professional since 1910, DeBeck had worked on the staffs of several Midwest news-papers before finding a job in his hometown. While the strip was nicely drawn in a simple, scratchy style, it gave little hint of the impressive sort of work DeBeck would be turning out just a few years later. *Married Life* was about a bickering middle-class cou-ple named Aleck and Pauline and their fairly hum-drum urban existence. Aleck, balding, bulb-nosed and the owner of a scraggly mustache, was, like a great many of the husbands to appear in later domestic strips, old and weary looking. Pauline was the traditional shrew of stage and screen, whose favorite words for describing her woebegone hus-band were wretch, idiot, and whelp. She was also fond of hurling heavy objects, such as vases and flatirons, at his nearly hairless head. Hearst, who

The Gumps, *Sidney Smith. Andy and Min take time out from continuity to bicker over spilled salt in this sample.* ©1920, Chicago Tribune, Inc.

was said to be very fond of DeBeck's work, bought the *Herald* in 1918 and turned it into the *Herald and Examiner*. DeBeck continued drawing *Married Life*, daily and Sunday for the new paper.

After working with polite, middle-class family life in strips like *The Newlyweds*, George McManus turned to other social levels for what was to be his major work. In *Bringing Up Father* he took Jiggs, a lower-class Irish roughneck, and Maggie, his shrew of a wife, made them suddenly rich and thrust them into high society. Endowed with a serviceable but very basic sense of humor and a fondness for the obvious, he was able to turn out hundreds of gags a year using small variations on a few simple situa-tions. There were the social pretensions and aspira-tions of Maggie and their pretty young daughter, Jiggs' lowbrow reactions to culture, his undying preference for such trappings of his former hodcar-rier life as the saloon, the pool hall, and corn beef and cabbage, and his less than enthusiastic encounters with the rich and famous. All these pro-vided McManus with endless inspiration, as did the embarrassment Jiggs' crude behavior caused his family. And Maggie's rolling pin, used frequently to chastise Jiggs and to goad him into adopting man-ners more suited to his new upper-class standing, was a recurring source of comedy. McManus never tired, too, of the sight of Jiggs wandering around in his undershirt in his vast art nouveau mansion. That this exaggerated allegory of assimilation had enormous appeal to readers is proved by the fact that *Bringing Up Father*, which officially began in January, 1913, continued to be an enormously suc-cessful strip for generations after the Irish had ceased to be an immigrant class. One of King Features most popular offerings, it made its creator even richer than Jiggs.

Jimmy Murphy's *Toots and Casper* was very much in the newlyweds tradition when it started in the *New York American* and other Hearst papers at the end of 1918. Originally Casper Hawkins was a very small, ugly middle-aged man with a pretty young wife. Murphy, a former political cartoonist, produced a very shakily drawn and weakly written effort at the start and the strip vanished in February, 1919. Something inexplicable happened offstage and when *Toots and Casper* returned in May, it was greatly improved in both art and copy. Casper was now taller and younger, Toots was even prettier, and the strip dealt with the foibles of middle-class, young married life. Murphy allowed the couple to have a baby in 1920. The little fellow was nicknamed Buttercup and he remained a cute little toddler for over twenty years. Casper worked in an office and Toots was a very stylish housewife. The couple squabbled and argued, but there was no physical violence at all. Like the later Blondie, Toots was an expert at manipulating her husband and there was, therefore, no need for a rolling pin. One of Casper's major flaws was an overdeveloped, almost a Shakespearean, strain of jealousy. He

imagined numerous affairs being indulged in by his always innocent wife and this gave Murphy plots for numerous continuities. Toots had a slight cruel streak and was not above teasing her husband with hints that his latest suspicion was well-founded.

The cartoonist was always up-to-date on the latest fads and fashions and he began fairly early in the strip to let his readers have some say in the events of his characters' lives. In a 1924 sequence, for instance, Toots was contemplating having her hair bobbed—an important issue in many families of the period. He included a large panel one day, showing Toots modeling eight different bobs, including the Boyish Bob, the Dutch Girl Bob, and the Vamp Bob. When Casper yelled, "I won't let you bob your hair!" Toots, in an obvious aside to the audience, replied, "What's your idea of the best way to have one's hair bobbed?" Readers took the hint and wrote in their opinions. In subsequent years, Murphy went even further, directly asking readers to write him about story lines and what actions his people should take. He became increasingly preoccupied with suspense and storytelling, and *Toots and Casper* ceased to be just a joke strip and became instead an early prototype, though still humorous, of a soap opera.

Among the other middle-class family comedies that came along in the period were *Pa's Son-in-Law*, a bland, low-key effort by C. H. "Duke" Wellington, and *Joe's Car* by Vic Forsythe, which alternated between family life and the husband's preoccupation with his automobile.

Toots and Casper, Jimmy Murphy. From the early days of Buttercup's long-running babyhood. ©1921, King Features Syndicate, Inc.

Jerry on the Job, *Walter Hoban. A portion of a daily strip, complete with railroad station and a falling-over take. ©1915, International News Service.*

George Herriman, though now gainfully employed with *Krazy Kat*, continued with *The Dingbat Family* until the first week of 1916. The strip had occasional lucid moments devoted to an only mildly cockeyed view of married life, but Herriman couldn't keep away from fantasy and burlesque. The World War had started in Europe and in one of the last Dingbat sequences Herriman did a parody of trench warfare. He had the Dingbats occupying separate trenches out in a field and carrying on chiefly verbal combat with each other. He also threw in various peacemaking delegations. In 1919 he tried a more conventional family strip, *Now Listen, Mabel*. Using his wife's name in the title did not bring him luck and the strip ended before the year did. It took one more unsuccessful family effort, a 1926 Sunday called *Us Husbands*, to convince King Features that Herriman, like Tarzan, was more at home among the animals.

Both Tom McNamara and his *Us Boys* are long forgotten, yet it was this early kid strip that was the major source of inspiration for Hal Roach's *Our Gang* comedies, and it was McNamara himself who helped put together the first silent short films in Hollywood. In 1912, after working as a reporter, photographer, and cartoonist for assorted papers around the country, touring in vaudeville, prospecting for silver, and teaching roller skating in Paris, he settled down in Manhattan to cartoon for the *Evening Journal*. His two closest friends on the newspaper became Tad Dorgan and George Herriman. In the book *Krazy Kat: The Comic Art of George Herriman*,

there is a photo of McNamara and Herriman at the Grand Canyon. In a photograph of some of the art staff, McNamara is this time identified as his old nemesis Harry Hershfield, further proof perhaps that the lack of recognition he felt throughout his life was real and continues even after his death.

He was never much of a cartoonist, but he had a strong understanding of what it was like to be a kid growing up on the streets of a big city. The title *Us Boys* was stuck on his daily strip by editor Rudolph Block, another person McNamara was not especially fond of. He felt the Sunday page title *On Our Block* was somewhat better. Both daily and Sunday dealt with the same gang of kids. The bunch included Shrimp Flynn, who was more or less the star, his pal, the fat kid named Skinny Shaner, and Eaglebeak Spruder, a somewhat mysterious and aloof boy who had, when he wanted to use it, a knack for leadership and was also an expert at all the street and sandlot sports. McNamara shunned ready-made gags, preferring to try to get his laughs from the feuds, problems, yearnings, and escapades of his big-town kids. There were assorted little girls in *Us Boys*, some of them tomboys and some of them more sedate. They often served as the objects of desire for Shrimp and his colleagues and could be the cause of friction when two boys were smitten with the same girl. This was not an idealized vision of youth nor a nostalgic one and McNamara showed abusive parents and tearful unhappy kids. He was also an early practitioner of continuity and involved his gang of kids in a variety of adventures, including being marooned on a desert island after a shipwreck. Some word experts credit the strip with introducing the word "movie" to the American language. Fittingly then, McNamara moved to Hollywood in 1922 to work for Roach. He later became a story man and assistant director for Mary Pickford on such films as *Sparrows* and *Little Annie Rooney*.

Another resident of the *Journal* bullpen was Walter Hoban. An excellent artist with an appealing, lively style, he doubled as sports cartoonist and comic strip artist. His *Jerry on the Job*, which started across the country in 1913, was a very fanciful strip about a very small kid who, while just two heads high, possessed the wiseacre vocabulary and wisdom of a teenager. The brash, slangy, and lazy little Jerry worked at various jobs and never went near a school. He served a long stretch as an office boy before settling down as a boy-of-all-work at a suburban railroad station where most of the travelers and commuters were interested in buying tickets to the town of New Monia. Hoban had little interest in reality and Jerry was nothing like a typical little boy. In fact, it is possible Hoban considered him a midget adult. He filled his panels with eccentric furniture, bizarre buildings, and eccentric people. The trains themselves, which might have been designed by Rube Goldberg, bordered on the surreal. There was a vaudeville aspect to the strip as well and after his players had delivered the day's gag, one of them was almost certain to do a take that involved falling over, usually backwards, with the feet going up in the air, amidst a huge cloud of dust.

Somewhat closer to real life was Elmer Tuggle, the ten-year old boy who inhabited A. C. Fera's *Just Boy*. Fera apparently worked out of Southern California, but his *Just Boy*, which was introduced by one of Hearst's syndicates in 1916, was set in what was obviously a midwestern small town. Elmer's parents, Clem and Ella Tuggle, were quite elderly in appearance and he was their only child. Though considered a mischievous brat by his parents and their black servant Lottie, Elmer was usually closer to Swinnerton's Little Jimmy than he was to Hans and Fritz. A good deal of his mischief was inadvertent. On the daily that ran on December 25, 1918, for example,

Just Boy, A.C. Fera. *Poor Elmer once again precipitates violence.* ©1919, *Newspaper Feature Service, Inc.*

Elmer had been sent out on an errand and returned with a gift-wrapped necktie. His bald, white-whiskered old dad, who'd been trying to repair the family stove, burst out with, "I'll 'swell neck-tie' you! Wot in thunder do you mean?—I sent you for a stovepipe!" Elmer replied, "Why, Pa, it's for your Christmas—You oughtn't to kick." His father decided the boy still needed a sound thrashing for disobeying orders, but since he'd just been given a present, he delegated the job to his wife. Taking the boy into another room, the two pretend that Elmer's getting a violent spanking. Since it was Christmas Day, Elmer got off easy. But on most occasions the beating he got for his misdemeanors was real. Fera continued with the feature, which was a Sunday only for much of its run, until 1925. The reliable Charles "Doc" Winner, a syndicate bullpen stalwart, took over and the title was changed to *Elmer*.

Later a realist, Frank King indulged in fantasy from 1915 to 1919 with his *Bobby Make-Believe* page. Another daydreamer, Bobby escaped the perils and perplexities of boyhood by imagining himself in adventurous settings. Many of his reveries owed something to the burgeoning field of the movies, since Bobby usually cast himself as an aviator, a secret agent, a cowboy, a big league ball player or a jungle explorer. *Terry and Tacks* was a more down-to-earth feature, although it did center on a little boy and his parrot. It was a Sunday page by Joe Farren, who later deserted comics to become a serious illustrator for such pulp magazines as *Detective Fiction Weekly*.

One of Gene Carr's specialties had always been the drawing of children. His most successful effort in the previous decade was *Lady Bountiful*, an odd page about a wealthy young society woman who was alternately the patron and the victim of a gang of tough-talking, unruly street kids. He was still doing *Lady Bountiful* intermittently up to 1920. He also created a half-page, *Chub's Big Brother*, for the *World*'s Press Publishing Co. syndicate. This was a quieter, gentler feature, closer to reality, about an amiable little five-year-old boy and his moderately

mischievous ten-year-old brother. Milt Gross, who would come into his own during the Roaring Twenties, began his newspaper career as the office boy in the *New York Evening Journal* art department. Before he was twenty Gross was drawing an assortment of strips and panels. Among them were *And Then The Fun Began*, which showed readers the moment just before the focal character got into trouble, and *In The Movies They Do It*, built around the notion that in real life things don't turn out the way they do in motion pictures. For a short while Gross also drew a kid strip called *Frenchy* about a little French war orphan.

A native of the little Midwest town of Nappanee, Indiana, Merrill Blosser had known from childhood that he wanted to be a cartoonist. While still a boy, he signed up for the Landon School, one of the most popular of the many mail-order cartooning academies. He became one of the correspondence school's star pupils and in 1915 he sold the NEA syndicate *Freckles and His Friends*. The sale

Percy in Stageland, H. C. Greening. Enrico Caruso helps the robot pretend to be a singer in this panel from a Sunday page. ©1919, New York Herald Co.

was no doubt helped by the fact that C. N. Landon was also the NEA feature editor. In later school brochures Landon used young Blosser as a shining example of what the world might offer his graduates, describing *Freckles* as a strip "which daily amuses millions of newspaper readers and earns for Merrill Blosser a yearly salary well in the five figures." The Newspaper Enterprise Association syndicate offered its clients, mostly small town papers, a blanket service and a packaged page of strips. *Freckles* was part of the package, which also contained, over the years, such strips as *The Doings of The Duffs*, *Salesman Sam*, *Wash Tubbs*, *Alley Oop*, and *Our Boarding House* with Major Hoople. Freckles was, when the strip began, a boy of about eight. He lived in a small town, no doubt based on Nappanee, called Shadyside. Blosser built his daily gags on the activities of Freckles and his kid buddies, including his best friend Oscar, and the redheaded little boy's rather placid home life. Blosser's drawing style improved as the strip went along and Freckles added a few years to his age.

A number of fantasy pages aimed primarily at children were introduced in the teens. William Donahey invented *The Teenie Weenies* in 1914 and the page originally appeared exclusively in the *Chicago Tribune*. His little people were about three inches high and had such generic names as Old Soldier, Cowboy, Chinaman, and Lady of Fashion. They inhabited a tiny world built of discards from the full-grown world, old shoes, cigar boxes, cups, and cans. According to Donahey, their enclave existed behind a rosebush in a backyard. He never explained where his Teenie Weenies came from or why they were so small. The usual format was one large, detailed panel and a block of copy telling the day's story. Though mild in tone, *The Teenie Weenies* occasionally offered the sort of thrills that were the staples of later Shrinking Man movies. This would happen when a cat or a frog blundered into the village, looking like a giant. In 1923 Dohaney's page went into national syndication.

The *New York Herald*, which was partial to fantasy, introduced *Mr. Twee Deedle* by Johnny Gruelle in 1910. This was the year before Winsor McCay quit the *Herald* to go to work for Hearst and took Little Nemo with him. Gruelle's page was a blend of handsomely colored illustration panels and typeset copy. It recounted the fantasy adventures of a polite little blond boy named Dickie, his girl pal, and his friend and guide, an elf named Mr. Twee Deedle. The amiable elf guided Dickie into all sorts of strange adventures. Some took place right in his own back yard, such as the occasion when Twee Deedle shrank the boy down so he could witness the fierce battle, complete with banners and a marching band, between the courageous ants and the nasty potato bugs. Others transported Dickie off to distant realms of fantasy where he interacted with such creatures as the Mirage Moodles. Gruelle drew the page for over ten years and later did a comedy page titled *Brutus*, but he is remembered today mostly for his Raggedy Ann books. Toward the end of the teens the *Herald* tried a similar page, *Bubble Land* by R. D. Highet. Deficient in both writing and drawing, it was about a little boy and girl team who were guided through a mild fantasy world by a child-sized, stuffed, patchwork cat named Mr. Calico.

Squirrel Food, Gene Ahern. Otto Auto continues to overcome the traps readers suggest.

The first robot to star in a Sunday page of his own came along several years before the word "robot" had been coined. His name was Percy and in the feature, which debuted in October of 1911, he was referred to as a "Mechanism Man." The *Percy* page was the work of H. C. Greening, and the robot was the invention of a nameless old inventor with the sort of thick, stage-Dutch accent the Katzenjammer clan had made popular in the funnies. It was the professor's notion that Percy would perform all sorts of menial tasks and thus relieve mankind for better things. Somehow, though, Percy, who was a tin woodman sort of fellow with a metal derby, always fouled up. The professor, who suffered Dr. Frankenstein-like defeats and disappointments week after week, continued to have faith in his mechanism man and summed up his innovative invention's chief flaw with the phrase, "Brains he has nix."

Greening had been successful as both a magazine and a newspaper cartoonist since before the turn of the century. On the *New York Herald* payroll from about 1910, he produced several features. Percy went on hiatus for a time, but returned before the decade was over. In 1919 Greening added temporary wings to Percy, turning him into a sort of airplane, and the robot entered the Great-Race-'Round-The-World. The prize was one million dollars, and Percy's pilot was real-life, World War I ace Capt. Eddie Rickenbacker. Later in the year, the title was changed to *Percy in Stageland*, and the trouble-prone robot began fouling up in a show-business setting. Real life personalities showed up here, too. Enrico Caruso did a turn on November 16, 1919, and also contributed four caricatures of Greening. All in all, *Percy* was an unusual feature.

A wide assortment of other funnies came along in this period. *Asthma Simpson the Village Queen* was a feature that began in December of 1914. The artist was Billy Liverpool, who drew like a Bud Fisher with talent, and the setting was a hinterlands farm community. Asthma, a pretty young village belle, had two competing suitors. One was the honest, upright, and fairly dense Luke and the other was a

Slim Jim, Stanley Armstrong. Jim remains ahead of the posse in this panel from an early twenties page.

slick "city-chap" named Con Traffic. With his waxed mustache and tophat, Con resembled Rudolph Rassendale, the house villain of *Hairbreadth Harry*. In Liverpool's triangle, however, the good guy rarely won and Con would usually outwit and outmaneuver him to end up kissing the fair Asthma at the annual husking bee or escorting her on a hay ride. Luke almost always finished out of the money.

Gus Mager revived his burlesque Holmesian sleuth for *The World* in 1913. Now operating under the title *Hawkshaw the Detective*, he became a regular part of the *Funny Side* Sunday comic section. The original Hawkshaw was a detective in the nineteenth century Victorian stage melodrama *The Ticket-of-Leave Man* by Tom Taylor, and Mager borrowed the name to rechristen Sherlocko. Initially Dr. Watso became the Colonel. Mager added a Professor Moriarty sort of master criminal, naming him simply the Professor. A lowbrow fellow despite his title, the Professor spoke in underworld locutions: "Come acrost with the boodle," and "This'll toin the trick." He was clever enough, however, to outwit the great detective on more than one occasion. A master of disguise as well, on one notable occasion he got himself up in drag and turned out to be a ringer for Mama Katzenjammer. Mager sometimes carried cases over from week to week, but always gave each page a separate title, such as "The Sad Story of the Governor's New Year's Party and the Armadillo Soup" and "The Sprightly Episode of the Dishonest Servant and the Jewel Casket." Eventually such familiar regulars as Groucho and Tightwaddo returned.

Rube Goldberg's longest running page was *Boob McNutt*, which has been described as "an eclectic jumble of satire, burlesque, fantasy and cockeyed technology." It began in 1915 and centered on a naive, redheaded young fellow who went around in a tiny hat, a coat that was too small and too tight, and polka dot pants. Boob, as his named implies, was not a mastermind and he looked like such earlier fools of the funnies as Simon Simple as well as a

When a Feller Needs a Friend, *Clare Briggs. This line also appeared on the once-popular brand of pipe tobacco named after Briggs. ©1924, New York Herald, Inc.*

silent movie comedian. Goldberg thrust him into continuing situations that took him around the world, and sometimes off it, while kidding every sort of adventure tale. Eventually a lady named Pearl was added to the cast and she became the object of Boob's affection as well as the target for a grand assortment of fiends, crooks, and kidnappers. Other regulars included Boob's faithful dog, Bertha the Siberian Cheesehound, and the ever popular Mike and Ike. *Boob McNutt* was part of the Hearst Sunday comic sections for almost twenty years.

A young artist who was profoundly influenced by Goldberg was Gene Ahern. When the National Enterprise Association (NEA) decided to add daily strips and panels to their basic package, he was one of the men they brought to their Cleveland headquarters. As improbable as it may sound, Cleveland became over the next few years one of the nonsense centers of the country. The panels Ahern created in 1915 were *Fathead Fritz*, *Taking Her to the Ball Game*, and *Squirrel Food*. The following year he converted the latter into a strip. The recurrent character was Balmy Benny, described by comics historian Mark Johnson as "a chunky little guy who shared vaudeville patter with his straight man, George the Dog. Benny would alternate every few days with a satire on a given subject, usually related to events in the news." As best he could, Ahern imitated Goldberg's style—with an occasional side trip to borrow from Tad—and tried as well to duplicate Goldberg's screwball manner of thinking. His strip was crude but energetic. In 1918, it became *Balmy Benny*. Ahern also drew *Otto Auto*, which concerned itself originally with a compulsive driver who never got out of his car. Ahern remained devoted to nonsense throughout his career and to characters whom the world in general would consider, in the vernacular of the day, nutty.

Slim Jim was the premier feature of the World Color Printing Company's ready-print comic section and it usually appeared on the front page of the four-page supplement. Though the supplement appeared in some large towns and cities, it was mostly a staple of small-town newspapers. Slim Jim was an extremely long and thin vagabond, a former circus acrobat, who was pursued by the constabulary of the small town of Grassville for much of the life of the strip. Though Slim Jim's crimes were never more serious than the swiping of a pie off a kitchen windowsill or stealing a chicken out of a hen house, the Grassville force chased him as doggedly as though they were auditioning for parts in *Les Miserables*. They chased the elusive hobo not only around Grassville but, eventually, across the length and breadth of America and across Europe and Asia. The prankish Slim Jim obviously enjoyed this endless chase and used many of his old circus tricks to stay ahead of the posse or to escape once he'd inadvertently fallen into their temporary clutches. The feature lasted from 1910 to 1937.

The first artist was George Frink, who'd drawn an almost identical feature called *Circus Solly* from 1904 to 1910. Solly, also a former circus acrobat, spent most of his time being chased by the same cops who later chased Slim Jim. There were usually three of them. In 1911, an exceptional artist named Raymond Crawford Ewer, an early disciple of the gifted German artist Heinrich Kley, took over *Slim Jim*. He excelled at complicated action shots and intricate crowd scenes and experimented with unconventional page layouts. He left in 1914, followed eventually by Stanley Armstrong, who chronicled Slim Jim's peregrinations for the rest of the run.

Another popular feature in a growing number of daily papers was the panel cartoon. Some of the early

Outdoor Sports, Tad Dorgan. The little stick figures, seen here in the vicinity of the signature, also appeared for a time in a feature of their own titled Daffydills.

ones had begun as adjuncts to early political cartoons. Like Frederick Opper, John T. McCutcheon was often called the Dean of American Cartoonists. He was the *Chicago Tribune*'s chief political cartoonist from 1903 to 1946. In addition, he drew hundreds of panel cartoons that poked gentle fun at small-town and rural America. He drew in a simple, homespun style and with his non-politicals, as Richard Marschall writes in the *World Encyclopedia of Cartoons*, he "led the way for Dwig, Briggs, Webster and an army of later cartoonists." McCutcheon established the ground rules for this sort of thing. Some of his panels expressed a nostalgia for the simpler world of childhood and the simpler pleasures of the good old days. He proved that cartoon humor did not have to be rowdy or slapstick. Quite a few of his panels could be classified as heartwarming.

Clare A. Briggs was a friend and protégé of McCutcheon. He worked with him on the *Chicago Tribune* from 1907 to 1914, then headed East to join the *New York Tribune* staff. He drew a daily panel, with a different recurring title on each. Briggs made use of the established formulas McCutcheon had pioneered, but added some of his own. There was

Krazy Kat, *George Herriman. Cosmic speculations and a touch of science fiction in a 1922 Sunday. For most of its life the page appeared in black and white elsewhere than the comic supplement.*

nostalgia, as in the recurring *The Days of Real Sport*, a sympathy for the perils and embarrassments of childhood, featured in *When a Feller Needs a Friend*. Briggs sometimes would use this latter title for a panel about the plight of a mistreated dog, too. He was also amused by social climbers, phonies, petty businessmen, and pompous civic officials. He devoted at least one panel per week to what James Thurber would later call "the war between men and women." Some of his other favorite departments were *Ain't It a Grand and Glorious Feelin?*, *Somebody's Always Taking the Joy Out of Life*, *Golf*, and *It Happens in the Best Regulated Families*. Briggs alternated formats, sometimes doing a single big panel and other times drawing a two-tier, six-panel strip. Among his favorites for the strip treatment were *Real Folks at Home*, *Wonder What...* (*Wonder What a Girl in the Chorus Thinks About*, *Wonder What a Dog with a Fancy Knit Blanket on Thinks About*, etc.) and *Movie of ...* (*Movie of a Man at a Country R.R. Station*, etc.). A very popular cartoonist, by the early 1920s Briggs' work was appearing in nearly 150 newspapers in America plus another two dozen in Canada. He even had a pipe tobacco named after him.

Harold T. Webster was Briggs' leading rival, and he covered much of the same ground. After a series of newspaper jobs, he went to work for the same newspaper, the *New York Tribune*, a year or so before Briggs. All three of these panel cartoonists, as well as their many imitators, were chroniclers of the middle class that was growing ever larger in this country. The men they drew had steady jobs and wore suits and ties to work and were married to women who were content to be housewives. They lived comfortably in the city and in the right suburbs, could afford in most cases to have at least one servant, and filled their leisure hours with such pastimes as golf, bridge, and social activities at the country club. There were few pranksters among them, few iconoclasts, and not a single beggar or hobo. Briggs and Webster especially practiced a polite, middle-class humor and represent one of the important transitions the funnies were going through as they struggled to grow up and at the same time attract wider audiences. Webster's recurring titles for his daily panel were *The Thrill That Comes Once in a Lifetime*, *Life's Darkest Moments*, *How to Torture Your Wife/Husband*, *Bridge*, and *The Timid Soul*, which gave the world Caspar Milquetoast. The Timid Soul worked compulsively to be politically and socially correct at all times and harbored every fear ever experienced by his class. His existence may indicate that Webster was not as fond of his average reader as might be supposed from his other series. For many years, starting in the 1920s, Webster's assistant, and sometimes ghost, was a talented book and magazine cartoonist named Herb Roth.

Tad Dorgan was much more hardboiled (a slang word he coined and popularized in his panels) than the likes of Webster and Briggs. He ignored the trials and heartaches of childhood and never suffered even a twinge of nostalgia. His daily panel began in the century's second decade and had the alternating titles of *Indoor Sports* and *Outdoor Sports*. He tackled hypocrisy, pomposity and plain baloney (another word he made popular). *Outdoor* took a jaded look at such popular pastimes as baseball and boxing, at both the players and the fans. *Indoor* dropped in on locations ranging from the parlor to the pool hall, from the office to the street corner. Tad's ear for the way everyday citizens expressed themselves was exceptionally accurate and, though he wasn't as skilled a draftsman as some of the competition, nobody could match him when it came to suggesting attitude, whether it was a nervous clerk asking for a raise or an oafish ballplayer bragging about his prowess. The characters who populate his world would never be invited to dine with any of Briggs' people or sit down to a friendly game of bridge with Webster's. Tad would often draw little stick figures along the lower edge of his panel, usually in the vicinity of his signature. They'd tell each other bad jokes or utter one of the many catch phrases that Tad was fond of repeating: "Yes, we have no bananas," "Quick, Watson, the needle," "Blow your whistle, you're coming to a crossing," "Woops, my dear," etc.

Hooray! Dirks' Kids Are Back!
San Franciscans Laugh With Boys

Originator of Katzenjammers, Always a Master of Fun, Now Drawing Exclusively for The Chronicle in San Francisco

The Captain and the Kids, *Rudolph Dirks. Similar stories appeared in newspapers across the country in June, 1914, after Dirks had won the right to draw the Katzies for Pulitzer.*

George Herriman began a new daily strip, *Baron Bean*, in January 1916, and, more importantly, in April of that same year started his *Krazy Kat* Sunday page. *Baron Bean* was peopled with humans and centered around the Baron, a tall, mustached, poseur and freeloader who was a refined version of the earlier Baron Mooch. He was accompanied by a short rotund sidekick named Grimes who served as his valet at times. On the surface the strip looked quite a lot like *Mutt and Jeff*, but Herriman usually shunned conventional jokes and it exhibited some of the graphic eccentricities to be found in more abundance in *Krazy Kat*. The Baron did not ingratiate himself to newspaper readers, despite some affinities to the later and extremely popular Major Hoople of Gene Ahern. The strip ended in January 1919. When the *Krazy* Sunday began on April 23, 1916, Herriman had already moved his cast, including Ignatz Mouse and the dogged Officer Pupp, to the strange desert location that was a

curious blend of Arizona and Wonderland. The eternal triangle was in place by then. Ignatz lived chiefly to conk the Kat's dome with a flung brick, Krazy forever interpreting the tossed dornick as an expression of love, and Pupp, unrequitedly smitten with Krazy, dedicated to protecting the cat and putting the mouse in his adobe jailhouse. Herriman was able to build countless narratives on this basic situation.

It was on the Sunday page that Herriman began to experiment with layout even more than he had with his daily features. He ignored the conventional breakdown into rows of ruled panels, preferring go from dozens of tiny panels one week to one huge one the next. At times he ignored panel divisions entirely. His drawing grew more inventive, too, and his scratchy pen lines conveyed a tremendous energy. He continued experimenting with dialogue and dialect: Krazy spoke in a sort of Yiddish patois; Ignatz's speeches were a mix of Tad Dorgan slang and Shakespeare imagery. Since the setting was now the Southwest, some characters spoke in Spanish. The backgrounds in Coconino County, a real place though not the way Herriman drew it, were in constant flux and sometimes gave the impression they were on rollers, like the backgrounds in early silent movies. This heady mix of elements delighted William Randolph Hearst and a certain percentage of the readers. In the 1920s critics like Gilbert Seldes would single out Herriman's *Krazy* as a masterpiece that intellectuals could take to their hearts. Most of the public, though, would not have voted it onto any top-ten list and it never achieved a very large list of newspapers. The Sunday, for most of its run from 1916 to 1944, appeared in black and white in another part of the paper and was exiled from the colored comic supplements.

This is the decade in which the Katzenjammer boys began having legal problems, not because of their terrorist activities, but because of difficulties that arose between Rudolph Dirks and the Hearst organization. Behind much of the trouble was the old familiar Pulitzer-Hearst feud. In this case it was the *New York World* that hired an artist away from the *New York Journal*. Years later the United Feature Syndicate, which took over the Dirks page after the *World* folded, sent out a canned autobiographic piece that contained Dirks' account of what had happened. Actually the piece was swiped from a magazine article by Martin Sheridan with "I" substituted for "he," but it gives a fairly accurate description of the events leading up to the fracas:

> After working almost continuously for fifteen years," said Dirks, "I decided that it was time for a vacation. I wanted a real rest and planned to spend a year in Europe with my wife. During that period I resolved to draw no comics but to catch up on my first love, oil painting. My contract with the Journal was about to expire, so I told my editor that I would sign a new one upon my return. The Journal didn't like the idea of letting the strip drop out completely for a whole year and asked that I double up on the work until the pages were a year ahead of schedule. This I began to do but soon gave up when certain difficulties arose. So I packed up and sailed with Mrs. Dirks for Europe. Cablegrams and Journal correspondence followed me all over the continent requesting that I send in some more drawings. I mailed in Sunday pages for about six months. Then I accepted an offer to work for the New York World on the condition that I would not begin until my contract was cleared with the Journal. Meanwhile, the latter paper sought to secure a restraining injunction against my working for the Pulitzer interests. When the case was first heard, I was declared the loser. My appeal, however, brought a reversal of that decision, allowing me to work for the World but leaving the title The Katzenjammer Kids with the Journal.

The legal actions stretched from 1913 to 1914 and for roughly fourteen months of that time, the Kids went on hiatus and did not appear in anybody's newspaper.

On Saturday, May 16, 1914, the Pulitzer paper was pleased to run a news story with the headline "Law Gives Dirks Right To Draw World Pictures." The law also, however, awarded Hearst the right to *The Katzenjammer Kids* title and the characters. While Dirks was free to draw them for the *World*, he could no longer use the old familiar title. The following month his new version began appearing amidst considerable fanfare, in newspapers. In the first months after the split, Dirks did not exactly have a title. A typeset head at the left of the page read simply *Here Dey Iss!*, and on the right, in equally large type appeared "By Rudolph Dirks, Originator of The Katzenjammer Kids." In January 1915 Dirks began using *Hans und Fritz* for his title. In 1918, probably because of World War I and the fact that things German weren't especially popular, the name was changed to *The Captain and the Kids*. This had the added advantage of sounding, if said rapidly and slurred a little, quite a bit like *The Katzenjammer Kids*.

Hearst eventually hired H. H. Knerr who was, as noted earlier, the leading Dirks imitator in the country, to carry on his *Journal* version. He did not assume his duties until November 29, 1914. From May through November, the Hearst version was drawn anonymously. Katzenjammer authority James Lowe has speculated that Opper may have been one of the artists who filled in during those months. The title was changed to *The Original Katzenjammer Kids* to drive home the point that this was the genuine article, even though Dirks had moved on. Knerr, for some reason lost in the mists of time, switched the names of the two boys. In the Dirks pages, Hans had always been the blackhaired one and Fritz the blond. But Knerr had Hans the fair-haired boy and Fritz the dark. Dirks continued with the original designations and few readers or editors apparently noted the discrepancy. The Hearst concession to anti-German feeling involved changing the name of the page to *The Shenanigan Kids* in June of 1918 and calling Hans and Fritz Katzenjammer Mike and Aleck Shenanigan. This might have fooled somebody had everybody in the page not continued to talk in thick accents full of Dod-gasted, dollink, dumbkopf, and similar locutions. The Kids posed as Dutch boys with Irish names until the spring of 1920.

Among the other durable features that emerged in these years was Fontaine Fox's *Toonerville Folks*. A crudely drawn panel, always using a modified bird's eye perspective, it dealt with life in a small town and had a rotating cast that included a tough kid named Mickey (Himself) McGuire, an almost superhuman servant named the Powerful Katrinka, and an irritable fellow known as the Terrible Tempered Mr. Bang. There was also the Skipper who piloted the Toonerville Trolley. Begun as a local feature in the *Chicago Post* in 1908, it was picked up for syndication by John Wheeler in 1913. Fox continued it until 1955.

Edwina Dumm's *Cap Stubbs and Tippie* (originally *Cap Stubbs*) began in 1918 and was a strip about a small town boy, his dog, and his grandmother. Though a quiet and gentle strip, it struck the fancy of Hearst, and he shared the syndication of it, offering the Sunday while the smaller George Matthew Adams operation took care of the daily. Edwina, one of the relatively few women in newspaper strips in the early years, drew in a warm, homey style and was especially good with animals.

Chapter 4

Flappers and Philosophers

The twenties really began in 1918, ushered in at about the same time in November that Armistice Day parades were being held across America. The country's losses in the Great War had been relatively small. Of an estimated nine million battlefield deaths, a little over fifty thousand had been American servicemen. But the disillusionment and the sense of discontinuity with the past that spread across Europe on the eve of the third decade of the century profoundly touched the United States as well, especially the young. Of the changes the world was undergoing, historian Samuel Hynes said, "Men and women after the war looked back at their own pasts as one might look across a great chasm to a remote, peaceable place on the other side."

The patterns of life in America changed rapidly as the Victorian Age was finally buried and automobiles, radios, phonographs, movie palaces, and newspapers proliferated. In January 1920, Prohibition went into effect and it was no longer legal to drink alcoholic beverages. The Nineteenth Amendment, at long last giving women the right to vote, was proposed by Congress in 1919 and ratified in August 1920. That meant that women shared the blame for voting the handsome, ineffectual, and casually corrupt Republican Warren G. Harding into office as President in 1920.

Discontent and a strong conviction that just about everything was in a state of flux affected most of the popular art forms, particularly novels and motion pictures. Many works containing a strange mix of optimism and cynicism, and what might be called a guarded euphoria, started turning up. There was not, however, a Lost Generation of comic artists and the twenties produced no examples of disillusionment, nihilism or sexual revolution in the comic strip format. But the funnies did change in many ways. Women began to assume more and more starring roles, especially as working girls and flappers. The amount of out-and-out nonsense increased while boyish pranks and dialect jokes diminished. Family life became an increasingly popular theme for comic strips and more contemporary satire appeared. As the decade progressed more and more strips became fascinated with the possibilities of continuity. The notion that you could tell a straight adventure yarn, of the sort to be found in pulp fiction magazines and on the silver screen, took hold. Constrained by the moral, religious, political, and social views of each and every client newspaper, no strip of the decade matched *The Great Gatsby*, *The Sun Also Rises*, or even a Clara Bow movie for candor and realism. But some interesting creations flourished.

The Affairs of Jane, *Chic Young.*

The real-life flappers of the decade were, first and foremost, aggressively emancipated. "Young women of the post-war generation appeared eager to abandon all social restraints on their behavior," writes historian Michael E. Parrish, "by taking to heart the idea equality meant enjoying the pleasures customarily reserved for men." The typical flapper, as described everywhere from the pages of *The Ladies' Home Journal* to an F. Scott Fitzgerald novel, went in for "a seemingly endless round of drinking, smoking, and flirting." Flappers wore short skirts, rolled silk stockings, and quite often, not a stitch of underwear. They enjoyed bad posture, too, and never stood up straight when they could slouch. Obviously the young women who began showing up in the comic sections of the day were more subdued than their contemporaries in the real world, but some managed to come as close to the popular flapper stereotype as they could in a polite medium like the newspaper.

One of the first flapper features was C. A. Voight's *Betty*, a Sunday page that began in 1920. Handsomely drawn in Voight's loose, sketchy, illustrative style, it dealt humorously with beautiful, up-to-date Betty Thompson and her rather mindless interactions with her rich and idle young friends. The main settings were parties and social gatherings, at mansions, country clubs, and beaches. Though a fairly liberated young lady, blond Betty came across as a rather dull social butterfly and it was difficult to determine exactly what Voight himself thought of his paper doll. He certainly dressed her fashionably and well. A required member of the cast in such enterprises seemed to be the unattractive yet persistent boyfriend; the sap, the goat, the born loser, who had much in common with the stock cuckold of farce. In *Betty* he was Lester DePester, a short, chinless, and charmless fellow who was the butt of endless jokes and pranks and of Betty's disdain and indifference for the entire near quarter-century run of the strip.

Chic Young, who was to become a multimillionaire by glorifying the American girl, made his first try at drawing about a liberated young woman in 1921. Hired by NEA and working out of the syndicate bullpen in Cleveland, Ohio, he produced *The Affairs of Jane.* Not quite as old as the century and still signing himself Murat Young, he drew the new daily in a simple, slightly awkward version of the standard correspondence school style of comic art. But the youthful Young was already displaying a good sense of how to structure gags as well as an eye and an ear for how flappers dressed and talked. Jane, a high school dropout, devoted her time to a string of weak-chinned beaus and an assortment of polite, small-town golddigging schemes. Young was paid twenty-two dollars a week, a sum he never forgot, and he abandoned *Jane* after six months in a dispute with his bosses over a raise.

In 1922, Young went to work for the Bell Syndicate and turned out *Beautiful Bab.* This new daily also starred a pretty brunette, but this time, in addition to gags, there was some continuity. The credit over the strip read, "A Serial, by Murat Young." Another polite golddigger, Bab was staying at a summer camp for young women when the story began. In need of $15.60 to buy a new riding habit and denied the sum by her exasperated dad, she devised a scheme for raising it. That involved renting out her soon-to-arrive beau, Oliver Gimble, by the hour to the man-starved other girls at camp. Since Oliver, like most of the leading men in Young's work, was lacking in charm and grace, Bab's plan did not work smoothly. *Beautiful Bab* came to an end after just four months, but better things lay ahead for the cartoonist and he was getting ever closer to turning into the successful Chic Young.

Accepting next a job with King Features, Young moved east to work in the syndicate art department in New York City. Apparently Hearst himself had been noticing his strip efforts, short-lived as they were. In 1924 the cartoonist created *Dumb Dora*, taking the name from a slang expression popularized by Tad, and started signing his work Chic Young. His name change also seemed to change his luck, and the new strip got off to a much better start than those that had preceded it. Dora Bell was a cute, dark-haired flapper, and this time Young, who had never been near a campus, picked a college coed for his heroine. Dora, despite her nickname, was actually clever and always got her way. She could, in the charming, scatterbrained manner of so many 1920s ingenues of stage and screen, manipulate just about anyone. After realizing what happened, they exclaimed, "She's not so dumb." The less than handsome, clumsy boyfriend in this strip was plump, redheaded, Rod Ruckett. There were, to be sure, a great many other more handsome beaus.

Young often utilized simple continuities, but his main goal was a gag each day. He remained with Dora and company until the spring of 1930 and then moved on to a new pretty girl, this one named Blondie.

Edgar Martin's *Boots and Her Buddies* became part of the Newspaper Enterprises Association package in 1924. Boots was a blond college flapper, complete with ukulele, in her first years in print. Then she became successively a working girl, married woman, and mother. Though fairly independent in her coed phase, Boots was, as one critic has observed, "never either a rebel or a flirt" and she was "chastely sexy." Martin had a brisk, uncluttered way of drawing and kept his heroine and all her buddies dressed fashionably. Indicative of what was most important in his work was the title Martin selected for the Sunday page, which started in 1931. It was called simply *Girls*.

An army of other flappers invaded the funny pages during the twenties, most of them not hanging around for long. Among the short-run flapper strips was *Dulcy, the Beautiful Dumb-bell*. It had a Hollywood setting and was illustrated by Loren Stout. The continuity was credited to movie actress Constance Talmadge. One of the three Talmadge Sisters, she was a major comedy star in silent films. At this time she was the sister-in-law of Buster

Petey, *Charles A. Voight. His daily strip often contained Betty type flappers in the twenties.*

Keaton and a friend of Anita Loos. Loos had written several screenplays for Constance, including an adaptation of the Marc Connelly and George S. Kaufman Broadway hit *Dulcy*. It's quite possible she had a hand in the writing of this unsuccessful newspaper effort. A versatile young woman calling herself Virginia Huget was responsible for several strips in the flapper category. In the summer of 1926, she very briefly drew *Gentlemen Prefer Blondes* for the Bell Syndicate. This was an adaption of Anita Loos' best-selling book of 1925. The book had been illustrated by Ralph Barton, and Huget based her versions of the blond Lorelei Lee and her brunette chum, Dorothy, on his. She was only with the comic strip a few weeks and then was replaced by a gentleman named Phil Cook for the remainder of its short life. The following year, in a style that blended elements of Barton and Ethel Hays, she produced *Babs in Society*, a Sunday page about a brunette department store salesgirl who inherited millions. Next came a daily strip that was known at various times as *Molly the Manicure Girl* and *Campus Capers*. Both versions featured blond Molly and brunette Gertie.

Ethel Hays was one of the more successful women cartoonists of the twenties. After studying art in both Los Angeles and New York City, she took the Landon mail-order cartooning course. This proved to be most beneficial, since C. N. Landon himself got her a job with the *Cleveland Press* art department. Hays drew in an appealing, decorative style that was obviously influenced by the work of Russell Patterson and John Held, Jr. Now and then she threw in some Nell Brinkley frills and filigrees. Her most widely seen feature, syndicated by NEA, was *Flapper Fanny Says*. It was a one-column daily panel, in the *Abe Martin* format. Each day readers got a cute drawing of dark-haired, fashionable Fanny with a clever saying printed below it. As might be expected from a panel with a double entendre in its title, *Fanny* specialized in smart sayings that sometimes bordered on the risqué. The drawings often showed Fanny in her lingerie, getting out of

FLAPPER FANNY SAYS:
REG. U. S. PAT. OFF.

In winter the mercury is down up north and up down south.

Flapper Fanny, Ethel Hays. Hays deserted her creation at decade's end, but Fanny continued through the thirties. ©1930, NEA.

bed or even relaxing in the tub. On a typical day she might say, "Too many gentlemen prefer blondes after marrying brunets," or "You can't expect a car to get anyplace when it's always stalling around." Hays dropped the panel in 1930, relinquishing the job to Gladys Parker.

Jefferson Machamer, forgotten today, was one of the principal depictors of flappers during the 1920s, right up there with Patterson and Held. A former Kansas City newspaper artist, he transplanted himself to New York City and was hired by *Judge*. He provided the weekly humor magazine with pictures of pretty girls, drawn in an appealing, scratchy version of the Patterson style. He also covered Broadway and the speakeasy circuit as an artist and, sometimes, writer. In 1928, he was noticed by Hearst and began, in late April, doing a flapper strip for King Features. Briefly titled *Patty the Playful*, it soon became *Petting Patty*. Patty was a pretty, long-legged member of the Manhattan smart set, described in syndicate publicity as "dazzling ... captivating ... irresistible," and her natural habitats included night clubs, cocktail parties, country houses, private beaches, and country club golf courses. Machamer had a rudimentary sense of humor and depended on glib remarks rather than structured gags. He frequently dabbled in continuity, once having Patty arrested as a masked burglar and another time chronicling her kidnapping by a gang that locked her in a mysterious mansion known as Black House. In addition to a string of handsome suitors, Patty also came equipped with the requisite foolish boyfriend. In this case he was Tubby Van Sillywill, who addressed her by such nicknames as "Patty-pooh." The strip collapsed at about the same time as the stock market in 1929.

Beyond doubt, the cartoonist most closely identified with the twenties and its basic iconography was John Held, Jr. He started depicting flappers and their boyfriends as the decade began, and his distinctive drawings were soon continuously on view in *Life*, *Vanity Fair*, *Collier's*, *College Humor*, numerous advertisements, and on the book covers of works by such Jazz Age chroniclers as F. Scott Fitzgerald. He was one of the few cartoonist millionaires of the era. Held, after working briefly on a panel titled *Oh! Margy!* for United Feature, signed up with King Features. His *Merely Margy*, a daily strip and Sunday page started in October 1929, starred a typical Held blonde, "an awfully nice girl." Like all Held girls, Margy was frequently seen crossing her legs and revealing the tops of rolled stockings and the lace of her teddy. Quite probably Held waited too long to jump into the funnies. The feature, as comics historian Dennis Wepman points out, "captured the fleeting humor of the period already disappearing; the sleek vamp Margy, her devoted but perennially broke swain Arab and his muscular stooge Bull were

by the end of the 1920s something of an anachronism, and with the Stock Market crash in 1929 their humor was doomed." *Margy* didn't make it through 1930 and in the grim new decade Held ceased to fare especially well.

Etta Kett started in 1925 as a strip aimed at giving etiquette tips to young people. It was by Paul Robinson, who'd spent several years working in animation before switching to newspaper cartooning. He was one more artist who drew in a simple linear style that owed a good deal to the example set by Russell Patterson. As a later press release put it, "Paul found that social usage had little appeal—and his good-looking girls plenty. He threw out the Emily Post touch." *Etta Kett* became a flapper strip, but a very mild-mannered one in which youth was tepid rather than flaming. Interestingly enough, Etta outlasted all of her roaring twenties competition and didn't exit the comic sections until late in 1974.

Not all the young women who frequented the funnies during these years were members of the leisure class. The decade also saw the continuing emergence of the working girl. During World War One thousands of women had moved into areas of employment that were traditionally male, particularly into industry and agriculture. But, as historians like Michael E. Parrish have pointed out, "wartime employment gains for women proved to be very short-lived, as figures from the 1920s demonstrated. Between 1920 and 1930, two million females joined the labor force, but the number of women actually employed grew only a single percentage point, from 23 to 24 percent.... The 1930 census listed American women in an extraordinary number of occupations from lawyers to steeplejacks, but the vast majority of those women who worked out-

Merely Margy, *John Held, Jr. Two panels from a promotional drawing. Note Margy's rolled stockings.*

side the home remained segregated in five low-paying, low-status jobs, as before—nursing, teaching, domestic service, clerical, and sales." The working women who showed up in the comic strips of the 1920s had an even narrower choice of occupations and most of them labored in business offices.

The earliest working girl strip was A. E. Hayward's *Somebody's Stenog*. It began in 1916 in the *Philadelphia Ledger* as *Somebody's Stenographer* and in 1918, under its new, shorter name, went into national syndication. The stenog in question was a slim, practical blonde named Cam O'Flage. She toiled as a secretary for a nuts and bolts company headed by short, roly-poly Sam Smithers and her best friend as a short roly-poly secretary named Mary Doodle. Although, as Mark Johnson has noted, "many of the strip's gags and continuities were based on office life, the characters also went on outside adventures, including a lark in Atlantic City in which Cam won the Miss America crown and another in Paris where a giant nut from the Smithers company pulled down the Eiffel Tower." Hayward developed a new style for this strip, using a simple line approach that avoided details, shading or much in the way of backgrounds. While *Somebody's Stenog* never came in near the top of any popularity polls, it did run throughout the 1920s and 1930s and managed to outlive Hayward by two years.

The Chicago Tribune-N.Y. News Syndicate's working girl strip began in September 1920. Titled *Winnie Winkle the Breadwinner*, it was the work of

Petting Patty, *Jefferson Machamer. That's Tubby Van Sillywill on the right.* ©1928, King Features Syndicate, Inc.

Martin Branner. While very much in the *Somebody's Stenog* vein—for a time pretty blond Winnie even had a short, plump girlfriend who was a ringer for Mary Doodle—the new strip added some elements of melodrama to the comedy. Winnie was the sole support of her family, which included her amiable mother, her unemployable and sometimes drunken father, and her little brother Perry. Rip Winkle, her ne'er-do-well father, was content to live off her earnings and he frequently advised her that she ought to marry a rich man: "Ye'd be fixed fer life!" After trying various jobs, Winnie settled down as a secretary with the Bibbs Pin Co. "In the early years, the daily strip recounted the events of a working girl's life with reasonable fidelity," notes Dennis Wepman. "Winnie deftly sidestepped the mashers who pursued her, humored her hypochondriacal boss Mr. Bibbs, and tactfully managed her shiftless and occasionally bibulous father." Branner produced a livelier, better looking feature than Hayward and *Winnie Winkle* was considerably more successful. Branner, with the help of his wife, kept Winnie dressed fashionably and sporting the latest hairstyle and that no doubt contributed to her popularity with women readers. If readers had thought about it, however, they'd have realized she had a great many more frocks than most secretaries could afford. For most of the 1920s the drawing was by a ghost named Royal King Cole.

Owing something to both Cam O'Flage and Winnie Winkle was Tillie Jones. She was the leading lady in Russ Westover's 1921 King Features effort, *Tillie the Toiler*. In its early years, this was an office-based strip and Tillie, a pretty and fashionably

dressed brunette, was portrayed as a somewhat flighty and scatterbrained secretary. She was a flirt and a moderate golddigger, and work was usually the last thing on her mind. Her

employer was named Simpkins, and he ran a fashion business, which gave Tillie the chance, eventually, to do some modeling as well. Working in the same office was Clarence J. MacDougall, better known as Mac. As the strip progressed, Mac began to shrink until he was the size of such comic strip shrimps as Abie the Agent and Wash Tubbs. He became the goat, the poor sap whom Tillie took advantage of, borrowed money from, and stood up for dates when a better looking guy came along. Unlike such characters as Lester DePester, Mac was somewhat likable, and many readers took to hoping that Tillie would eventually give him a break. Westover apparently never considered that as a possibility, and once told an interviewer, "Personally, I can not picture a pretty girl like Tillie marrying a deadpan half-pint like Mac, can you?" As *Tillie* continued through the 1920s, continuity began to creep in and stories unfolded outside the workplace. Like Branner, Westover paid close attention to fashions and always saw to it that Tillie was up-to-date in her outfits. When a *Tillie the Toiler* movie was made in 1927, William Randolph Hearst's great good friend Marion Davies appeared in the title role.

Fritzi Ritz, started by Larry Whittington in 1922 for the *New York Evening World*'s syndicate, underwent a transition from flapper to working girl strip in the middle of the decade. For quite awhile Fritzi led an idle life, letting her businessman widower father support her in style and dating a succession of bland young men, one of whom was a bootlegger. Then she became interested in acting and began pursuing a career in the movies. In the twenties there

Somebody's Stenog, A. E. Hayward. This sample is from 1930, hence the concern with the state of the nation's business.

was still considerable film activity in the East, and the pretty brunette did not have to leave her Manhattan home to work in that branch of show business. Hearst continued his habit of raiding the staff of the *World*, and in 1925 Whittington, an artist endowed with a very minor talent, was hired away by King Features. For them he fashioned a similar strip called *Mazie the Model*. Both the strip and the artist soon faded away.

Fortunately for Fritzi, the artist who assumed her strip was Ernie Bushmiller. A talented, redheaded twenty-year old from the Bronx, he'd been on the *World* staff for several years and had worked his way up from office boy. He had moved into the art department and was doing everything from spot drawings to puzzle pages. The Bushmiller version of *Fritzi Ritz* was immediately better looking and funnier. A born cartoonist and one of the best gagmen around, the young artist had now found a suitable outlet for his abilities. He turned the strip into a winner and in 1929 a Sunday page was added. Early in the next decade, as we'll see, he introduced Fritzi's little niece to the strip and turned it into an even bigger success.

Among the other working girl strips were Sals Bostwick's *Hello, Hattie*, about an office switchboard operator, and *Polly of the Follies* by magazine cartoonist Chester Garde, which followed a young woman who came to New York seeking a career on the stage. Not quite in the same pattern was Ken Kling's *Katinka*. Drawn in the style he'd developed while ghosting *Mutt and Jeff*, the strip was about a large, ungainly young woman who worked as a cook and housekeeper, at a salary of $40 a month, for a middle-class couple named Gessitt. Some of the jokes dealt with Katinka's housework and others with her bumpy romance with her boyfriend Ferdie, who was a borderline four-flusher.

America became increasingly urbanized as the 1920s progressed, and the public in general grew more sophisticated. A fascination with small-town life continued to grow, however, in popular entertainments. Some works were nostalgic, others satirical or critical. Sinclair Lewis's bestselling novels *Main Street* (1920) and *Babbitt* (1922) viewed small-town life and Midwestern businessmen with what has been called "photographic distaste." Others took a more positive view. Harold Lloyd, for example, usually played a likable small town go-getter in his feature comedies, notably in such films as *Grandma's Boy* (1921), *Girl Shy* (1924), *The Freshman* (1925), and *The Kid Brother* (1927). Glenn Hunter portrayed a slightly more serious but similar character in *West of the Water Tower* (1924) and *Merton of the Movies* (1924). This latter was based on Harry Leon Wilson's 1922 novel about a young man who leaves his Midwestern small town to seek fame and fortune in Hollywood.

The small-town boy also showed up in the funnies, and there was a mild flurry of them in the middle of the decade. Sals Bostwick was a graduate of the Federal Schools correspondence course in cartooning and had worked as assistant to

Tillie the Toiler, Russ Westover. Mac does an impressive take in this daily from the strip's first year. ©1921, King Features Syndicate, Inc.

Frank King on *Gasoline Alley*. After doing strips of his own for the *Chicago Trib*, he was hired away by the rival *Chicago American* at a yearly salary of $15,000. His first effort for Hearst was *Main Street Jed*, a daily that began in March 1926. When readers first met Jed Simpkins, the lean, chinless young man was just one of the loafers in the little community of Birdville. The town was populated chiefly by the types who'd been hanging out in *Abe Martin* for years, although some of the young women were flappers. A quiet place, Birdville was making the same transitions that many real-life hamlets were undergoing. Citizens were trading in their horses and buggies for automobiles and while they attended church socials, they also frequented the town movie house and listened to the radio. Jed's judgment of Birdville was that it was not "such a dull town to live in 'cause you are always sure of two big days—Friday when the paper comes out and Saturday when Emery Squires gets drunk."

In May he got a job at a nearby summer resort, after explaining to his prospective boss that "all of the work there is in me is still in 'cause I never worked any of it out." When he collected his first weekly salary of fifteen dollars, Jed was elated: "This is the first time I've ever had enough money all at once to buy a new suit, a hat, a pair of shoes, and still have some change." While working at the resort, Jed met a rich, big-city girl named Floradora. He politely courted her, even though he had a plump girlfriend back home. Floradora was fond of Jed, yet could not help thinking of him as "a country rube." Nothing came of the romance, and later in the year Jed made his first trip to the city. He found it a frenzied, unfriendly place and was glad he'd bought himself a round-trip ticket. Back in Birdville, Jed became a reporter for the *Gazette*. He took Miss Vaughn, "Birdville's pretty school teacher," to a dance and that caused a scandal. The School Board was ready to fire her, since single teachers were not allowed a social life, but Jed's friend, bewhiskered old Uncle Al, spoke up and saved her job. *Main Street Jed* was a quietly amusing strip, and Bostwick drew in his own version of the simple Chicago style favored by King, Walter Berndt, and Frank Willard. He was fond of soliloquies, a habit he probably picked up while working on *Gasoline Alley*, and his characters were often to be found talking to themselves.

In 1927 writer Bill Conselman, under the pen name Frank Smiley, teamed with artist Mel Cummin to produce *Good Time Guy*. This one was about a hefty, freckle-faced small town young man, a "well-meaning bumpkin," with "a heart as big as a pump-

Main Street Jed, Sals Bostwick. ©1926, Evening American Publishing Company.

kin, only softer." Guy had two big ambitions: "To see everyone has a good time and to give uke lessons in Hawaii." He lived with his widowed mother in Cornhay City and was too shy to pursue pretty, blond, Mary Laffer, even though "she has eyes only for Guy—and what eyes!" October 1927 saw the advent of a similar strip, *Big Hearted Otis* by Fred Fox. Otis Galahad Gay was a good-looking, dark-haired young fellow who lived in the small town of Jaydunk—"It's such a slow town that even radio programs come in a day late"—with his maiden aunt and worked at a blacksmith's at a salary of seven dollars a week. Otis dreamed of the days of King Arthur and yearned to do good deeds himself. After saving a young flapper from a runaway car, Otis decided to leave Jaydunk to seek adventure in the outside world. For the remainder of the strip's brief life, he sought adventure and fortune and didn't do that badly. He won a couple of rewards for his good deeds and he ran into the girl he'd rescued, Elaine Fair was her name. If *Big Hearted Otis* had lasted longer a romance would not doubt have blossomed between the two. Fox later worked briefly on *Good Time Guy*, and then he and Conselman established a long term relationship on *Ella Cinders*, which we'll encounter in the next chapter.

The family homesteading of the comic section continued in the 1920s. The majority of these new neighbors were comfortably middle class and they dealt in more genteel forms of humor, scorning pranks, pratfalls, and fireworks. A model for many of this breed was Clare Briggs's *Mr. and Mrs.* A Sunday page he began doing for the *New York Tribune* in the spring of 1919, it was widely syndicated in the 1920s. The feature was devoted almost entirely to Joe and Vi and their little son. Joe was the prototype for many comic strip husbands. He was middle-aged, round-shouldered, balding, weak-chinned, and sported a scraggly mustache. Vi was a plain woman who dressed sensibly and wore her hair in a bun. Joe did some sort of office work and they owned their own home in the suburbs. Briggs favored a fixed point of view for his drawing, and every panel was a medium shot of the domestic stage. The majority of the pages took place in their home and what they excelled at was bickering. Vi thrived on a low-key sort of nagging: "I thought you were going to start the garden today," "You go right down and *demand* a raise." Joe's favorite pastime was sitting in his armchair, reading his paper, smoking his cigar, and avoiding all of his household responsibilities. Each of them loved to get the better of the other, and when a spouse caught the other spouse in an awkward situation or a fib, the standard response was, "Ha ha ha ha." Arguments and squabbles sometimes continued for hours and Briggs frequently ended a page with a black panel that indicated the darkened bedroom. Only talk balloons showed and a caption that read, "And so—far-far into the night." At the conclusion of bicker sessions of shorter duration, their son, who seemed to serve no other function, would inquire either, "Mama love papa?" or "Papa love mama?" This pioneering dysfunctional family survived until 1963. Briggs died early in 1930 and was replaced initially by writer Arthur Folwell and artist Ellison Hoover.

Early in the 1920s, Tad Dorgan, possibly at the suggestion of *New York Journal* edi-

tor and Hearst henchman Arthur Brisbane, started a Sunday page that bore a strong resemblance to *Mr. and Mrs.* Webster Blink, the husband in Tad's *For Better Or Worse*, was balding, middle-aged, and the owner of a nondescript mustache. His wife, Lil, closely resembled Vi. Webster worked in an office, and the childless couple resided in the suburbs either in or near a new development called Hopeville by the Dump. Tad was rowdier than Briggs, and did not abandon his fascination with slang for this domestic endeavor. Lil Blink was heard to utter such expressions as "Rats!" and "You're as funny as a glass eye." Sunday situations were built around such events as Webster's getting into a fist fight with a surly plumber or being tossed into the loony bin after he and an old chum caused a disturbance in a restaurant. Tad, as noted earlier, sometimes indulged in ethnic humor. One page that could not have been done after the twenties had Webster overhearing a black woman speaking in Irish dialect: "Git out of me sight I says—It's the likes of you that spoils parties…. Begorra." Unaware that the woman "was raised down by Paddy's market," he assumes he's suffering hallucinations caused by some bad liquor: "I'll swear I heard that darky with the brogue."

The most successful family strip to be introduced during this period was *The Nebbs*. It came along in 1923 and had several affinities to the popular *The Gumps*. Sol Hess was running a thriving wholesale jewelry business in Chicago when he met Sidney Smith in 1917. Both men frequented Stillson's, a saloon favored by newspaper people. Fairly soon, the gregarious and inventive Hess was contributing gags to *The Gumps* and eventually

The Nebbs, *Wally Carlson. Adventures and get-rich-quick schemes were suspended for the holidays.* ©1925, the Bell Syndicate, Inc.

came to write most of the continuity. According to an account Hess gave to Martin Sheridan for his 1941 book *Comics and Their Creators*, "Even with the meteoric rise of the cartoon, Sol continued to give his services as though he were paid for them, content merely with the realization of the success of his efforts." It was when Smith signed his first million-dollar contract with the *Chicago Tribune* in 1922 that Hess began thinking about doing a strip of his own.

John Wheeler, whose Bell Syndicate distributed *The Nebbs*, gave a somewhat different account of the events leading up to the genesis. "Smith, however, made one big mistake. When his contract ran out with the *Tribune*, he held out for big figures and got them, as well as a Rolls Royce as a bonus," he wrote. "Then he offered Hess $200 a week to continue to write the comic. Knowing the facts, Hess was insulted and told Smith he was going to quit." Sensing an opportunity, Wheeler rushed from Manhattan to Chicago. He made a deal with the disgruntled Hess to come up with a new version of *The Gumps*. "We hired a young artist named Wally Carlson to do the drawing. I guaranteed Hess 6 percent against a guarantee of $800 a week."

Carlson was born in St. Louis, but grew up in Chicago. Self-taught, he was something of a prodigy, having "graduated from newsboy to cartoonist on the *Chicago Inter-Ocean* at the age of fifteen." After the morning newspaper failed, he moved into animation, working for Essanay and then Bray. In 1919 he started the Carlson Studios in the Windy City, whose chief output was a series of Gumps animated cartoons. That was how he met Hess. Carlson was, even at the start of the strip, a much better cartoonist than Smith.

"The name Nebb had been used a number of times in *The Gumps*," Hess told Sheridan.

"It comes from the Jewish word 'nebich,' a reference of contempt for a 'poor sap.' The name Rudy was very popular at that time, at least its distinguished owner was, so we chose the famous movie idol Valentino's first name." Rudy Nebb was similar in looks and attitudes to Andy Gump, except he was not chinless. He had a plump, goodhearted wife named Fanny, a teenage daughter, and a preteen son called Junior. The stories Hess fashioned for his own strip were similar to those he had turned out for Smith. There were domestic problems, mysteries, and frequent plots involving Rudy's attempts to make some kind of financial killing. Junior Nebb, like the similar Chester Gump, led a separate life of his own in the Sunday pages and it was a life filled with action, intrigue, and adventure. He got involved with lost gold mines, circuses, Western outlaws, crooks, spies and most of the other Saturday matinee staples. Wheeler was an exceptional salesman and even managed to approach his rival, William Randolph Hearst, and show him samples of *The Nebbs*. "He okayed it for his whole string of papers at a price that got us off the nut," Wheeler explained. "From then on it grew, and we all prospered." The feature eventually achieved a list of over five hundred newspapers.

The New York Tribune, Inc. continued to add domestic comedies to its list. An early entry was *Clarence*, a Sunday page by magazine cartoonist Crawford Young. This was, though it adhered to the basic family format, much more in tune with the twenties. Clarence, head of the household, was a plump fellow in his middle years with a mustache and not much hair. His wife was a slim blonde with bobbed hair and a fashionably boyish figure. They had a son named Jasper and a college-age daughter named Mabel. A definitely liberated young woman, the brunette Mabel saw to it that the page was livelier than some of its neighbors. She regularly shocked her parents with her ideas about petting, companionate marriage, and sex in general. In between more traditional gags, Young would toss in one involving the thoroughly modern Mabel.

The majority of father figures in most of the other domestic strips that blossomed in these years resembled that standard husband doodle perfected by Briggs and Tad. The theme of R. W. Satterfield's *The Bicker Family* was summed up in the title. Syndicated by NEA

Reg'lar Fellers, Gene Byrnes (with Tack Knight). Jimmie, Puddinhead, and company in two panels from a 1925 Sunday page.

in 1922, it was drawn in a fairly close approximation of the Briggs style and Milt Bicker was a double of Joe from *Mr. and Mrs.* Milt Gross, before he began experimenting with the joys of Yiddish, drew a family strip for the *New York World*'s syndicate in 1923. It was called *Hitz and Mrs.* and derived its humor from the trials and tribulations of urban apartment living. Fowler Hitz, the man of the house, was a shorter, squatter version of the Briggs stereotype. He and his plump wife Harriet got along pretty well, and the daily gags were often wackier and more screwball than those to be found in other domestic comedies. Vic Pazmino, who always signed himself VEP and drew in the manner of a gifted twelve-year-old, began *The Figgers Family* for the Central Press Syndicate in 1927. Pa Figger was a fatter version of the standard dad and the daily came equipped with Ma, flapper daughter Betty, little son Teddy, and mutt dog Rusty. VEP alternated jokes with simple continuities. Among the many other similar strips were *The Gabbs* by Barrie Payne, another Briggs impersonator, and *Adam and Eva* by Cap Higgins, which concerned a young, married couple in the suburbs.

Further family gatherings included H. T. Webster's *The Man in the Brown Derby*, a Sunday page very similar to *Mr. and Mrs.* in look, content, and pacing. Webster drew it from 1923 until the end of the *World*. Joe Cunningham drew *Roofus McGoofus*, and Bud Counihan did *The Little Big Family* (also known as *Little Napoleon*). Another NEA entry was *Mom 'n Pop*,

which got going in December, 1924. The family name of the leading characters was Gunn, meaning that the head of the household was known as Pop Gunn. Loron Taylor, a former telegraph operator in a small Ohio town and a graduate of the Landon Course in Cartooning, was the creator. He concentrated chiefly on a gag-a-day approach. At Taylor's death, early in 1928, Wood Cowan inherited the strip. A onetime sports cartoonist, Cowan already had several strips to his credit, including the flapper effort *Carrie and Her Car*. He brought continued stories and suspense to the feature.

Included in the flood of other family-based strips were *Main Street*, a Sunday drawn in an imitation of the McManus style by Gus Mager; *So This Is Married Life* by Al Zere (the lifelong pen name of Alfred Alblitzer); *The Potters* by J. P. McEvoy and a succession of artists; *The Featherhe ds* initially by L. F. Van Zelm and then by F. O. Alexander using his middle name for the alias Osborne; *Eddie's Friends*, based on characters from Jean Knott's poker panel, *Penny Ante*, and drawn by Knott and, on occasion, various of his colleagues, including Frank Willard and Cliff Sterrett.

The children who invaded the comic pages were different from most of their predecessors of earlier decades. Neither pranksters nor dreamers, nor excessively cute, they were, for the most part, just kids. The new strips were closer to the sort of thing Tom McNamara had pioneered in *Us Boys*, and dealt with the everyday concerns of everyday kids. Often adults would not appear at all, and when a parent or a teacher or a relative showed up, it was rarely as the target of an assault. Things like marbles and baseballs and homemade wagons replaced fire-crackers and wildcats as standard props and figuring out how to come up with a nickel for an ice cream soda replaced plotting ways to sink a boat or dress a chimpanzee in a tuxedo. These new comic strip children of the twenties were regular fellows.

The strip that helped establish the new precedent had actually started during World War I. Gene Byrnes, one more Landon graduate, first did his *Reg'lar Fellers* as a panel. By late 1920 there was a *Reg'lar Fellers* daily strip and Sunday page. Although looking and talking like big-city street kids, Byrnes's bunch lived in a pleasant suburban neighborhood. Jimmie Dugan, who always wore a black, short-pants suit and a checkered cap, was the focal youth and came closer to any of the others to being leader of the half-dozen or so boys who made up the pack. Next in line was pudgy Puddinhead Duffy. Aggie Riley was Jimmie's girl, but she did not hang out with him, Puddinhead, and the other regulars. While many of the kids had Irish names, there was nothing ethnic about the strip. Byrnes, who had considerable help on the strip from George Carlson and Tack Knight, built his gags around the common pursuits and concerns of children in the ten-year-old range: school, home, food, girls, and games.

Skippy, Percy L. Crosby. ©1938, Percy L. Crosby.

Frequently, the boys would exchange opinions about topics ranging from the meaning of life and what it would be like to be rich and famous to whether or not cowboy actors could really ride horses. Most of the discussions took place while the cast was in motion, since all the children were hyperactive. They rarely sat still, and whenever they went racing someplace they stirred up clouds of dust on peaceable suburban streets.

Walter Berndt took a somewhat different approach to childhood. In his *Smitty*, begun late in 1922 for the *Trib-News* syndicate, he built many of his jokes on the working life of his young protagonist. Augustus Smith was a thin blond lad in his early teens and he labored daily as an office boy for a plump avuncular boss named Mr. Bailey. Unlike *Jerry on the Job*, there was no nonsense in the strip and Smitty had a homelife. He lived with his mother and father and lisping little brother Herby. Unconcerned about the pros and cons of child labor, the strip went its jovial way. As Dennis Wepman has observed, "there isn't a mean bone in any of their bodies and it was not surprising that America took the genial strip to its heart for over half a century."

An artist with a very modest ability was Arthur Daniels Carter, who always signed his work Ad Carter. In 1922 he produced King Features' imitation of *Reg'lar Fellers*. It was called *Just Kids*, and in it Carter even swiped Byrnes' format and his backgrounds. His central character was Mush Stebbins, who'd appeared in the previous decade in a short-lived strip titled *Our Friend Mush*. Mush's gang of kid pals had the requisite fat boy, Fatso by name, but departed from the norm by including a Chinese kid.

The most impressive comic strip kid to emerge in the twenties was Percy Crosby's *Skippy*, who became not only a hit in newspapers but eventually in books, radio, movies, and merchandising. The oddly dressed little boy, who went around in a smock, floppy bow tie, short pants, woebegone shoes, and a movie comedian's checkered hat, made his debut in 1923 in the humor magazine *Life*. He appeared there in full-page, black-and-white halftones with dialogue running in type beneath the sequential panels. When *Skippy* became a newspaper strip in 1925, Crosby converted to hand-lettered balloons. He was an excellent artist and drew in a manner that had little to do with the accepted cartoon style of the correspondence schools or the styles of his contemporaries. "Crosby's sketchy, unlabored line had a ferocious energy," observes comics historian R. C. Harvey, "the vitality born of pen tearing breakneck across paper, and Crosby's subjects were imbued with that energy even if drawn in repose."

Percy Crosby, who had grown up on Long Island in a town his biographer Jerry Robinson describes as typical of "leisurely paced suburban America at the turn of the century," had early become fascinated with slum kids and tenement life. He drew them frequently in his magazine cartoons. Crosby treated these descendants of the residents of Hogan's Alley much differently than had Outcault. He was much closer to these ragged children and empathized with them. Unlike Outcault, who always drew kids from an adult distance, Crosby never forgot what he'd felt while making the difficult journey from child to adult. His first syndicated comic strip, begun in 1916, was *The Clancy Kids*. He was in tune with these children, too, though they lived in better circumstances than the street urchins of his magazine drawings. The artist served overseas during World War I as a first lieutenant in the AEF. He also managed to draw a daily cartoon panel, *That Rookie from the 13th Squad*, which was published in American newspapers. "How I did it, I'll never know," Robinson quotes

Crosby. "I conceived humorous events from the Front and drew them up and sent them to my syndicate. Six a week."

Skippy was set in the suburbs and Skippy Skinner lived a life that was outwardly comfortable and serene. But readers who got to know him soon realized that he was a very complex boy and that he had a much wider range of emotions than the other kids on the comic pages. Skippy was often seen sitting on a curbstone alone and addressing himself to one of the mysteries of life. Crosby frequently touched on topics that none of his colleagues in the 1920s risked getting involved with. He did strips about death, God and politics. In addition, of course, he dealt with the more acceptable problems of childhood—school, parents, romance, etc. Skippy was neither a brat nor an angel child and he took a pragmatic approach to many of the moral and social dilemmas of youth. Once, while walking by an outdoor fruit stand, he reflected, "Hm! Nobody around the fruit stand, but I don't think it's very nice to steal." After strolling on by, he added, "Besides, ya never know who's watchin'." On another occasion, when he spotted a little girl he was interested in at work sweeping the sidewalk in front of her

Mr. Dinglehoofer und his Dog, H. H. Knerr. A sketch done in response to a 1948 fan letter. Schnappsy is responding to a sketch I'd had the temerity to send Knerr.

Salesman Sam, C. D. Small. ©1930, NEA Service, Inc.

house, Skippy paused and told her, "Gee, kid, I hate to see you work so hard." Not offering to help her, he walked on, observing, "Oh, well, maybe someday I'll be able to take her outa all this." Crosby was one of the first strip artists to ignore the conventional daily format of four panels of equal width. He broke up his space to fit the joke, sometimes using three panels, sometimes two, and, now and then, just one long panel that stretched across the whole strip. *Skippy*, owned outright by Crosby, became increasingly popular. It had started out with a small syndicate but by the end of the decade Crosby was being distributed by King Features.

Among the other kid strips were *Chubby* by Jack Farr; *Snoodles* by political cartoonist Cy Hungerford; *Buttons and Fatty*, created earlier by Al Zere but carried on in the 1920s by M. E. Brady; *Muggs McGinnis* (later known as *Muggs and Skeeter*) by Wally Bishop; and *Bringing Up Bill*, also by Jack Farr. Charles "Doc" Winner drew a simple boyhood gag strip called *Tubby* for United Feature in 1923. He next went to work for King Features, becoming one of their two colorists for Sunday pages and also the syndicate's most dependable ghost artist. Winner also took over the *Elmer* page in 1925 and got back into the kid business. Jerry Costello, very briefly, drew a rather strange page titled *The Topsy-Turvies*. The premise was explained in the subtitle *If Children Were Grown-Ups and Old Folks Were Young, What a Funny World 'twould Be*. This strip had kids dressing and acting like adults while their elders behaved like

children. In the latter part of the decade Dwig abandoned all of Mark Twain's characters and converted *Tom Sawyer and Huck Finn* into *School Days*. A boy named Tom continued to be central to the strip, but now he lived in a contemporary small town and his best buddy was named Ruff instead of Huck.

The original brats of the funnies, Hans and Fritz, continued to be popular, in both the Dirks and the Knerr versions. Along with Mama, the Captain, and the Inspector, they undertook a series of around-the-world peregrinations. In Harold H. Knerr's *The Katzenjammer Kids*, the duo practiced mischief and mayhem in such far-flung locales as Brazil, Europe, Africa, and the North Pole. Rudolph Dirks's *The Captain and the Kids* did not travel as extensively, but in the course of these ten years the characters moved from an urban setting to, after some adventuring on the high seas, a permanent home on one of the Squeejee Islands. This was a tropical isle where the majority of the population was black. Dirks was fond of having odd characters, including an exiled South American dictator, a pompous pedagogue, a Svengali-like hypnotist, the perennial pirate Long John Silver, and the Herring Brothers drop in on the island of a Sunday. Besides being inventive pranksters, Dirks's Hans and Fritz were also iconoclasts and social critics and they often used their skill constructing explosive devices and sundry engines of destruction to deflate a pretentious visitor. The Captain, a conformist at heart despite his rather unorthodox life style, rarely appreciated the kids' work as revolutionaries and administered the same sort of spanking for an act of icon-oclasm as for the theft of fresh-baked pies.

Both Dirks and Knerr were exemplary cartoon-ists. Knerr was a shade ahead of Dirks in the con-structing of mechanical devices that wrought havoc amongst the kids' targets and he was exceptional at drawing the variety of animals—including elephants, monkeys and large quantities of wildcats—that many of Hans and Fritz' schemes required. Dirks, however, became increasingly adept at dialogue and dialect. For quite a spell in the middle 1920s, he took to ending his pages with a panel showing the boys, usually hiding out to avoid punishment, dis-cussing the events of the day. These dialogues usu-ally ran to hundreds of words.

Fritz: If it vosn't for der spanking I could be sorry for dot bunch but on der odder hand maybe not. You got to look at it fum both sides like a fried egg only dem is bad eggs und it vouldn't make no dif-ference. It's all so complexity! Sumtimes everyt'ing iss so simple und den again it's all ge-mixed und you can't t'ink! Chust now I can't t'ink vot I vos going to say!

Hans: Vell dot is der best news in a long time! Chust keep on t'inking und I vill do der saying. For impstance if sumbody don't dry up I might hand him a biff on der beezer. Dot vould be simple und I vould haff no more to say.

Hans: Did you heard der vun about der vild cat und der porcumpine? Dot's too bad, neither did I! In vun vay you iss a lucky liddle stiff on account you got such a smart brudder but on der odder hand why brag? In fact why mention it? Life is queer in some vays und so iss your Aunt Sarah, den vhy not be a sport und owe me fife dollars?

Fritz: Belief me, I vill keep your secret! Der only vorry I got is dot you won't haff gas enough to take you home! So play safe und dry up, Luffingly yours, Fritz!

In the early 1920s, King Features tried a daily *Katzenjammer Kids* strip, but it did not catch on. The artist was Oscar Hitt, who'd worked as an assistant to Dirks.

In the early months of 1926, the number of fea-tures in many of the Sunday comic sections sudden-ly doubled. The Hearst organization was the first to come up the idea of having most of the artists work-ing for its syndicates split their pages in two and add a second feature. These new additions, eventually called toppers, usually occupied from a fourth to a third of the total space. Most used a two-tier for-mat. At no extra cost, since the cartoonists did not earn extra pay for the new features, and no increase in overall page count, the Hearst Sunday comic sec-tions could advertise that readers were now getting up to twice as many funnies as before. Supplements that once had promised eight pages of color funnies started proclaiming, "16 Comics in Color."

The new top strips included *Dot and Dash*, an animal pantomime that moved in over *Polly and Her Pals*; *It's Papa Who Pays*, a domestic comedy about a middle-aged couple, which accompanied *Toots and Casper*; *Bill*, a domestic comedy about a young man who lived with his folks, that served as the topper to *Boob McNutt*. Many of the cartoonists on the Hearst payroll did not waste their time bothering to think up a brand new feature. Segar revived *Sappo*, featur-ing his suburban couple John and Myrtle Sappo. Over the years, as Segar became increasingly preoc-cupied with science fiction, the topper turned into a fantasy. Jimmy Swinnerton went back again to *Mr. Jack*, his strip about a tiger who was a philanderer and a sexual harasser, and installed it as a top strip to *Little Jimmy*. George McManus brought back *Rosie's Beau* to sit atop *Bringing Up Father*, and Percy Crosby made use of *Always Belittlin'*, formerly a one-panel daily cartoon, to accompany *Skippy*.

One of the more inventive cartoonists was H. H. Knerr, who created *Mr. Dinglehoofer und his Dog Adolph*. A pleasant humorous continuity, it was much gentler than *The Katzenjammer Kids* downstairs. Otto Dinglehoofer was a plump bald bachelor with a small white mustache. He spoke in the Katzenjammer dialect. Knerr authority James Lowe has suggested that in appearance he was a caricature of the artist's physician father. In the early thirties an orphan boy named Taddy became Dingy's ward and a regular member of the cast. In 1935 Adolph was dropped, no doubt because the rise of Hitler was making the name Adolph unpopular. A new dog, a dachshund named Schnappsy, replaced him.

Other syndicates joined in, and eventually such features as *Maw Green*, *Old Doc Yak*, *Ain't Nature Grand?*, *That Phony Nickel*, and *Phil Fumble* were sharing the page with *Little Orphan Annie*, *The Gumps*, *The Captain and the Kids*, *Gasoline Alley*, and *Fritzi Ritz*. The Chicago Tribune-N.Y. News Syndicate ran its second features at the bottom of the page instead of the top and limited them to a single tier.

Animal strips continued to appear. Rabbits, for some reason, multiplied considerably. First, in 1919, there was the kindly rabbit gentleman Uncle Wiggily. The creation of writer Howard R. Garis, he'd originally hopped into view in 1910 by way of a newspaper column that recounted bedtime stories. Uncle Wiggily Longears wore a tophat and tailcoat and lived in comfortable quarters in Animal Land. His devoted muskrat housekeeper was Nurse Jane Fuzzy Wuzzy and his wide circle of friends included a goat named Uncle Butter and a pig known as Floppy Twistytail. Several villains also resided in the middle-aged rabbit's woodsy neighborhood, including the Blue Nosed Baboon, the Skillery Skallery Alligator, Bob Cat, the Pipsiewah, and the Skeezicks. To a man they were intent on doing away with Wiggily so that they could obtain a mysterious substance called souse that was found in his ears.

All the characters of the stories were transferred to the Sunday *Uncle Wiggily's Adventures* page, syndicated by McClure, that started in 1919. The format consisted of illustration panels with the story in type below them. The artist was Lang Campbell, the same gentleman who'd been providing the drawings for the daily bedtime stories. An excellent cartoonist, Campbell had long specialized in animal cartoons and was a regular contributor to *Judge* and *Life*. He obviously enjoyed drawing not only animals, but birds and even insects. Lady bugs were a favorite of his and could be found in almost every page he did. A daily strip, titled *Uncle Wiggily's Tricks* and distributed by the McNaught Syndicate, began in the early 1920s, but was drawn by a succession of others. Garis threw in a dramatic change in his Sunday version in the spring of 1925, when he got rid of Nurse Jane and had Uncle Wiggily marry a widowed bunny lady with six small offspring. The tone changed and Mr. and Mrs. Wiggily took to bickering in the manner of *Mr. and Mrs.* while the half dozen stepbunnies emulated Hans and Fritz. The printed text was dropped later in the year, replaced by dialogue balloons. By 1929, all the funny paper versions of the Uncle Wiggily saga had ceased. Lang Campbell carried on for awhile with a sort of spinoff Sunday page for McClure. It was called *Paddy Pigtail* and starred a porker who was, from tam cap to colorful trousers, a ringer for Wiggily's old chum Floppy.

Another notable bunny, thoroughly domesticated from the start, was Peter Rabbit. His Sunday page commenced in 1920. This Peter derived not from the books of Beatrix Potter, but from a series of bedtime stories by Thornton W. Burgess. His Green Meadow tales, which appeared in magazines and books, were illustrated by Harrison Cady. Another master of animal drawing, Cady got sole credit for the *Peter Rabbit* Sunday page, which was syndicated by the *Herald Tribune*. His businessman bunny lived a life of quiet desperation in the suburban community of Carrotville with his wife and twin little sons, who were both pranksters. Bill Holman, while still a lad in his teens, drew *J. Rabbit, Esquire* for NEA, starting in November 1921. This was a simple joke-a-day strip, with an urban rabbit and his animal friends, yet it lacked the high nonsense content of Holman's later work. After it folded in 1922, he then produced *Birdville Birds*. A cozier rabbit family strip was *The Dumbunnies* (originally titled *In Rabbitboro*). It was the work of Albertine Randall and was syndicated by George Matthew Adams. Randall's drawings looked like those of an amateur, but she was the mother of Ed Wheelan, whose *Minute Movies* was a notable Adams success. Her strip ran from 1924 to 1927.

Nize Baby, Milt Gross. Two panels from a Sunday during the Feitlebaum's stay in the movie capital. That's Looy running in with the cramp cure. ©1928, Press Publishing Co.

The most popular 1920's animated cartoon character prior to Mickey Mouse's advent late in the decade was Felix the Cat. Indeed, many of Walt Disney's early animal characters, notably Oswald the Rabbit and Mickey Mouse, were patterned on the famous feline. The feisty, inventive Felix was a product of Pat Sullivan's cartoon studio and first showed up in movie palaces in 1919. Sullivan had been a newspaper cartoonist, first as assistant to Billy Marriner and then doing some unsuccessful Sunday pages of his own. Once he moved into animation, Sullivan left most of the drawing to the gifted and unsung Otto Messmer. King Features, who would later license many of the Disney characters, including Mickey, introduced a Felix Sunday page in 1923. Messmer drew it, but Sullivan signed it and took all the credit. A daily strip was added in 1927, also ghosted by Messmer. He drew in a lively and distinctive style and ranked high among the many excellent animal cartoonists of the period.

The leading George Herriman impersonator in the 1920s was a Canadian cartoonist named Arch Dale. The trouble with trying to become a surrogate Herriman is that while it is theoretically possible to approximate his drawing style, there is absolutely no way to emulate his thought processes. Born in Scotland, Dale came to Canada while in his teens. He left Winnipeg in 1921, where he'd

been a staff cartoonist for the *Free Press*, and moved to Chicago to do a Sunday page for the Thompson Feature Service. This was about the community of Dooville where a small population of very odd and diminutive people dwelt. Prominent among them was Officer Flannelfeet, who was a human version of Officer Pupp. Most of the weekly gags had to do with his encounters with an enterprising little fellow named Nicky Nutt who owned an elephant known as Tiny. All of Dale's jokes involved simple physical violence: Nicky shoots Tiny with a slingshot and then gets squirted by the elephant's trunk, or Nicky plays a prank on the cop and ends up getting beaten with a nightstick, etc. Dale did better at copying his idol's artwork, and all his background buildings and trees are swipes from *Krazy Kat*. *The Doo Dads* was never widely circulated and Dale gave it up in 1927. He returned to the *Winnipeg Free Press* and was their political cartoonist for more than twenty-five years.

A variety of other strips with a high nonsense content came and went in the years after World War I. *$alesman $am* was unleashed upon the world by NEA in the autumn of 1921. The artist George Swanson, who signed himself Swan, became a specialist at this particular blend of vaudeville jokes and silly trappings, and we'll encounter other similar works of his through the next several decades. The Sam strip centered on a go-getter named Sam Howdy, who spent most of his career working in the general store owned by J. Guzzlem. The emporium was the stage for the daily gag, often involving Sam and a customer and followed by a reaction take that might included falling over, turning a backwards somersault, and raising a huge cloud of dust. The store was also a comedy element itself, being festooned with odd signs and props. The signs changed daily, often from panel to panel: "Pants Included With Each Suit," "Shoe Sale—98 cents Each—3 for $3," "Henfruit From Our Own Orchard," and "Try Our 'Choo-Choo' Chew For Engineers." When Swan moved to King Features in 1927 to draw the comparable *High Pressure Pete*, Charles D. Small came from the NEA bullpen to become the new Salesman Sam perpetrator. He carried on admirably in the Swan tradition until well into the thirties.

Gene Ahern, a zany encountered earlier, began a new panel called *The Crazy Quilt* in February 1921. Two months later, it became a strip, broken into an assortment of sections, including a sometime invention corner and the adventures of a drunk named Homer Brew. Each day part of the space was given over to *The Nut Bros.—Ches & Wal*. The Brothers Nut, though not twins, were obviously inspired by Rube Goldberg's *Mike and Ike*. They told venerable jokes and riddles while traveling through surreal surroundings. Goldberg was producing his own brand of nonsense during these years, including such daily strips as *Rube Goldberg's Boobs* and *Rube's Ramblings*.

Herriman's major moonlighting effort in the 1920s, drawn in addition to *Krazy Kat*, was *Stumble Inn*. It got going as a daily in October 1922, with a Sunday page added in December. The daily version succumbed the following May, but the Sunday hung on until January 1926. Uriah Stumble, with the help of his wife Ida, ran a large country inn. He was a short form version of the standard husband doodle. The other recurring character was Owleye,

a house detective who came equipped with the standard gumshoe props of derby and cigar. The page was nicely drawn and, as Richard Marschall has noted, "overflowed with bizarre and eccentric characters." It avoided the imaginative layouts of *Krazy Kat*, however, and was not especially funny, more proof that Herriman's strong suit was animals. After *Stumble Inn* folded, Herriman turned to simple domestic comedy with *Us Husbands*, a beautiful but dumb Sunday page that didn't quite make it through the year.

Gallagher and Shean was a nonsensical daily introduced by King Features in 1923. Loosely based on the routines of the popular comedy team of Edward Gallagher and Al Shean, who also happened to be the uncle of the Marx Brothers, it was one of the few strips written in verse. Though the team had been together for many years and appeared frequently on Broadway, their greatest popularity came while they were working in the *Ziegfeld Follies of 1922*, a review that also starred Will Rogers and the noted shimmy dancer Gilda Gray. This edition of the Follies introduced "Mr. Gallagher and Mr. Shean," a patter song that included the exchange "Absolutely, Mr. Gallagher?" "Positively, Mr. Shean." The strip based all its jokes on rhymed variations of the song. Each sequence would start with Shean, the short one in the fez, saying "Oh, Mr. Gallagher, oh, Mr. Gallagher ..." and then asking the setup question of the day. A typical daily dealt with a gent who was going on an around-the-world cruise and Gallagher's mentioning that he'd asked him to write him frequently. After some rhymed badinage, Shean asks, "Are you a relative, Mr. Gallagher?" "No, a stamp collector, Mr. Shean," is the reply. This sort of material, which apparently wowed them on Broadway, was not the stuff of hit funnies, and the team had a short run in the newsprint medium. The writer of the ill-fated feature was Jo Swerling, who later had a hand in the screenplays for such movies as *The Whole Town's Talking*, *Pennies from Heaven*, and *The Pride of the Yankees*. The artist, who received no credit, was Charles Dunn.

Milt Gross went to work for the *New York Evening World* in the early 1920s and soon came out of the ethnic closet. In 1923, in addition to drawing such strips as *Banana Oil*, he undertook a weekly column called *Gross Exaggerations*. "Here at last Gross was able to introduce his hilarious version of the Bronx Yiddish dialect (essentially the lingo of the first-generation Jewish immigrants struggling gamely with English)," Bill Blackbeard observes. The column used dialogue exchanges to recount the goings on in a four-story Bronx apartment building. The central characters were the Feitlebaum Family. Gross also retold and converted into dialect fairy tales, great moments from history, and notable poems in the column. The material became popular with big city audiences, and Doran collected it in a series of very successful hardcover books, including *Nize Baby* (1926) and *Dunt Esk* (1927). In 1926, Gross began *The Feitlebaum Family*, a daily strip using the column characters. The family itself consisted of small, irascible Morris; his large, calm wife; his lazy, college-age son Looy (usually referred to as "Looy, dot dope"); younger son Isadore; and an infant who was always addressed as "nize baby." Everyone except Looy spoke in dialect: "So how iss by you, Messus Feitlebaum?," "Nize baby, giff a look de moofing picture!!!," "Who needs a doidy ocean I should get dere sunboined." Gross added a Sunday page version early in 1927. The daily, its title changed to *Looy Dot Dope*, continued for several years, but with Johnny Devlin as the artist. Gross kept on with the Sunday and after concentrating on apartment life and other big-town pastimes, he moved the family West in 1928 and had them become involved with the movie business in Hollywood. Gross himself also moved to Southern California and worked for the movie studios. In February 1929, possibly tiring of dialect, Gross dropped *Nize Baby* and replaced it with *Count Screwloose of Tooloose*. There was but one simple premise in operation here. The little cross-eyed count was an inmate of the Nuttycrest Asylum and he was continually going over the wall into the out-

side world. The fads and follies of real life, ranging from marathon dancing to big business, always proved to be much crazier than anything he encountered inside the asylum. He would then climb back inside the place and tell his waiting hound, a faithful mutt in a Napoleon hat, "Iggy, keep an eye on me." Gross drew in a loose, rapid style and his work was always compelling and fun to look at. But the one-note gags of pages like *Count Screwloose* soon became tedious. Gross climbed back over the wall into the Hearst organization in 1930, bringing the count with him.

One of the first, and few, strips to star an adult African-American was *Tempus Todd*. Syndicated by McClure in 1923, it was drawn by H. Weston Taylor and written by Octavus Roy Cohen. Cohen was a Southern white, a former attorney, who specialized in humorous fiction about Negroes. He also wrote detective novels. His early books include *Highly Colored*, *Assorted Chocolates*, and *Dark Days and Black Knights*. Taylor, an illustrator whose work appeared in such slicks as the *Saturday Evening Post* and *Good Housekeeping*, drew the all-black cast in a casual, sketchy style and depicted his characters as individuals, avoiding the minstrel doodle that was the standard of the day. Tempus Todd was a cab driver and the daily gags were built around his encounters, sometimes bizarre, with assorted passengers. His social life now and then also played a part. Cohen was sympathetic, though somewhat patronizing, and the characters spoke in the sort of dialogue he'd developed in his book and magazine fiction— "Hol' on tight, folkses!," "Hot dam! I never knowed before that my taxi-cab had airplane blood in it."

Speaking of cab drivers, the *Amos 'n' Andy* radio show dealt with Amos Jones and Andrew H. Brown, who owned and operated the Fresh Air Taxi Company. It consisted of one rattletrap cab. Amos, portrayed by Freeman Gosden, did all the driving, and Andy, played by Charles Correll, did not do much of anything. The fifteen-minute daily comedy show first aired in March 1928, and by the early 1930s, it was just about the most popular program

NO, MA'AM—THERE'S NO MAIL FOR YOU = THESE ARE ONLY FAKE PARCELS I'M CARRYING SO'S I'LL BE WARMED UP TO THE RUSH WHEN CHRISTMAS COMES.

PAUL FUNG 8·18

Bughouse Fables, *Paul Fung. ©1931, King Features Syndicate, Inc.*

in the country. Since radio was a blind medium, it did not bother many listeners that Amos and Andy, as well as dozens of other Harlem residents, were being played by two white actors. Late in 1928, the *Chicago Daily News* began syndicating an *Amos 'n' Andy* comic strip. Gosden and Correll were broadcasting out of the studios of Station WMAQ in Chicago and it was owned by the *Daily News*. They were credited with writing the strip and each daily was linked with the show episode to be broadcast that night. Charley Mueller, who spent many years assisting on and then ghosting *Smitty*, was the artist. He drew most of his all-black cast in the traditional way, using large white lips and big round eyes in totally black faces. Some of the women characters were colored by pen shading and their features were allowed to show. The strip used the popular catch phrases from the program, such as "I'se regusted," but never gained much popularity. It ended in 1929.

Among the many other humor strips were Jack Callahan's *Freddie the Sheik*, which politely covered the Jazz Age young set; *Samson and Delia*, written by

humorist H. C. Witwer and dealing with the social life of a prize fighter; *The Guy from Grand Rapids*, by Paul Fung, about a lonely out-of-towner in the big city; *Dizzy Dramas*, by Joe Bowers, a tiny strip in which stick figures with cartoon heads told jokes; and *Otto Watt*, by Fred Neher, one of several strips about radio fans.

Panel cartoons proliferated as well. Two of the most popular came from NEA, Gene Ahern's *Our Boarding House* in 1921 and J. R. Williams's *Out Our Way* in 1922. When Ahern's panel replaced his *Crazy Quilt* strip in September 1921, the boarding house's star boarder was not yet in residence. Major Amos Barnaby Hoople did not move in until the beginning of the next year. He claimed to be a veteran of the Boer War, which explains his rank. Martha Hoople, the hefty no-nonsense owner of the place was his wife, and the major had it in mind to devote himself to living off her. Though essentially a windbag, a freeloader, and a con man, Major Hoople did dabble in professional life now and then and make a pretense of working. He, for example, managed a prize fighter or two and owned a race horse for a time. Ahern's view of communal life was not an especially rosy one and he depicted most of the perennial residents in the Hoople establishment, including bachelors Buster, Mack, and Clyde, as a sour and conniving lot. Only Alvin, the Major's young nephew, ever evidenced any faith in him and that was a transitory thing. During the early years of the panel, Major Hoople grew in stature and girth and took to wearing a fez around the house. He added several stock phrases to his vocabulary, among them "Fap!" and "Egad!" When he cleared his throat to gain attention, his "Hrummf—hakkaff!" never failed to produce results. According to the NEA guidelines for later writers, the Major lived "in a middle-western town that is not too big for old-fashioned, neighborly people, and not so small as to be without many metropolitan features such as a race track." Of his creation, Ahern once said, "To me, the Major is a real person. There are thousands of Major Hoople's in the world, and I think the world is better off because of them." Such was the success of Major Hoople that Ahern, who had taken up residence in Hollywood, was hired away by Hearst and King Features in the middle 1930s.

J. R. Williams was a man who knew what he was drawing about. He'd been a cowboy in his youth, then worked in a factory in the Midwest. Though his folksy drawing style gave the impression he was self-taught, Jim Williams had taken the Landon correspondence course. And it was Landon who hired him to do his *Out Our Way* panel for NEA. Williams used several rotating topics in his panel, including *Born Thirty Years Too Soon*, which looked back into the past at small town life; *The Worry Wart*, devoted to a forlorn and messy little boy who was a source of irritation to his older brother and to himself; *Why Mothers Get Gray*, dealing with contemporary life from the point of view of a frazzled mother; and *The Bull of the Woods*, starring a crusty factory foreman. Williams also usually did at least one panel a week about life on the range. The Sunday *Out Our Way* page was about a contemporary family named the Willits. It had little of the charm and quiet humor of his daily work. That was because he neither wrote nor drew it and it was ghosted from the start, for many years by Neg Cochran.

There were numerous other panels. Lee Stanley's *The Old Home Town*, started in 1920, was about life in an old-fashioned Midwest small town and focused on the activities of such characters as Marshal Otey Walker, Aunt Sarah Peabody, handyman Ed Wurlger and beautician Emma Flight. Billy DeBeck did a simple panel in which characters acted against type—cops paid for the apples they took from fruit stands, and kids demanded more spinach for dinner. It was called *Bughouse Fables*, and

DeBeck eventually turned it over to Paul Fung. *Embarrassing Moments*, as its title indicates, also was built around a very narrow premise. A great many artists drew it over its long run, including Ed Verdier, Jack Farr, Charles Dunn, and George Herriman. *And Then the Fun Began* was another one-note panel, always showing the moment just before something dire happened. Milt Gross started it in the previous decade and Fred Faber carried it on in the 1920s.

An exceptional artist, one who could capture the attitudes and emotions of his characters with a few deft lines, was Gluyas Williams. He was a frequent contributor to *Life* and, from the time it started in 1925, to *The New Yorker*. He did spot drawings, full-page drawings, two-page spreads, and also illustrated the pieces of such humorists as Robert Benchley and Corey Ford. His style, in the words of Richard Marschall, was "marked by a sophistication and a distinguished reserve." Williams was the younger brother of Kate Carew, who'd drawn *The Angel Child* page. He began a daily panel, initially for McClure and then the Bell Syndicate, in the early 1920s. It had no official name and each day bore a different title. Some were recurrent, like *The World at Its Worst* and *Suburban Heights*, others were one-shots, like *Snapshots of a Man at a Football Game*. Williams might devote his entire panel to one large drawing or he might break it up into as many as a dozen small sequential drawings. He was especially good at finding humor in the simplest of every day situations, such as looking for a misplaced telephone number or helping a small child get dressed to go out into the snow. A modest man, Williams summed up his newspaper career to date in an early 1930s *Who's Who* with the single phrase "also series daily newspaper cartoons for Bell Syndicate."

Chapter 5

To Be Continued

Suspense has been an important component of the storyteller's craft at least since that long ago evening when a shrewd caveman told the rest of the gang gathered around the fire that they'd have to come back tomorrow night to hear the next installment of his narrative. And for untold centuries the phrase "to be continued" has been highly effective in getting the paying customers to come back to find out what happens next. The idea of continuity was present in comics almost from the start, with Sunday pages like *Little Nemo* using story lines that were carried over from week to week. And while most of the funny paper pioneers did not bother with it much and were content to work at getting a laugh a day, some of them did resort to continuity now and then. Adventure strips began to develop in the 1920s and were to have their heyday in the 1930s and 1940s. This has caused some cultural historians to conclude that continuity was the exclusive property of the more serious comic strips. Actually, some of the most successful humor strips also used cliffhanging techniques and the "continued tomorrow" approach.

Some of the early users of continuity were more interested in mockery than in building suspense. C. W. Kahles, creator of *Hairbreadth Harry*, was one, and another was Harry Hershfield with his *Desperate Desmond* and *Dauntless Durham of the U. S. A.* A some-

what more serious believer in continuity was Sidney Smith, who made suspense an important part of *The Gumps*. The most successful exponent of humorous continuity in the 1920s was Billy DeBeck, yet it took him quite awhile to discover how effective the phrase "to be continued" could be. When his *Barney Google* was introduced in the summer of 1919, it concentrated on unrelated gags built around home and office. In its first years, the new strip was not much different from DeBeck's earlier *Married Life*. Although *Barney Google* ran on the sports page of newspapers and had begun with Barney's attending the Dempsey-Willard heavyweight bout in Toledo, DeBeck hadn't devoted much subsequent time to sporting life. That changed in 1922, when Barney became the owner of a woebegone race horse named Spark Plug. While all that readers usually saw was a silly-looking nag covered with a horse blanket, there was no reason to believe a winner was hidden beneath the covering. DeBeck at this point must have been struck by the notion that he might have fun playing against his readers' expectations. He had Barney enter Sparky in a race called the Abadaba Handicap. The horse won, and Barney collected a $50,000 prize. This all took several days to unfold and proved that if you built up suspense you didn't need a surefire joke each day. During the twenties he and his horse and his faithful black

jockey, Sunshine, made a rambling journey through America and even oversaw racing, gambling, and romancing. The plots got trickier as DeBeck involved his cast with all the fads and fancies of the Roaring Twenties. At one point Sparky even swam the English Channel.

DeBeck had developed into an excellent cartoonist by the time Spark Plug became a national hit and the Sparky and Barney toys, games, books, and other types of lucrative merchandising proliferated. Throughout the twenties and for most of the thirties his *Barney Google* was a model of what a comic strip should be, a combination of good drawing and good writing. DeBeck's fascination with suspenseful continuities led him in the later 1920s to begin constructing long, intricate plots for his strip, such as mock melodramas in which Barney impersonated a wealthy playboy, was hounded by a mysterious secret organization, and got tangled in a murder mystery involving a femme fatale. As a topper feature to his Sunday page he introduced *Parlor, Bedroom & Sink* in May of 1926. This eventually came to star a little tyke named Bunker Hill, Jr. Dressed in a baby bonnet and nightshirt, Bunky roamed the world and had a series of melodramatic adventures that mixed elements of Dickens, Mary Pickford movies, and every lost orphan story ever done. Bunky had a nose like comedian Jimmy Durante and spoke in the flowery language of silent movie title cards. With both *Barney Google* and *Bunky* (*Parlor*'s later title), DeBeck established that you could make fun of suspense and cliffhangers and still get readers to

Barney Google, Billy DeBeck. His increasing fascination with continuity prompted DeBeck to toss in a synopsis like this every now and then to keep his readers informed on what was going on. ©1927, King Features Syndicate, Inc.

come back next time to see what was going to happen.

Another quintessential lowlife strip, and originally the Chicago Tribune-New York News Syndicate's answer to *Barney Google*, was Frank Willard's *Moon Mullins*. A friend and former assistant to DeBeck, Willard had worked in the King Features bullpen and had done some unsuccessful features of his own before getting hired by Captain Patterson to produce a roughneck strip to compete with the Hearst effort. Moonshine Mullins and his cronies began in June 1923, roughly a year after DeBeck had introduced Spark Plug and boosted his strip's circulation. Though taller than Barney and without a mustache, Moon had many affinities to his rival. He was insolent, disrespectful, and coarse, though he lacked Barney's redeeming sentimental streak. Nonetheless, he became extremely popular and the strip eventually appeared in over 250 newspapers across the country. Willard, with considerable drawing help from his gifted assistant Ferd Johnson, offered sporting life continuities, stories set in the circus, and assorted intrigues centered around life in the boarding house where Moon resided. It was run by the spindly, shrewish Emmy Schmaltz and peopled by such perpetual tenants and employees as Uncle Willie, Lord Plushbottom, Mamie, and Moon's kid brother, Kayo. The derby-wearing Kayo gave the impression that if he ever grew up, he'd be an even bigger lout than his elder brother. He slept in a drawer of Moon's bureau.

Harry Hershfield maintained his obsession with *Hairbreadth Harry* and burlesqued melodrama into the 1920s. He wrote, but did not draw, three more variations for assorted Hearst syndicates. One was *Vanilla and the Villains*, an updated *Desperate Desmond*, drawn by Darrell McClure. *Gerald Greenback*, illustrated by Ray McGill, covered similar ground. *Hard-Hearted Hickey*, begun in 1927, offered a slight variation. Its hero was a small, feisty fellow who behaved like a tough, hardboiled guy even though he was built along the lines of Barney Google. The promotion copy for the new feature said, "There is a distinctive comic realism to this daily adventure strip." McClure also drew this one.

A much more interesting humorous continuity strip was *Gus and Gussie*, introduced by King Features in 1925 and written by longtime newspaperman Jack Lait, and drawn by Paul Fung, former assistant to Billy DeBeck. It was a fairly sophisticated strip, despite the fact that its two leading characters were named Gus Donnerwetter and Gussie Abadab, and displayed a big city sensibility. Gus was a short, self-confident young man with a sheepdog haircut that hid his eyes and a vocabulary that mixed slang and malapropisms: "How long did it took Shookspeare to knock out 'The Merchant of Venus'?," "After thinkin' an' thinkin' a suddent unspiration came to me," and "An' how's the world's mos' charmin' cigar-peddlar an'

Gus and Gussie, Paul Fung. At this point they were working in the movie business. ©1927, King Features Syndicate, Inc.

theayter ticket bandit on this here glorgeous day?" Gussie was a slim, bright, and self-assured brunette and, like Gus, she was street-smart and cynical. The continuities were built around their adventures in employment. At one point Gus would be a busboy and Gussie the hatcheck girl at the same restaurant. Later they'd move on to jobs aboard an ocean liner, work in the movies, do an act in vaudeville. There was also a supporting cast of two other young women and a little girl who served as a mascot. They'd always get jobs along with Gus and Gussie and were an important part of the odyssey. While Gus had an ongoing crush on Gussie, she thought of him usually as just a good friend. Lait got several sequences out of Gus's unhappiness over Gussie's falling for a handsomer and taller young man. Nobody, however, in the strip's five-year run ever managed to part the team for long. Fung made an important contribution to the strip. As one critic has pointed out, he "had one of the liveliest cartoon

styles around and, unlike many of his Jazz Age contemporaries, he'd mastered perspective and anatomy. Nobody could draw women better than Fung, in action or, even more difficult, in repose."

Another wisecracking humorous continuity strip was *Ella Cinders*, the joint creation of writer Bill Conselman and artist Charlie Plumb, both Los Angeles newspapermen when they began their Jazz Age Cinderella saga in 1925. Ella, thin, wide-eyed, and freckled, lived with her mean stepmother, two ungainly stepsisters, and a likable though mischievous little brother Blackie. As overworked as the original Cinderella, she entered a magazine beauty contest that promised a job in the movies. Ella won on a fluke, since she was not exactly a beauty, and ended up in Hollywood. After considerable complications she found her long-lost father, Sam Cinders, heading up a movie studio and did indeed get into silent pictures. It was a premise of the early years of the strip that its skinny heroine was jinxed and that her successes would always be short-lived. Ella, with brother Blackie usually in tow, moved up and down the social and financial ladder. She'd go from a menial job to a part in a Broadway show, then, after another fall from grace, return to Hollywood to star in a talkie. For awhile she was a movie director and at another time a waitress. Blackie sometimes figured as a plot device, getting kidnapped or disappearing and becoming the object of a quest. Conselman was fond of building suspense by pretending that even he did not know what was going to happen next. Frequently, a daily would end with copy addressed to the reader: "So that was Ella's big idea! Wonder what'll come of it??" or "Who can this be who is sending gifts to Ella? It surely can't be Mr. X again!" He'd also solic-it input, "Letters of advice are pouring in to Ella. But she wants to hear from you."

Plumb drew in a stiff, correspondence-school style, and fairly early in the strip's life began to hire assistants and ghost artists. The first was a youth named Hardie Gramatky, who frequently won the amateur cartoon contests in the *Los Angeles Times*. Gramatky, best remembered for his children's book *Little Toot*, started penciling the strip in the late 1920s and stayed on until the early 1930s. He was the first of a long line that included Fred Fox, who both drew and wrote *Ella Cinders*, Henry Formhals, who ghosted the Sunday page for many years, and Jack McGuire, who drew both the daily and Sunday from the late 1930s into the 1940s. Conselman and Plumb had luck in Hollywood themselves, and in 1926 sold *Ella Cinders* to the movies. Colleen Moore, very popular at the box office, starred in the film, which was about how "the kitchen slavey becomes a movie vamp." Conselman devoted much of his time in the 1930s to screenwriting, which is why Fox came in to write the strip. Among the movies Conselman worked on were *Pigskin Parade*, which starred Patsy Kelly, Jack Haley, and a very young Judy Garland, and *On the Avenue* with Dick Powell, Alice Faye, and the Ritz Brothers.

By the middle 1920s some comic strips began taking the idea of continuity seriously. There were also several that began to make a gradual change from jokes to suspense. One transitional figure was

Ed Wheelan, who began the decade using continuity in a humor strip burlesquing the films of the day and ended it doing fairly serious suspense narratives. In 1921, Wheelan left Hearst, an event he always believed put him on the Hearst blacklist for the rest of his life, and went to work for the George Matthew Adams syndicate. He converted his *Midget Movies* to *Minute Movies* and added a cast of regular actors. This included handsome, leading man Dick Dare, lovely golden-haired, leading lady Hazel Dearie, and consummate portrayer of villains, Ralph McSneer. Using films as a takeoff point, Wheelan cast his company of actors into every kind of story. He worked in several of the categories adventure strips would use, from western and detective to aviation and sports. He made use of long shots, closeups, and other camera-inspired setups. Although Wheelan was casting his stock company in burlesques and parodies of current motion pictures, he felt he was not poking fun at the movies. "Instead, I laugh with them," he told a 1922 interviewer. "As a matter of fact, I attend motion picture shows quite frequently for I must keep up with them.... To me the space devoted to these little drawings is a real screen, and I do my work with the sincerity of a producer instead of a cartoonist." Wheelan also admitted that "having discovered long ago that I couldn't be funny every day, I try to be interesting instead." The *Minute Movies* strip ran in two tiers, meaning Wheelan was producing a miniature Sunday page each day. As the strip progressed, the movies got longer, lasting two or three weeks. Since Wheelan did not present a movie in a single day, he had to break up the story and that made continuity and suspense inevitable. Between serials, Wheelan ran mock travelogues, mock newsreels, glimpses of Follywood, the town from which Wheelan Pictures, Ink allegedly operated. All his productions were directed by Art Hokum. Late in

Vanilla and the Villains, *Darrell McClure. All three of the major characters show up in these sample panels—the virtuous Vanilla, the sinister Master Mind and the heroic Stonewall. ©1929, King Features Syndicate, Inc.*

the twenties, Wheelan had Hokum address his readers directly to explain that "our serials have changed. They have become longer and we have stopped trying to make them funny, in an endeavor to make them thrilling and interesting." In addition to longer and more serious continuities, Wheelan tried adaptions of the classics, including *Ivanhoe, Treasure Island* and even *Hamlet*. He was assisted on these more sober efforts by an artist named Nicholas Afonsky.

When E. C. Segar's *Thimble Theatre* began in December 1919, it was intended to be in the vein of *Midget Movies*. It was, as R. C. Harvey points out

supposed to parody movies and stage plays, and its cast consisted of actors who would take parts in lampoon productions: Willy Wormwood, a mustache-twirling villain akin to Desperate Desmond; the pure and innocent Olive Oyl; and her boyfriend, Harold Hamgravy. After a few short weeks of daily or weekly productions along the intended line, Segar abandoned the original plan in order to focus on the actors and their real life adventures. He introduced Olive's pint-sized brother Castor, whose get-rich-quick schemes motivated the action for the next 10 years.

Segar remained throughout his career a rather primitive cartoonist, almost a folk artist. He never mastered perspective or anatomy. He apparently never noticed, for instance, that when people walk or run the right arm goes forward while the right leg goes back and most of his characters move with matching arm and leg to the front. But what Segar had a definite talent for was screwball continuity that made fun of all the basic tenants of adventure stories as well as much of what was going on in the world. A fan of fantasy and science fiction, he also filled his work with odd inventions and strange beings. In January 1929, he introduced a crusty, one-eyed sailor named Popeye to the cast of *Thimble Theatre*. Though Popeye had taken nearly ten years to get on stage, he was the undisputed star from then on. A pragmatist with muscles, Popeye had, as Harvey notes, "a perfectly logical sense of justice. Rather than redress a wrong with words and sweet reasonableness, he simply walloped it on the nose." In the 1930s, Segar's superhuman sailor became one of King Features' most lucrative merchandising properties as he turned up in books, in animated cartoons, as toys, and on dozens of products.

A lesser Hearst effort was *Fillum Fables*, which got going in the middle 1920s. It was by Chester Gould, who was destined for better things. "I cannot claim originality for it," Gould once said. "We already had a very capable man doing a strip like that—*Minute Movies* by Ed Wheelan." Gould got to practice with continuity on his strip and to do parodies of such popular movie stereotypes as cowboys and detectives.

By 1916, Mary Pickford was earning $10,000 a week in films. She remained "America's sweetheart" for over twenty years, retiring as one of the richest women in America. What brought Pickford and her movie studios large amounts of money were films in which she portrayed children. "When she had reached twenty and stood ready to impersonate young love, Famous Players began to cast her as a child. It was an immediate and furious hit," wrote Will Irwin in his biography of Adolph Zukor. "Put her in pinafores and she was eight years old again." She played every sort of kid, from Pollyanna to Little Lord Fauntleroy and plucky orphans were her specialty. The basic ingredients of Mary Pickford's films and character inspired a good many kid adventure strips in the 1920s. Another influential screen child was Jackie

Minute Movies, Ed Wheelan. These autographed pictures of the Wheelan Pictures, Ink stars were drawn for The Cartoonist *magazine in 1922.*

Coogan, who for a few years after appearing with Charlie Chaplin in *The Kid* was enormously popular. Gradually a new sort of kid character took to the comic pages, a kid who owed something to the Horatio Alger, Jr., tradition, something to the newer pulp fiction magazines, and a good deal to the movies of Mary Pickford and Jackie Coogan. These serious, or at least semi-serious, strips were of two basic kinds: those utilizing waifs and orphans and those given over to feats of heroic young boys.

The champion waif of the twenties and thirties was Little Orphan Annie. Heartland born, cartoonist Harold Gray found his way to Chicago and a position in the *Tribune* art department. "One strip I feel indirectly to have had a tiny part in was *Little Orphan Annie*," the noted *New Yorker* cartoonist Garrett Price once explained. "My friend from Purdue, Harold Gray, and I lived with the same private family in Chicago. We had afternoon and evening jobs in the art department of the *Chicago Tribune*. Mornings we played tennis. Harold got fired. One day Sid Smith asked me if I would assist him with Andy Gump. My ambition was to be an illustrator and I declined. Did I know anybody he could get? Yes, Harold Gray." Price believed that the

five years Gray served on *The Gumps* taught him almost everything he needed to know about how to produce a successful strip. It's also probable that Captain Patterson had something to do with the creation of Orphan Annie, since he was a firm believer that the movies were a barometer of mass public taste. "He used to go to the movies and watch very closely what the audience laughed at, what they like and didn't like," Walter Berndt once recalled. *Little Orphan Annie* was a composite of the most successful Pickford films. There was, as in her movies, the tough little orphan lass taken into a palatial home, her backtalking and joke playing and her slangy honesty, and there was the gruff millionaire who became her mentor and protector.

The strip started in August 1924, and the regulars, Daddy Warbucks and the faithful hound Sandy, were soon part of the cast. "In the office *Little Orphan Annie* was anything but popular," remembers Price. "At the first opportunity it was left out of the paper. The *Tribune* was bombarded with phone calls, all of which could not have been made by Harold. From then on *Orphan Annie* was pushed and it never faltered." Gray always remained ambivalent toward his red-haired, blank-eyed, little heroine. In interviews he tried to disarm his critics by attacking the melodramatic elements of the strip himself. He often referred to Annie as "our lovable little monster" and maintained that "in those days she was *East Lynne, Over the Hill to the Poorhouse,* and all the other favorites rolled into one and modernized. She was not a 'comic.' Life to her was deadly serious."

Minute Movies, *Ed Wheelan. This daily from the middle 1920s served as a trailer for the serial to follow. Hazel Dearie frequently played Hazel Knutt, the lady sleuth, but this is the first time she did it with bobbed hair.*

The increasing popularity of Gray's moppet inspired imitations. In 1927, King Features introduced them in batches, offering both *Little Annie Rooney* and a strip with the no-nonsense title of *Two Orphans.* This latter was the work of Al Zere, who covered all the bases and peopled his new strip with one little girl orphan and one little boy orphan plus a dog. True to the Harold Gray tradition, both little Tess and little Bub had no pupils in their eyes. The dog didn't either. Despite all this, *Two Orphans* did not last long. *Little Annie Rooney* had better luck. The link with motion picture moppets was somewhat more direct here. Mary Pickford had made a movie called *Little Annie Rooney* in 1925. Tom McNamara, who was associated with the Pickford organization in the middle twenties, tried to interest King Features, for whom he was drawing *Us Boys,* in doing a comic strip version while the film was still in production. King was not interested at the time. McNamara always maintained that the 1927 strip was an unacknowledged swipe of his original pitch.

The initial artist on *Little Annie Rooney* was Ed Verdier, who signed himself Verd. His Annie was a feisty, glib orphan living with an old gentleman she called Uncle Bob. "By 1930 Annie Rooney had wandered a lot," according to one comics historian, "had even put in some time working with a circus and was

Ella Cinders, *Charlie Plumb (and Fred Fox). Ella and her kid brother encounter a seeming ghost in this melodramatic sequence.* ©1930, *Metropolitan Newspaper Feature Service, Inc.*

wrote borrowed from the numerous pluck-and-luck, onward-and-upward novels that Horatio Alger, Jr. and many of his dime novel colleagues had

being looked after by Aunt Aggie and Uncle Paddy, an overwhelmingly good-hearted pair." Ben Batsford was drawing the strip by that time. Soon after, Darrell McClure became the artist. The writer since the late 1920s was Brandon Walsh, former scriptwriter for *The Gumps.* Annie now fell into the clutches of Mrs. Meany, a cruel orphanage proprietor, who pursued her every time she managed to escape. Walsh's continuities were full of paranoid fantasies, with poor Annie never able to enjoy happiness in a foster home for more than a few weeks before the relentless Mrs. Meany caught up with her. The ruthless harpy frequently exclaimed, "I'd do anything to get my hands on that little brat!" Like Orphan Annie, Annie Rooney traveled with a dog who was her friend and confidant. His name was Zero. Gray's orphan made the phrase "Leapin' lizards!" part of the language and for a time Annie Rooney's favorite exclamation "Gloryosky!" gave it some competition. Walsh also invented a malady for his Annie to suffer from, a state of mental and physical unease called the wim-wams: "Gee, Zero, I got the wim-wams awful bad. I keep tryin' to pretend I ain't scared of Mrs. Meany, but I know I am." The passage of time did not help Annie Rooney, either, and she did not have the chance of the usual escape from an unhappy childhood. She remained forever on the brink of adolescence, and Mrs. Meany continued to pursue her through the 1930s and into the 1940s.

Writer, radio commentator, and entrepreneur Jay Jerome Williams turned to a more venerable waif tradition for part of his inspiration. The strips he

ground out in the nineteenth century. He also mixed in some movie action and thrills. He went so far as to use the pen name Edwin Alger on both his strips, *Phil Hardy* and *Bound to Win* (a Horatio Alger, Jr. title if there ever was one). His *Phil Hardy*, which started in November 1925, dealt with a plucky lad who ran away to sea. The artist was George Storm, embarking on his first nationally syndicated strip. Phil, "a bright boy of fifteen," was not an orphan but was fatherless and the sole support of his widowed mother. Shanghaied while hunting for work, Phil found himself on the steamer *Black Castle* and headed for South Africa. The strip was somewhat rougher and tougher than what had come before and went in for violence and bloodshed. Just prior to Storm's resigning from the strip, its title was changed to *Bound to Win* and after he left a new adolescent boy hero was introduced. His name was Ben Webster and he wandered from adventure to adventure accompanied by "his faithful dog Briar." He wasn't the usual ragged, shortpants boy hero and always appeared in a suit and tie with his hair neatly brushed. Edwin Alger was the only credit on the strip and several anonymous artists drew it.

In March 1927, George Storm went into business with an orphan of his own. Storm had developed a highly individual style of drawing, part illustrative and part cartoon. There was an energy to this work, an expert use of black and a sense of movement that owed something to the movies. His work had an easy-going tenseness, a sort of casual power. Before the strip was many days old, Bobby ran away from the small farm where his guardian, a man named Jed Flint, mistreated and overworked him—"When I was a lad I didn't lay abed till four in the morning." Bobby remained on the road for most of the ten-year run of the strip, taking part in adventures with rumrunners, aviators, cowboys, seafaring men, and, as a relief from all the action, sometimes hanging out with a gang of boys in an idyllic small town.

In 1928 Gus Mager, a very unlikely man for the job, started drawing a straight adventure strip that aped *Bobby Thatcher* and the earlier *Phil Hardy*. Done for the McNaught Syndicate, *Oliver's Adventures* treated seriously all the melodramatic conventions that Mager loved to kid in *Hawkshaw the Detective*. His Oliver had adventures similar to those Bobby Thatcher was enjoying, though he managed to get further afield and spent some time in South America. His constant companion was a burly pilot named Captain Breeze. When the strip folded in 1934, it had toned down considerably and was operating under the tamer title of *Oliver and His Dog*.

The strip that was a major contributor both to ending the domination of the joke-a-day feature and to the explosion of adventure strips in the 1930s began quietly and unobtrusively in 1924 under the title *Washington Tubbs II*. The work of a twenty-two-year-old Texas youth named Roy Crane, it took awhile to get going. Crane was not even sure at first what kind of strip he was doing. Once he

Thimble Theatre, *E. C. Segar. Popeye is already exhibiting a tendency toward invulnerability a few months after his debut in the strip.* ©1929, *King Features Syndicate, Inc.*

found out, there was no stopping him. He began to write and draw like nobody before. There was an ease and grace to his stuff, an admirable pace. He mixed action, humor, and romance. There were pretty women, brawls, chases, and sound effects. It was like the movies.

When Royston C. Crane was fourteen and growing up in Sweetwater, Texas, he had signed up for the C. N. Landon mail-order cartooning course. By 1924, Landon was also comics editor for NEA. "My early investment of $25 in the Landon course paid off," Crane later observed. After dropping out of a few colleges, riding the rods, serving as a seaman on a freighter, and studying art in Chicago, Crane got a job in New York assisting H. T. Webster. He also tried a panel of his own called *Music to My Ears.* After it flopped with United Features, they suggested he try their Cleveland affiliate NEA. Crane's old correspondence course teacher didn't like the panel, but he asked his pupil to come up with an idea for a comic strip. The strip, which would eventually be called *Wash Tubbs*, began running in the early months of 1924 under the title *Washington Tubbs II*. It was originally intended to be a gag strip with simple, if any, continuity. "The funny situations worked out by Crane," explained the promotion copy, "bring in Wash's employer, the owner of a grocery store, and Dotty Dimple of the movies, who is Wash's best girl. Of course, there is a rival which leads to amusing complications." These amusing complications did not always readily occur to young Crane and he was soon unhappy with the way the strip was going. Crane remained dissatisfied. "The problem was what the hell to do," he once said.

"Ideas like Billy DeBeck or *The Gumps* or what?" Working in the NEA offices in unromantic Cleveland, Crane dreamed of adventures in faraway places. "I wanted to be a hell of a long way off. About the furthest off I could think of was the South Seas. One his favorite books was *Treasure Island*, and the first of Wash's real adventures was inspired by it. In the middle of August 1924, Wash suddenly disappeared. He showed up a weeks later in San Francisco, having, like Crane in his youth, ridden the rods. He'd figured out that a mysterious paper he'd been handed back home was actually a treasure map. He joined the crew of a freighter bound for Australia, hoping somehow to get to the South Sea island he was seeking. He got shipwrecked on a desert island, which turned out to be the one he was after. He found the treasure and went back home to "strut his stuff." The Wash Tubbs who began to emerge was very much a 1920s hero, the sort of character that Harold Lloyd was developing in his comedy films, the "eager and bumbling young man" who is determined to succeed. Crane knew what he was doing now and he abandoned the gags and the grocery store for good to concentrate on adventure. Over the next two years Wash got involved in both foreign and domestic intrigues. He even picked up a sidekick, a slick, mustached young man named Gozy Gallup. Gozy shared Wash's interest in get-

Little Orphan Annie, Harold Gray. Throughout her career Gray's waif spent considerable time on the road. ©1936, Chicago Tribune—N.Y. News Syndicate, Inc.

rich-quick ideas, treasure hunts, and dimpled young women. But he was not much better in a fight than the not quite five-foot tall Wash.

After a stint with a circus, during which Wash fell temporarily under the spell of a tough lady tiger-tamer named Tango, he and Gozy fought bandits in Mexico and then went on another island treasure hunt. It was there they met Bull Dawson, a thick-necked and lowbrowed sea captain who was brutal, cunning, and hypocritical. To the rowdy Dawson everybody was a softie. While successfully beating up both Gozy and Wash, he boasted, "Ain't never seen the day I couldn't handle the likes o' you pretties by the boatload an' call it fun." It was the resolution of a desert sequence in the autumn of 1928 that led to the creation of Crane's most successful character. Wash and Gozy went up against the sinister Hudson Bey in order to save Princess Jada. When the two men got lost in the vast Sahara, a black harem slave named Bola found them. He later helped them overcome Hudson Bey and when Wash and Gozy fell into the hands of Sheik Bumfellah, it was Bola yet again who rode off to return with a band of French colonial troops. Crane once explained that his brother-in-law kidded him about this particular continuity. "He told me you shouldn't have a eunuch save them," Crane recalled. "What you need is a two-fisted guy." Crane felt Wash was an underdog, somewhat like Jim Hawkins in *Treasure Island*, who "obviously had a hell of a time taking care of himself." In the spring of 1929, Crane introduced Captain Easy to the

AS SOON AS CAPTAIN BENT GAVE HIS "NO SURRENDER" MESSAGE TO THE MUTINEER THE LOYAL BAND TOOK POSTS OF VANTAGE ON THE BRIDGE—PHIL WAS POSTED PORT-SIDE COMMANDING A CLEAR VIEW OF THAT PART OF THE SHIP

HERE COME SOME OF THEM!

FIRE!

THE SKUNKS DON'T LIKE LEAD! FIRE, LAD, WHENEVER YOU SEE ONE—REMEMBER YOU'RE ON THE SIDE OF LAW AND ORDER—IT'S THEIR LIVES OR OURS—

strip and "since this brother-in-law of mine suggested it, I used him as a model." Easy was not a Texan like Crane, but "a Southern gentleman." He almost did not get named Easy: "I was thinking of a name for him while walking from the studio up to get a streetcar," he once said. "And I thought of his name, but I didn't have anything to write it down with." By the time Crane got around to jotting it down, he wasn't sure he remembered it correctly. He put down Easy, but later admitted "I believe it was Early."

Wash first encountered Easy in an ancient fortress called the Black Castle. This was in the small European country of Kandelabra, where he'd been helping Jada, who had turned out to be the rightful heir to the throne. After being imprisoned in the fortress, Wash managed to escape and, while wandering around, comes across a hook-nosed unshaven man who's locked in a cell. Locating a crowbar, Wash helps him get free. Wash introduces himself, saying, "My name's Wash Tubbs—G. Washington Tubbs. Wot's yours?" "Easy. Just call me Easy." It turned out that Easy had also been working for Jada. He was posing as a captain in the artillery, and Jada was the first person in the strip to call him Captain Easy. Actually, Easy had been serving as the head of the Kandelabran Intelligence Service. After ending the country's civil war and putting Jada on the throne, Easy and Wash refused high positions in her kingdom and slipped quietly out of the country. Easy and Wash, with only a few breaks and separations, would roam the world together, going from rags to riches several times, for

Phil Hardy, George Storm. Such action and violence were rare at this point in the Jazz Age. ©1925, the Bell Syndicate, Inc.

the next decade and more. Bull Dawson would recur on several occasions and he and Easy would tangle. Sometimes Easy would win, sometimes Dawson. Captain Easy was more complex than the average two-fisted hero of pulp fiction and the movies. He didn't always win and he wasn't always right. Although the title of the daily strip remained *Wash Tubbs* until well into the 1940s, there was no doubt that Easy was the star and responsible for its increasing success.

A cowboy feature that began late in the decade as a half-serious continuity strip and later switched to the gag-a-day format was *Mescal Ike*. "In the late Twenties S. L. Huntley and I got together and started *Mescal Ike*," cartoonist Art Huhta recalls. "The *Chicago Daily News* had launched a syndicate and we were lucky, they took us on. The syndicate lasted about three years and folded. We got offers from both Bell and United Features. We chose Bell.... Huntley worked in an ad agency writing copy, later he wrote soap opera for radio.... We did our *Mescal Ike* ideas over the telephone and between horse races. He liked the races. At times I wound up doing the ideas as well as the art." Always drawn in a cartoon style, the strip pursued continuity in its early years. White-hatted Mescal was the hero, his shaggy partner was Dirty Shirt Mulloney, and cantankerous, bewhiskered Pa Piffle was another regular. The adventures took place in and around the Southwest desert town of Cactus Center. The action was built around searches for lost mine deeds, run-ins with bandits, and other conventions of Western melodrama. There was also considerable joke cracking and by the early 1930s only the jokes remained. Another early Western strip was *Broncho Bill*, which started in 1928 as *Young Buffalo Bill*. It was also known as *Buckaroo Bill* for a spell. The artist was Harry O'Neill, a onetime circus acrobat and another graduate of the Landon school. The strip was drawn in an illustration style and centered around Bill, a clean-cut blond young fellow who worked to bring law and order to a movie-type Old West.

Most of the early adventure strips, even those with fairly straight continuity, were drawn in a cartoon style. Both Roy Crane and George Storm had proven that this simple, direct method of drawing would work in an adventure context. The illustrative approach had thus far been usually reserved for more serious comics projects. In the middle 1920s, several syndicates began offering what they called educational strips. These appealed, according to Walter Vogdes, who was in charge of that sort of thing at King Features, to the increasing number of newspaper readers who had a "powerful desire for *knowledge* and *mind stimulation*." King attempted to stimulate minds with adaptations of both fiction and nonfiction. They offered Will Durant's *The Story of Philosophy*, Dickens's *Oliver Twist*, Sir James Frazer's *The Golden Bough*, Shakespeare's *The Taming of the Shrew*, and Ida M. Tarbell's *The Life of Napoleon Bonaparte*.

The strip format called for four panel-size illustrations with the text in blocks of copy underneath. The adaptions were models of conciseness—both *The Taming of the Shrew*

and *Oliver Twist* were squeezed into just six dailies each. One of the most famous scenes in the Charles Dickens novel was presented in one drawing and the following text: "Each foundling boy was given a small bowl of gruel. But this was not enough, so Oliver was chosen by lot to ask the cook for additional food. He approached timidly, bowl in hand, and said, 'Please, sir, I want some more.'" Vogdes, writing in the King promotional magazine *Circulation*, emphasized the fact that the artwork for the educational strips was provided by people like George Kerr, "one of America's celebrated illustrators." Other syndicates made similar offerings with

Skylark, Elmer Woggon. Demonstrating the cartoony style Woggon later regretted. ©1928, United Feature Syndicate.

Wash Tubbs, *Roy Crane. The recently formed team of Tubbs & Easy in action. ©1929, NEA Service, Inc.*

short run continuities based on everything from the life of Christ to the Lindbergh solo flight across the Atlantic. In the interim, between his leaving *Bound to Win* and commencing *Bobby Thatcher*, George Storm drew a twenty-two-week comic strip version of *Swiss Family Robinson* for the McClure Syndicate. Major Malcolm Wheeler-Nicholson, who in the middle of the next decade would found the comic book company that became DC Comics, syndicated a comic strip version of *Treasure Island* in the middle 1920s. In 1924, J. Carroll Mansfield began writing and drawing *Highlights of History*, initially a daily strip. His format was similar to that of the shortrun educational

features, except that he hand-lettered the text. A talented though unimaginative illustrator, Mansfield covered American history in the daily continuities. A success for John Wheeler's Bell Syndicate, *Highlights of History* ran until the early 1940s.

The earliest full-time detective strip came along in 1926 and was laid out like the educational strips. *Craig Kennedy* was distributed by the McNaught Syndicate and written by Arthur B. Reeve. Kennedy, a Columbia professor who used scientific tools and even psychoanalysis to solve crimes, was already a very popular character at the time. He'd first appeared in 1910 in the pages of *Cosmopolitan*, and in 1912 moved into hard cover books. By the 1920s, Reeve's novels had a large following in this country and he was the best-selling American mystery writer in England. The Craig Kennedy short stories also showed up in *Detective Fiction Weekly*, *Detective Story*, and *Adventure*. Just prior to World War I, Craig Kennedy began appearing on the silver screen in several serials that starred Pearl White and an actor named Arnold Daly. Among them were *The Exploits of Elaine*, *The New Exploits of Elaine*, and *The Romance of Elaine*. One of the side effects of these chapter plays was the introduction of such memorable villains as the Clutching Hand and the insidious Wu Fang.

Reeve was not an impressive writer, despite his popular success, and the Kennedy stories and novels are all but forgotten today. Unlike the cliffhanger silents he'd had a hand in, Reeve's comic strip was slow, stodgy, and extremely talky. An average daily contained two hundred words or more, an unusually large number for a comic strip even in those more spacious days. Kennedy, who wore pince-nez glasses, didn't

Flying to Fame, *Russell Ross. Aerial action and conversation about the plot. ©1930, Register & Tribune Syndicate.*

come across as a man of action and seemed to like nothing better than to sit around for days at a time discussing the case with whomever was handy. As in the magazine stories, which provided the continuities for the strip, the scientific detective made frequent use of the latest gadgets and inventions to solve his cases. In *The Green Curse*, for example, he utilized a sound detector and an otophone—"it hears light"—to clear up the mystery of some museum thefts and a haunted mummy case. The strip was illustrated in a sedate style by Homer Flaming, a veteran magazine cartoonist. In the next decade, Fleming would be one of the first artists to work in the new comic book field. *Craig Kennedy*, while paving the way for later and livelier detective comic strips, did not manage to last out the year.

A new sort of popular hero came into being during the First World War—the aviator. He was initially an ace, taking incredible risks in a rickety biplane and shooting down enemy aircraft. Then in the Jazz Age, he went on to become a barnstormer and a breaker of records. This latter aspect was perhaps best personified by Charles A. Lindbergh. Aviators, back when flying wasn't something just a bit more interesting than a bus ride, were taken up by the popular media in the 1920s. They appeared in novels, pulp fiction magazines, and movies—most notably in such films as *Wings* (1927) and *Lilac Time* (1928). The flyer became a hero in the comic pages of the 1920s, too.

Young Lindbergh's successful solo flight across the Atlantic in May 1927 made him an internation-

al hero and caused just about every American who wasn't air-minded already to become that way. Over the next two years several aviation comic strips took off, adding a new genre to the funnies. In January of 1928 came *Skylark*, an adventure strip drawn in a very basic cartoon style by Elmer Woggon, staff artist on the *Toledo Blade* at the time. The writer credit went to Eddie Stinson, a record-setting pilot and, later, an aircraft designer and manufacturer. This United Features daily centered around ten-year-old Billie Lark, nicknamed Skylark because of his intense interest in flying. The continuity involved him with helpful Pilot Pete, Captain Bruce of the Air Patrol, and the pursuit of a gang of smugglers and their Phantom Plane. Skylark got to go up in the air on several occasions and there were dogfights, parachute jumps, and kidnappings. The strip, however, lasted only a few months. "Woggon admits that *Skylark* never really got off the ground," the artist, speaking of himself in the third person, said many years later. "He admits that *Skylark* may have survived longer in the illustrative style."

A considerably more durable flying hero was introduced in *Tailspin Tommy*, which came along a few months later. Tommy Tomkins looked to be in his late teens— "A modern American youth who lives in Littleville. His ambition is known all over town. He has talked 'airplane' so much that the village 'wit' has nicknamed him 'Tailspin Tommy.'" Glenn Chaffin once recalled, "Lindbergh and some others were preparing to fly the Atlantic and the Dole pineapple people were sponsoring a flight from the West Coast to Honolulu, so aviation was a red hot topic." Chaffin, a former reporter and press agent, was living in Hollywood when a rep for the Bell Syndicate got him together with a cartoonist named Hal Forrest. According to the biography, fashioned by Forrest, he had been a flyer with the 144th Pursuit Squadron during World War I and then worked several years as a barnstormer. In reality, says newspaperman and comics historian Jay Maeder, while "Forrest did in fact become a licensed pilot at some point ... his later claims to have been a World War eagle and a barnstorming stunt flyer were quite fanciful." The syndicate man told them that the country was ready for a serious adventure strip about flying. Chaffin and Forrest agreed to try one. Starting in four newspapers in the spring of 1928, *Tailspin Tommy* "took off like a rocket and by the end of the year we had fifty or sixty."

Fairly soon, the main characters in the strip were in place. In addition to Tommy, who quickly got his wish and became a pilot, there were Skeeter, his freckled flying sidekick, and Betty Lou Barnes, herself a capable aviator possessed of "more nerve than most men." The trio was employed by the Three-Point Airlines, but was often too involved with sky pirates, crazed inventors, lost races, and hidden treasures to put in much time with the airline's routine activities. While Forrest was a somewhat stodgy artist and drew people stiffly, he was not bad with planes. "We had about 250 daily papers and 200 Sunday papers when I sold out my interest to Forrest in 1933," said Chaffin, who'd never gotten along especially well with his pilot partner. After they parted, Forrest continued *Tailspin Tommy* solo.

In 1929 author Lt. Lester J. Maitland and artist Lt. Dick Calkins teamed up to produce *Skyroads*. Both of them were aviators. In June of 1927, Maitland and a fellow Army lieutenant had made that first flight from California to Hawaii, a 2,400 mile nonstop hop in a Fokker trimotor. Calkins had been a pilot and a flight instructor with the Army Air Service toward the end of World War I. He usually signed himself Lt. Dick Calkins, Air Corps Res. More didactic than any of its predecessors, the strip mixed a great deal of educational material with its narratives. The strip initially centered around former warbird Ace Ames and young Buster Evans who "form a partnership—'Skyroads, Unlimited.'" Their new biplane was purchased for them by Buster's dad and part of setting up business involved Ace's teaching his youthful partner to fly. Maitland and Calkins often included diagrams and footnotes: "When the 'stick' is pushed forward, the elevators drop, raising the tail and putting the plane into flying position." In addition, many of the dialogue exchanges were of an informative nature. While they were flying an emergency airmail job, for instance, Buster asked, "Why is the propeller in front instead of in back, as it is on a boat?" His mentor replied, "Because the air in front is free from swirls caused by the plane, so the 'prop' gets better pull."

Skyroads also included helpful hints on everything from how to execute an Immelman to how to

Windy Riley, *Ken Kling. Kling manages to cover a whole round of the bout without showing it.* ©1929, McNaught Syndicate, Inc.

avoid propwash. In addition, Lt. Maitland cordially invited any and all readers to get in touch with him—"I will be glad to answer questions about aviation. Address me care of this paper." Many of the characters the two pilots encountered were equally airminded. A pretty young heiress they rescued from a flood remarked that "I took a fifty-hour flying course while I was visiting auntie." Even an escaped prisoner who stole a seaplane the partners were using confided to his fellow con that flying was a cinch—"See? All you do is pull back the stick." As the strip progressed, Maitland let up on the instruction some and by the end of the third month Ace, Buster, and the heiress were winging their way to Brazil where they encountered a lost civilization.

Calkins, who was not a master draftsman, also served, as we'll see, as head artist on *Buck Rogers*. He had two assistants to help him out on both projects. They were much like the heroes of some of the aviation strips, eager kids who loved flying. Both Russell Keaton and Zack Mosley went on to do aviation features of their own and both became licensed pilots. Keaton was actually nicknamed Buster and may have served as the inspiration for the Buster of the strip. After Maitland and Calkins left *Skyroads* in the early 1930s, Keaton took over the writing and drawing. The strip switched central

Buck Rogers, Dick Calkins. In the opening daily Buck goes to sleep in 1929 and wakes up 500 years later in a world filled with war, gadgets, romance, and racism. ©1929, John F. Dille Co.

characters several times during its run. Later heroes included Hurricane Hawk, Speed McCloud, and Clipper Williams.

Flying to Fame started in November 1929, done originally by Ernest Henderson. The Register and Tribune Syndicate daily offered a trio of young fellows, Curly McKay, Slim Saunders, and Tubby Harris, all of whom were interested in flying. Within a matter of months Henderson was replaced by writer John Welch and artist Russell Ross. More of an illustrator than his predecessor, Ross improved the looks of the strip. While Welch included air races and flying circuses in his narratives, he was obviously more interested in the sort of story elements then prevalent in adventure pulps and action movies. One typical continuity had the trio helping the blond Pat Rowe, "adventurous girl flier," keep possession of "the valuable but dangerous Rajah Ruby." Although cursed—"No one has owned it five months and lived!"—the gem continued to be much sought after. A crooked pilot, a sinister Oriental, and the ruler of an island kingdom all tried to swipe the thing. In most instances, they kidnapped Pat while making off with the stone. Slim, Tubby, and Curly, hopping into their plane, flew to Pat's rescue more than once. Eventually Curly dropped out of the proceedings and the strip became *Slim and Tubby*. The two heroes continued in business to the end of the next decade, but by 1933 had lost all interest in the romance of flying.

Several continuity strips dealing with sports showed up in the twenties, often running in isolation in the daily sporting section. *You Know Me Al,*

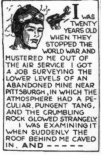

Gasoline Alley, *Frank King. King used the one-panel format in the daily in which Skeezix got his name. ©1921, Chicago Tribune.*

offered by the enterprising and experimenting Bell Syndicate, started in the fall of 1922. The writing was credited to Ring Lardner and the strip was based on the short stories, later collected in *You Know Me Al*, that he'd written for the slick *Saturday Evening Post* from 1914 to 1919. The comic chronicled the adventures on and off the diamond of Jack Keefe, a naive and self-centered bush-league baseball player. As in the stories, the strip was narrated by Keefe in the form of ungrammatical letters to his friend Al back home in Indiana: "Well Al I dident sleep a wink all night and lade awake worring about my little actress friend that got fired out of her show on acct. of trying to do me a flavor and I am going down to the hotel where she is stopping at and pull a few of my gags on her and try to cheer her up and make her forget." The initial artist was Will B. Johnstone, a political cartoonist for most of his career. Johnstone was also a writer and, in 1924, he wrote the book and lyrics—his brother Tom Johnstone provided the music—for the Marx

Brothers Broadway debut show *I'll Say She Is*. He did a lackluster job on the strip and his Jack Keefe was an unappealing oaf. Dick Dorgan, Tad Dorgan's less talented brother, was the second artist on the strip and did no better. Lardner's writing on the strip, if indeed it was his, was flat much of the time and conveyed little of the vernacular charm of his fiction. The strip ended in 1925. After *Al*, Dick Dorgan drew a short-lived boxing strip called *Kid Dugan*.

After leaving his job as ghost on *Mutt and Jeff*, Ken Kling tried a variety of strips. In 1923 he started *Joe Quince*, a sporting life effort. In it he recycled the notion that Bud Fisher had used nearly twenty years earlier, having the lead character bet on the races. Kling had Joe wager on real nags, but, according to his later accounts, originally made no effort to pick winners. When his early random picks began to win, the popularity of the strip increased. After adding a wisecracking black stableboy to the cast, Kling changed the name of the strip to *Joe and Asbestos*. He drew Asbestos in the traditional minstrel manner. The strip, syndicated by Bell, flourished for several years. A great number of his readers used the strip as a tip sheet and "when his choices began to lose, Kling took it to heart and worried," reported Martin Sheridan in *Comics and Their Creators*. "He spent thousands of dollars to secure 'hot tips' from race-track and stable employees. At the end of his contract, he dropped *Joe and Asbestos* and took a year's vacation."

Kling returned to the sports arena in the summer of 1929, signing with McNaught to do *Windy Riley*. This daily, obviously influenced by both *Barney Google* and *Moon Mullins*, was concerned with its brash, cigar-smoking young hero's efforts to establish himself as a boxing promoter in New York City. He arrived from the small town of Scramsburg with his little brother Roughhouse, who was a Kayo Mullins minus derby. The directors of Madison Square Garden fell under Windy's spell and commissioned him to find them a new heavyweight of the Firpo, Carpentier, Schmeling mold—"Dig up some foreign fighter." Windy, with his brother in tow, headed for England, but got somewhat off-course and ended up in Tibet. There he signed a 350-pound Oriental fighter and brought him home. Kling then held a contest to have his readers provide a name for the boxer and settled on Chop Mup. The heavyweight got KO'd his first bout, but did better subsequently; so well, in fact, that Windy bragged to Roughhouse, "When I get finished exploiting this baby all I'll have to do for the rest of my life is sit back and manufacture cigar ashes." According to Kling, many readers of the strip, which usually appeared on the sports page of the one hundred or so papers it ran in, were convinced that he was again passing along turf information. "Like every cartoonist," he once explained, "I marked the releases with date figures—7/5 meaning July 5. As soon as the strip appeared, dozens of horse players telephoned, insisting that I was still giving tips and saying that the numbers 7/5 meant a horse with seven letters in the fifth race." He eventually threw in the towel on Windy and returned to *Joe and Asbestos*, where he openly gave out betting tips once more.

The first time they tried to sell *Tarzan* as a newspaper strip, nobody bought it. That was in 1928, when an advertising man named Joseph H. Neebe formed Famous Books and Plays, Inc. to peddle a strip adaptation of *Tarzan of the Apes*. The Neebe version was in the style of the educational strips, consisting of illustrations with the Edgar Rice Burroughs copy set in type below. Neebe had been a Tarzan enthusiast since the apeman debuted in the pulpwood pages of *All-Story* in 1912. J. Allen St. John, who illustrated many of the Burroughs hardcovers, was not interested in doing the newspaper strip. After being turned down by him, Neebe approached Harold R. Foster, then a commercial artist. "Joe Neebe had the idea of putting famous books and plays into newspaper comic strips," Foster later explained. "I'd done a lot of work for him as he was with an advertising agency I did work for, and he thought of me when he got this idea. He wanted to raise the tone of comics and Tarzan was the first." Foster was an excellent artist, working in a style that

grew out of the work of Howard Pyle and N. C. Wyeth. Without doubt he was the best serious illustrator to work in comics thus far.

Burroughs's Tarzan was by this time a formidable property. Each novel as it appeared in hardcover became a bestseller. They were serialized in newspapers and translated into numerous foreign languages. The apeman became a movie hero in 1917, with chesty Elmo Lincoln portraying him. A comic strip seemed like a great idea. "Neebe prepared very elaborate promotion and hired a staff of advertising salesmen to sell the feature to newspaper editors," said George A. Carlin, general manager of United Features. "Apparently this approach of high-powered advertising salesmen was precisely not what was needed, because at the end of the campaign no newspaper had bought the feature." Neebe went next to the Metropolitan Newspaper Service and let them try to sell *Tarzan*. Metropolitan, which later merged with United, did a better job and on January 7, 1929, the adaption of *Tarzan of the Apes* began in "a small but important list of newspapers." The novel was broken down into sixty dailies and, when these ran out, editors were instructed to ask readers if they wanted to see further adventures of the jungle lord. Metropolitan must have had a hunch they would, since their trade ads, as early as November of 1928, were promising that the first adaptation would be "followed by 10 others, each to run from 10 to 12 weeks." The reaction was favorable, but a problem turned up. Hal Foster did not think much of the medium or of Tarzan, and he decided to return to advertising. His final panel shows Tarzan kissing Jane's hand as he took his leave of her: "Knowing he could have had Jane if he had told her of the proud name he bore, he still refused to do so. For Tarzan's pride was great. Sorrowfully he bids her farewell."

The syndicate was able to find another artist, also a former advertising illustrator, right in the Metropolitan bullpen. Rex Hayden Maxon, though no match for Foster in ability, was willing to take on the job of drawing the strip. He started with the

eleventh week with the serialization of the second novel in the series, *The Return of Tarzan*. "A great ocean liner was nearing France. Aboard her was Tarzan of the Apes," read the copy under Maxon's maiden panel. "Thinking, rather sorrowfully, over the past few weeks, he wondered if he had acted wisely." In 1933, *Fortune* estimated that the strip was earning $2,000 a week, of which Burroughs got about $1,200. By the middle thirties United Features was claiming over three hundred papers for the feature.

By chance, *Buck Rogers* and *Tarzan* made their funny paper debuts on the same day, Monday, January 7, 1929. This was less than a year before the stock market collapse that would send the country into the Great Depression. Like the jungleman, Rogers had previously been a pulp magazine hero. The character, under the name Anthony Rogers, had appeared in the August, 1928 issue of *Amazing Stories* in a novelette entitled *Armageddon 2149 A. D.* by Philip F. Nowlan. In the manner of many another traveler to the future, Rogers had accidentally been put in a state of suspended animation—in his case by way of a mine cave-in. He awoke five hundred years later "to find the America I knew a total wreck." The wrecked United States was now ruled by the Mongol Reds, the twenty-fifth century version of the Yellow Peril, "cruel, greedy and unbelievably ruthless." Rogers joined the guerrilla forces to battle these cruel rulers of his homeland. John F. Dille, who operate the syndicate of the same name,

The Bungle Family, *Harry Tuthill. This particular get-rich-quick scheme involved a missing sacred Siamese elephant and a good deal of bickering. ©1927, McNaught Syndicate, Inc.*

noticed the pulp story and contacted Nowlan to suggest he use it as the basis for a comic strip. Dille didn't like Anthony as a first name for a futuristic hero, so he borrowed one from the popular movie cowboy Buck Jones.

Whereas the *Tarzan* strip had been handsomely drawn, *Buck Rogers in the 25th Century* was rendered in a clumsy cartoon style by Dick Calkins. That didn't seem to matter. The strip was a success and inspired multitudes of small boys, among them future scientists and writers of science fiction. The potency of the idea of looking into the future was such, especially in those months when America was heading inexorably for the Wall Street crash, which very nearly wrecked America five hundred years ahead of Nowlan's predicted date, that *Buck Rogers* very quickly became a very popular feature. "What, specifically, did Buck Rogers have to offer?" Ray Bradbury once asked.

Well, to start out with mere trifles, ... rocket guns that shot explosive bullets; people who flew through the air, ... disintegators which destroyed, down to the meanest atom, anything they touched; radar-equipped robot armies; television-controlled rockets and rocket bombs.... In 1929

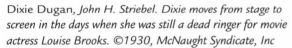

Dixie Dugan, *John H. Striebel. Dixie moves from stage to screen in the days when she was still a dead ringer for movie actress Louise Brooks. ©1930, McNaught Syndicate, Inc*

> *our thinking was so primitive we could scarcely imagine the years before a machine capable of footprinting moon dust would be invented. And even that prediction was snorted at, declared impossible by 99 percent of the people.... I am inclined to believe it was not so much how the episodes were drawn but what was* happening *in them that made the strip such a success.*

When Buck woke up in the future, he met Wilma Deering, a member of the guerrilla group that was trying to overthrow the Mongols. She put him in touch with the Orgs, an organization of resistance fighters. Wilma was unlike some early adventure strip heroines in that she was independent, tough, and smart. She liked Buck, but she considered herself his equal. Buck Rogers's America, in the early years while Nowlan and Calkins were still getting used to the future, was a contradictory place. There were flying women soldiers who toted rocket guns and wore jumping belts, there was television, and even electro-hypnotic machines. Yet when Buck wanted to look for the missing Wilma, his other new friends helped him into the cockpit of a 1920s biplane. The Sunday page began some months after the daily and was drawn from the start by Russell Keaton, although Calkins signed his name to it. It featured Wilma and her teenage brother, Buddy, and Buck rarely made

an appearance. Like the daily, it was narrated in the first person, in this case by Buddy: "I, Buddy Deering, had joined the Boy Air Scouts division while my sister Wilma and Buck Rogers were in Mongolia," began the premier Sunday. Martians were first seen in the strip in 1930 and from then on *Buck Rogers* became more of a space opera. It was to have several imitators in the thirties.

A gifted and inventive cartoonist with a spare, appealing style, Frank King earned fame and fortune as much for his characters as for his drawing skill. When *Gasoline Alley* began in 1918, it was a panel about a group of guys who were interested in cars. Originally it was one of the segments of a black and white Sunday page titled *The Rectangle* that King was turning out for the *Chicago Tribune*. In the summer of the following year, *Gasoline Alley* became a daily panel of its own. It sometimes ran in strip form and branched out to reflect on other aspects of everyday life in a quiet Midwestern town. On Valentine's Day in 1921, Walt Wallet, a large plump bachelor who was one of the guys who hung around the alley, found a baby left in a basket on his doorstep. "Joseph Patterson decided that the feature would be even more popular if something in it appealed to women," R. C. Harvey has pointed out. "He told King to get a baby into the story fast." From that suggestion, King developed a longlasting and fairly realistic account of American life throughout several decades. Readers watched the abandoned baby, named Skeezix, grow through childhood and then into adolescence. They got to know him, his friends, his girlfriend Nina Clock, and many of the other citizens of the town. *Gasoline Alley* was a gentle sort of soap opera, and it depended on continuity and a quiet suspense to keep readers coming back day after day and year after year. Sometimes underrated as an artist, King had a strong gift of design and a flair for fantasy. His Sunday pages in the late 1920s and well into the 1930s were often given over to flights of fantasy and are among the most attractive of the period.

One of the more eccentric dabblers in family continuity was Harry J. Tuthill. In 1918 he began a domestic strip with the deceptive and ironic title of *Home, Sweet Home*. By the middle 1920s the strip had become *The Bungle Family*. The central characters were George, Josie, and a daughter in her early twenties. George and his wife were another bickering couple, but in their case the squabbling often took on a near Dadaist quality as their debates detached from reality and went off into realms of fantasy. Never owning a home of their own, the Bungles lived in a succession of rented flats. These grim locales inspired many of Tuthill's continuities. George's intricate feuds with his neighbors and his tangles with landlords often took on a surreal quality. The bleak hallways and stairs of the apartment buildings, where other tenants—or their nasty pets—lay in wait to ambush George, and the ghostly cellars, where anything from rats to a homicidal neighbor might lurk, became familiar settings. The plots became increasingly bizarre, and the continuity funnier, as the decade progressed. George's endless quest for the perfect get-rich-quick scheme caused him to interact with dubious millionaires, amorous widows, robots, explorers who were heading expeditions into the jungle, and even scientists who were traveling to the future. Assassins, revolutionaries, and pixilated little visitors from other dimensions helped make *The Bungle Family* one of the most unusual and entertaining family strips ever to grace the comic sections. Tuthill drew with a quick, scratchy style and he was one of the best dialogue writers of his day. Some popular radio shows of the 1930s, notably *Fibber McGee and Molly*

and *Lorenzo Jones*, were quite probably inspired by Tuthill, although neither risked being as odd and quirky as he was.

The McNaught Syndicate introduced one more flapper late in 1929, just as the first effects of the stock market crash were starting to be felt. Written by reporter and playwright J. P. McEvoy and drawn by magazine illustrator John H. Striebel, the original title of the new strip was *Show Girl*. McEvoy based it on his *Liberty* magazine serial and novel of the same name. There was also a *Show Girl* musical, which opened a few months before the start of the comic strip and starred Ruby Keeler in the title role, with music by George Gershwin. The Dixie of the printed page was a flighty chorus girl, very much in the Lorelei Lee mode, except that she was a brunette and not a blonde. Striebel drew her, both in *Liberty* and the funny papers so that she looked very much like Louise Brooks, a show girl who'd become a silent movie star. The wisecracking Dixie lived with her folks and was good at wisecracks and at manipulating all sorts and conditions of men. The early continuities dealt with Dixie's life as a chorus girl, her small roles in the movies, her job at a radio station, and other tries at making it in show business. Not an instant success in that increasingly bleak era, the strip had its name changed to *Dixie Dugan*. The syndicate sent out salesmen again to try to sell it under its new title and managed to add papers to the list. As the Depression grew worse, Dixie and her blond best friend Mickey quit show business and tried various small business ventures, including opening a tea shoppe. McEvoy now began to introduce more mystery and suspense to the stories, and by the middle 1930s, *Dixie Dugan* had lost all traces of its Broadway beginnings.

Supposedly one of the salesmen who went out on the road to sell *Dixie Dugan* was a pugnacious amateur cartoonist from Wilkes Barre, Penn. The legend, as Ham Fisher recounts it in *Comics and Their Creators*, is that he "took the strip out during the worst period syndicates have ever known, paid my own expenses and sold *Dixie Dugan* to some thirty-odd newspapers in forty days, a syndicate sales record." Next he went out to sell a crudely drawn boxing strip of his own. "I took *Joe Palooka* on the road and sold the strip to twenty papers in three weeks.... *Palooka* became the largest feature in the history of syndication." Fisher exaggerated, but his strip about a heavyweight champion with a heart of gold did become highly successful. Not much of a cartoonist, Fisher soon hired ghosts, including Phil Boyle, Al Capp, and Mo Leff, to help him out with the drawing. But he usually wrote the scripts himself and relied on continuity to keep his readers coming back. He built suspense around whether or not Joe would win a fight and also tossed in all sorts of melodramatic entanglements for his hero and Knobby Walsh, Joe's salty manager. The strip began in April of 1930 and by the middle of the decade was a definite hit. And the undisputed best-selling sports strip ever.

Chapter 6

Armchair Marco Polos

The comic sections continued to grow more serious during the early years of the Depression, and the number of adventure strips kept increasing. Growing unemployment and even the fear of losing a job meant that the more expensive leisure time activities dwindled. More people took to the road looking for work, fewer traveled for fun. Like the talkies, adventure strips offered a depressed and hobbled public inexpensive entertainment. Funny papers increasingly provided not just laughs but escape. For the price of a daily paper—three cents to five cents usually—you could fly through the air in a biplane, have a tommy gun shootout with bootleggers, travel by tramp steamer to the exotic ports of the Orient or even hop a rocket ship to Mars. Through the medium of the funnies millions of Americans became armchair Marco Polos for a few minutes each day and traveled to strange and romantic places.

A new batch of aviation strips flew into view in the thirties. Yet another that was inspired by Lindbergh was *Scorchy Smith*, which began in 1930 as part of the package of new strips the Associated Press was offering to its news service clients. As with more than one of its predecessors, it centered around a small town young man who was determined to be a pilot. Though it was to have a major influence on adventure strips of every kind, it start-ed inauspiciously and unhandsomely. *Scorchy Smith* was the work of John Terry, a former political cartoonist and animator. Despite the clumsy look of the strip it was a substantial success by 1933, when tuberculosis forced Terry to stop drawing. Noel Sickles, then in his middle-twenties and working in the Associated Press (AP) art bullpen, was selected to continue the strip. A close friend of Milton Caniff, Sickles didn't have a very high opinion of Terry's work. "It was the worst drawing I had ever seen by anybody," he once said. He imitated his predecessor at first and then gradually worked into his own style. What he began to perfect was the impressionistic, boldly inked style that Caniff, as we'll see, took over and made enormously popular. All of Sickles' strip work shows an excitement and a love of drawing. He was able to draw anything—A New York street scene, stretches of jungle, a beautifully staged dogfight. He was a master of drawing any kind of airplane, from a World War I Fokker to a Boeing P26, and the aerial shots he created went unmatched in the decade. Many of the young artists beginning to work in the thirties had grown up with the movies. Sickles was one of the first to apply motion picture points of view to comic strips and he used long shots, close ups, and other movie setups. He did away with the fixed angle, proscenium staging that was still standard in most strips

Scorchy Smith, *Noel Sickles. Demonstrating Sickles' use of the cinematic style.* ©1935, The AP.

and cut from panel to panel the way a director would cut from scene to scene.

Scorchy himself had begun as a lanky lad very much in the Lindbergh mold and Sickles turned him into a more mature hero. He added several characters of his own. One of the most notable was Himmelstoss, a German ex-World War I ace who was briefly a heavy before switching to Scorchy's side and becoming his friend and sidekick. An admirer of Von Richtofen, Sickles saw Heinie Himmelstoss as a man who might've been a friend and colleague of the Red Baron. By the middle of 1936, Sickles was growing tired of the strip. Since he had some money saved, he decided to quit. After helping Caniff draw *Terry and the Pirates* in the late 1930s, he went on to become a magazine illustrator for *The Saturday Evening Post* and *Life*. When Bert Christman replaced Sickles late in 1936, he was just twenty-one. He'd been working on the AP art staff and freelancing for some of the early comic books that were starting up. At first his work had a shaky, hand-me-down appearance, but he soon improved and came up with a style of his own that made use of the techniques Sickles had developed. Christman only stayed with *Scorchy Smith* for a year and a half before becoming a Navy flying cadet. By 1941, he was a pilot with the Flying Tigers, and in January 1942, at the age of twenty-six, he was killed in an air battle over Burma.

The most successful funny paper flyer of the decade was Smilin' Jack, created by Zack Mosley, but when he first took to the air that was not even his name. And he required several more years to grow the mustache that made him a ringer for Clark Gable of the movies. He first showed up in 1933 in a Sunday page entitled *On the Wing*. The page was originally supposed to be a semi-humorous thing about three fellows learning to fly, though Mosley began to swing toward adventure and continuity quite soon. When *On the Wing* was barely aloft, Mosley was told by Captain Patterson of his syndicate to "Change the name of *On the Wing* to *Smilin' Jack*!" Mosley obliged, even though there was nobody in the strip named Jack. There was, however, a character named Mack and while he was airborne, flying a rescue mission in a blizzard, he became Jack.

No doubt influenced by *Dick Tracy*, Mosely started introducing a weird lot of crooks and scoundrels to the strip. Such villains as a bald Peter Lorre simulacrum known as the Head (it was as part of a disguise to catch him that Jack first grew the mustache), the one-armed Baron Bloodsoe, the sultry Teekeela and so on. Jack's cronies were an odd lot as well—the obese, button-popping Fat Stuff, the horny Downwind, whose face was never seen and who referred to all the pretty women he chased as de-icers. Jack's own romances, which often wiped the smile from his lips, were as ill-fated as those of any soap opera heroine. Helping Mosely in the early years of the strip (a daily was added in 1936) was Gordon "Boody" Rogers. Mosely became a licensed pilot himself and syndicate publicity often called him "the flying cartoonist." While he was up in his plane, Rogers was manning the drawing board.

Airplane strips continued to proliferate. *Ace Drummond* started early in 1935, dealing with yet another Lindbergh sort of young aviator who had aerial adventures in various parts of the world. A Sunday page, it was drawn by magazine illustrator and World War I aviator Clayton Knight. The writing was credited to Capt. Eddie Rickenbacker, the World War I hero of the 94th Aero Squadron with twenty-six German kills to his credit. It's likely Rickenbacker did little more than approve the scripts. By late 1937 Knight was drawing only the topper to the page, a nonfiction series called *Hall of Fame of the Air*. An artist named Royal King Cole was drawing the adventures of Drummond in a style that was much more cartoony than Knight's. *Barney Baxter in the Air*, handsomely drawn by Frank Miller, took off in 1935. Barney was an apple-cheeked, freckle-faced lad when the strip began, but he soon grew up and became a full-fledged pilot. Miller was a champion of aviation and he obviously enjoyed drawing real planes, such as the GeeBee and the P-40, as well as experimental jobs of his own design.

Flyin' Jenny, a daily and Sunday strip, began in October 1939. It was the work of Russell Keaton who, as noted, was a graduate of *Skyroads* and *Buck Rogers*. He was a few hours from his pilot's license when *Jenny* commenced. Initially, he wrote his own continuities, but then Frank Wead came in to do the scripting. Wead, a former Navy pilot, was the author of such movies as *Hell Divers* and *Ceiling Zero* and later became the subject of the John Wayne film *The Wings of Eagles*. Jenny Dare, the blond heroine,

got into as many air races and aerial intrigues as her male comic page contemporaries, and for young female readers Keaton tossed in paper doll cutouts every few Sundays.

The 1930s was a good decade for mystery fans. You could find detectives in just about every popular medium, from movies and radio to books and pulp fiction magazines. And you also encountered them in great quantities in comic sections. The most auspicious detective strip of the period was *Dick Tracy*. The strip began in 1931, the same year Al Capone was tried for income tax evasion, and was the work of a thirty-year-old cartoonist named Chester Gould. Living in the Chicago area, Gould had sources of inspiration close at hand. "Chicago in 1931 was being shot up by gangsters," he once recalled, "and I decided to invent a comic strip character who would always get the best of the assorted hoodlums and mobsters." What was needed was a detective who "could hunt these fellows up and shoot 'em down." Besides being tough and impatient, although not much on civil liberties, Dick Tracy was unreachably honest. An honest cop was much needed in places like Chicago and New York City, to name but two cities with less than spotless police departments at the time. Gould's new strip was soon a success in these markets, as well as in other urban areas. Heroes who were impatient with red tape, particularly nice-guy vigilantes like Tracy,

Smilin' Jack, *Zack Mosley (and Boody Rogers). Jack marooned with a group of de-icers.*

were extremely popular in the Depression years. Gould's plainclothesman rose to success in the same years in which Clark Gable, Jimmy Cagney, and John Dillinger became national celebrities.

"Gunplay is part of the strip, and was from the very beginning. That is natural," Gould once explained. "The law is always armed. Back in 1931 no cartoon had ever shown a detective character fighting it out face to face with crooks via the hot lead route. This detail brought certain expressions of misgiving.... However, within two years the sentiment had faded to the point where six other strips of similar pattern were on the market." While gunplay had something to do with the popularity of the strip, it was the increasingly violent and bizarre methods of dispatching crooks and cops that attracted readers and news magazines. As the strip progressed, undercover agents were frozen alive in refrigerator trucks, smuggled aliens were sunk in the ocean with their own chains as anchors, rival crooks were doused with cleaning fluid and set afire, and midget thugs were roasted in steam baths. There were also shootings, floggings, throttlings, bludgeonings, and an occasional amputation. Gould was ingenious, too, at devising ways to almost kill Tracy himself. Villains tried dynamite, decompression chambers, sulfur fumes, exploding furnaces. They even dipped him in paraffin once.

"I try to keep the detective deduction angle the main theme of underlying interest," Gould maintained. "Pursuit, deduction and action are the ingredients that I stress." Although he was a pioneer in the police procedural detective strip, it was the

Barney Baxter in the Air, Frank Miller. From early 1935, when the strip was running only in Denver and Miller was using the penname David.

crooks and villains and not the authentic means used to track them down that put *Dick Tracy* at the top of the popularity polls from the middle 1930s on. After a few years of relatively conventional gangsters and hoodlums such as Larceny Lu, Stooge Viller, and Cut Famon, Gould started experimenting with more flamboyant and exotic, not to mention uglier, criminals: the Blank, the Mole, B. B. Eyes, Little Face Finny, the Brow, Pruneface, and Flattop. *Dick Tracy* was one more successful strip that had been discovered and nurtured by Captain Patterson of the N.Y. News-Chicago Tribune Syndicate.

The success of *Dick Tracy* did not go unnoticed, and other syndicates began bringing forth imitations. In 1933, the Publishers Syndicate launched *Dan Dunn* by Norman Marsh. A former Marine, boxing promoter, and Treasury department agent, Marsh had been a friend of Gould's until his new strip began. He did not draw very well, but he managed to come up with a hero who looked quite a bit like Tracy. He had a similar profile, but his hat was floppier. That may have been because of Marsh's limitations as an artist. Dunn worked, for reasons never explained, as both a city cop and a counterespionage agent. Also known as Secret Operative 48, he handled both big city crimes and international intrigues. He had a dumb sidekick named Irwin Higgs who was even denser than Tracy's early sidekick Pat Patton. While *Dan Dunn* never equaled

Gould's strip in popularity, it did manage to build up an impressive list of nearly 150 newspapers by the middle 1930s.

Always aware of successful trends, King Features was eager to have some crime and detective strips of its own. To that end they went after Dashiell Hammett late in 1933. A former Pinkerton detective and pulp fiction writer, he was becoming increasingly popular as an author. Knopf had published his *The Maltese Falcon* in 1929 and *The Thin Man*, originally published in *Redbook*, was due out early in 1934. Hammett agreed to go to work for Hearst, signing a contract that guaranteed him $500 a week. What Hammett came up with was *Secret Agent X-9*, who was a loose composite of Sam Spade, the Continental Op, Nick Charles, and, since he was given to lounging around in ornate smoking jackets at times, a touch of Philo Vance. It was never made clear by Hammett just what sort of secret agent his nameless hero was. Eventually, after Hammett had left the strip, X-9 turned out to be an FBI man. Rumors have persisted for years that Hammett never actually wrote the strip at all, but simply lent his name to it and farmed out the scripting to an old pulp colleague named James Moynahan. That would explain why the strip lacked the spark of Hammett's other work. The artist was young Alex Raymond, who was paid $20 a week. He

drew *Secret Agent X-9* in a vigorous drybrush style that suggested pulp magazine illustration.

By 1935, Hammett was off the strip. According to a contemporary account, he was fired by syndicate head Joseph Connolly because "he lagged behind schedule with ideas that lacked the power of his printed work." Alex Raymond stayed with the strip, and Leslie Charteris, mystery novelist and creator of Simon Templar (the Saint), became the scriptwriter. Then Charles Flanders, a syndicate staff artist who would make a career of imitating Raymond's drybrush illustration style, took over. King had other teams warming up to do the strip, and samples exist of a version of *X-9* drawn by staff artist Joe King and writer William Ritt. Nicholas

Dick Tracy, Chester Gould. Tracy treated 'em rough in the Depression years and Tess was no exception. ©1932, News Syndicate Co., Inc. Reprinted with permission: Tribune Media Services.

Afonsky, who was drawing the *Little Annie Rooney* Sunday page, was Flanders's unlikely replacement in the spring of 1938. The continuities of this period are an odd mixture of melodrama, flowery speech, and sidewalk reality. *X-9* and his bumbling partner Wild Bill sometimes go after dealers in marijuana, referred to as muggles, and at other times are hunting sinister masterminds like the mysterious Dr. Deel, who killed his victims by sending them envelopes filled with a deadly poison gas. The somewhat pretentious quality of the prose suggests that Afonsky's *Annie Rooney* scriptwriter, Brandon Walsh, was also helping him on this project. Afonsky was

replaced in November of the year with Austin Briggs, a talented magazine illustrator who'd been working as Alex Raymond's assistant and sometimes ghost. The writer credit on *Secret Agent X-9* had been reading Robert Storm for some time, but there was actually no such person. After listing Hammett and then Charteris as author, King Features decided they wanted some stability. Robert Storm was a house name under which several scripters did business. The man who did the most Storm work was probably Max Trell, a former newspaperman and movie scriptwriter. Trell remained writer when Mel Graff took over the drawing of *X-9* in May 1940.

For readers who wanted to get even closer to real life there was *War on Crime*. It dealt with true, or nearly true, crime and was based on FBI files. An early blurb described the daily strip as offering "True Stories of G-Men Activities, Based on Records of the Federal Bureau of Investigation—Modified in the Public Interest." The scripts were by Rex Collier, a *Washington Star* reporter as well as a friend and confidante of J. Edgar Hoover. The modifications were made by an FBI agent assigned by Hoover to go over each continuity. The strip,

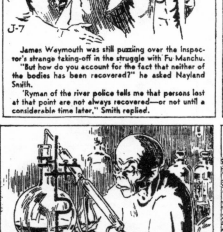

J-7

James Weymouth was still puzzling over the Inspector's strange taking-off in the struggle with Fu Manchu.
"But how do you account for the fact that neither of the bodies has been recovered?" he asked Nayland Smith.
'Ryman of the river police tells me that persons lost at that point are not always recovered—or not until a considerable time later," Smith replied.

There was a faint sound from the room above. The news of that tragic happening in the mists of the Thames had prostrated poor Mrs. Weymouth.
"She hasn't been told half," James Weymouth said. "She doesn't know about the poisoned needle. What kind of a fiend was this Fu Manchu?" he demanded of Smith.

"Dr. Fu Manchu was the ultimate expression of Chinese cunning," Smith replied, "a phenomenon such as occurs but once in many generations. He was a superman of incredible genius who, had he willed, could have revolutionized science...."

"There is a superstition in China according to which an evil spirit of incredible age may enter into the body of an infant born near a deserted burial ground. I have not been able to trace the genealogy of the man called Dr. Fu Manchu. But I have sometimes thought that he was a member of a certain very old Kiangsu family—' and that the peculiar conditions I have mentioned prevailed at his birth."

Fu Manchu, *Leo O'Mealia. Not only illustrations but an ample sampling of Sax Rohmer prose.*

I'VE BEEN WANTING TO SEE YOU FOR A LONG TIME, KARPIS. I SEE YOU RECOGNIZE ME!

SURE, I KNOW YOU! I'VE BEEN LAYIN' TO GET YOU-TOO!

KARPIS, HUNTER AND THE LATTER'S GIRL FELL INTO THE F.B.I. NEW ORLEANS TRAP SET BY J. EDGAR HOOVER.

© Ledger Syndicate   D 96

distributed by the Ledger Syndicate, began in 1936 and ended in 1938. For most of the run the artist was the gifted and unduly forgotten Kemp Starrett. While the stories dealt with the more colorful and violent of the Depression era public enemies—Dillinger, Alvin Karpis, Pretty Boy Floyd, Ma Barker—much of the copy was bland. The violence was toned down and there was never any mention of mistakes FBI agents might have been guilty of in real life. According to Collier, though, the real reason for *War on Crime*'s demise was simple—"We ran out of public enemies."

Several other tough cops and government agents broke into the comic sections in the middle 1930s. Will Gould's *Red Barry*, another King Features entry, was about a hardboiled and humorless police undercover man who operated in a melodramatic, pulpwood version of Los Angeles. Will Gould, who was in no way related to Chester Gould, had a rapid energetic style that suggested both the sports cartoons he used to draw and the illustrations in the detective pulps which inspired many of his plots and a good deal of his dialogue. King Features also picked up *Radio Patrol* in 1934. The strip was about Sergeant Pat and his plump partner Stuttering Sam, who shared a radio patrol car.

War on Crime, *Kemp Starrett. J. Edgar Hoover appears in person in the strip to help capture Alvin "Creepy" Karpis. Though never mentioned by name, the head of the FBI would later show up regularly in* Secret Agent X-9.

There were also Molly, a plainclothes policewoman, and an amateur boy sleuth named Pinky Pinkerton and his dog. Written by Eddie Sullivan and drawn by Charlie Schmidt, both staff members of Hearst's *Boston Daily Record*, the strip had started in the Boston paper in 1933 under the title *Pinkerton, Jr.* Another view of the FBI was to be found in *The G-Man!*, which originated in the *New York Daily Mirror* and was written by George Clark and drawn by Lou Hanlon. It also dealt with kidnappers and bank robbers and an occasional anarchist but in a fictionalized way. The hero was an FBI man named Jimmie Crawford, who looked to be about nineteen years old. For its Scotland Yard police strip, King Features apparently raised the dead. When *Inspector Wade* began running in 1935, the author credit went to Edgar Wallace. One of the most prolific and successful mystery writers of the era, and the co-creator of King Kong, Wallace had been dead for three years. The quiet, mundane strip was based on one of his novels, and the actual writer was Sheldon

Jim Hardy, Dick Moores. ©1938, *United Feature Syndicate.*

Stark. Lyman Anderson was the first artist, followed in 1938 by Neil O'Keeffe.

Several other, and much better known, fictional sleuths came to the funnies as well. John Wheeler's Bell Syndicate offered a *Sherlock Holmes* strip in the early 1930s. This was done in the Great Books format, with the copy set in type beneath the drawings. Leo O'Mealia, a meticulous illustrator, provided the drawings. After the strip ended, Wheeler and O'Mealia returned with *Fu Manchu*. It started in April 1931 and was based on Sax Rohmer's wildly melodramatic and unintentionally hilarious thrillers about the insidious Oriental menace. "Imagine a man, tall, lean and cat-like, with long, strange magnetic eyes, the brow of Shakespeare and the face of Satan...Invest him with the cruel cunning of an entire Eastern race, with all the resources of science, and vast wealth—imagine that awful being, and you have DR. FU MANCHU, the Yellow Peril incarnate in one man!" read the copy beneath the first panel of the first daily. The Devil Doctor's nemesis was Nayland Smith of Scotland Yard, surely one of the great all-time bumbling detectives and a man, for all his reputation as a brilliant sleuth, who never failed to walk into every trap the doctor set for him. Each sequence of continuity had a title, such as *The Needle of Madness*, *The Coughing Horror*, *The Hulk of the Marsh*, and *The Giant Toadstools*. There was new interest in the Yellow Peril in the early 1930s and Rohmer's char-

acter had been appearing in a series of movies starring Warner Oland as a plump and strangely likable insidious doctor.

Philo Vance had made his first appearance in S. S. Van Dine's *The "Canary" Murder Case* in 1926. Other novels followed and the character became immensely popular. He came to the screen in 1929, with William Powell as the first Philo. In the early 1930s there was a briefly seen daily comic strip. It was drawn, and possibly written, by a young man who signed himself R. B. S. Davis. His work was quite shaky at that period and the strip was not a success. Davis went on to write pulp detective stories and in the late 1930s, as Bob Davis, worked in comic books as an artist. In 1938 a detective known for his patient gathering of clues as well as for his aphorisms came to the comics. The *Charlie Chan* strip by Alfred Andriola owed more to the successful motion pictures, also starring Warner Oland, than it did to the six novels by Earl Derr Biggers that featured the Chinese detective. Andriola, who'd worked as secretary to Milton Caniff and Noel Sickles, turned out a strip that was in their style. In fact, both men later admitted to having helped the young artist prepare the samples that won him the job.

Two of Chester Gould's erstwhile assistants turned to crime in the decade. Dick Moores, who'd worked with Gould in the early thirties, started *Jim Hardy* in 1936 for United Feature. It was about a newspaper reporter and dealt with crime and violence, yet in a quieter, more small-town way than *Dick Tracy*. Russell Stamm replaced Moores on the Gould staff, and in 1940 began a strip of his own called *Invisible Scarlet O'Neil*. Scarlet had acquired the ability to become invisible at will and used the talent to fight crime, clear up domestic problems, and generally do good.

Zane Grey of Zanesville, Ohio, gave up his dental practice in 1904 to follow a literary career. By 1915 his Western adventure novels were hitting the bestseller lists and they remained there throughout the 1920s and 1930s. Some of his titles, notably *Riders of the Purple Sage*, sold millions of copies. His works were frequently translated into movies and many of them were serialized in newspapers. Early in the 1930s, the Register & Tribune Syndicate introduced a strip that offered a series of adaptions of several of his novels, including *Nevada* and *Desert Gold*. The copy was set in type beneath the illustrations, and the artist was Jack Abbott, whose work has been described as "undistinguished." A New York entrepreneur named Stephen Slesinger had a hand in packaging

several comic strips about the West. Around 1934, he'd come up with the idea for a contemporary horse opera to take place farther North and deal with the Royal Canadian Mounted Police. He christened it *King of the Royal Mounted*, set about trying to recruit a famous action writer to front it, and finally persuaded Zane Grey to take credit for the adventures of Sergeant King. He hired a journeyman illustrator named Allen Dean and sold the project to King Features in 1935. The redcoat saga was a success and in 1936 the team of Slesinger, Grey, and Dean came up with *Tex Thorne*. This Sunday page, set in the standard Old West, chronicled the good deeds of its freelance gunslinger hero. Tex, who looked something like movie cowboy Randolph Scott, roamed Texas looking for trouble and then cleaned it up.

White Boy, *Garrett Price. The top half of a tabloid Sunday page. ©1934, News Syndicate Co., Inc.*

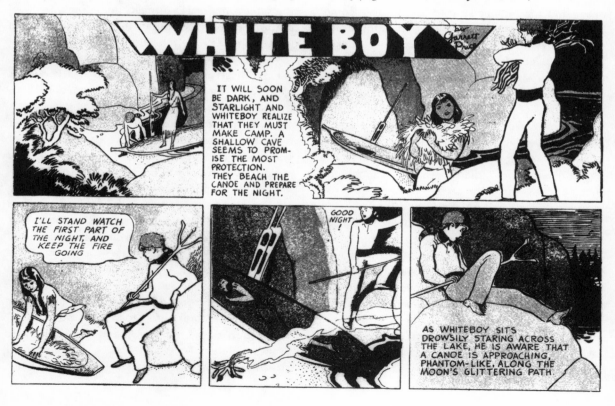

King of the Royal Mounted, *Jim Gary.* ©1940, *King Features Syndicate, Inc.*

One artist who'd actually been on a horse was Fred Harman. He grew up on his dad's ranch in Colorado. In the middle 1920s, he wandered to Kansas City and got into newspaper work as an artist. He became interested in the burgeoning art of animation and for a time was in partnership with another Kansas City cartoonist, Walt Disney. A few years later, having acquired a wife and son, Harman decided to try a comic strip to add to his income. He called it *Bronc Peeler* and tried syndicating it himself. Bronc, who traveled with a mustached sidekick named Coyote Pete, was a redheaded youth. Although it had an Old West look, the strip was actually set in the contemporary world, as an occasional sequence involving a car chase or an airplane dogfight attested. Late in the strip's life Harman added a boy sidekick named Little Beaver, in hopes of winning a larger audience among juveniles. He was a Hollywood Indian both in costume and speech: "Me sneakum away to tailum," "You betchum." Shortly after the advent of Little Beaver, Harmans's work came to the attention of Slesinger. Inviting Harman east, Slesinger had him convert Bronc into Red Ryder. Little Beaver remained Little Beaver and became Red's saddle sidekick. Stephen Slesinger, Inc., sold the strip to NEA in 1938 and subsequently promoted the *Red Ryder* property into serials, B-movies, comic books, novels, toys, and a radio show. Harman knew his West and in the new version he kept the locale the Southwest but moved the time period back to the late nineteenth century.

In spite of the Saturday matinee plots and medicine-show Indians, *Red Ryder* had the look and feel of the real West.

A well-drawn and unusual Western was Garrett Price's *White Boy*, a Sunday page that started in the fall of 1933. One of the stars of *The New Yorker* at the time, Price had been approached by the *Chicago Tribune*, where he'd once worked in the art department, to develop a Western feature. Price had grown up in Wyoming, Oklahoma, and South Dakota, and he once said that his developing of a cowboy page was "hampered by my authentic knowledge of the West." Set in the last century, his handsome page was about a blond adolescent who was captured by the Sioux and then rescued by a rival tribe. White Boy was befriended by an Indian girl named Starlight and two young braves, Chickadee and Woodchuck. The pages were drawn in an imaginative style that managed to be both gentle and bold and exhibited a great fondness for the subject matter. Eventually, under pressure from the syndicate, Price shifted to more conventional matter. In 1935, he relocated his hero in the present, bid farewell to Native Americans, and had White Boy settle in a trouble-prone area known as Skull Valley. By the time the feature ended in 1936, it was called *Skull Valley*.

Not the first masked cowboy by any means, but one of the most successful, the Lone Ranger got going in, of all places, Detroit, Michigan, in 1933. In radio shows scripted by Fran Striker, with considerable creative input from others on the broadcasting staff, the masked man first captured the hearts and minds of American youth by way of Station WXYZ. He, along with the great horse Silver and his faithful Indian companion Tonto, was soon being heard across the country. A great deal of licensing and merchandising followed. In the autumn of 1938, King Features introduced a Lone Ranger newspaper strip. The adventures unfolded in the same post Civil War period as the radio program, and the earliest locales included Texas and Mexico. A commercial artist named Ed Kressy was chosen to illustrate and

Striker got the writing credit. Not at home on the range and possessed of a light cartoony style that did not exactly suit the subject matter, Kressy had problems getting the details right. In his very first daily, for instance, he showed the Lone Ranger mounting Silver from the wrong side. In early 1939 Kressy was put out to pasture, replaced by Charles Flanders, fresh off of *King of the Royal Mounted*. Flanders drew in a more forceful, illustrative style. The stories were much the same as those on the airwaves, basic white-hat-versus-black-hat stuff, but there were more pretty young women on view. Tonto gave the impression he'd learned English at the same school as Little Beaver—"Me hearum talk with Barton! You try killum Lone Ranger!"

A quite reasonable facsimile of the masked man's strip—in fact, it was superior in the art department—came along in 1939. It was offered by a small Manhattan-based syndicate owned and operated by Bob Farrell. With admirable chutzpah, the strip was titled *The Lone Rider*. The young artist who drew it was then signing himself Lance Kirby, but he would soon be changing his name again to become Jack Kirby. Instead of a domino mask, his Lone Rider wore a dark hood to hide his face and his horse Lightnin' was grey rather than white. The initial action took place in that same post-Civil War time frame. Kirby didn't remain with the strip long and after he quit the venue, abruptly, changed to the present. Frank Robbins was the new artist.

The first science fiction strip to pop up after *Buck Rogers* was *Jack Swift*, which came to the daily comic pages in the autumn of 1930. Written by Cliff Farrell and drawn by Hal Colson, it excelled in neither script nor illustration. Jack, who was

possibly a poor relation of Tom Swift, was a clean-cut young man noted for his brilliant inventions. Chief among them was a rocket ship that was "a combined airship, streamlined bus, sea vessel and submarine." Jack's associates included his girlfriend Joan, his mentor old Professor Lucius Long, his best pal Jimmy Smith, and Jimmy's sweetheart Una. After saving Earth from an assortment of perils that included giant penguins, they set out to explore the rest of the universe. Out in space they encountered even worse problems, everything from giant Ionians to runaway asteroids. Jack wasn't especially broadminded and didn't think much of the alien peoples he met, usually referring to them as "those freaks."

Brick Bradford was introduced in August 1933 by the Central Press Association, the small town division of King Features. Although Brick did appear in some of the larger papers in the Hearst chain, it was in the many lesser sheets that he made his initial impact. The syndicate was offering a *Frank Merriwell* strip at the same time and there is something of that strong-jawed, clean-living leftover from an earlier era in the redheaded Brick. The writer was William Ritt, who had put in time on several newspapers and kept his job as an editor and columnist on a Cleveland paper during his tenure with the strip. A student of history and a borrower from the fantasy works of Edgar Rice Burroughs and A. Merritt, Ritt concocted some of the most complex, prolonged,

Flash Gordon, Alex Raymond. Dr. Zarkov, Dale, and Flash discover why the forests of Mongo are not a popular tourist spot. ©1936, King Features Syndicate, Inc.

and often wacky science fiction continuities of the 1930s. The artist was Clarence Gray, a redhead like his hero and a longtime newspaper artist. The two men had never met until shortly before the strip started and apparently never became close friends.

In his first years Brick Bradford led two separate lives, at the very least. "It was seldom less than a staggering multitude of strips," comics historian Jay Maeder points out. "The Sunday page dabbled in futurism early on.... The daily strip employed a separate set of conventions." In the daily adventures Brick started off as a daredevil aviator. Soon, however, he was involved with a lost city in South America and he went on to tangle with crazed Asians bent on world conquest, got himself reduced to teenie weenie size by a Shrinking Sphere, and defeated a titanic robot. The tabloid-style Sunday page, introduced in August, 1935, tossed Brick into fantastic swords and sorcery situations. He spent his early Sunday time in the Land of the Lost, a locale rich with monsters, damsels in distress, and pirates: the sort of location Merritt had been offering guided tours of in the pages of the Munsey pulps for the past decade or more. As the 1930s wore on, the Sunday Brick visited other out of the way places such as the Middle of the Earth, the reign of Queen Anne, and the year 6937. This time-traveling he did after gaining access to the Time Top. Designed by Professor Horatio Southern, the Time Top was designed to "unravel the secrets of the past and

probe the mysteries of the future." Southern and his marvelous machine had originally appeared in a topper to *Brick Bradford* called *The Time Top*. Shortly thereafter Southern, his lovely daughter April, and the time machine moved downstairs and joined Brick for adventures in time and space.

King Features wanted a Buck Rogers of its own and in 1933 contacted Don Moore, who was a writer and the editor of the popular Munsey pulp *Argosy*. Moore had edited the works of dozens of SF writers, including A. Merritt, Edgar Rice Burroughs, and the Burroughs imitator Otis Adelbert Kline. What Moore came up with was a mixture of Burroughs, Merritt, and elements of the recently published novel *When Worlds Collide* by Philip Wylie and Edwin Balmer. For an artist Alex Raymond was again pressed into service and he got the only credit on the new Sunday page. When *Flash Gordon* started on January 7, 1934, readers were told that a strange new planet was rushing toward Earth and that certain doom was inevitable. After parachuting from a damaged airliner Flash Gordon, a handsome blond young man described as a "Yale graduate and world-renowned polo player," and fellow passenger, beautiful Dale Arden, meet a scientist named Dr. Hans Zarkov who has built a rocket ship of his own and plans to take it out in space and use it to deflect the onrushing planet. In the 1930s the notion that the space program would be undertaken by private companies and eccentric lone recluses was common in pulp science fiction and apparently it never occurred to Moore to suggest that something like this would be so costly that it would almost certainly have to be a government venture. The beard-

Speed Spaulding, *Marvin Bradley. Speed and the professor talk about who will be chosen to escape the collision of worlds.*

Adventures of Patsy, *Mel Graff. The Phantom Magician, Thimble and Patsy. This is probably the first flying masked man seen in the funnies.*

ed Zarkov forced Flash and Dale to join his crew. Like many early space argonauts, the Zarkov party goes astray and lands on an Earthlike planet called Mongo. The planet, with its castles and deep forests, had an 1890s Ruritanian look. But the preoccupations of the decade—wars, famines, invasions, and dictators—were also to be found there. Ming, the merciless emperor of much of the planet, was an embodiment of the Yellow Peril, a kind of galactic Fu Manchu. Flash, Dale, and Zarkov were to spend several years dodging the power of Ming, joining assorted resistance groups, and visiting strange kingdoms. Moore was not an inspired writer of prose, but Raymond, influenced by such magazine illustrators as Matt Clark and helped by his assistant Austin Briggs, turned in a extremely good-looking page. The Earth, by the way, never did get smacked by that runaway planet and Flash and his friends returned for a visit some years later. The topper for the page was *Jungle Jim*, another Raymond and Moore effort. For good measure King decided they might as well have something to compete with *Tarzan*, too. Jim was a white hunter and an adventurer in places like the Malay Peninsula.

In 1935 the *Brooklyn Eagle*, tired of the way it was being treated by syndicates, started its own. John E. Watkins, formerly with the Ledger Syndicate,

was put in charge. The Watkins Syndicate offered a small list of strips, including *Gordon Fife and the Boy King* and *Bill & Davey*. The Watkins challenge to Flash and Jungle Jim was a handsome Sunday page, drawn by Carl Pfeufer and written by Bob Moore. The full title of the science fiction effort was *Don Dixon and the Hidden Empire*. Don started the strip as a teenage boy with a Zarkov surrogate named Dr. Lugoff as a companion. Don soon matured into a broad-shouldered young man and had a series of adventures in the lost kingdom of Pharia. The woman in his life was the blond Princess Wanda whose trouble-plagued life provided the basis for many of the continuities. The decor was Early Ming, with lots of marble columns and towers. The men wore the same sort of light opera uniforms as did most of the residents of Mongo and the women dressed like runway queens. Up above *Don Dixon* ran *Tad of the Tanbark*. Tanbark is the material they spread in circus arenas and young Tad's early adventurers involved him in circus life with his father. Later they relocated in the jungle, the better to impersonate *Jungle Jim*.

One of the least circulated science fantasy pages of the decade was *Rod Rian of the Sky Police*. It was written and drawn by Paul H. Jepsen as part of an eight-page, ready-print tabloid comic section produced by the George Matthew Adams Syndicate in the middle thirties. The section, which also contained *Ted Strong*, a cowboy page by Al Carreño, and *Loco Luke*, another humorous cowboy page by Jack Warren, ran in a few small town newspapers and didn't last long. In the first page Rod was assigned to catch some space pirates who've "cost the Earth seven transport ships, many men and billions of earthons in Tellurium." After he'd been drawing the page a few weeks the young artist, who was getting $25 for the job, changed the spelling of his last name to Jepson. His wife was interested in numerology at the time.

In 1939 that runaway planet started heading straight for Earth again and a smashup looked inevitable. "The Earth will be shattered into frag-

Mandrake, *Phil Davis.*
Lee Falk's master magi-
cian up to his old tricks in
Hollywood. ©1938, King
Features Syndicate, Inc.

War II and lasted just over a year. "No comic strip ever concluded in a more impressive way than *Speed Spaulding*," a comics historian observed. "Speed and his selected friends clambered aboard their spaceship hours before Alpha was due to strike Earth. They blasted off, using atomic engines. In the final panel of the final strip the world blew up."

Although the possibility of a Second World War became increasingly strong in

ments by the collision," shouted a headline. "NO LIVING THING WILL SURVIVE." This time it wasn't another borrowing from Wylie and Balmer. The John F. Dille syndicate, hoping to come up with another *Buck Rogers* of its own, turned *When Worlds Collide* into a daily and Sunday comic features. They gave it the title *Speed Spaulding*, although there was no character of that name in the novel. Balmer and Wylie got the writing credit, though it's unlikely they prepared the scripts, and Marvin Bradley did the drawing. Again there was a privately built rocket ship, this time one that would, like the Ark, take a select few to safety. Speed was working with Professor Bronson, the man in charge of the escape project. The strip was a grim one and it showed American civilization breaking down as the killer planet came ever closer. It didn't succeed in taking people's mind off impending involvement in World

the thirties, out-and-out military adventure strips were not especially popular. Watching a grinning Errol Flynn riding bravely off to the Little Big Horn or charging with the Light Brigade was about as close as most Americans wanted to get to a shooting war. But battles involving our own soldiers, sailors, and marines had less appeal. The most successful character in the uncrowded field of service strips was Don Winslow. *Don Winslow of the Navy,* introduced by the Bell Syndicate in 1934, was put together by Frank V. Martinek and one of its purposes was to encourage interest in the Navy among young men. Especially young men in landlocked states where recruitment wasn't faring all that well. Teaming with artists Leon Beroth and Carl Hammond, Martinek created an action strip that emphasized intrigue, spychasing, beautiful women, and villains with names like Dr. Centaur, the Dwarf, and the Scorpion. A former Naval Intelligence officer and newspaperman, Martinek was still in the Naval reserve and signed himself Lt. Frank V. Martinek. Beroth got the only art credit. Besides Hammond, the uncredited artists in the thirties included Ed Moore and Ken Ernst.

Bell Syndicate seemed intent on representing every branch of the service. They got around to the Marine Corps in the fall of 1937, when they introduced *Sergeant Stony Craig*. "Stony Craig is the typical Marine Sergeant ... hard-boiled, tough, a disciplinarian, but underneath, a great fellow and soldier," stated promotion copy. "With his group of Marines, he has some strange advents and exciting action ... on land, at sea, in the air, the Marines keep the situation well in hand." The new strip was the work of two career Marines, Sgt. Frank H. Rentfrow and Lt. Don L. Dickson. Renfrow, a pulp writer and former editor of the Marine magazine *Leatherneck*, provided the continuity. Dickson, a reserve officer and commercial artist, drew the strip in a no frills style. Both artist and writer maintained in interviews that "the strip contains no propaganda for the Marine

Corps." A couple of years before the Marines landed in the funnies, Bell had offered an Army strip of sorts. *Wiley of West Point* was by Lt. Richard Rick and it followed the career of young Bob Wiley from the time he left his small town home to enter West Point. Such was his eagerness that when the bus he was riding broke down, he chartered an airplane and parachuted out over the parade ground. Badly drawn and written, the strip soon faded away.

Kid heroes, following in the footsteps of Bobby Thatcher and Orphan Annie, continued to appear. *Tim Tyler's Luck* by Lyman Young, brother of Chic Young, had actually started in 1928. But it wasn't until the early 1930s that it became an illustrational adventure strip. Originally, blond Tim and his dark-

Connie, *Frank Godwin. Connie is about to explore a mysterious satellite in this mid-1930s daily.*

The Blue Beetle, Jack Kirby. This 1940 strip offers an early example of Kirby's approach to superheroics.

haired pal Spud were two plucky orphan lads in their early teens who ran away to find adventure. By 1932 the boys were in Africa, where they joined a uniformed police group called the Ivory Patrol. This was the movie Africa full of jungles, wild animals, shirty white hunters, savages, white goddesses, and nasty witch doctors. Wisely realizing that his drawing abilities weren't up to this sort of thing, Lyman Young hired a ghost to do his work for him. In the early 1930s it was the young Alex Raymond and he was followed by Charles Flanders, Burne Hogarth, and then Nat Edson. Physically handicapped, Edson had begun working for King Features as an office boy and then moved into the art department. He developed an effective and personal variation of the Raymond style and drew *Tim Tyler* from the middle 1930s to the middle 1940s. While working for Young, Edson created the Sunday topper page *Curly Harper*, which began in March 1935. It was originally about a college athlete; then, in 1937, Curly quit school to become a cub reporter.

Among the other child hero features was Stanley Link's *Tiny Tim*, which began as a Sunday page in July 1923. Tim was an orphan lad and, at the outset of the strip, was built along the lines of a Teenie Weenie. As R. C. Harvey has noted, "the protagonist's minute size quickly proved more a hindrance than a useful novelty in developing gags and stories." Link let Tim grow a few inches more and eventually Tim became a full-sized boy. Link had long been doing most of the drawing for Sidney

Smith on *The Gumps* and he took to using Gump approaches in his strip. "Heart-rending stories." Harvey observes, "in which Tim's happiness was continually threatened by a parade of greedy, slavering landlords or selfish foster parents or crazed scientists ... ending each weekly installment with trumpeting cliffhangers or overwrought suspense." When Smith was killed in an auto accident in 1935, Link briefly assumed full responsibility for *The Gumps*. An apparent disagreement with the *Chicago Tribune* over salary caused Link to be replaced by the less gifted Gus Edson. Link stayed with Tim until his death in the late 1950s.

After he was bounced off *Little Annie Rooney* and replaced by Darrell McClure, Ben Batsford soon returned with another waif. The unfortunate child this time around was a boy, a curly-top kid named Frankie Doodle. Batsford had begun his new strip, syndicated by United Feature, as *The Doodle Family*. Apparently feeling more comfortable with orphans, he soon killed off everybody but Frankie and put the strip in his name. Not only was Frankie Doodle a put-upon orphan, he was, like so many waifs in nineteenth century novels, "the heir to a great fortune." During his wanderings, Frankie was pursued by a shyster lawyer named Mr. Shady, who was after the fortune. Even nastier than Shady was Mrs. Krule. She was the proprietor of an orphanage, run in the same manner as Dotheboys Hall, from which little Frankie was repeatedly escaping. Another troubled lad was Joey, who guest starred in the Sunday *Little Annie Rooney* and was looked after by a Chinese aphorist named Ming Foo. The pudgy Oriental came from the same school as Chester Gump's mentor Ching Chow, a character Brandon Walsh had invented before moving on to write the Rooney strip. In March 1935, *Ming Foo* became a separate feature, running above *Little Annie Rooney*. Nicholas Afonsky drew both pages. Joey and Ming Foo had livelier adventures than Annie and traveled all over the world in quest of melodrama.

What Jackie Coogan and Mary Pickford did for comic strips in the 1920s, Shirley Temple repeated in the 1930s. Pushed into movies at the age of three, Shirley Temple became a major star before she was six. In 1934, no less than nine of her films were released. She is credited, along with Will Rogers, with saving the Fox studios from bankruptcy in the middle 1930s. Naturally enough, syndicates began thinking about winsome little tots during these same years. *Adventures of Patsy* began in March 1935. Mel Graff was the artist, and the daily strip was part of the Associated Press package. The early continuities were whimsical fantasy, involving dark-haired little Patsy in adventures in the kingdom of Ods Bodkins. She had a small boy pal named Thimble, and her protector was the Phantom Magician, who wore a domino mask, tights, and a cape. Among the magical things the Phantom could do were fly and become invisible. It has often been pointed out that Graff had brought into existence a year before the Phantom and three years before Superman the first costumed superhero in comics. The public was not receptive to either whimsy or superheroics, and Graff decided to change his strip. "She was my own idea and was supposed to be an *Alice in Wonderland* strip," Graff once explained. "But it didn't jell, so I worked *Patsy* into a Temple movie moppet." Graff changed his style when Patsy became more serious,

showing the influence of fellow Associated Press artists Noel Sickles and Milton Caniff. Like them, he became fascinated with the effects of light and shadow and with how to convey a sense of place and time and even weather. Graff did some impressive work during this period, as he followed Patsy's career as a child movie star, mixing studio politics, filming in exotic locations, and mystery and suspense elements into his stories. "I never did live in Hollywood," he said later, "though many studios sent me slick action photos." In 1940 Graff was hired by King Features to draw *Secret Agent X-9*. The artists who followed him on *Patsy* included Charles Raab and George Storm.

Fanny Cory was a well-established children's illustrator, having begun her career with *St. Nicholas* magazine in the 1890s. In 1928 she had begun a one-column panel called *Sonnysayings*, which featured a cute drawing of a kid with a clever remark below it. In the middle 1930s, she entered the comic strip field. Her first effort was *Babe Bunting* for the Ledger Syndicate. Babe fit the Shirley Temple mold, and the strip promotion copy promised that "the child playing the title role has the very maximum of beauty. This insures 100 percent more appeal than offered by other children's strips featuring youngsters that are either comic or grotesque." Despite being so much cuter than Little Orphan Annie, Babe Bunting apparently didn't succeed. The strip, however, surfaced a couple of years later, drawn now by Roy L. Williams. The new Babe wasn't as salty as the Babe of the Cory version. She had the requisite

The Red Knight, *Jack W. McGuire. The creators of this strip had obviously been studying comic books for inspiration.*

shaggy dog, named Buttons, and her life was filled with all the paraphernalia of small town drama, including mortgages, lurking hobos, and girls cast out into the snow. Cory, meantime, fared better at King Features, where she succeeded with *Little Miss Muffet*. The artist didn't do the scripts and she was not above expressing her dissatisfaction with the continuities she was forced to illustrate. "There are no gangsters, or divorces or anything like that in her adventures, so she must be a relief to mothers," she once said. "But sometimes I think she's too pure."

Writer Lee Falk created two indestructible adventure strips. The first was *Mandrake the Magician*, which began in 1934, and the second *The Phantom*, introduced in 1936. He sold them both to King Features. Falk himself drew the sample strips that sold *Mandrake*, but then he brought in a friend from St. Louis, commercial artist Phil Davis. The art on *The Phantom* was by Ray Moore. Both artists came fairly close to imitating the illustrative drybrush approach of Alex Raymond, which was already becoming the house style at King. Fairly early in *Mandrake* Falk made it clear that his dapper hero, who dressed like a traditional stage magician in top hat and tails, had no real magical powers and relied entirely on his prodigious talent for hypnotism. The caption "Mandrake gestures hypnotically" was frequently used. The adventures that he and Lothar, his huge African companion, endured, however,

were fraught with the stuff of fantasy and science fiction. They took them to other planets and strange dimensions and pitted them against witches, robots, werewolves, and other unrealistic antagonists. The idea of a suave magician hero with terrific hypnotic powers was moderately popular in the early 1930s. A rival mystic, Chandu the Magician, was heard on the radio from 1932 to 1936 and seen in the movies in 1932 with dapper, mustached Edmund Lowe gesturing hypnotically.

Though Falk has stated he was not a reader of pulp fiction magazines, the Phantom began life covering ground similar to that of such pulpwood mystery men as the Shadow, the Phantom Detective, and the Spider. He wore a mask and a costume, moved mysteriously through large cities to strike when evil was afoot, fought against kidnappers, jewel thieves, and such exotic foes as a gang of beautiful lady air pirates. Nobody knew who he really was nor how, in many instances, the Phantom found out a criminal act was underway. After several years of dealing with urban criminality, he settled in a mysterious section of Africa known as the Deep Woods that was populated with a tribe of amiable pygmies. From then on, the Phantom operated as a sort of fully-clothed Tarzan. It was thereafter that Falk introduced the legend of the Phantom, explaining that there had been a Phantom for countless generations and that the role of the altruistic avenger, along with the costume and the Skull Ring, was passed down from father to son. The seeming longevity of the hero earned him the title of the Ghost Who Walks.

Sparky Watts, Boody Rogers. *A somewhat less serious approach to the idea of a superman.*

An underlying element in both strips was a long-running romance with a young woman who was seemingly unobtainable. In Mandrake's case it was Princess Narda and for the Phantom it was Diana Palmer. Falk's pair of heroes became very popular throughout the world and are still flourishing. The Phantom especially maintains an enthusiastic following in Europe. From country to country, by the way, the color of his costume changes. In America it is a lavender hue, but in Europe it is brown, red, or grey.

The King Features raiders continued to be active in the 1930s. Impressed by Hal Foster's work on the *Tarzan* Sunday page, the syndicate approached Foster to do something for them. Since the money offered was substantially more than drawing the apeman paid, Foster went to work in his spare time on a new idea. A history buff, he preferred to dwell in the past and what he came up with was a historical epic he initially called *Derek, Son of Thane*. Not an especially catchy title, it was changed by the syndicate to *Prince Valiant*. The new page was handsomely done, though a bit stiffer and more formal than his jungle work. It began in February 1937. The action was supposed to take place during the reign of King Arthur, but Foster set it several hundred years later than the time the alleged monarch might have sat at the Round Table with his brave knights. The costumes and pageantry were better in the Middle Ages.

Another good-looking strip was Frank Godwin's *Connie*. Begun in the late 1920s as a flapper strip, it changed in the Depression years to a serious adventure feature. The slender blond Connie Courage worked as a private investigator, joined expeditions to find lost civilizations, visited far planets and traveled through time to the thirtieth century. Godwin was one of the master pen and ink artists of his day and his Sunday pages were especially well done, rivaling those of Hal Foster for scope and skill. Unfortunately, *Connie* was distributed by the Ledger Syndicate, which fell far short of King Features and other majors when it came to get-

ting its stuff into newspapers. Then, too, Godwin's scripts never matched his artwork. Considering the amount of work he put into his strips, Godwin was surprisingly prolific. At the same time he was turning out *Connie*, he took over the daily *Roy Powers, Eagle Scout*. Another Ledger feature, this was advertised as "the thrilling adventure story of Roy Powers and the Beaver Patrol. Produced with the official consent and cooperation of the Boy Scouts of America." Artist Kemp Starrett and writer Paul Roberts (using the penname Paul Powell) started it in 1937 and Godwin took over as artist early in 1938. Unlike the usual Boy Scouts, handsome Roy and his fat friend Chunky journeyed to far-off places like Africa and fought against mad scientists, sky pirates, and master criminals at home.

Another lady adventurer was to be found in *Myra North, Special Nurse*. Syndicated by NEA, the strip was the creation of two cartoonists. Charles Coll, a longtime newspaper artist, did the drawing and Ray Thompson, who drew in a lighter style and would later create Pud and the other kids who flourished in the comics accompanying Fleer's Dubble Bubble gum, provided the scripts. Few of the pretty blond Myra's escapades had much to do with hospital routine and she was more likely to get mixed up with mad scientists, crazed apes, invisible men, international intrigue, and sinister Orientals. The strip began as a daily early in 1936, with a Sunday page added a few months later. The daily ended in 1939, the Sunday not until 1941. The writing was a blend of girls' series book and horror pulp prose, and the drawing was also in the pulpwood tradition.

Little Mary Mixup began in the *New York World* in 1917. It was by R. M. Brinkerhoff and originally was about a bright and now and then mischievous little girl. But by the 1930s, when the strip was being syndicated by United Feature, Brinkerhoff had turned Mary into a spirited teenager in the Nancy Drew mold. No doubt intending to put her in contention with the various orphaned Annies of the funnies, Brinkerhoff had his spunky auburn-haired heroine mixed up with kidnappings, treasure hunts, and other staples of melodrama. He modified his sketchy style to suit the new content.

Not until the late 1930s, after the advent of Superman in *Action Comics* in the spring of 1938, did comic books start to become big business and attract the attention of the newspaper syndicates. The McClure Syndicate had turned down writer Jerry Siegel's and artist Joe Shuster's creation before DC Comics decided to take a chance with the Man of Steel. But in 1939, impressed by the continually climbing sales figures of *Action*, they had second thoughts and launched a newspaper strip. The initial dailies look to be the work of Shuster himself, but a number of other artists drew the feature in the funnies. They included Paul Cassidy, Dennis Neville, John Sikela, and Wayne Boring. Boring would inherit the strip in the late 1940s when Siegel and Shuster were legally separated from their creation. The enterprising Victor Fox, accountant for Detective Comics, Inc., had been inspired by the flourishing sales of Superman to quit his job and start his own comic book empire. Less than a year after the arrival of the first issue of *Action*, he introduced *Wonder Comics* starring Will Eisner's Wonder Man. DC's attorneys promptly suggested that the new hero infringed on Superman's copyright. The resourceful Fox immediately gave up Wonder Man, but not on his conviction that there was big money to be made from superheroes. In his *Mystery Men Comics*, another 1939 effort, he tried more of them. The most successful proved to be the Blue Beetle. Clad in azure chainmail and empowered with a super elixir called Vitamin 2X, the Beetle combated some pretty mundane criminals yet somehow managed to become a hot property. In January 1940, a *Blue Beetle* daily strip began. Its chief distinction was that it was drawn by a young and exuberant Jack Kirby. Fox also offered as Sunday page version of his vitamin-propelled hero, but it was actually only old comic book pages recycled. Neither version lasted long.

The impressive sales of the flamboyant kind of adventure fantasy offered in the upstart comic

Captain Storm, Ed Moore. One of the samples Moore used to get a berth on the Trib's Comic Book Magazine.

books caused some syndicates to fear that sales of Sunday papers, which were bought mostly for the four-color funnies, would be hurt. Victor Fox had the ear of the *Editor & Publisher* trade journal, and he was continually issuing dire predictions under such headlines as *Fox Sees Adventure Comics in Ascendancy* and *Format Change Won't Help Comics, Says Fox*. It was Fox' theory that what everybody wanted now was the type of "thriller" material that only comic books, especially those in the Fox line, could deliver. In addition to a *Blue Beetle* strip and recycled Sunday pages, Fox promised a sixteen-page comic book section as well, but there is no evidence that this ever made it into a newspaper. The *Chicago Tribune*, however, added a special *Sunday Comic Book Magazine* of their own in the spring of 1940. Apparently, nobody at the Tribune Tower knew exactly what a comic book was. Early issues contained a revived *Texas Slim* by Ferd Johnson, along with reprints of Gaar Williams's *Mort Green & Wife* and Frank King's *Bobby Make-Believe*. Gradually, more adventurous comic book fare began to appear, including a heroic fireman strip by Jack Ryan called *Streamer Kelly*, a seagoing page by Ed Moore titled *Captain Storm*, a mystery man strip, *Mr. Ex*, by Bert Whitman, and Dale Messick's *Brenda Starr, Reporter*, which started on June 30, 1940. *Brenda* was the only feature to become a hit and was eventually transferred to the regular comic sections.

Later in 1940, Will Eisner began producing a sixteen-page booklet for the Register & Tribune Syndicate. Titled *The Spirit*, it was a mini-comic book that starred Eisner's baggy-pants masked crimefighter. The backup features were *Lady Luck* and *Mr. Mystic*. In 1940, two superheroes created expressly for the newspapers made their debuts. *The Red Knight* was by writer John J. Welch and artist Jack McGuire, the team who'd been doing the prizefighting strip *Bullet Benton*. This had previously been a Western strip and before that was known as *Slim and*

Tubby. Prior to that it was the aviation strip *Flying to Fame*. The Knight wore the upper half of a suit of armor, plus a sort of kilt and a plumed helmet. He got his powers after being charged with Plus Power by a maverick scientist named Dr. Van Lear. Though the Red Knight had milder adventures that his funny book colleagues, the Register & Tribune Syndicate was obviously going after the newsstand audience. "Mystery! Action! Adventure! Suspense!" promised the ads. "Made for 'the kids' who have zoomed the sale of comic books featuring just this type of thriller!" Covering all bets, the copy added that the new strip also contained, "just the right number of beautiful blondes and gorgeous brunettes!" Far less serious was Boody Rogers' *Sparky Watts*. Sparky was a blond young man who went around in a sweater

and slacks and wore a pair of glasses that branded him as mild-mannered. Unlike Clark Kent, he didn't take them off to perform super deeds. He didn't even have a costume. He'd come by his powers through having been exposed to a cosmic ray machine invented by an amiable old inventor named Doc Static. The cosmic ray machine looked suspiciously like a box camera with a light bulb stuck atop it, but it seemed to work and Sparky spent the next few years enjoying fantastic adventures that both rivaled and spoofed those of the comic book supermen. Rogers had been ghosting his friend Zack Mosley's *Smilin' Jack* for several years and he drew his mock heroic epic in the same style. This gave it a respectable facade for its slapstick burlesquing of the whole idea of superhuman heroes.

Dickie Dare, *Milton Caniff. ©1934, The AP.*

Miss Fury, a serious Sunday page that brought the action and violence of comics to newspapers, began on April 6, 1941. Syndicated by Bell, it was written and drawn by a young lady calling herself Tarpe Mills. She'd originally been just plain June Mills. From the late 1930s on she'd turned out such comic book features as *Daredevil Barry Finn*, *Fantastic Films*, and *The Purple Zombie*. Her newspaper page was hardboiled, full of activity and rough stuff. Miss Fury (originally called Black Fury) possessed no super powers but did very well without them. By day she was lovely socialite Marla Drake, and by night she slipped into a black leopard skin costume to fight crime. Mills seemed to have been influenced by bondage literature as well as comic books and many of the traditional elements—whips, branding irons, spike-heel shoes, men beating women, women tearing each other's clothes off, and all sorts of frilly lingerie—abound on the page.

During World War II, Miss Fury was continuously involved with espionage and intrigue, dealing with beautiful blond spies, handsome and dashing secret agents, and sadistic villains. Chief in this latter category was bald, monocled Bruno Beitz, a Nazi spy of the worst sort, who combined the best qualities of such movie bad guys as Eric von Stroheim and George Sanders. He slapped women, carried a sword cane, loved to use a branding iron on human flesh, and once tried to assassinate an enemy by taping a bomb to a cat. After the war, the strip grew somewhat tamer and it ended in 1952.

A mystery man from the pulp fiction magazines and radio had a brief run as a newspaper hero about this time, too. In 1940 the Ledger Syndicate introduced *The Shadow*. The prolific Walter Gibson, who'd written most of the Shadow pulp novels up to that point, under the alias Maxwell Grant, provided the scripts and Vernon Greene, fresh from ghosting *Polly and Her Pals*, did the drawing. Needless to say, Greene used a different, more realistic style for the adventures of wealthy man-about-town Lamont Cranston. As in the popular radio show version, Cranston had, years ago in the Orient, picked up the knack for clouding men's minds so that they could not see him. A comic book about the invisible crimebuster was also launched in the same year and did much better than the strip.

Early in the Depression Milton Caniff managed to get himself hired by the Associated Press and moved from his hometown of Dayton, Ohio, to Manhattan. He'd been a newspaper cartoonist since he was in his teens. He worked five years on the *Columbus Dispatch* art department. His mentor there was Billy Ireland, one of the most popular cartoonists in the Midwest. Caniff was attending Ohio State during most of his stint with the paper. He majored in fine arts, was editor of the campus humor magazine, *The Sundial*, yearbook art director, starred in several campus plays, and joined a touring stock company now and then. "I became quite adept at this odd triple life—and learned quite a bit about entertainment," Caniff said. "I had more irons in the fire than the village blacksmith." Noel Sickles, a couple of years younger than Caniff, was also a protégé of Billy Ireland and Caniff first met him in the offices of the paper's star cartoonists. Both were excellent artists, but Caniff had to work harder at it. Sickles was a natural and when Caniff first saw the younger man's samples, he was much impressed. Before Caniff moved on to New York, he and Sickles ran an art service in Columbus.

At the AP, Caniff drew an assortment of features. "At one point," he recalled, "I was writing and illustrating a four-line, daily, single-column jingle called *Puffy the Pig,* a three-column panel called *The Gay Thirties,* a six-column strip, and ghosting another daily and Sunday strip at night." The strip he ghosted was *Dumb Dora,* which his friend Bill Dwyer found himself not up to doing. His own strip was *Dickie Dare,* which began in 1933. It was originally about a boy who imagines himself having adventures with real and fictional heroes, including Robin Hood, Aladdin, General Custer, and Robinson Crusoe. Tiring of his notion after awhile, and noticing that *Dickie Dare* wasn't especially popular, Caniff turned it into a contemporary adventure strip. He had found his métier and for the rest of his life Caniff would draw strips dealing with action and intrigue in the real world. He gave the darkhaired Dickie a grownup companion, blond Dan Flynn. A roving author who traveled "around the world writing stories of his adventures," Flynn became a surrogate uncle to Dickie as they began to travel into adventurous territory. The style Caniff was using on the strip was a mix of illustrations and cartoons and showed the influence of Billy Ireland. Sickles, meantime, through Caniff's touting him to the Associated Press, was given a job there, too. The two men shared a studio in the Tudor City apartment complex on 42nd Street. Sickles, who was already experimenting with a cinematic approach to laying out a story and an impressionistic way of inking, had a strong influence on his friend. Caniff left the strip in 1934 and it was ably carried on by Coulton Waugh, who was a painter as well as a newspaper cartoonist.

The traditional story Caniff told about how he came to do *Terry and the Pirates* involved Captain Patterson's assistant Mollie Slott recommending him because her sons loved *Dickie Dare.* This may well have been so, but it was Caniff himself who saw to it that the captain was supplied with samples of his strip. *Terry* was, when it started in October, 1934, a reasonable facsimile of *Dickie.* Young Terry Lee, another twelve-year-old, was blond instead of brunette. Pat Ryan, who fulfilled the Dan Flynn function, was dark-haired instead of blond. Several things, though, gave the new strip an edge over Caniff's original. Patterson had suggested that China would make an interesting locale and told Caniff that pirates still operated there. China, which Patterson must have been aware of, was also being torn apart by war and as the thirties progressed

Mary Worth's Family, *Dale Conner Ulrey. Soap opera already dominates the strip in 1940.*

would be in an accelerating conflict with Japan. The events that were happening in China forced Caniff to mature and he abandoned the melodramatic boys' book plots, such as Terry and Pat arriving in the Orient with a treasure map. Caniff also paid more attention to his supporting players and invented such characters as the Dragon Lady, and the wisecracking Burma, both ladies having piracy in their resumes. He added, as well, such villains as Papa Pyzon, Captain Judas, and the Charles Laughton simulacrum, Sandhurst. The drawing improved, too, till it matched the storylines in sophistication. "My job was not dull, but it consumed the physically available day," Caniff once said. "It was not until Noel Sickles ... worked out a means of delivering illustration quality pictures on a seven-day basis that I was able to buck some of the chains of the working schedule while dramatically improving the all-over value of Terry." Sickles gave more than advice and inspiration—he helped with the drawing, too. Many of the panels, especially the long shots of ships, artillery, and planes, were rendered by Sickles. Caniff used the pen less and less, switching to brush and the liberal use of black. He gave much more attention to the staging of his events and, like Sickles, made use of motion picture approaches. He introduced long shots, close-ups, boom shots. He became infected with a curiosity similar to Sickles'. What did a train look like from a hundred feet directly above it? What was the difference between the light of early morning and that of midday? Most importantly, what shot would best punch up the story and the action? Caniff also allowed Terry to grow up, fall in love, and become involved in the anguishes of the teenage years. And his dedication to authenticity got him into the war against Japan several years ahead of anyone else in the United States.

Many of the elements of what would soon become one of the most popular new comic strip genres first showed up in an advertising strip. Advertising funnies came into their own in the Depression years and the real Sunday funnies began

to share their space with sponsored strips advertising soap, cereal, cigarettes, and other mass market products. The ad strip that came closest to being the prototype for what was to come later in the strips without sponsors was the one featuring Mr. Coffee Nerves, a Desperte Desmond personification of the problems of too much coffee drinking. Begun in the middle 1930s, it was taken over in 1936 by the team of Milton Caniff and Noel Sickles. They used the penname Paul Arthur—Caniff's two middle names reversed—for this page dedicated to selling the coffee substitute Postum. Dedicated movie buffs, Sickles and Caniff staged these domestic melodramas of people brought to the brink of social ruin by coffee habituation in slick and perceptive, big-budget, motion picture fashion. No one was more prop conscious, more determined to get the interior and exterior of everything exactly right, and the two young artists—with Sickles penciling and Caniff inking—got the look and feel of middle class life in the thirties exactly right. Not only were the settings accurate, the problems prefigured those that would soon show up in the soap opera strips. How to get into the country club, how to marry a millionaire, how to shine on Broadway.

At the end of the decade writer Allen Saunders had a hunch. He'd taken over scripting *Apple Mary*, which had been created in 1934 by Martha Orr and was unofficially inspired by the character Apple Annie in Frank Capra's 1933 Depression comedy *Lady for a Day*. Saunders felt the strip needed to be more sophisticated and ought to use some of the elements of the very popular radio soap opera serials. It needed "a linking character, who provides continuity by tirelessly meeting interesting people." Many of these interesting people that the streamlined Mary met were the upper class, actors and actresses, fashion models, business tycoons, spoiled heiresses, and men-about-town. He changed the title to *Mary Worth's Family* and converted the venerable strip into a sort of Mr. Coffee Nerves without commercials. Dale Conner Ulrey, who'd been assisting and ghosting for Martha Orr, became the official artist. She drew in a much slicker and more illustrative style. But she came to believe that the Saunders continuities, while building readership, were tawdry and vulgar. Eager to try a strip of her own, Ulrey quit in 1942. She was replaced by Ken Ernst, a friend and emulator of both Sickles and Caniff. He was much better at depicting the haunts of the rich and famous and in creating the slick, sexy women that Saunders was now writing about. The strip became *Mary Worth* and continued to climb in sales. It would have considerable influence on the funnies in the next two decades.

One of the first to realize that there was room for more than one soap opera strip in the funny papers was Elliot Caplin. A brother of Al Capp, he'd held on to the family name and in the late 1930s gone to work as a writer for King Features. Inspired by the popular radio soaper *Young Dr. Malone* and the Dr. Kildare movies, starring the boyish Lew Ayres, which MGM started producing in 1939, Caplin came up with *Dr. Bobbs*. King started syndicating it in 1941. A daily, it was drawn by James McCardle, an illustrator who'd graduated from the pages of pulps like *Spicy Detective*. Young Stephen Bobbs was cleancut, boyish and, unlike strip heroes

of the day, he wore glasses. The stories dealt with the traditional hospital drama problems and there were also murders, civic scandals, and romance to contend with. Caplin also wrote *Abbie an' Slats*, a homespun adventure strip United Feature introduced in 1937. Al Capp had originated the idea and provided the early scripts about a tough city young man named Slats who comes to live with the small town spinster Abbie. Raeburn Van Buren, a noted magazine illustrator, drew the feature.

Allen Saunders' other 1930s strip was originally called *Big Chief Wahoo*. It started in November 1936 and was drawn by Elmer Woggon. It was a continuity feature with considerable humor and focused on a pint-sized Indian and a W. C. Fields-like con man named the Great Gusto. Growing tired of the humorous approach, Saunders introduced Steve Roper, a roving magazine writer and photographer, into the strip in 1940. The stories became more serious and the chief was eventually eased out and the name changed to *Steve Roper*. Woggon wasn't up to providing the type of drawing needed for the updated version and he used a series of ghosts that included Don Dean and Pete Hoffman.

Chapter 7

Laughing at the Depression

It wasn't all suffering orphans, superheroes and high adventure in the newspaper strips of the thirties. There was a great deal of comedy to be found there, too. Just as humor flourished amid daring deeds and romantic interludes on the radio and in the movies, it also held its own in the comic sections of the Depression. Some of the most popular, and durable, funny features were born during these grim years.

In 1930, when Chic Young switched flappers, he had no intention of creating the most successful domestic comedy strip of the century. What he wanted, simply, was more money. His *Dumb Dora* was still a moderate success, but Young felt that a new feature, one that he might possibly own, would provide him and his wife a more secure financial life. After threatening to quit, and actually sailing for Europe, Young was offered a new deal by Joe Connolly, the general manager of King Features. This resulted in a new strip titled *Blondie*, which started on September 8, 1930. At the offset pretty Blondie was a giggly, featherbrained Roaring Twenties type, another goodhearted golddigger. One of her suitors happened to be Dagwood Bumstead, the amiable and not too bright heir to a railroad fortune. Young moved away from the gag-a-day format to use continuity. The plot centered around Dagwood's determination to marry Blondie. He met strong opposition from his snobbish parents and, at times, from Blondie herself. His persistence caused him to be tossed out of his palatial family home and forced to go to work. Undaunted, he told his father, "I'm happy for the first time in my life—independent—and as soon as I get a little better job, Blondie and I will be married."

The suspense continued into 1933, with time out for a few subplots. Finally, on February 17, 1933, the wedding took place. A working stiff now, Dagwood had to take an office job and Blondie, who no longer giggled, became a model housewife. She also proved to be considerably brighter than her spouse and very efficient at sweetly manipulating him. Their first child, called Baby Dumpling, was born on April 15, 1934. Young had been narrowing the scope of *Blondie* and he continued to have much of the action take place in and around the Bumstead household, with side trips to the office. Similar approaches can still be seen on many television sitcoms. There was little continuity anymore and Young became an expert at delivering domestic jokes. Certain objects, such as Dagwood's monumental sandwiches and the living room sofa he loved to nap on, became familiar recurrent props. *Blondie* climbed in popularity and number of newspapers throughout the decade. By the early 1940s, as Richard Marschall has pointed out, it "officially

became the most popular comic strip in the world." To help him get out the strip, Young had early on hired Alex Raymond and most of the wedding sequence is his work. Later he employed Ray McGill and Jim Raymond, Alex' brother.

Dumb Dora continued with Paul Fung as the artist. The looks of the strip improved greatly and Dora shed most of her flapper mannerisms. Redheaded Rod Ruckett continued to pursue her even after she ceased to be a coed. There was continuity in the dailies and quite probably Jack Lait, who'd worked with Fung on *Gus and Gussie*, was doing the scripting. One of the earliest imitations of

Blondie was John Devlin's *Honey Dear*. A daily that began in the middle 1930s, it was about a newlywed couple consisting of cute, blond Honey Dear and dark, boyish Bill. Devlin, who'd done *Looy Dot Dope* for United Feature, drew this domestic effort in a slightly more realistic style.

Impersonations of *The Gumps* continued in the Depression years. The Associated Press included one such, *Homer Hoopee*, in the original package of daily strips it made available to its clients in 1930. The work of Fred Locher, it mixed humor with continuity in dealing with the dramatic ups and downs of Homer, his wife Helen, and assorted kin. Like

Blondie, *Chic Young. ©1941, King Features Syndicate, Inc.*

Andy Gump, Homer was a lean, mustached, self-important, go-getter who talked to himself and to anyone else who'd listen. This being a bleak decade, many of his more inspired schemes had to do with attempts to get rich quick. Locher was even more melodramatic than Sidney Smith and crew and, as one comics historian has pointed out, "in a typical year Homer might start a detective agency, go to Hollywood, get shipwrecked, suffer from amnesia, and find buried treasure." Also in the Gumps and Nebbs mode was *The Boomers* by Dick Richards, which began in 1932. A daily, it centered around Bert and Myrt Boomer and their offspring. A tall plump fellow with the required father image mustache, Bert was a well-meaning and impractical sort, described by a disapproving neighbor as "a wild-eyed crank." Richards did pay attention to the real world and in one sequence dealt with "Bert's great scheme to beat the Depression." The humor was of a quiet and obvious kind and other continuities turned around such problems as the family's vacation at a haunted seaside hotel and with Bert's being suspected of carrying on with the pretty neighborhood widow.

In the fall of 1933 the Chicago Tribune-N.Y. News Syndicate introduced a batch of new Sunday pages. Among them was Al Posen's *Sweeney & Son*, a family saga that emphasized the father-son relationship. Young Sweeney remained about six years old for the long life of the strip. Pop was one more example of the plump, balding father with a fuzzy mustache. Similar in appearance, though with a bit more hair, was Mort Green, the head of the household in Gaar Williams' *The Strain on the Family Tie*, a 1934 Sunday effort by the veteran panel cartoonist. Jack Callahan drew a mid-1930s Sunday called *Home Sweet Home*, recycling some of the characters from his earlier family strips.

In addition to an assortment of families, a whole gang of kids stormed the comic sections in the thirties. The unsinkable Dwig returned to the

funnies in 1931 with *Nipper*, done for the *Philadelphia Ledger* syndicate. This was another one about small town kids and featured most of his standard types, all updated for the new era. Even Ophelia, with her slate, was in the cast. Nipper was a lean blond youth of about ten, an organizer and a leader of men. That his plans didn't always work out was one of the sources of humor. The Sunday page was devoted strictly to gags, but the daily often indulged in the sort of wild and woolly adventure yarns that appealed to Dwiggins. The bottom strip on Sunday was *Footprints on the Sands of Time*, which offered a bird's eye view of a section of a small town with dotted lines indicating the route taken by its protagonist Bill while carrying out a chore. Bill never appeared, nor did any other person, large or small. All that Dwig showed were buildings, foliage, assorted props, and Bill's meandering footprints. The basic premise was that the boy never got to where he was heading without considerable delays and distractions along the way. A typical strip would begin with "Bill's Aunt Het sends him running to the radio store for a $3 tube so she can learn how to fry an egg—Here he goes—" Bill never believed that a straight line was the best way to travel and the trail of his weekly journey would be annotated with such comments as "Goes into Sally's house to phone Uncle Zeke that Aunt Het's left the lights on in the car—Plays game of Authors with Sally," or, "Soaks Spike with apple core." Bil Keane has now and then used a similar notion in his current *Family Circus* Sunday pages.

Clyde Lewis came up with something completely different in the way of kid strips with his Sunday page *Herky*. A former political cartoonist, Lewis was assisting on *Alley Oop* when he sold his creation to NEA in 1935. Initially Herky, whose nickname was short for Hercules, was a superbaby, capable of walking, talking, telling off grownups, and performing feats of strength. The notion of a feisty little tot in a diaper holding his own in the adult world apparently didn't appeal to a large audience. The blond baby was soon allowed to mature into a cute six-year-old and lose all his powers. He started having regular funny childhood encounters with a perfectly conventional circle of peers. Had Lewis been a more serious fellow, he might have had his superbaby grow up into Superman, thus becoming rich and famous.

For awhile in the early 1930s the Register and Tribune Syndicate had a strip called *Alec and Itchy* on its list. It was unusual for its time, since Alec was white and Itchy was black. The two pint-size boys, drawn in a simple style by Ed Mulholland, specialized in a joke a day and with no mention of their respective races. Beyond the fact that his kids dressed less eccentrically than Percy Crosby's, George Marcoux's *Toddy* looked quite a bit like *Skippy*. This was understandable, since Marcoux had been Crosby's assistant. His own kid strip, daily and Sunday, got going in 1934 and was set in the same sort of middle-class locales. There was the usual philosophizing on the curb, the get-rich-quick schemes of long summer days, and the mild conflicts with parents. The gags weren't especially strong, which probably accounted for *Toddy*'s early demise. Marcoux moved on and in the early 1940s worked in comic books, where he created the fairly popular kid feature, *Supersnipe*.

In a rather unusual move, the *Chicago Tribune* introduced two new kid Sunday pages in the spring of 1930, yet made clear to readers that only one of them was going to survive. They were *Little Folks* by Tack Knight and *Teddy, Jack and Mary* by Tom McNamara. A ballot appeared on each of the pages, requesting "all children under 15 years of

age" to tell their newspaper editor "which group you like better." The pages alternated during the polling period. McNamara, recently put out to pasture by King Features, came up with another strip about poor street children. Redheaded Teddy and blond Jack had a somewhat uneasy relationship with blond Mary, who was a tomboy. Not a master draftsman, McNamara drew only a bit better than a ten-year-old himself, but he had a good sense of what childhood was all about. Knight, at the request of Captain Patterson, produced a strip that was a close imitation of *Reg'lar Fellers*, which he'd been ghosting since the middle 1920s. In *Little Folks*, however, there were more girls in the basic gang. He was a slicker cartoonist than his rival and a more traditional gagman and that probably accounts for why he beat McNamara at the polls. Knight was rewarded with a contract and a daily strip was added. *Little Folks*, despite its impressive start, never took hold and folded in 1933. More than twenty years later McNamara was down on his luck and living in a Tenderloin hotel in San Francisco. Knight, comfortably retired, was also living in the city and he and McNamara became friends.

Fuzzy-headed little Nancy Ritz moved in with her Aunt Fritzi in 1933. Thin and rather shy at the offset, she gradually increased her weight and her self-confidence. The new Nancy was clever, conniving, chubby, often pushy, and yet appealing; a more amiable version of the lovable brat Jane Withers was playing in the movies at the time. Nancy eventually came to dominate the daily and Sunday *Fritzi Ritz*. Early in 1938 she met Sluggo Smith and the team proved to be too much for her aunt. That same year the name of the daily was changed to *Nancy*. Fritzi

Nipper, *Clare Dwiggins. A daily from the middle thirties.*

retained a Sunday page and Nancy got one of her own. Phil Fumble was relieved of his Sunday when that happened and moved into Fritzi's page as her regular fellow. Ernie Bushmiller drew *Nancy* in his simple, direct style and he remained one of the best constructors of gags in the field. Although he later said the way to make certain that a strip reached a large audience was to "dumb it down," he obviously took pride in what he was doing in the 1930s. Before it was five years old, *Nancy* was one of the most popular strips, appearing in hundreds of newspapers.

Its influence was felt throughout the 1930s, as other feisty dark-haired little girls popped up to compete with Nancy. Al Zere was on the scene in 1937 with his reasonable facsimile. *Flossie* was probably the closet *homage* to Bushmiller and, except for the frizzy hair, the title character looked like a close relative of Nancy Ritz. McEvoy and Striebel added a somewhat more mischievous Nancy surrogate, Imogene by name, to *Dixie Dugan* at about this time, mostly on Sunday. Rounding out the decade in 1940 was Syd Hoff with *Tuffy* for King Features. Leaner than her comic page sisters, Tuffy lived in the same lower-middle-class, big-city apartment milieu that Hoff had been celebrating in his *New Yorker* cartoons for several years. She even had the Hoff trademark, a fat, mustached father who sat around in his undershirt.

J. Carver Pusey—the first initial stood for nothing more exotic than James—had been on the art staff of the *Philadelphia Inquirer* and the *New York World* and had drawn a 1920s feature called *Cat Tales* before starting *Benny* in 1929. Running daily

Footprints on the Sands of Time, *Clare Dwiggins. As it appeared at the bottom of the* Nipper *Sunday page.*

and Sunday until the middle 1930s, it was a very low-key pantomime effort about a small hapless blond little guy who shuffled through a large city wearing a baggy black overcoat. Unemployed, often homeless, and usually friendless, Benny was one of the champion losers of the comics. It's difficult to imagine that his downbeat encounters with a basically heartless urban world could have cheered up many depression era readers. Some have suggested that Pusey was trying to produce something Chaplinesque. If so, he fell considerably short of his goal.

The quiet art of pantomime, judging by the number of new strips and pages that emerged, increased in popularity in the 1930s. Now that the movies had learned to talk, some comic strips were falling silent. King Features was especially hospitable to these wordless, or nearly wordless, strips. In 1934 it added three to its permanent roster: *Henry, The Little King,* and *Sentinel Louie*. The bald, silent Henry was first seen in a gag panel series in *The Saturday Evening Post* in 1932, drawn by the venerable Carl Anderson. A *Henry* daily strip, arranged for by William Randolph Hearst himself, started on December 17, 1934, and a Sunday page was added on March 10, 1935. By that time Anderson, who'd been a professional cartoonist since the 1890s, had celebrated his seventieth birthday. Few cartoonists have started a new feature at such an advanced age. Not an especially likable kid, the hairless Henry was an ingenious loner, a pint-sized conman who

Little Folks, *Tack Knight.* ©1930, *the* Chicago Tribune.

loved to outwit and exploit his peers and all of the adult world, too. The appeal of *Henry*, for those who could tolerate its endless small variations on a very narrow range of themes, lay in the amusing and cunning ways the bald little boy went about taking advantage of society and, almost always, getting his way.

Otto Soglow, a fine arts student gone astray, established himself as a magazine cartoonist and illustrator in the 1920s in such magazines as *Judge*, *Life*, and *The New Yorker*. For the latter publication he created the Little King character in 1931. He, too, was hired by Hearst and in 1934, after having done a short-lived pantomime page called *The Ambassador*, moved his Little King into the Sunday funnies. The topper for the page was another nearly speechless strip entitled *Sentinel Louie*. Soglow's style has been described as being "stark, almost diagrammatic ... devoid of shading but always alive with action." He never seemed to tire of drawing the pomp and circumstance of the mythical kingdom over which his small monarch ruled. As conditions in Europe grew worse during the decade, Soglow even kidded war and dictators. In *The New Yorker*, his feature had been a true pantomime, and not a word was spoken. For the comic sections, though, Soglow often allowed other characters, but never the king, to speak in order to set up a gag situation. Anderson, too, used bits of dialogue to establish jokes, and in the strip's earliest days, even Henry was known to utter a sentence now and then.

A handsomely drawn yet only minimally amusing pantomime strip was Clifford McBride's *Napoleon*. Syndicated by Lafave Newspaper Features, it began as a daily in June 1932 and added a Sunday page in 1933. Napoleon, the huge gawky dog, and his portly bachelor owner, Uncle Elby, had started showing up from time to time in a black and white pantomime page McBride had turned out for McNaught in the late 1920s. Lafave had decided they should star on their own. An impressive penman and capable of drawing his misguided and disorderly hound in a multitude of appealing poses, McBride was possessed, alas, of a very simple sense of what was funny. For him the sight of the pompous Uncle Elby falling face down in the mud, putting his foot into a bucket of water or getting hopelessly entangled in a line of hanging wet wash was considered sufficient to provoke his readers into helpless laughter. Not strictly a wordless feature, but close to *Napoleon* in look and spirit was Arthur Poinier's *Jitter*, a daily and Sunday that started in 1936. Jitter was a chimpanzee who'd escaped from a zoo, wearing the keeper's cap and red jacket. He eventually became the ward of Susie and Fred Fuddle and for the next several years plagued them with his monkey tricks. Jitter was the only silent one in the strip. Though cute to look at, the chimp was entirely destructive and most of the jokes revolved around his doing damage or making noise. While not seen in many papers, *Jitter* was reprinted in the widely circulated *Famous Funnies* comic book that was published from the late 1930s into the 1940s and reached a large audience. Poinier left the chimp in 1943 to devote full time to his other career as a political cartoonist.

John Rosol's *The Cat and the Kid*, as the title implied, focused on a small boy and his pet cat. Drawn in a simple, uncluttered style, it was essentially a pantomime strip, although the kid did occasionally speak. It was syndicated in the middle 1930s and was characterized by, in Bill Blackbeard's phrase, "gentle humor and a homey setting." Rosol drew gag cartoons for magazines like *Collier's* also, often about cats. Another middle thirties pantomime was Bill Sakren's *Mortimer Mum*. A Sunday page, it followed the silent adventures of a small professorial looking fellow.

A sturdy, though bland, pantomime page was Rolfe Mason's *Brenda Breeze*, which became part of the NEA Sunday package in October 1939. Brenda

Teddy, Jack and Mary, *Tom McNamara. Top portion of the Sunday page that lost out to* Little Folks, *including the fateful ballot.*

was a pretty blonde, with no visible means of support, who spent most of her time vacationing, shopping, or being flirted with and ogled. Rolfe's page, in its earliest years, was very mildly risqué and Brenda was frequently to be seen in skimpy bathing suits and other politely revealing outfits. She held on until October 1962.

The gag cartoon, a form of graphic humor that was flourishing in dozens of magazines, including the mass-circulation slick weeklies *Collier's* and *The Saturday Evening Post*, became an increasingly popular format for newspaper features. Unlike earlier panels, such as *Our Boarding House* and *The Old Home Town*, most of the new entries used neither continuing characters nor dialogue balloons. George Lichty, who'd begun selling magazine cartoons while in high school, was working as a staff artist on the *Chicago Times* when he created *Grin and Bear It* in 1932. It started as a Sunday page, then branched out to add a daily panel. United Feature picked it up in 1934. Lichty drew in a loose, scratchy style and covered a wide range of topics, from domestic life to sports to politics. When he defected to Field Enterprises in 1940, United hired Abner Dean to do a very similar feature, *Funny Side Up*. Dean's new Sunday page used a layout template that was iden-

tical to the one Lichty had developed and his gags were pretty good, but the replacement was not a hit. Among the other gag panels and pages that got going in these years were Fred Neher's *Life's Like That*, Ed Reed's *Off the Record*, Bill Holman's *Nuts and Jolts*, Jefferson Machamer's *Gags and Gals*, and George Clark's *The Neighbors*. This last one was basically Clark's *Side Glances* under a new name and for a new syndicate. The earlier panel was continued by William Galbraith Crawford, one of *The New Yorker*'s star contributors. Magazine cartoonist Fred Balk drew a kid gag panel called *Punky* in the middle thirties. Punky was a politely mischievous blond youth of about eight, who usually wore a shirt and tie. Balk's feature was one of the few that included a black child as a regular.

The mass media dealt with rural poverty and illiteracy in some unusual ways during the Depression. Erskine Caldwell's best-selling novel, *Tobacco Road*, was adapted for the Broadway stage in 1933 and became a much talked about hit. Radio shows like *The National Barn Dance* and, later, *Grand Ole Opry* sent out country music and hillbilly humor across the country. Rustic comedy shows like *Lum and Abner*, begun in 1931, and *Uncle Ezra*, started in 1934, specialized in hick comedy. The image of the lazy mountaineer, usually with long beard and a wife in her early teens, was frequently seen in magazine gag panels and animated cartoons. Billy DeBeck became interested in the folklore of the mountain people of Appalachia. He put together a large library of books on folk customs and folk humor, including many on Ozark life. According to Professor M. Thomas Inge, DeBeck "traveled

Fritzi Ritz, Ernie Bushmiller. Though still slim, Nancy is already upstaging her aunt. ©1933 by United Feature Syndicate, Inc. Reprinted by permission.

through the mountains of Virginia and Kentucky, talked to the natives, made numerous sketches, and read everything he could lay his hands on that treated mountaineer life."

In June 1934, Barney Google learned that he'd inherited property in North Carolina. Barney's estate turned out to be a tumble-down cabin and he soon found himself a bystander in a rural romance and wedding. One of the guests at the wedding was a rough, tough little mountaineer called Snuffy Smith. The same size as Barney, he was twice as cunning and three times as ornery. Almost at once he, with some help from his large nurturing wife, Lowizie, began to take a star spot in DeBeck's strip. Throughout the decade the strip, which eventually changed its title to *Barney Google and Snuffy Smith*, dealt in hillbilly humor and continuities. There was quite a bit of fantasy, too, notably in a long sequence dealing with an enclave of mysterious little flying rustics known as the Feather Merchants.

About the same time that Barney Google was venturing South, United Feature was advertising a forthcoming comic in the pages of *Editor and Publisher*. "A hilarious and human new comic strip by Al Capp," the syndicate announced, "the story of a real hill-billy boy." His name was Li'l Abner Yokum, and he was a big, amiable nineteen-year-old rustic who was about to leave his cabin in the southern hills to visit "New Yawk." The strip started in August 1934 with Capp utilizing a classic theme, one that had been used for countless centuries—that of the country bumpkin in the big city. The narrative opened in Dogpatch, Kentucky, and introduced Mammy and Pappy Yokum and pretty blond Daisy Mae, who from the start had a crush on the rather dense Abner. Abner's wealthy Manhattan aunt wrote inviting him to live with her. "He could mingle with society and enjoy all the advantages of wealth and luxury." Bidding a tearful Daisy Mae goodbye and putting on shoes, Abner headed East. After nearly a year among the rich and famous, he returned to Dogpatch. Capp had perhaps sensed that his real strength was barnyard humor and that Dogpatch presented a fertile field for rowdy burlesque and broad satire.

Born in New Haven as Alfred Gerald Caplin in 1909, Capp lost his left leg when he was run over by a trolley car at the age of nine. His family later moved to Boston. In his teen years, unable to participate in sports or such social activities as dancing, he "looked for other diversions." Capp once said, "I wonder if it wasn't because of the wooden leg, slowing me down, that I had patience to study art." In addition to reading a lot, particularly humorist novelists like Twain, Smollet, and Dickens, the young Capp was also a dedicated fan of the funnies. He listed among his favorites Rube Goldberg, Fred Opper, Milt Gross, Rudy Dirks, and the now-forgotten Maurice Ketten. Capp managed to get a job in the Associated Press art bullpen in Manhattan in 1932. He drew the *Mister Gilfeather* panel for a few months, then quit with the AP's blessings. He went home to Boston, got married, and returned to New York for another try at the cartoon markets. He was hired by Ham Fisher to assist him—which meant ghosting—on *Joe Palooka*. Both men were endowed with enormous egos and their relationship over the years became extremely bitter and acrimonious and quite probably led to Fisher's suicide. Early on Capp publicly pretended that he admired his onetime employer. "I owe most of my success to him, for I learned many tricks of the trade working alongside of him," he told an interviewer in the early 1940s. A few years later, writing in the pages of *The Atlantic Monthly*, Capp said, "I regard him as a leper, a veritable goldmine of swinishness." It was while working alongside the swinish Fisher that Capp came up with the notion of using hillbilly characters. In 1933 he came up with a rowdy mountaineer boxer called Big Leviticus and his rowdy relatives. These hillbilly characters acted and talked like Dogpatch denizens and Capp later maintained that they were loosely based on real mountain people he'd encountered on a trip he took to Tennessee while a teenager. Fisher used Big Leviticus after Capp had left his employ and never missed a chance, once *Li'l Abner* had become a hit, to remind his many readers that the first funny hillbillies in the comics were created by none other than Ham Fisher.

Capp's wife, Catherine, has said that he was also inspired by a hillbilly vaudeville act they'd seen one night in New York. "We thought they were just

Li'l Abner, Al Capp. Marryin' Sam presides over the unusual aftermath to a Sadie Hawkins Day. ©1938, United Feature Syndicate, Inc.

Barney Google, *Billy DeBeck. Barney does not yet suspect that Snuffy will soon be the star of the strip.* ©1934, *King Features Syndicate, Inc.*

hilarious," she said. "We walked back to the apartment that evening, becoming more and more excited with the idea of a hillbilly comic strip." After leaving Fisher, Capp drew up six complete weeks of *Li'l Abner*, signing the first two dozen with the name Al G. Cap. He tried the new feature out first on King Features, then sold it to Monte Bourjaily at United. His strip started in a handful of papers but soon began to pick up more and more customers. *Li'l Abner* proved to be the syndicate's most successful strip of the thirties. Originally Catherine Capp helped her husband on the strip: "I drew the backgrounds: all of the outdoor country scenes were mine—the trees and log cabins and such." Early in 1935 Mo Leff, who was working in the syndicate bullpen, became Capp's assistant. A much better artist than his new boss, Leff improved the looks of the strip. He added such basic props as automobiles and trains, which were beyond Capp at the time, and improved the appearances of all the female characters, including Daisy Mae.

Capp, freed from some of the drawing burden, was able to concentrate on the writing. Like his friend and colleague Milton Caniff, he was a dedicated fan of the movies. Many of his storylines in the early years are either parodies of motion pictures or imitations of them. He would make fun of a typical

Hollywood horror film with a sequence wherein a mad doctor tries to transplant Pappy's brain into the skull of a gorilla, then try his hand at emulating the popular screwball comedies with a continuity in which Abner teams up with the ghost of a Manhattan playboy. The humor continued to broaden. Characters like Marryin' Sam, Lonesome Polecat, Hairless Joe, and the pig Salomey entered the action. More and more people with names such as Barney Barnsmell, Cecil Cesspool, and Moonbeam McSwine became part of the ensemble. In 1937 Capp introduced Sadie Hawkins Day, an annual event that allowed the unmarried women of Dogpatch to chase and capture, if they could, the unmarried men of the community. Daisy Mae tried year after year to catch Abner.

On December 5, 1932, a primitive man was introduced to the readers of a few dozen small newspapers across the country. The next day his humorous prehistoric adventures began with the line, "Early one morning a million years ago a hungry fellow met a little bear and thereby hangs this amazing tale." The hungry fellow was named Alley Oop. Vincent T. Hamlin was in his early thirties and his career up to then had not been notably successful. When he finally managed to sell his *Alley Oop* strip to the fledgling Bonnett-Brown syndicate of Chicago, Hamlin was running the art department of the *Des Moines Register & Tribune*. This early version of the strip introduced the prehistoric kingdom of Moo, where dinosaurs and cavemen co-existed, along with Oop's one true love, Ooola, and his pet dinosaur, Dinny. When Bonnett-Brown collapsed in April, 1933, Oop was homeless for a spell. NEA became interested, however, and *Alley Oop* started all over again on August 7, 1933. A Sunday page followed on September 9, 1934.

Like Capp, Hamlin favored continued stories. After a few years of doing business exclusively in Moo and environs, he expanded his interest in the past. He introduced, at his wife's suggestion, a time machine to the strip. Dr. Elbert Wonmug—his last name a punning translation of Einstein—inventor of the time machine had a deep interest in the secrets of the fourth dimension. While testing his new invention, he plucked Alley Oop and Ooola out of their own era and into the twentieth century. That took place in April 1939, and from then on Oop was able to enjoy escapades in such locales as ancient Rome, Troy, Cleopatra's Egypt, the Spanish Main, contemporary America, and prehistoric Moo. All this gallivanting through history seemed to inspire Hamlin and he produced some of his best work after his hero became a chronic argonaut.

Oaky Doaks combined the best qualities of both Li'l Abner and Alley Oop. He was a simple, goodhearted country boy who was stubborn, persevering and impressively strong. He dwelt in an unspecified period in the past when knighthood was in flower and he left home at the beginning of the feature to work as a sort of freelance knight. He wore a suit of armor he'd made from tin swiped from the roof of one of the sheds on his father's farm and his noble horse was Nellie, who formerly pulled a plow. *Oaky Doaks*, which started as a daily in 1935, was undoubtedly the Associated Press's answer to *Alley Oop*. It was drawn by Ralph B. Fuller, one of the most prolific magazine cartoonists for over two decades, and written by Bill McCleery, who was AP comics editor. Fuller, as one comics historian has pointed out, "had an impressive pen and ink style and could draw anything the strip called for, including gloomy castles, lovely damsels in distress, armored knights, fiery dragons and galloping steeds." McCleery had Oaky meet up with King

Cedric, the neighborhood monarch, early in the story and they began a series of mock adventures that involved them with pirates, amazons, dark knights, wizards, and ambitious ladies. Cedric was an amiable, maladroit fellow who looked like an overweight Ed Wynn. Their picaresque wanderings were amusing and entertaining and McCleery managed to slip in quite a bit of contemporary satire. In both 1936 and 1940, for example, Oaky and Cedric got involved in presidential elections. One involved a beautiful blond candidate who appeared on her campaign billboards wearing a bathing suit. Cedric left the strip in 1940 and McCleery seems to have taken his leave about that time as well. At any rate, some of the fun went out of *Okay Doaks*. By 1941 Okay had found his way to Camelot and joined up with King Arthur.

Harry Haenigsen's *Our Bill*, which the *Herald Tribune* began syndicating in 1939, was a harbinger of things to come. A humorous Sunday page, it centered around a clean-cut blond teenager who was the only child of a decidedly middle-aged couple. Though mild and gentle, Haenigsen's new strip helped introduce the world of jitterbugs to the comic sections. Adolescents had only recently been discovered to be a separate tribe, a large segment of the population whose antics and rituals could be exploited for entertainment purposes and who had money of their own to spend. College youths had

Napoleon, *Clifford McBride. A good example of McBride's drawing ability and sense of humor.*

become popular culture stereotypes back in the Roaring Twenties, but high school kids didn't really get much attention until the thirties. Swing music and the jitterbug craze helped put them on the map. Whenever you have a group getting attention you also have an older group that looks on with shock, dismay, and disapproval and you have a younger group who can't wait to grow up and be just like them. There was, therefore, a large audience for the teen-based entertainments of the late 1930s and early 1940s.

Henry Aldrich, the well-meaning but bumbling teen who was the inspiration, along with Andy Hardy, for much of the later adolescent entertainment, had first appeared in 1938 in Clifford Goldsmith's Broadway play *What a Life*. Henry and his pal Homer jumped next to radio and then into movies. Jackie Cooper, who'd earlier played Skippy, was the first screen Henry in 1939. Less frantic than the Aldrich saga and less maudlin than the Mickey Rooney Hardy epics, *Our Bill* was definitely in that tradition. Haenigsen drew in a minimalist cartoon style and built his gags around teen life—the soda shop, dating, school—and Bill's relationships with his folks, especially his plump, balding, white-haired dad. Many more teenagers would invade the funny papers in the next decade.

The top-rated radio comedy show in 1937, 1938, and 1939 wasn't *Bob Hope* or *Jack Benny*. It was *The Edgar Bergen and Charlie McCarthy Program*,

Alley Oop, V. T. Hamlin. *A sample of the earlier version of the strip.* ©1933, Bonnet-Brown.

sponsored by Chase & Sanborn coffee. The feisty, top-hatted dummy had first reached a national audience late in 1936, when he and his ventriloquist partner made a series of very popular guest shots on the *Rudy Vallee Show*. In the spring of 1937 the unusual team was given a show of its own and earned an impressive 39.4 Hooper rating the first season out. Benny, the runner up, only managed a 34.0. The sudden popularity resulted in movie appearances and considerable merchandising. The McNaught Syndicate gave a comic strip, daily and Sunday, a try in July 1939. Called *Mortimer and Charlie*, it costarred another Bergen dummy, the rustic buffoon Mortimer Snerd. Bergen was also a character and his creations were drawn as if they were real people. Ben Batsford, who by now had several comic strips to his credit, was the initial artist. The opening continuity involved the ventriloquist and the boys in a cross-country drive to visit their syndicate editors in Manhattan and attend the World's Fair. Moderately amusing, *Mortimer and Charlie* didn't have the spark and audacity of the radio program and it won no ratings contests in its short career. Despite its limited life, the feature used up two cartoonists. Carl Buettner was the second.

Just before he struck it rich with *Dick Tracy*, Chester Gould did a humor strip called *The Girl Friends*. This 1931 daily, syndicated by the *Chicago Daily News*, centered around two pretty young women, blond Dot and brunette Bebe. They both worked as salesgirls, and sometimes models, for Madame Batiste's dress shop. Drawn in the same sparse cartoony style he would use in the early years

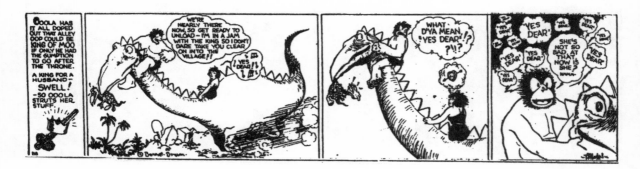

Oaky Doaks, *Ralph B. Fuller. Oaky and King Cedric in a typical predicament.* ©1935, The AP.

of his detective feature, *The Girl Friends* went in for simple continuities and each strip ended with a punchline. A depression era combination of a working girl comic and the earlier flapper funnies, it only survived for a few months.

Don Flowers was one of several artists who based his style pretty much on that of Russell Patterson. Quite open, as well as whimsical, about his sources of inspiration, Flowers once told an interviewer, "Any claim to fame that I might have I owe to diligent swiping right and left and staying sober at the drawing board." In addition to Patterson, he listed British cartoonist Gilbert Wilkinson and *New Yorker* regular Garrett Price as his favorites. In the late 1920s, he worked on the art staff of the *Kansas City Star*, a paper that had earlier employed Ralph Barton and Jefferson Machamer. Moving on to Manhattan, Flowers signed with the Associated Press and in 1930 began doing a daily pretty girl panel titled *Modest Maidens*. He also produced *Oh Diana*, a prosaic pretty girl humor strip. He later admitted that he had "hated every minute" of the twelve years he devoted to Diana and her crowd.

The comic sections of the depression years also made room for strips that traded in burlesque and nonsense. A long-time nonsense provider was Gene Ahern, who was obsessed with nuts and squirrels. As a companion piece to his Sunday *Our Boarding House*, he'd drawn *The Nut Bros., Ches & Wal.* When he switched to Hearst's King Features in 1936, his main effort was a Major Hoople imitation entitled *Room and Board*. The Sunday topper to that was *The Squirrel Cage*, a surreal effort whose only continuing character was a small fullbearded hitchhiker in tamoshanter and long overcoat. He spoke exclusively in a language that Richard Marschall has tentatively identified as "some vague, burlesque-style Slavic dialect." The hitchhiker's most frequently uttered line was the tantalizing query, "Nov shmoz ka pop?"

One of the old masters of nonsense, and the man who profoundly influenced Ahern, was Rube Goldberg. The thirties didn't prove an auspicious period for him and he spent most of the decade gradually falling out of favor with the public. After his long-running burlesque picaresque, *Boob McNutt* folded in 1934, he tried a melodramatic straight strip, *Doc Wright*. Goldberg, then in his middle fifties, returned to humor in 1936. *Lala Palooza* was done for the small Frank Jay Markey syndicate and centered around the plump, wealthy Lala and her

Dave's Delicatessen, *Milt Gross. One of Gross' several unsuccessful strips of the depression years. Dave's nephew, seen singing here, had quite a few similarities to the earlier Looy Dot Dope. ©1931, King Features Syndicate, Inc.*

lazy ne'er-do-well brother Vincent, who bore some resemblance to Wimpy both physically and spiritually. The daily offered rather flat comedy continuities and the Sunday was for gags. Now and then Vincent would come up with a Goldberg invention. The feature lasted until 1939.

Goldberg's final effort in the thirties was also to be his last comic strip. *Side Show*, a Sunday page composed of a variety of different features, was distributed by the Register & Tribune Syndicate. It included a *Weekly Invention* section, wherein the cartoonist returned again to the thing that had made him famous. There were also *Little Butch*, a panel about a precocious and prankish baby, and *Twisted Tales*, another version of the *Life's Little Jokes* doggerel narratives: "A very sad lad was T. Merriwell Totem," "A stylish and social young lady named Maud." Other departments that came and went within the page included *Blame It on Wilbur*, *Crackpot College*, and *Dopey Behavior Dept.* Fairly soon Goldberg started devoting half his weekly space to *Brad and Dad*, a two-tier father-and-son strip that went in for mock adventure continuity. The page, never widely distributed, ended in 1941. Goldberg had considerable help in the drawing from his assistant, John Devlin.

Milt Gross declined in popularity during the 1930s, too. He left the *New York World* in 1930, having already abandoned the use of dialect in his comic

strip work, to draw a new version of the *Count Screwloose* Sunday page for King Features. In addition, he drew a daily strip that alternated three uninspired single gag premises; *Draw Your Own Conclusions*, *I Did It and I'm Glad*, and *The Meanest Man in Town*. The following year the trio gave way to *Dave's Delicatessen*. A natural born patsy, Dave was continually being taken advantage of by his customers, his family, and his friends. Growing tired of delicatessen situations, Gross threw Dave into mystery stories and adventure tales, providing his own slapstick and irreverent version of this type of material. After awhile Dave took over the Sunday page and the Count and his dog Iggy moved upstairs to the topper. By 1935 Dave was gone from the Sunday and Count Screwloose was back in charge. Dave's daily ended as well. All of these efforts by the restless cartoonist were drawn in his usual loose, cockeyed style and were lovely to look at, but not that funny to read. Gross had lost some of the audacity and zaniness that he exhibited back in the heyday of *Nize Baby*. He left King in the middle 1930s, and showed up in the Sunday funnies a bit later doing a tabloid page for the *New York Mirror*, another Hearst enterprise. He revived Count Screwloose and also did a *That's My Pop!* page, devoted to a shiftless father and his doting little son. Resettled in Hollywood and writing and drawing for the movies, Gross had little time for his comics. Most of the *Mirror* material was ghosted by Bob Dunn, with some work done by an artist named John Calcagno. Gross, who'd always been considered essentially a big-town cartoonist who didn't go over in the hinterlands, left newspaper comics as the decade ended.

Walter Hoban's last go-round was *Needlenose Noonan*, a King Features Sunday page that got going in late September 1933. The hero was a diminutive blond fellow, just barely tall enough to qualify for the police force and thus follow in the footsteps (size 12D) of both his father and grandfather. Drawn in the same appealing style he'd used on *Jerry on the Job*, the page delivered Hoban's brand of broad gags and regularly had someone falling over backward in a cloud of dust by way of reacting to the punchline. The police station, like Jerry's railroad station, attracted a colorful bunch of eccentrics and was always plastered with odd signs and posters. For a topper to his new page Hoban introduced *Discontinued Stories*, a rather strange series of humorous fables in which each week's protagonist, usually an animal, ended up dead. A rabbit, for example, became dissatisfied with his rural life, journeyed to the big city and wandered into the back entrance of a restaurant. In the final panel a waiter is recommending hasenpfeffer to a customer. Hoban, though still drawing as well as ever, no longer seemed in tune with the times. Needlenose faded away in 1935. Later in the decade Jerry returned in a series of advertising strips for Grape-Nuts, but many of those were ghosted. Hoban died in 1939.

A prince of screwball cartoonists and one of the undisputed masters of the pun was Bill Holman. He'd worked in the NEA offices alongside Gene Ahern and George Swanson in the early 1920s, which must have made that particular corner of Cleveland a hotbed of zaniness. In 1935, with several strips and hundreds of magazine cartoons to his credit, he sold *Smokey Stover* to Captain Patterson for his Chicago Tribune-N.Y. News Syndicate. For much of its life the feature was Sunday only, but briefly in the middle thirties there was also a daily. Although Smokey was a fireman, he devoted most of his time to nonsensical encounters around the firehouse and at home. His boss was Fire Chief Cash U. Nutt, no doubt an *homage* to Ahern. What made Holman's work fascinating was all the extras he stuffed into it. In the thirties, fascinated by the word "foo," Holman inserted it into various nooks and crannies of his pages. Mice scampered by carrying signs reading, "3 blind mice. See how they foo," Holman signed himself "Doctor of Foolosophy," and dogs popped up toting signs that urged, "Let us now be up and fooing." And from the late thirties onward, after foo faded out, there were pictures on the walls illustrating outrageous puns. One showing a pair of snoring two-bit pieces was labeled "Sleeping Quarters," a dog peeking out of a mailman's bag was designated "Mail Pooch," two bottles of milk clasping hands was a "Milk Shake." Puns abounded elsewhere, too. A cow bore a tag saying "Barn Dora." Smokey rushed in on one occasion carrying a Love Ladder. He picked up Gun Drops at a firecracker store, kept some puppies in a crate made of dogwood, and used a vacuum cleaner called Li'l Sweep Heart. On top of all that, Holman never tired of hanging up signs that read "Notary Sojac" at least once per Sunday. He was also quite fond of the phrase "1506 Nix Nix." He once explained that 1506 was the number of the hotel room of his bach-

Smokey Stover, Bill Holman. Smokey and over a half dozen puns in this top half of a Sunday. ©1944, News Syndicate Co., Inc.

elor friend, cartoonist Al Posen, and that he was using this method of warning women to stay away from the place. In moments of stress or when reacting to some overwhelming punchline, Holman's players would leap clean out of their shoes. Their hats would pop high into the air, sometimes deconstructing, and even their hair might fly around the room. In addition they would often shed objects that looked like the metal nuts that accompany bolts. Holman got away with this obvious visual pun for years. As an accompaniment to Smokey and his fearless foofighters, Holman produced *Spooky*, a page about a disreputable cat.

Gus Mager brought his burlesque Sherlock Holmes back to the Sunday funnies toward the end of 1931. That was when *Hawkshaw the Detective* became the top strip to Rudolph Dirks' *The Captain and the Kids*. A close friend and sometimes ghost for Dirks, Mager was drawing the straight adventure strip *Oliver's Adventures* for another syndicate at the time and so he used Watso, the name of Hawkshaw's Watson, for his penname. It was Dirks who hired Mager for the job and not United Feature. Mager drew *Hawkshaw* in his old familiar style and didn't ape George Storm this time. Once again the sinister Professor and his minions cooked up fiendish schemes to plague decent people and befuddle the great detective. As in former days one-note characters such as Groucho, Tightwaddo, Coldfeeto, Humbuggo, and Henpecko turned up. There were sultry sirens, hairbreadth escapes, ingenious plots, and masterful detection. Mager would sometimes have Hawkshaw solve a case in a single Sunday, other times he would stretch a mystery across several weeks. He selected titles for each episode that would have made Conan Doyle envious: "The Peculiar Episode of the Snoozer," "The Singular Affair of the Purloined Pants," and "The Droll Denouement of the Stuffed Goose."

When Dirks left *The Captain and the Kids* in 1932, Mager had to give up *Hawkshaw*. The syndicate press releases pretended that Dirks, after a long, happy career, had decided it was time to retire and devote himself to painting. In reality, Dirks had asked editor Monte Bourjaily for a raise and was turned down. Angered, he'd quit. Since Mager was working directly for Dirks, he had to quit, too. From out of the bullpen came the dependable Bernard Dibble, who had ghosted for Dirks in the 1920s and worked on a variety of other strips, including *Danny Dingle* and *Looy Dot Dope*. For nearly a year, Dibble drew both the Kids and the detective. Dirks was persuaded to return in 1933 and Mager resumed drawing his own creation.

When Dirks came back, a daily *Captain and the Kids* strip was launched. Soon tiring of the extra work, he turned the daily over to Dibble. The younger cartoonist proceeded to create one of the great wacky adventure sagas of the decade. It was a frenzied stew of Saturday matinee melodrama, broad satire, and Marx Brothers anarchy. For the first extended adventure Dibble explained that the Captain had a miniaturized treasure map tattooed on his back, unbeknownst to him. A criminal mastermind known as the Brain, who wore a robe, face mask, and top hat, ordered him kidnapped by two lowlifes named Burlington Bertie, a name borrowed from the title of an old English music hall song, and Barkis, a name lifted from Dickens. Hans, Fritz, Mama, and the Inspector all became involved in an odyssey that took them eventually to Egypt and a scientific treasure hidden in a pyramid. There they encountered a Marxian detective named J. Rollo Coalscuttle. The narrative would pause now and then for looks at the personal lives of its main characters. One day, for instance, the Brain decided to go out and buy himself a crown, anticipating that he would soon be King of the World. Deciding to wear the impressive new crown home, he stepped out of the haberdashery shop to discover it was raining. He walked off muttering that it never failed to rain when he bought a new hat. Dibble, who never got a credit on the strip, kept this sort of thing up for years, mixing the Captain and the kids in encounters with pirates—the mild-mannered little Captain Bloodshot was one such—and cannibals and other stock menaces.

United introduced several tabloid Sundays in the middle thirties. The two humorous ones were a bit unusual. Initially *Billy Make Believe* was a fantasy aimed at children. The artist was Harry Homan, who'd previously worked in advertising and as a political cartoonist. His little blond hero was one more kid who enjoyed imaginary adventures, most of them, which he shared with his girlfriend Dolly and his buddy Bub, were of a fairy tale nature. Eventually the fantasy gave way to more mundane yarns and the page was canceled in 1938. A second Sunday, introduced in 1934, was *Cynical Susie*. At first glance, it, too, looked to be a kid strip, but its tiny heroine was actually a midget. The diminutive dark-haired Susie's goal was to get into the movies and become a Hollywood star. Not the typical aspiring ingenue, Susie was often to be seen riding around the movie capital on her pet cow, Lily Whey. The page was by Laverne Harding, a top animator with the Walter Lantz studios, who drew in a simple, uncluttered animated cartoon style. She left the job early on and was replaced by the dependable and busy Bernard Dibble. Under him the strip grew even stranger as Susie became the stand-in for cinema star Thistle Feather and was courted by tall, dark, handsome leading man Milo Maize. Later on she left Hollywood to roam the country, even joining a circus for awhile. By the late 1930s she was permanently at liberty.

Mickey Mouse wasn't even two years old when he moved into the funny papers and Walt Disney wasn't even a millionaire when he started signing his name to the new King Features daily strip. The likable rodent had begun his climb to fame in the *Steamboat Willie* cartoon short in 1928. The strip began on January 13, 1930. Disney had had considerable help in creating Mickey from a gifted artist and animator named Ub Iwerks. Disney contributed gags to the dailies and Iwerks penciled them and was, due to an oversight, allowed to sign the earliest ones. Win Smith inked *Mickey Mouse* and became its artist when Iwerks returned to his animation chores a few weeks later. Smith had a falling out with Disney and was replaced by a young cartoonist named Floyd Gottfredson. An excellent artist, Gottfredson was an admirer of Roy Crane and he modeled his Mickey after the plucky, optimistic Wash Tubbs and converted the Mouse strip into a comedy adventure continuity. He had a hand in the writing in the early years and saw to it that, in the words of one comics historian, "the plucky mouse went up against mad scientists, ghosts, Western bandits, air pirates and racketeers. He searched for lost treasure, impersonated royalty, served a stretch in the Foreign Legion, dwelled with cavemen and visited the far future. Minnie Mouse costarred in many of the stories and Mickey's usual sidekick was Goofy. The most frequent villain was Peg-Leg Pete." Gottfredson remained with Mickey for over four decades. Win Smith, by the way, returned briefly to the funny papers in 1934, when he ghosted a *Bosko* strip attributed to High Harman and Rudolph Ising and based on the character who was starring in their Warner Brothers *Looney Tunes*.

A *Mickey Mouse* Sunday was added in January, 1932 and for a top strip the *Silly Symphony* title was used. Stories related there and on September 16,

The Captain and the Kids, Bernard Dibble. Including Mama, the Kids, the Captain, the Inspector and Captain Bloodshot. ©1935, United Feature Syndicate, Inc.

1934. the noted fowl Donald Duck made his comics debut in the page. The fourteen-week sequence was an adaption of *The Wise Little Hen*, the June 1934 animated short that had introduced Donald to the screen. The artist was Al Taliafero, who'd worked as an inker on the Mickey strip. As a cartoonist he was nearly Gottfredson's equal and he was one of the best ever to draw the duck in comics. By 1938 Donald had a daily strip of his own, with a Sunday added in 1939. Bob Karp was the chief writer and, unlike Mickey, Donald avoided continuity and concentrated on a joke each and every day. Several other Disney properties showed up in the Sunday comic sections in the 1930s, usually in the *Silly Symphony* slot. Among them were *Snow White and the Seven Dwarfs*, *Bucky Bug*, *The Three Little Pigs*, and *The Ugly Duckling*.

Chapter 8

Wartime

From 1940 onward the comic section was not the place to turn to forget the spreading World War. An increasing number of established strips were beginning to deal with the conflict that was sweeping across Europe and Asia. In addition, many of the new comics that were launched in the early forties dealt directly with the war and military service. Once the United States officially entered Word War II in December 1941, just about every newspaper strip was caught up in the war effort. No other war, before or since, was so widely reflected in the funnies.

Joe Palooka was the first adventure strip character to join the service. With his manager Knobby Walsh by his side, the champ enlisted on November 29, 1940. This was a little over six weeks after the Selective Service Act, establishing the Draft, had gone into effect. Ham Fisher, the mastermind behind the Palooka enterprise, was a longtime Roosevelt supporter—he'd even used the president as a character in the strip—and he was eager to use his extremely popular feature to help the administration. "He had asked Colonel Magruder, in charge of recruiting in the Second Corps Area, if he could help the urgent drive for recruits," reported a contemporary interview. "Colonel Magruder said he thought it was a great idea. Ham visited Fort Dix in New Jersey and spent much time in getting the

authentic background." Joe Louis, the real-life heavyweight champion entered the service in 1942 and attained the rank of sergeant. Palooka, who remained the in Army until 1946 and saw action overseas, never rose above Pfc.

When *Hap Hopper, Washington Correspondent* began in 1940, it centered around the activities of a handsome blond bumpkin of a reporter who worked "amid the glamour and comedy of the nation's capital." The copy for the new adventure strip was supposedly edited by Drew Pearson and Robert S. Allen, nationally renowned at the time for their muckraking column "Washington Merry-Go-Round." William Laas, the comics editor at United Feature Syndicate, wrote the actual scripts and Jack Sparling, who'd been a staff artist and political caricaturist with the *Washington Herald*, was the artist. Editors around the country, many of whom had been young reporters at one time, were not taking kindly to a strip where the young reporter was depicted as being several percentage points denser than Li'l Abner. Hap was made brighter and, for good measure, handsomer and, as Sparling once explained, "the strip began to pick up papers."

Hap entered the U.S. Army in December 1940 as a private. He divided his time for the next several months between camp routine and tracking a saboteur who called himself Pierre LaVichy. At one point the sinister LaVichy even slipped Hap's girlfriend, Holly Woode, a drugged root beer in order to establish an alibi for himself. Pleased with Hap's eventual exposure of the spy, the Army transferred him to G-2 and suggested he go after "the men higher up in this desperate international game." He was told to return to Washington, D.C., and pose as a reporter. "A Washington correspondent again?" exclaimed the young newsman. "Yipp-ee!!" Until America actually entered the war, the country of origin of the international conspirators who were out to sabotage America's defenses was never specified.

Captain Easy officially entered the service on December 30, 1941, when he was given a special commission as a captain in Army Intelligence. Early in February of the following year, he was captured by the Japanese while attempting to fly to Chungking. He escaped with the help of an exotic dancer named Liska, and in mid-April arrived in the Philippines to fight alongside the guerrillas. Later in the year he was transferred to Air Intelligence and shifted to the European Theater of the war. Roy Crane was tapped to create a new strip for Hearst, as we'll see, and he left *Wash Tubbs* and the *Captain Easy* Sunday page in May 1943. Leslie Turner, who'd been ghosting just about all the dailies since the late 1930s, took over officially with the daily of May 31. The Sunday was taken over by Walt Scott.

Skeezix of *Gasoline Alley* turned twenty-one on Valentine's Day in 1942, and in June he enlisted in the Army. Frank King followed him through induction and basic training, alternating service sequences with glimpses of the other characters doing their bits back home. Nina, for example, took a job working on a farm and said of the war—"I wish I were a man. I'd like to be in it." Skeezix kept close to his roots and was assigned to Ordnance, which is defined as "the branch of the army that procures, stores and issues weapons, munitions and combat vehicles." He was sent overseas and saw combat in Libya. Home on leave in 1944, he married Nina and the following year the couple became the parents of a son named Chipper. "A rumor spread," according to columnist Paul Gallico, "that Frank King ... was going to kill Skeezix off in the war. For three days the switchboards of the *Daily News* in New York and the *Chicago Tribune* were clogged with calls saying, 'Don't you dare,' until the rumor proved unfounded."

Harold Teen, who'd been a teenager since 1919, finally reached manhood in 1942. His creator, Carl Ed, put him in the Navy and thereafter alternated service and homefront continuities. Zack Mosley served in the Civil Air Patrol while his mustached daredevil Smilin' Jack flew for the Air Force in the Pacific. Interestingly enough, these two strips, as well as *Gasoline Alley* and *Terry*, were products of the Chicago Tribune—N.Y. News Syndicate. Both Colonel McCormick of the *Trib* and Captain Patterson of the *News* had been staunch isolationists and opposed to American involvement in any way with the war in Europe and Asia.

Although *Terry and the Pirates* had been involved in the war since the late thirties, Terry Lee himself

Hap Hopper, *Jack Sparling.* ©1941, United Feature Syndicate, Inc.

Captain Easy, Leslie Turner. ©1943, NEA Service, Inc. Reprinted with permission.

didn't officially enter the service until the end of February 1943. By that time, readers of Milton Caniff's picaresque adventure strip, as noted earlier, had been through several years of land and air fighting in Asia. While Terry flew with the Army Air Force, his mentor Pat Ryan served as a lieutenant in the Navy. Caniff kept several story lines going during the war years, crosscutting between Terry and Pat and bringing back such supporting players as the Dragon Lady, April Kane, Burma, and Sanjak. He also introduced a batch of new characters, most notably Flip Corkin. Based on his longtime real life friend Colonel Phil Cochran, Colonel Flip Corkin of the Air Force served as a surrogate Pat Ryan. A hard-boiled yet humorous man, Corkin helped Terry through the transition from boy to man. Charles C. Charles of Boston didn't land in the strip until 1944, but once he did he came close to stealing it. On the small side, redheaded, and freckled, a wiseguy and a would-be womanizer, he was nicknamed Hotshot Charlie. A first-rate pilot, he became Terry's closest friend and his irreverent attitude toward love and war kept Terry from taking himself too seriously.

The *Scorchy Smith* strip had changed hands again in May 1939. The new artist was Frank Robbins, a gifted young man in his early twenties. In May 1942, he had Scorchy join up as an Army pilot after stumbling onto a secret U.S. base in the South American jungle. Later Scorchy became a lieutenant in the Air Force and fought against both the Japanese and the Germans. The Associated Press added Sunday pages rather late in the game. *Scorchy Smith* got going at the

end of 1941 and Robbins was the first cartoonist to do it. He turned out an especially strong Sunday sequence set in Russia, and showing the influence of Eisenstein's *Alexander Nevsky*. His work, which was definitely of the Caniff school, caught the attention of King Features and that led to a new aviation strip of his own in 1944.

Snuffy Smith, who had been dominating what had once been the just plain Barney Google strip for some time, got into the service ahead of all his humor strip colleagues. Although he didn't meet the height requirement, he was given a special dispensation from a colonel whose life he happened to save. As of November 13, 1940, Snuffy was an Army buck private. Billy DeBeck concentrated for quite awhile on boot camp life and took to calling Snuffy a yardbird. The term, indicating a raw recruit assigned to menial camp chores, became a popular one in the war years and was even the source of jazzman Charlie Parker's nickname. Now a definite second fiddle to his hillbilly associate, Barney didn't get around to joining up until September 1941 and he went into the Navy. When DeBeck died late in 1942, his longtime assistant Fred Lasswell, after some filling in by the King Features bullpen, took over the strip. He sent both Barney and Snuffy into combat in the Pacific.

After two decades of office work, Tillie Jones enlisted in what was initially called the Women's

Terry and the Pirates,
Milton Caniff. ©1943,
News Syndicate Co., Inc.

stylized version of the Woman's Army.

Elza Poppin was one more strip that made a transition from civilian to military life. The comedy review *Hellzapoppin'*, concocted by and starring the screwball comedians Ole Olsen and Chic Johnson, opened on Broadway in the autumn of 1938 and ran for a record-breaking 1,404 performances. A sort of surrealist burlesque show, it was converted into a Universal movie, starring Olsen & Johnson and Martha Raye, in 1941. King Features introduced the *Elza Poppin* daily, with writing credited to Olsen & Johnson, in July 1939. Elza, who was not a character from the show, was a tall, thin blond young lady built along Olive Oyl's lines. She hung out with a small bald fellow named Squeaky and devoted herself to delivering a joke, and not always a fresh one, each and every day. Bits of business from the review, such as the woman who kept calling for Oscar and the man carrying a plant—sometimes a tree—to deliver to Mrs. Jones, appeared as background elements. Ving Fuller, a veteran cartoonist of the sec-

Army Auxiliary Corps in the summer of 1942. Russ Westover's *Tillie the Toiler* became the first comic strip to deal full time with the W.A.A.C. Gladys Parker had begun her *Mopsy* panel in 1939, featuring a feathercut, featherbrained young woman who resembled her creator in looks though not intellect. In 1944 Mopsy started serving in a very

ond rank, was the initial artist. By 1940, George Swanson, who'd pioneered screwball comics with *Salesman Sam* back in the 1920s, was doing the drawing. The following year Elza, a brunette now, joined the Army. Since this was before the United States entered the war and a year before the W.A.A.C., she functioned as a kind of secretary in uniform. All traces of the Broadway show had long since vanished and the strip purveyed simple army gags until it folded in 1942.

The established servicemen strips all went to war, too. In December 1941, Don Winslow of the Navy had finally gotten around to proposing to his longtime sweetheart, Mercedes Colby, but before anything could be done about it, Don and his side-kick, Lt. Red Pennington, were off to the Pacific to fight against the Japanese. Ken Ernst, who'd recently graduated from comic books, was now doing most of the drawing on the strip. Don Dickson, the artist on *Sergeant Stony Craig*, was recalled to active Marine Corps duty at the end of 1940. A succession of other artists, including Bill Draut, saw the sergeant and his crew into World War II and through the fighting in the Pacific. *Navy Bob Steele*

also shifted its action to the Pacific theater upon America's entry into World War II.

Yankee Doodle, an aviation adventure strip by Frank Tinsley, had begun in the fall of 1940. Its handsome blond civilian hero entered the Marines in 1942 and was soon leading a special unit of airborne commandos. In June of that year the strip's name was changed to *Captain Yank*. It had more ghost artists than most any other strip of the period and they included Jack Lehti, Mart Bailey, and Lou Fine. On Sunday, September 7, 1941, exactly three months before the Japanese attack on Pearl Harbor, a new NEA Sunday page made its debut. *Biff Baker*, by Henry Lee, had for its hero a handsome young fellow who was a "college senior, football star and amateur aviator." The Henry Lee pen name covered NEA comics editor Ernest "East" Lynn, who did the writing, and Henry Schlensker, who drew the page in a commendable illustration style. It may be that Lynn had planned this as a military strip all along. At any rate, in June 1942, after graduating from Midwestern University, *Biff* was accepted by the Air Corps. By following the military careers of Biff and his erstwhile college friends, the page was able to deal with combat situations in both Asia and Europe. When Schlensker was drafted, the dependable bullpen wizard Walt Scott became the artist.

War clouds cast their shadows on Secret Agent X-9 fairly early. As an FBI operative, he was busily

Scorchy Smith, *Frank Robbins. Scorchy is fighting side by side with Russian partisans in these panels from a 1943 Sunday page.*

tracking down saboteurs and enemy agents throughout 1940, and in the summer of 1941 he went on a secret mission into what was obviously Nazi Germany to arrange an escape from a concentration camp. Up until December 1941, however, Germany and the Axis powers were never referred to by name and the details of the uniforms were blurred. The veteran undercover man underwent another change of appearance in May 1940, when Mel Graff took over as artist. Graff's work on *Adventures of Patsy* had impressed King Features and, according to him, "Ward Greene, at King, both phoned and wired me" to carry on the strip after Austin Briggs's departure. Under Graff, the strip swung even further from the Alex Raymond look. Having worked with both Caniff and Sickles at the Associated Press, Graff had developed his own individual version of their style. His first few years on *Secret Agent X-9* were impressive. He favored the use of doubletone board and he was very good at drawing the planes, trains, and automobiles that the action called for. He was also effective at depicting more static situations, such as office conversations and restaurant confrontations. He had worked for years as a caricaturist as well, and his secondary characters and his villains are not stock types but come across as varied people.

After the war officially broke out, X-9 continued his pursuit of spies and saboteurs. Now, though, the

Yankee Doodle, Frank Tinsley. Captain Yank is briefed on an espionage plot while flying over the N.Y. World's Fair in this prewar strip.

Nazis were specifically labeled as such and swastikas finally showed up in spy headquarters. X-9 did such things as crack a spy ring in Washington, D.C. and thwart a Nazi plot to assemble bombers in a secret facility within the Untied States. He also returned again to Germany to impersonate a spy school trainee in Berlin. It seems likely that Max Trell, who continued as script writer, and Graff were impressed by such contemporary movies as Carol Reed's *Night Train to Munich* (1940), Alfred Hitchcock's *Foreign Correspondent* (1940), and *Saboteur* (1942). During the war *Secret Agent X-9*, despite a few touches of humor, was a decidedly downbeat strip and it displayed many of the qualities that would soon be associated with *film noir*.

Several new service strips, in both the adventure and humor categories, were also introduced in the early and middle 1940s. A United Feature entry into the uniformed ranks was *Race Riley of the Commandos*, which got started in 1942. Drawn by Milburn Rosser, it concerned itself with American Riley's service in a British commando unit. Race's military career was unconventional even for a commando. After a raid or two, he took to working with the underground in occupied France. The fact that he was an American through and through, no matter what sort of uniform or disguise he donned, was emphasized by his speech patterns. "Sizzlin' sassafras!" he'd cry out in moments of stress. He was also fond of "What's cookin'?" and he would never say "you" when he could slip in "ya." While the Gestapo was closing in on him on one occasion, he radioed England to report, "I'm hotter'n a fire-

cracker in this burg!" A former pulp illustrator, Rosser supplemented his *Race Riley* income by drawing Sunday advertising strips for such clients as Camel cigarettes.

The shortest-lived war strip was the one produced by Alfred Andriola for King Features in 1942. *The Yankee Rangers* ran for just six weeks. It was while Andriola, who'd just quit the *Charlie Chan* strip, was negotiating with Publishers Syndicate for a new strip that King approached him with the suggestion that he cook up a miniseries about fighting men for them. He obliged with *The Yankee Rangers*, but was not able to recall in later years why he or the syndicate had been interested in such a short run venture. Since it ran toward the end of the year in some papers, it's possible it was originally intended as some sort of seasonal strip, although there's no mention of Christmas or any other holiday and the strip certainly wasn't festive. The Rangers were yet another elite commando unit, this one operating in occupied Europe. Their duties, as outlined by their commanding officer, included being able to "dynamite and sabotage—handle rifle, tommy-gun, grenades and a razor-sharp trench knife against a ruthless enemy, employ jiu jitsu and guerrilla warfare—go for days without food or water, and swim long distances with an 80-pound pack on your back!" The three heroes of the strip were Rex Rand, the dark, handsome one, Riff Rafferty, the big, tough bruiser and Chunky Tubbs, the jovial fat one. Their first, and only, mission took them to the Netherlands. There they met a pretty blond young woman who fought as a guerrilla, tangled with the

Secret Agent X-9, Mel Graff. One of the earliest and one of the few mentions of concentration camps in the funnies. ©1941, King Features Syndicate, Inc.

Nazis, and paved the way for an invasion. The strip ended with the Rangers sailing away into the sunrise while the blonde waved a tearful farewell.

As we've noticed, William Randolph Hearst was doing some wartime recruiting of his own. His biggest coup of the period was luring Roy Crane away from NEA and over to his King Features Syndicate. In November 1943, Crane's *Buz Sawyer* commenced. Crane had been moving away from the Ruritanian adventures of the 1930s *Wash Tubbs* and toward more realistic storylines and settings long before he signed up with Hearst and he moved even closer to reality with his new venture. "It was during World War II, so I decided to make Buz a Navy pilot," Crane later explained. "It promised lots of action, and I also felt that I would be making a contribution to the war effort. Before actually starting the strip, and to ensure authenticity, I did a great deal of research. I've always loved to travel, so I went to many different places in search of information ... I even spent some time aboard an aircraft carrier."

Buz was a Lt. (jg) on the carrier Tippecanoe when readers first encountered him, in the Pacific and "bound for action." A clean-cut young man, not a weather-beaten rowdy like Easy, Buz was a more typical handsome adventure hero. His comic sidekick was Rosco Sweeney, an easygoing roughneck who served as gunner on the plane Buz flew. By

Buz Sawyer, Roy Crane. Crane also dealt with the problems servicemen encountered while home on leave.
©1945, *King Features Syndicate, Inc.*

the end of the year Crane had them, after being shot down by a Japanese Zero, stranded on a tropical island. In addition to Japanese soldiers and assorted natural hazards, the island also came equipped with a lovely young woman in a sarong.

When Crane was first approached by Hearst, he assumed that his longtime assistant/ghost Les Turner would stay with him for the new strip. But Turner chose to take over *Wash Tubbs*. Crane was able to hire former gag cartoonist Ralph Lane to work with him on the strip, daily and Sunday, and in 1944 a teacher named Ed Granberry joined the team as chief script writer.

Frank Robbins' *Johnny Hazard* started one day prior to D-Day, on June 5, 1944. Robbins, too, had been recruited by the Hearst organization. The first time around they'd offered him the opportunity to draw *Secret Agent X-9*. But the gifted young artist saw that as another Associated Press type of dead-end, so he held out for a new feature of his own. He got his wish with *Johnny Hazard*, although it was actually a very close approximation of what he'd been doing with *Scorchy Smith*. The Robbins hero was less lean and lanky, less well-groomed than many and looked more like a working stiff in those days. Robbins' effective impressionistic style definitely showed the Caniff-Sickles influence, and also a touch of the influence of his painter friend Jack Levine. But it

was, nonetheless, his own and, coupled with his increasing attention to the ordnance of the war, resulted in making *Johnny Hazard* a striking wartime adventure strip.

Late in June 1942, an unusual man in uniform joined the comic strip ranks. He was introduced at the controls of his pursuit plane, flying over the North Atlantic. This was Captain Midnight, "a secret, unofficial American fighter for Freedom—off to aid the United Nations against the Axis." The new strip was distributed by the Chicago Sun Syndicate and copyrighted by the Wander Co., who were the makers of Ovaltine. The captain had begun life as a radio serial hero in 1939, broadcasting out of Chicago. By 1940 his fifteen-minute weekday show was being heard all across the country during the children's hour of 5 to 6 P.M., sponsored by Ovaltine. With the help of two teenagers, Joyce Ryan and Chuck Ramsey, and a mechanic named Ichabod M. Mudd, Midnight managed an organization known as the Secret Squadron. This was a vigilante group of aviators that operated, with full government approval, against the enemies of the nation. After appearing in Big Little Books and comic books, Captain Midnight and his crew next showed up in a newspaper strip.

The pen name signed to the daily and Sunday *Captain Midnight* was Jonwan. This masked writer Russ Winterbotham and the artist Erwin L. Hess, who'd already collaborated on the Big Little Books issued by the Whitman Publishing folks. It seems obvious that the strip was also produced by Whitman, especially since the other most frequently seen artist was Henry E. Vallely, who did an enormous amount of work for the Racine, Wisconsin, outfit. An artist named Donald Moore also took a turn with the dailies for a stretch. Hess drew in a variation of the Caniff style and produced some very striking pages.

The captain's uniform consisted of a black aviator helmet and a midnight blue uniform with an insignia depicting a winged clock with the hands at midnight emblazoned on the chest. He was accepted by Allied military leaders everywhere. None had any problem working with him and the Secret Squadron, and confided in him or let him take part in both combat and intelligence missions. Midnight concentrated on fighting the Nazis in occupied Europe and his chief antagonist was an ambiguous secret agent they called the Moon Woman. Also known as Luna White, she was strangely affected by moonlight and could be both helpful and detrimental to Captain Midnight. There were times when she tried to kill him, times when she saved his life, and a few times when she made it quite obvious she was in love with him. Needless to say, this was an aspect of the captain's life that wasn't touched on during the kid radio show. The strip ended just before the war did in 1945 and readers finally learned that Luna had been on the Allied side all along. This didn't allow for a getting together with Captain Midnight, though. The final caption said, "And so these two fighters for freedom, proven friends at last, go their separate ways."

One of the earliest strips to deal with the lighter side of life as a conscript was *Draftie*, which began in 1940 and was the work of writer Paul Fogarty and, for most of its life, artist William Juhre. It was syndicated by John F. Dille, best known for distributing *Buck Rogers*. Draftie, whose first name was Lem, was a small-town rube from Cider City. His early Army career was one more enactment of the country boy amid the slickers routines. Soon teamed up with a little Brooklyn hustler named Oinie, Draftie's maiden adventures took him through the then relatively unfamiliar routines of induction and basic training. For awhile Fogarty aimed for a joke, or a reasonable facsimile, every day. When the real war got underway, the continuities grew a bit more serious. The two comrades served in various war zones and they destroyed both German and Japanese opponents with wisecracking exuberance. Although the copy was never especially strong, Juhre was an interesting artist. Back in the 1930s he'd drawn the *Tarzan* daily strip for several months. On *Draftie* he developed a looser, more cartoony approach and may have been the only comic strip artist ever to have been influenced by the noted British political cartoonist David Low. In 1944 the strip changed its name to *Lem and Oinie*.

There were also service related gag panels. They all started after the draft and before Pearl Harbor. Herc Ficklen's *You're In The Army Now* specialized in Army life jokes but didn't concentrate on a single character. Quin Hall's *Strictly Private* dealt with the

Captain Midnight, Erwin L. Hess. The captain gets his first glimpse of the notorious Luna White (a.k.a. the Moon Woman). ©1942, The Wander Co.

Army experiences of Private Peter Plink, and Clyde Lewis' *Private Buck* starred a diminutive draftee of that name. Dave Breger had been drafted early in 1941 and his *Private Breger* was a loosely autobiographical panel about a died-in-the-wool civilian who finds himself expected to act like a soldier.

The first *Vic Jordan* Sunday page appeared on December 7, 1941. Although the strip, which debuted the previous Monday, had a civilian hero, it was definitely a war strip. The opening sequence took place in Paris in the summer of 1940 and an early caption explained, "Summer has come to Paris. So have the Nazis!" Jordan, a good-looking, fast-talking American publicity agent, was working for a musical revue that was playing in the German-occupied city. A stunt involving the French leading lady doing a satirical impersonation of Hitler resulted in a riot and audience cries of "Down with the Nazi dogs!" Vic soon found himself unemployed and in trouble with the Gestapo. Very soon, rather than returning to America, he joined the resistance movement and was committing acts of sabotage and writing anti-German propaganda.

Vic Jordan, syndicated by the liberal *Newspaper PM*, was written by Kermit Jaediker and Charles Zerner under the name Paine, a nod to Tom Paine. Elmer Wexler, who drew such second-string comic book superheroes as the Black Terror and the Fighting Yank, was the first artist. He went into the

Marines in the spring of 1942 and was replaced by Paul Norris.

When *Claire Voyant* started on May 10, 1943, it was very much involved with the war. Another *PM* offering, the new strip was by Jack Sparling, fresh from *Hap Hopper*, and it began in the Atlantic as a fogbound Merchant Marine freighter sighted a drifting lifeboat, "its occupants more dead than alive." The two were apparently survivors of a Nazi torpedo raid, but the reader never learned the details since the man died and the pretty young brunette turns out to have amnesia. Overhearing the ship's cook speculating about her and using the word "clairvoyant," she took that as her name. Explaining his strategy in creating a strip of his own, Sparling said, "I picked a girl hero here because it has appeal in the papers. I picked a girl with amnesia because we were in the middle of the war and I didn't want to give her any family ties after the war was over."

Claire remained aboard the ship for the first months of the strip. Two of the handsomest crewmen, redheaded Tex and dark-haired Spike, fell for her amidst a string of adventures that included the ship's being torpedoed by a Nazi sub. Sparling portrayed his leading lady as shrewd and capable, and she was fond of making suggestions that helped save the crew from danger: "I have a sort of a plan." Eventually the locale was shifted to the Orient. By 1945, when the *Chicago Sun* had taken over the syndication of the strip, the young lady was being touted as having the "power of seeing into the future …

Flyin' Jenny, Russell Keaton. ©1944, Bell Syndicate, Inc.

Vic Jordan, Paul Norris. ©1942, Field Enterprises.

the charm to lead men to the far-away corners of the earth ... and the 'know how' to chart the course of their lives!"

One of the gloomiest of the new war-inspired strips was *Spunkie* by Loy Byrnes, a daily that was introduced by United Feature on December 16, 1940. Spunkie was a nine-year-old blond boy who lived in a European country called Bombardia that was under attack by an invading army. Before the first week was over the boy had seen his home destroyed by bombs and his mother and father killed. After burying them himself, Spunkie was advised by the burgomaster to go to America, "where the lights of liberty burn bright!" He joined a forlorn parade of refugees. When enemy planes strafed the refugees, the boy escaped injury. But soon, weary and hungry, he collapsed on the roadway and was left for dead. He was finally helped by a refugee relief station and just managed to squeeze aboard a yacht that had been chartered to carry wealthy children to safety in America. Spunkie helped save the ship from being torpedoed, but got no credit for his efforts.

After arriving in the United States, he was left sitting unclaimed in the offices of the Refugee League. Turning to the readers, Spunkie pleaded, "Nobody in whole America want Spunkie? Please!!" The following week he was adopted by a plump, kindly widow named Mrs. Weeds and taken to live with her in the pleasant little town of Hopeville. Like many comic strip orphans before him, the boy was not destined to have a happy time of it. Mrs. Weeds turned out not to be a widow after all, and her ras-

cally husband came back to Hopeville to plague her and the boy. Then, agents from Bombardia tried to drag Spunkie back to his occupied homeland. On the run, he paused long enough to route a gang of spies and saboteurs. Then he was on the run again and he disappeared for good and all on March 21, 1942. The final caption, gloomy to the end, said, "And there goes little Spunkie ... alone ... friendless ... helpless ... into the sunset and shadows again."

Byrnes, who'd been handicapped since childhood, worked his way up from art department office boy at the *New York World*. After a stint at Tom Johnstone's advertising strip shop, he became assistant and eventually ghost for Gus Edson on *Streaky*. When Edson moved up to *The Gumps*, Byrnes took over *Streaky*. He drew his new strip in a cartoon style that did not completely suit its grim content. Never successful, *Spunkie* was picked up by less than a dozen newspapers across the country. Byrnes' old boss would have better luck a decade and a half later when he recycled the same basic notion as *Dondi*.

By the spring of 1942, references to the war could be found throughout the funnies. One week Felix the Cat would be gathering old pots and pans for the scrap drive and the next be seen as a mascot at a WAC camp; *They'll Do It Every Time* added boot camps and foxholes to its locales; many of the young men hanging out with Etta Kett and her girlfriends were in uniform; Nancy and Sluggo collected for the paper and scrap drives; Donald Duck had to

Spunkie, *Loy Byrnes. The gloomy third daily of the opening week of the strip.*

cope with gas rationing and his girlfriend Daisy did volunteer work; Buck Rogers and his gang battled off-planet invaders who looked suspiciously Japanese and had huge rising sun symbols emblazoned on their rocket ships.

Mickey Mouse was preoccupied with war-related activities, too. He worked on a farm to help food production, caught a saboteur, captured the crew of a Nazi sub, helped the government test a new superplane called the Bat, got kidnapped and taken to Berlin, and became the guardian of a trio of war orphans. The dastardly Peg-Leg Pete, Mickey's perennial nemesis, was at his worst during this period. He sold out to the Nazis and worked as a spy.

Harold Gray's *Little Orphan Annie* made several early contributions to the war effort. After giving his factory and "every dime I have" to the United States, Daddy Warbucks became a lieutenant colonel in what was apparently the British Army. Punjab and the Asp joined up, too. In the middle of June 1942, Annie organized a kid group called the Junior Commandos. One of their jobs was to "gather up every scrap o' paper—all th' old iron, 'luminum, ever' bit o' junk you can find." Annie was a dedicated patriot and she told her young comrades, "This is war, kids—*our* war, just as much, or more maybe, than anybody else's—we're *givin'* all we can to help those who are *givin' ever'thing* for us!"

As the war progressed, the number of working women kept increasing. "By the fall of 1943," reports historian Geoffrey Perrett, "with war production at its peak, 17,000,000 women made up a third of the total work force, and of those about 5,000,000 were in war industries. In some plants, particularly the airplane factories, women did most of the work while men did most of the supervising." Despite this, the majority of comic strip women stayed out of the factory labor force and you never saw Blondie, Maggie, or Fritzi Ritz punching a time clock. Briefly in the summer of 1944, King Features tried a Sunday page about a young woman who worked in a war plant. *Rosie Rattletrap* by Wilson Cutler dealt with a pretty redhead who wore slacks and was a riveter at the Northwood airplane factory in an unspecified southern California town. The page was humorous in intent, and Cutler drew in a slick style that bore many similarities to that of Russell Patterson.

Many strip cartoonists also did volunteer drawings for the government, using their characters. Secretary of the Treasury Henry Morgenthau, Jr. put a lot of them to work doing special newspaper panels to promote the sale of War Bonds and Stamps. Among the many characters doing their part for the bond drives were Smitty, Joe Palooka, Hap Hopper, Dick Tracy, Superman, Flyin' Jenny, the Timid Soul, Winnie Winkle—"What about it, girls? Have you started the payroll plan in your office?", Scorchy Smith, and Li'l Abner.

Though one of the most self-promoting cartoonists of his time, Al Capp made a long term anonymous contribution to the war effort. From 1942 onward he and his staff produced an unsigned biweekly Sunday page for Morganthau and the Treasury Department. Titled *Small Change*—originally *Small Fry*—it centered around a pint-sized young bumpkin and took place in a unnamed rural community that was obviously Dogpatch. Small Change's obsession was the buying of Yew-nited States War Bonds. In the first episode, after being turned down by the Army because of his height—"Thar hain't *enough* inches!!"—he was persuaded by his gorgeous girlfriend Tallulah, a brunette in a tattered red shirt and cutoff overalls, that by buying a bond "yo' helps win a battle as much as if you *fit* in it!!" The feature followed Small Change as he came up with schemes to earn the money to buy a bond and worked to persuade others to purchase one. There was often a fantasy element, with the diminutive hero transporting a smug civilian to the battlefront to convince him how important "just one li'l rifle bullet" could be.

The Office of War Information was established by order of President Roosevelt in June 1942. It's ostensible purpose was to "coordinate the dissemination of war information by all federal agencies." Basically the OWI, headed originally by newsman Elmer Davis, was a huge domestic propaganda

bureau that not only disseminated news but oversaw how the mass media presented that news and dealt with the war. Newspapers, radio shows, and especially movies were given a great deal of attention and advice. As might have been expected, the OWI found time to pay attention to the comics and their creators. On September 19, 1942, *Editor & Publisher* proudly reported that "the knights of the drawing board are doing their bit to help Uncle Sam speed the day of victory over the Axis." The trade weekly went on to report that "the nation's syndicate cartoonists whose material appears in newspapers over the land have enlisted for the duration to aid in doing the job of keeping up the morale of the fighting men and the folks here at home. And they're performing a valuable service, government officials say."

E&P went on to point out, "It's impossible to compute how many millions of dollars worth of War Bonds and Stamps have been sold through the constant plugging of the cartoonists in their daily releases, or how many pints of blood have been donated to the Red Cross through their efforts." The magazine singled out Ham Fisher and his *Joe Palooka* for special praise because of the positive treatment of Army life. "The Army's morale department has on many occasions requested Fisher's cooperation in bringing to the attention of the men various phases of training." Also cited for their efforts in "the morale effort" were all the artists of the NEA Service, including Roy Crane, Fred Harman, V. T. Hamlin and Herblock. *E&P* even mentioned that Henry Formhals, who was drawing the Sunday *Joe Jinks* at the time, was an air raid warden in Altadena, California.

In light of this, it must have been disappointing to many cartoonists and syndicate editors to see, just two months later, an article in the same magazine that was headlined "Comics Not Geared to War, OWI Analyst Says." It seemed that Edward Barnhart, a doctor of philosophy and "a noted psychologist"

Dick Tracy, Chester Gould. Dick and Junior help Uncle Sam sell bonds.

Small Change, *Al Capp (and staff). Selling war bonds Dogpatch style.*

had been hired, at a "sizable salary to read the funnies." Dr. Barnhart's job was "to tell whether they are carrying the right message or merely providing laughs." An admitted nonfan of the funny papers, he indicated to *E&P* that his findings convinced him that comic sections as a whole were "lacking sympathetic and serious treatment of the demands of war on the civilian populace." Obviously he hadn't been reading *Spunkie*. It's safe to say, looking back across more than half a century, that Dr. Barnhart may not have worked hard enough to earn his sizable salary. As we've seen, the majority of strips were caught up in the war and a great many characters were doing their bit, at the front and back home. According to a later account in the *Wall Street Journal*, the Barnhart report found that only *Terry* and *Joe Palooka* were representing fighting men anywhere near correctly. As for the funny strips, "The effect of the war on the civilian is only a subject for humor. The home front's actions and thoughts and the demands on the civilian, have yet to receive serious and sympathetic treatment." All of this appears to have had little effect on how the funnies continued to deal with the war. But it does indicate a certain ingratitude on the part of the government.

Quite a few new strips in various categories showed up during these years. There were, for instance, some new cowboy comics. The first, and certainly the most unusual, was *Ricky Mason, Government Marshall* by Jimmy Swinnerton. Turning his back on nearly a half-century of funny stuff, Swinnerton here assayed a straight adventure page. Replacing the venerable *Little Jimmy*, this Sunday-only feature started on August 24, 1941. The time was the present and the setting was the hot, dry Arizona countryside Swinnerton knew so well. Rocky was a tall, lanky, and taciturn blond. Like Red Ryder, he rode a horse named Thunder and had an Indian sidekick, Red Wing in this case, who spoke a movie redman patois; "Me follow gang to hideout." The plots seemed inspired by the Saturday matinee. The longest running villain was a masked man who called himself the Black Coyote and managed to elude the stalwart marshall month after month. Swinnerton, perhaps with a sigh of relief, abandoned the strip in 1945 and brought back Little Jimmy.

Another contemporary Western came along in March 1942. This one was called *Ramblin' Bill* and credited to Tex Bradley. The midwesterner hiding behind that name was Marvin Bradley, still a few years away from his hit soap opera strip *Rex Morgan, M.D.* Bill West, the tall handsome hero, was sometimes called a Special Defense Deputy and in charge of handling the "trouble brewing in the defense area you're assigned to." The area in question was Palomar, New Mexico, and environs; the trouble involved mysterious plane crashes and a Nazi saboteur who went around in a hooded robe. So modern was the strip that Bradley never got around to drawing a horse during his tenure.

Vesta West, created by Fred Meagher, was added to the lineup of the *Chicago Tribune*'s Sunday *Comic Book Magazine* in 1942. Vesta was the daughter of a ranch owner in the present day Southwest. Her horse was a black stallion named Traveler and she had a pudgy sidekick known as Pinky. Meagher left the feature after only a few weeks and was replaced by Ray Bailey, who was working as Milton Caniff's assistant at the time and gave Vesta and her colleagues a certain *Terry and the Pirates* aura.

Comic books had their most successful period in the war years. Numerous titles sold hundreds of thousands of copies, and the most popular books, such as *Superman* and *Captain Marvel Adventures*, were selling over a million each issue. It was to be expected that the syndicates would try to adapt more proven funny book characters to the strip format. McClure, which had good luck with Superman, signed up another DC Comics hero in 1943. Created by artist Bob Kane and writer Bill Finger, Batman had debuted in *Detective Comics* a little less than a year after the Man of Steel and had proved very popular. According to Batman historian Joe Desris, King Features Syndicate had been interested in doing a Batman strip but nothing had come of it.

The McClure effort, officially titled *Batman and Robin*, was packaged at DC's editorial offices and involved, in addition to Kane and Finger, an assortment of other pencillers, inkers, and writers, among them Jack Burnley and Dick Sprang. A nicely done feature, the strip was, however, much more conservative than its comic book counterpart. The famous flamboyant villains were kept mostly on the bench. The estimable Joker appeared in exactly one daily sequence and once on Sunday. The Penguin showed up twice in Sunday continuities but never in a daily caper. Two-Face and Cat Woman each occupied one brief Sunday story. In one daily continuity, illustrated by Burnley, Batman did not show up at all, and Bruce Wayne did all the sleuthing. Never able to build up a sufficient list of subscribing papers, *Batman and Robin* ended in 1946.

After missing out on Batman, King Features decided to take a chance with yet another DC Comics, Inc. character. Wonder Woman was the concoction of psychologist William Moulton Marston, hiding behind the pen name Charles Moulton. She first appeared in *All Star Comics #8* at the end of 1941. Then she became the leading char-

Famous Fiction, *Chad Grothkopf. A panel from a 1942 Sunday adaptation of Lewis Carroll.*

ALICE IN WONDERLAND IS HAVING TEA WITH THREE OF THE QUEEREST PEOPLE -- A MAD HATTER, A MARCH HARE, AND A VERY SLEEPY DORMOUSE!

acter in the new *Sensation Comics*. The early Wonder Woman years were rich with the sort of bondage-submission fantasies that had hitherto been seen only in under-the-counter publications. Moulton's scripts offered wartime readers some of the wackiest continuities to be found in any funny book, a heady brew of whips, chains, and cockeyed mythology. H. G. Peter, the artist personally selected by Marston, brought it all to life. He'd been a professional cartoonist since early in the century and he gave the feature a slightly decadent, entertainingly unsavory feel. Peter got the solo art credit on the strip, but he had long since set up a shop, employing mostly women, to turn out the large volume of comic book work, and the strip looks like a shop product rather than pure unadulterated Peter.

The *Wonder Woman* newspaper strip, a daily started in 1944, was somewhat more sedate than the comic book version and it used more soap opera and less bondage. Diana Prince, WW's alter ego, suffered considerable heartache because of her unrequited affection for her boss Captain Steve Trevor, for example. In spite of his fondness for tying up women, Marston also championed feminism in his work. In the strip Wonder Woman was often to be heard making such statements as "Girls who realize woman's TRUE POWERS can do greater things than I have EVER done!" Not a hit, the strip folded in 1945.

True Comics had been started by *Parents' Magazine* early in 1941 to provide a wholesome alter-native to the wild and woolly superheroes who were invading the newsstands in multicolored hordes. Offering mild-mannered comics format accounts of history and present world events, the new comic book managed to sell 300,000 copies and up each month. In 1942, Jack Wheeler's ever venturesome Bell Syndicate introduced a *True Comics* newspaper strip, daily and Sunday. The initial announcement of the new venture in *Editor & Publisher* had given the impression that the strip would simply reprint material from the comic book, and Bell was quick to get a correction. Everything would be brand new. Elliot Caplin was editing the comic book by then, and he took charge of producing the strip. Some of the same artists and writers who worked on the magazine turned out the strip and few credits were given. Among the regular cartoonists were Ed Smalle and Jack Sparling. A very speedy artist, Sparling produced sequences of *True* at the same time he was doing *Hap Hopper* and then *Claire Voyant*. Unlike the comic book, the strip devoted itself chiefly to contemporary history, with emphasis on the heroes of World War II.

A Sunday-only companion to *True Comics* was the equally uplifting and beneficial *Famous Fiction*. Another product of the *Parents'* editorial offices, it was edited by Caplin and syndicated by Bell. Chad Grothkopf, who'd worked in both animation and comic books by that time, was the first regular artist and writer. *Alice in Wonderland* was his opening adaptation, followed by *Ali Baba and the Forty Thieves* and *Under Two Flags*. Most of the classics and near-classics turned into the comic strip format

Penny, Harry Haenigsen. © New York Herald Tribune, Inc.

SUCH A QUESTION—! AIN'T GIRLS THE DUMMERS!

The Toodles Family, *Rod Ruth.* ©1946, Chicago Sun Syndicate.

were scrunched into six to eight week versions. Even after Chad went into the service, he continued to get credit for the page. *Robin Hood*, *Ben Hur*, and *The Murders in the Rue Morgue* were among the other works offered, and Harry Anderson and Jack Binder, both from comic books, among the other artists.

While *Buck Rogers*, *Flash Gordon*, and *Tarzan* carried on, there was little new science fiction and fantasy in these years. John Carter of Mars, despite Edgar Rice Burroughs's fondness for him, always ran a poor second to Tarzan. Although he beat the apeman into print by several months, debuting in the pulpwood pages of *All-Story Magazine* in February 1912, he didn't reach the comic sections until a dozen years after Tarzan. The pulp serial had been published as a book in 1917, under the title *A Princess of Mars*. Burroughs, often referred to as ERB, went on to do a series of novels about his swordsman of Barsoom, which is what the residents called the red planet. Once Tarzan had made a hit in newspapers, ERB decided John Carter could do the same. Working with J. Allen St. John, who'd illustrated many of the Mars and Tarzan books, he prepared samples. The strips went first to William Randolph Hearst himself, but he rejected them for King Features. Other syndicates were equally unenthusiastic. It took Burroughs until 1941 to find a taker. United Feature, who distributed *Tarzan*, reluc-

tantly signed up the *John Carter of Mars* Sunday page. This was a new rendition, with art and script by ERB's son John Coleman Burroughs. Although the page didn't succeed and lasted just a little over a year, it was a noble and uncompromising effort. Edgar Rice Burroughs's whole extravagantly wacky version of life on a fantasy Mars was transferred to the strip. Readers who weren't familiar with the conventions of pulp science fiction simply had to fend for themselves. Here was a heroine whose named was not Wilma Deering or Dale Arden, but Dejah Thoris. There were strange creatures such as the woolas and the calots and the giant chicken men of Mars, in addition to huge green warriors with four arms. Carter traveled by a rocket craft, but often fought his enemies with a sword.

In January of 1942, King Features launched a new Sunday fantasy. It took up two-thirds of a page and, initially, told its story in captions in the manner of *Prince Valiant*. Titled *Aladdin, Jr.*, it was obviously intended for young readers. The page was drawn by William Meade Prince and written by Les Forgrave. Prince was a much respected illustrator and teacher, whose work was frequently seen in slick magazines like *Collier's* and *The Saturday Evening Post*, and Forgrave had been writing and drawing the *Big Sister* strip for years. The basic plot had a small-town boy of eleven or so inheriting a magic lamp and having a series of fantastic adventures with the rather feisty genie contained therein. This notion served British fantasist F. Anstey well some decades earlier in his very successful novel *The Brass Bottle* and in the 1960s television repackaged it as *I Dream Of Jeannie*. Forgrave, however, had a rather prosaic imagination and his Aladdin in overalls and the little genie in a purple loincloth devoted themselves mostly to playing obvious pranks on the townspeople. They always had right on their side, but that didn't make their exploits especially interesting or entertaining. *Aladdin, Jr.* soon shrank down to one-third of a page and then vanished entirely in the autumn of 1943.

Perhaps it was war-induced nostalgia, a desire for a kinder, gentler world far removed from combat and killing. Or maybe it was simply the fact that

Kerry Drake, *Alfred Andriola*. ©1944, Publishers Syndicate.

Chic Young's strip was now one of the most successful in the land. Whatever the reason, a swarm of domestic comedy strips, every one of them in the mode established by *Blondie* back in the middle 1930s, descended on the newspapers in the early 1940s. *The Berrys* by Carl Grubert was the Chicago Sun Syndicate's offering in 1942. Next came *Polly Pippen* by Hugh Chenoweth from the Publishers Syndicate. In 1944 it was *Dotty Dripple*, also from Publishers. Originally *Dotty* was written by Jeff Keate and drawn by Jim McMenamy, but it was soon taken over by Buford Tune. While the husbands in these strips weren't quite as dense as Dagwood, they were all wed to wives who were obviously superior to them in intelligence, common sense, and tactical skills. Each of these ladies was pretty, in the same unobtrusive way that Blondie was pretty and each had blond hair. Like today's sitcoms, the strips took place mostly indoors; in the kitchen, the living room, and, less frequently, the bedroom. Now and then the backyard showed up as a setting. Each family possessed an assortment of kids, pets, and politely eccentric neighbors. All the families were comfortably middle class, all the husbands held down white collar jobs, and all the housewives were content to be just that. The oft heard question "Don't you know there's a war on?" might not have gotten an affirmative answer in some of these neighborhoods.

The war years saw an influx of teenage girls, too. Hilda Terry, in her middle twenties, was contacted by King Features to produce a teen panel. Her work, mostly about adolescents, had been appearing in *The Saturday Evening Post*, *The American Magazine*, and *The New Yorker*. The feature she developed for the syndicate was titled *It's a Girl's Life* and it started on Sunday, December 7, 1941, and later she pointed out "its debut on the back pages of Pearl Harbor." Later on the feature changed its name to *Teena*. The invasion of the bobby-soxers continued with *Penny* by Harry Haenigsen. It started with the Herald Tribune Syndicate in 1943, replacing the venerable *Betty*. Basically the new strip was simply a variation on *Our Bill*, which Haenigsen had been turning out since 1939. Somehow, though, a girl spouting the latest slang, following the latest teen fads, and perplexing her parents proved more successful, and *Penny* became a hit. It was strictly a gag-a-day feature, and for much of its life the chief writer was Howard Boughner.

Marty Links started her *Bobby Sox* panel for the *San Francisco Chronicle* when she was just out of high school. It was picked up for national syndication in November 1944. She had a wispy style and a gentle sense of humor, and originally she alternately followed the lives and times of an assortment of skinny teenage girls, including one whose name actually was Bobby Sox. Eventually the daily panel and the Sunday page came to concentrate on a hapless teen named Emmy Lou, and the title was changed to her name. A similar, though slicker and more idealized, panel was King Features's *Susie Q. Smith* by Linda and Jerry Walter.

Much more of a pinup type was the brunette star of *Candy*. A daily by writer Ed Groggin and artist Harry Sahle, the strip began on October 2, 1944. Both men were comic book veterans and Sahle had worked on *Archie*. The character had made her comic book debut at just about the same time, initially as a backup in *Police Comics*, the home of such heroes as Plastic Man and the Spirit, and then in a title of her own. The strip offered the usual exasperated parents, confused boyfriend, and teen slang, but in addition to gags there was continuity. There were also a great many shots of Candy in bathing suits and skimpy clothes, and it seems likely the strip was aiming for adult as well as teenage readers.

Two family strips with soap opera elements emerged in these years. *The Toodles*, originally known as *The Toodle Family*, began in December 1941 and was created for Marshall Field's new paper, *The Chicago Sun*. A popular feature, it eventually appeared in close to three hundred papers. *The Toodles* centered around a middle-aged couple who had a son and a daughter of college age, and another son and daughter who were of preschool age, and twins. Mr. Toodle was a successful business executive, and the family lived a comfortable suburban life. An effective blend of humor, adventure, and soap opera situations, it was written by Betsy Baer and plotted by her husband, Stanley. Betsy Baer was the daughter of Sol Hess, creator of *The Nebbs*, and she and her husband had recently taken over the writing of that strip following the death of her father. The artist was Rod Ruth, who worked as an advertising artist in Chicago and was also an illustrator for such pulp fiction magazines as *Amazing Stories*. He had an effective, individual style of drawing and he was equally at home with the comic antics of the aggressively cute twins and with the mystery, romance, and action sequences involving the more mature members of the cast. Since the authors signed their work simply "The Baers," more

than one account of the strip refers to them as Rod and Ruth Baer.

The Goldbergs began as a daily radio serial over NBC in 1929, a soap opera of sorts with a comedy element. Gertrude Berg wrote, produced, and directed the show and starred as Molly Goldberg. The other members of the family were her patient husband Jake, their children Sammy and Rosalie, and the irascible Uncle Jake. In the early 1940s the show, which radio historian John Dunning describes as "the Jewish version of *One Man's Family*," was still popular. Bert Whitman was already doing a strip for the New York Post Syndicate and acting as its comics editor. He put together the team for a comic strip version of *The Goldbergs*. For the artist he picked Irwin Hasen, recently out of the Navy, who'd worked for Whitman in the comic book field before taking on such superheroes as the Green Lantern. Hasen's style, though lighter, was in the Caniff vein. Stanley Kaufman, now the long-time movie critic for *The New Republic*, was then an editor for the Fawcett line of comic books and he was brought in as the writer. Gertrude Berg's only participation was to okay the continuity.

The strip, which began in 1944, failed to capture the humor of the radio show and it lacked the ethnic flavor as well. Molly functioned as a kind of pushy Mary Worth, intruding into people's lives and lecturing and manipulating them until they got their problems straightened out. At one point Jake told his wife, "I hope you've had enough mixing ... learn from me ... don't mix!" Unrepentant, Molly reminded him that he mixed in people's business as much as she did. Not a winner, *The Goldbergs* ended in 1945, the same year the radio show left the air.

Dan Dunn, also known as Secret Operative # 48, having been inducted as a private into the Army, bid his readers farewell on Sunday, October 3, 1943. By that time he was looking considerably better than he had when Norman Marsh had introduced him as a clumsy imitation of Dick Tracy ten years earlier. After a violent argument with his syndicate, Marsh quit the strip and had gone off to join the Marine Corps in the spring of 1942. Allen Saunders, the dependable writer of *Mary Worth* and *Steve Roper*, was brought in to take over the scripting and Paul Pinson, a Chicago area commercial artist, became the illustrator. Dan and his associates immediately got better looking. Then in January 1943, the look of the strip improved again, when Alfred Andriola was put in charge of the artwork. This began a long, fiery, and basically unpleasant relationship between him and Saunders.

A small man with a large ego, Andriola was one of the most gifted entrepreneurs in the comics field. He'd already, as we've seen, parlayed a secretarial job with Milton Caniff into a job producing the *Charlie Chan* strip. Now, when approached by Publishers Syndicate to take over *Dan Dunn*, he later said he told them, "I was only interested in starting a detective character of my own." This resulted in his carrying on with the Dunn strip until its existing newspaper contracts ran out and then launching *Kerry Drake*. Throughout his lifetime, Andriola was diligent in taking complete credit for the new strip. Saunders, however, took a much different view. "Eventually, to avoid possible steps by Marsh to recover his abandoned property, it was decided to substitute in client papers an entirely new strip, *Kerry*

Drake. In 1943 this step was taken, with the loss of very few papers," he wrote in his autobiography. "As an artist partner I was teamed with Alfred Andriola, a Greenwich Village resident. Andriola demanded credit for the writing as well as the art work and in all the publicity identified himself as the sole creator of *Drake*. We differed often on plots and dialogue, exchanging argumentative letters or wrangling over the phone."

This uneasy collaboration nevertheless produced a successful product. *Kerry Drake* was an entertaining strip and it offered *Dick Tracy* type villains and action done in an attractive variation of the Caniff style. Although Andriola also took sole art credit, he always had considerable help. Drake was a handsome fellow with prematurely silver hair and he was originally a "private investigator who is attached to the staff of the district attorney." He had his own office, a pretty secretary named Sandy Burns, and a red-haired office boy known as Firetop. He later went to work directly for the DA and finally became a police department detective.

Among the other new adventure strips was Bert Whitman's *Debbie Dean*, a 1944 entry about a bored debutante who took a job as a newspaper reporter and went on to tangle with Nazi spies, boxing racketeers, and crazed cult leaders. Whitman once admitted that he'd been offered the chance to do *Brenda Starr*, but had turned it down. Apparently having second thoughts, he came up with this one. Another radio-based strip was *The Sea Hound*. The kid serial it was derived from was on the air from 1942 to 1948 and dealt with Captain

The Sad Sack, *George Baker. This sample appeared in a civilian newspaper. ©1944, Sgt. George Baker.*

Silver, his ketch *The Sea Hound*, and his crew. The strip started in 1944, with a script by Fran Striker and art by Jon L. Blummer. Though it offered standard action adventure fare, *The Sea Hound* emphasized understanding "the people of other countries" and concentrated on South America. The strip ended in 1945.

The humor crop included a new entry from United Feature, who'd had such impressive success with *Li'l Abner*. They tried another rural type, this time a fellow who lived in a small Mexican town and named Gordo. You didn't have to be a linguist to figure out that *gordo* meant fat, since the hero was a living definition of the word. He was also lazy and about the only things that roused him were food and "gorls." In the first day's strip, dated November 24, 1941, his little nephew Pepito stepped out from behind a cactus to introduce himself and his pet, Señor Dog. He then told readers about his uncle, "My Uncle Gordo ees the mos' bes' BEAN farmer in the WHOLE worl'. NOBODY can grow beans like Uncle Gordo. Nobody can cook beans like Uncle Gordo." In the final panel, Gordo was seen sitting at a table, consuming a bowl of chili beans. Pepito adds, "An'—NOBODY can EAT beans like Uncle Gordo!!"

Gordo was written and drawn by a young Arizona-born cartoonist named Gustavo Arriola. He'd worked in Hollywood animation, first at Screen Gems and then at MGM with Hanna and Barbera. The early strips had an animated cartoon look and the dialogue—laden with "ees," "dorty," and "I theenk,"—sounded like something out of Disney's version of *Ferdinand*. Within the first year, Arriola introduced several of his running characters, including Pelon the cantina keep and the Widow Gonzales, whose main object in life was to snare Gordo in marriage. At that point, Arriola was drafted, which he explained to his readers on October 28, 1942, and announced the strip was stopping so he could go off to war. As it turned out, he was assigned to animation work for the Air Force and that left him enough free time to do a *Gordo* Sunday

page. He returned in May 1943, and a post-war daily resumed in June 1946.

With government support, Walt Disney and a crew of writers, artists, and cameramen had traveled through South America in 1941, gathering material for a series of shorts to support the Good Neighbor Policy. With the world war spreading, it was important to keep the Latin American countries friendly to the United States. And with European markets being cut off, these countries also represented a potential market for Hollywood movies. The Disney pilgrimage resulted not in short subjects but in a 1943 compilation film, a mix of animation and live action, titled *Saludos Amigos*. After playing in South American countries, the picture opened in this country and gave Disney one of his few wartime hits. It grossed nearly $1,500,000. Donald Duck's costar was a new character, a smart and dapper Brazilian parrot named Jose Carioca. *The Three Caballeros*, a similar film that was released in 1945, reunited Donald and Joe and introduced a flamboyant Mexican rooster named Panchito.

Disney merchandising didn't rest during the war, and one result was a *Jose Carioca* Sunday page introduced in 1943. It was drawn by an uncredited Paul Murry and distributed by King Features. Peopled entirely by anthropomorphized birds, the feature dealt with mock adventures and a long continuity that had Jose searching the Amazon jungles "een quest ov a mysterious rubber which eez said to need no refining!" There were assorted "gorls" for the parrot to pursue, including one who kept reminding him he'd promised "to star me on the stage en yore beeg city." Getting a jump on the 1945 *The Three Caballeros*, Panchito, a sort of gun-toting barnyard cowboy, barged into Jose's strip in April 1944. Eventually, the title was changed to *Panchito*, and Carioca was seen no more.

The well-known Hollywood hare Bugs Bunny invaded comic supplements nationwide on Sunday, January 10, 1943. NEA was the syndicate, and most of the Warner Brothers cartoon company shared the page, including Elmer Fudd, Sylvester, and Porky and Petunia Pig. The Western Publishing outfit, which produced the *Looney Tunes* comic books, was in charge of packaging the strip, and the initial half-dozen were the work of Chase Craig. When Craig, who had also worked on the comic book version of Bugs, went into the Navy, he was replaced by young Roger Armstrong. For the handsome salary of $25 per week, Armstrong did "the writing, penciling, lettering, inking and mailing out." He was surprised, considering how much work he did for so little pay, to find himself suddenly replaced by Carl Buettner after two years. A daily *Bugs Bunny* was not added until the post-war year of 1946.

George Swanson, last seen perpetrating *Elza Poppin*, returned in 1943 with a lowbrow gag-a-day strip called *The Flop Family* and featuring Philander Flop, his argumentative wife, and three disrespectful children. Frank Beck continued his Clare Briggs impersonation with *Bo*, a 1940 domestic comedy dominated by the family dog. *The Right Around Home* Sunday page, which King Features began syndicating in the late 1930s, was unusual in format. It consisted of one large panel in which readers got a bird's-eye view of a large social gathering—a picnic, a backyard barbecue, a bridge, or club gathering. Artist Dudley Fisher managed to pack two dozen or more people into each page, along with an assortment of birds, dogs, cats, and other animals. The chief focal family consisted of Freddie; his wife, Susie; their little daughter, Myrtle; Bingo the dog; and Hyacinth the cat. Fisher had originally drawn *Right Around Home* for the *Columbus Dispatch*, the paper where Milton Caniff's mentor Billy Ireland had reigned for so many years, and Fisher's style showed many echoes of the older cartoonist's work. The popularity of the page prompted King to add a daily strip in 1942. Most of the Sunday cast was on hand and the weekday version was titled *Myrtle*.

One of the century's undisputed comic strip masterpieces also emerged in the early 1940s. The newspaper started syndicating *Barnaby* in the spring of 1942. Crockett Johnson, who'd come into the world thirty-six years earlier under the name of David Johnson Leisk, later admitted he'd tried a comic strip mainly because he was finding a way to make a steady living. He'd worked at department store advertising and hit magazines such as *Collier's* with pantomime cartoons. Johnson's style was simple and in the tradition Gluyas Williams, Rea Irvin, and Gardner Rea. There was no shading, crosshatching, or other fancy penwork. He rarely used a closeup and usually got no nearer to his characters than a medium shot would allow. Everything—people, animals, trees, buildings, automobiles—was drawn flat and without any dimensions. He achieved his illusion of perspective the way a paper cutout diorama does.

The two main characters of the strip were Barnaby Baxter, an intelligent and articulate five-year-old, and Mr. O'Malley, his garrulous and sometimes bungling Fairy Godfather. The same

Barnaby, Crockett Johnson. Mr. O'Malley discourses on pixies. ©1944, Field Publications.

height as Barnaby, the bombastic O'Malley wore an overcoat in all seasons, one that allowed his small pink wings to flap freely. An expensive Havana cigar served as a magic wand, and he also came equipped with a copy of *The Fairy Godfather's Handy Pocket Guide*. In the first strip, Barnaby, after hearing his mother read him a fairy tale, wishes he had a fairy godmother. The next day Jackeen J. O'Malley comes whizzing through the boy's bedroom window, ruining his cigar on landing. "Cushlamochree! Broke my magic wand!... Lucky Boy! Your wish is granted! I'm your Fairy Godfather! Yes, mob's, your troubles are over. O'Malley is on the job." After promising to return, O'Malley makes a colorful flying exit out the window. He then crashes in the shrubbery outside.

When Barnaby's parents come rushing up to see what's going on, he tries to explain his marvelous visitor—"He's got pink wings! He can grant wishes!" His father, adopting the attitude he'll hold for the run of the strip, tells him, "Try not to dream anymore, son." After they leave him, Barnaby remembers Mr. O'Malley's cigar. He hops out of bed and, sure enough, finds ashes on the floor. From that point on he and the reader know that O'Malley is real. Barnaby, by the way, didn't live in a fantasy world. He lived in a real world, as perceived by a smart preschool kid. It's a remarkable place, where reality and fantasy can comfortably coexist. Despite his parents' concerns and criticisms—and attempts to have child therapists help him—Barnaby was extremely practical and not a dreamer at all. And although he was fond of his extravagant Fairy Godfather, he could be critical of his follies, proposed or committed. One of Barnaby's oftfelt emotions was a sort of quiet frustration. He frequently knows the truth about a situation or the answer to a question, but he is rarely paid attention to or believed when he does get to speak up. His most frequently seen speech balloon over the years contained the single word "But—" that occurred in encounters with his parents.

"It's all right now, Barnaby. You were dreaming."

"But—"

And with O'Malley as well.

"If, and sometimes I doubt it, your parents actually do exist, I cannot but conclude they're avoiding me! Coincidence can only go so far ... I'm wrong, they can contact me at the club ... I am leaving, m'boy!"

"But—"

Johnson stacked the cards in Barnaby's favor. One of the quiet ironies of the strip was that all the fantastic events that cause the Baxters to worry and fret over their son's mental state were actually happening. What Johnson was saying is that to a child the world was a much more marvelous and wonderful place than adults notice it to be. That he did this without being sticky and fey was one of the triumphs of *Barnaby*.

The strip contained a varied cast of supporting characters. There was Gus the Ghost, an intellectual spook who wore glasses in addition to the traditional sheet, lived in a haunted house, and sometimes served as a ghost writer for O'Malley. Barnaby's dog was named Gorgon and he had the ability to talk, which he exercised only when it pleased him to do so. Called upon on one occasion to portray a dog on a radio drama staged by O'Malley, Gorgon was found unconvincing by several prominent critics of the day. The woodlands around the Baxter home were rich with ogres, pixies, elves, and other allegedly mystical characters. There was also a small Barnaby-size fellow who was an Intellectual Giant and an uncouth leprechaun named Launcelot McSnoyd. He was invisible and held a low opinion of O'Malley, greeting him with such remarks as, "Still working the Fairy Godmother racket, O'Malley?"

O'Malley's favorite hangout in the Baxter home was the kitchen, and his favorite dish, which Mrs. Baxter seemed to fix often, was roast lamb. He also hung out at Paddy's Bar & Grill, a congenial watering place that catered to all types, including pixies. O'Malley belonged to the Elves, Leprechauns, Gnomes, and Little Men's Chowder and Marching Society, and often regaled Barnaby with accounts of their social activities and their many snubs and slights to him. Neither Paddy's nor the Little Men's headquarters ever appeared on stage. Unlike the grownups, Barnaby's contemporaries had no trouble seeing O'Malley and all the other creatures. His closest friend, Janie Shultz, considered O'Malley something of a dope and a nuisance and preferred to get her excitement from *Captain Bloodbath Comics* and stories like the one "where the mad doctor saws off the top of Captain Bloodbath's head and steals a secret code he memorized." The targets of Johnson's quiet satire included not only the mass media, but politicians, rationing, and other fads and foibles of the period.

Before *Barnaby* was a year old, it had built up an impressive list of newspapers and caused a raft of intellectuals to fall under its spell. Dorothy Parker called it "the most important addition to American arts and letters in Lord knows how many years." Robert Nathan, Rockwell Kent, Louis Untermeyer, Norman Corwin, and William Rose Benet were all equally enthusiastic. *Time* and *Newsweek* raved; *Life* called it "a breath of cool, sweet air." W. C. Fields, who shared certain affinities with O'Malley, said, "Barnaby is a whiz."

Thanks to the Camp Newspaper Service and publications like *Yank* and *Stars and Stripes*, enlisted men and women, no matter where they were stationed, had access not only to several of their favorite homefront funnies but to a batch of GI-created features that were raunchier and more outspoken than the homegrown stuff. So in addition to following *Dick Tracy*, *Joe Palooka*, and *Li'l Abner*, they could also partake of *The Wolf*, *Sad Sack*, and Bill Mauldin's *Up Front*. While Leonard Sansone's *Wolf* never found its way into American newspapers, both George Baker's pantomime *Sad Sack*, syndicated by Bell, and Mauldin's panel about Willie and Joe, thanks to United Feature, were running in several American newspapers during the final years of the war. Both features, and several other GI favorites, would make the transition, sometimes an uneasy one, to civilian life.

Chapter 9

Back Home

Germany surrendered on May 7, 1945. A little over three months later, after the United States had dropped atomic bombs first on Hiroshima and then Nagasaki, Japan also surrendered. World War II was over and peacetime was back. On August 16 a special strip, rushed out by Roy Crane, appeared in many of the papers that carried *Buz Sawyer*. In the present continuity, Buz and Sweeney had just escaped from a Japanese sub and were about to participate in an air raid on Tokyo. The emergency daily showed the two happily discussing the fact that World War II had ended. Crane explained, "The current story sequence began before the Jap surrender. In reality, the action takes but a few hours. Its presentation in a strip, tho, requires several days. Can you bear with us while the episode runs its course?" While quite a few strips were caught in similar situations, others had anticipated a cease-fire and begun returning their characters to civilian life weeks, sometimes months, earlier. And several new strips featuring returning GIs got under way even before victory in Europe was declared.

The D-Day invasion and the subsequent liberation of Paris contributed to an increasing optimism in America. "By that summer of 1944 a new spirit moved through everyday life," observed one historian. "Almost everyone was convinced it would be the last summer of wartime.... On city streets discharged servicemen were beginning to appear, with an eagle lapel pin to show they were honorably discharged." In the spring of 1945, two honorably discharged servicemen, both former Air Force pilots, showed up in new comic strips. *Ayer Lane* started off with Major Lane being discharged from a military hospital and then returning to his hometown, the aptly named Hometon, to his widowed mother. A decorated hero—"a fellow that's flown on 80 bomber missions—shot down Japs"—Lane faced the same problem that millions of returning GIs would be facing over the next year—he had to find a way to make a living in the civilian world. Teaming with an old Air Force mechanic buddy, Ayer Lane tried first to establish a garage. But he soon found himself tangled up with crooked businessmen and politicians who wanted to exploit his medals and bright war record to front such crooked ventures as a shady airport investment scheme and a plane building con. Eventually, Ayer, with the help of an assortment of beautiful women who fell for him, was able to set up a charter line. One of his first jobs took him to Central America, a popular locale for postwar adventure strips. *Ayer Lane* was distributed by the Chicago Sun Syndicate. Dale Conner drew it in a bold, brushy, illustrative style and her husband, Herb Ulrey, wrote the scripts. A blend of action,

Bruce Gentry, *Ray Bailey.* ©1945, N.Y. Post.

adventure, and soap opera, it wasn't a long-term winner and ended in early September of 1947.

The hero of *Bruce Gentry* had served as a captain in Air Force intelligence. His new strip started, late in March, 1945, with Gentry's arriving in the capital city of the mythical South America country of Cordillera to act as a combination troubleshooter and pilot for the troubled Southern Cross Airline. The feature, which ran daily and Sunday, was syndicated by the New York Post Corp. and written and drawn by Ray Bailey. This strip, too, he rendered in a creditable version of the Caniff style. Obviously the *Post* had high hopes for *Bruce Gentry*, anticipating that papers across the country that couldn't run the very popular *Terry and the Pirates* for territorial or financial reasons would grab up this reasonable facsimile. The strategy apparently worked and the new strip was launched with a respectable list of newspapers. Advance publicity played up the points that there was no propaganda and no war to be encountered. "*Bruce Gentry* is not a strip with social significance. Mr. Bailey has no axes to grind," explained a release. Furthermore, the artist "feels that the readers are tired of battles, hence he has none."

Despite that, there was considerable action, intrigue, and romance. Initially Gentry teamed up with a local rep of the airline, a handsome Latino named Ricardo who had a hep Indian sidekick named Jive and who spoke in a perfect Hollywood Spanish accent—"Ees Jive pestering you? He probably wants to play hees box of juke for you." There was also a plenitude of sinister villains determined

to sabotage the planes, plus a mystery woman named Eden Cortez. As the strip went along Gentry worked with different associates, a couple of them former Air Force buddies who were definitely from the Hotshot Charlie school of sidekicks. The locales eventually shifted from South America to Alaska, Vietnam, and Manhattan. Like Caniff, Bailey saw to it that there were always plenty of beautiful and intriguing women around. These included, in addition to Eden, Tango, Bandy Muffet, Mandalay, Yukon, and Cleo Patric.

Bailey also did well on rendering the planes and other action props and he was pretty near the equal of his former employer when it came to jungle landscapes, impressive mountain vistas, and other scenic wonders. The scripts, however, tended to be somewhat routine and given to clichés and his characters never had quite enough individuality or life to them. Probably the major blow to his strip's chances for long-term success was the advent, in January 1947, of Caniff's new *Steve Canyon*. Caniff was the undisputed champ of the adventure and the appearance of a feature by him, using many of the elements of Bailey's effort, couldn't have made anybody at the Post syndicate especially joyful. *Bruce Gentry* limped along until January of 1951 and then ended with the wedding of Gentry and his longrunning girlfriend, Cleo Patric. Marriage then meant the end of adventure and readers in the few papers that were still carrying the strip must have realized, once they spotted Gentry carrying his bride over the threshold, that the strip wouldn't be back the following Monday.

What Coulton Waugh had in mind with *Hank* was something more than an adventure strip. "This was to be," he once explained, "a deliberate attempt to work in the field of social usefulness." When it began in the *Newspaper PM* on April 30, 1945, the lead character was still in the Army, fighting in the South Pacific. In saving the life of a downed flyer, Corporal Hank Hannigan lost his right leg. Before the end of the war Hank was back in the United States undergoing rehabilitation in a military hospital. Waugh followed his returned soldier, who was the sort of big, innocent, openfaced guy that Wayne Morris had played in such movies as *Kid Galahad* and *I Wanted Wings*, through the readjustment process. He pictured the physiotherapy, showed him being fitted for an artificial leg and allowed him to be openly depressed. When Hank met Sparks, a reporter for the *Daily Liberal*, he mentioned that he'd run into somebody who suggested he'd been a sucker to serve his country. "Can you tell me why I had to lose my leg?" he asked the newsman. "And can we dope it out so my son won't have to lose his?" Sparks replies, "That's a $64 dollar question, Hank. And millions of people are looking for the answer.... Maybe we'll find it."

A continuity then began in which Hank seemed to get lured into joining a vets' group called Veterans Forward. It was soon revealed to be backed by a bunch of former isolationists and was violently fascist and racist. But Hank was only pretending to fall in with the bunch and was actually gathering information for Sparks. With his

Hank, Coulton Waugh. Panels from an unpublished sample strip.

help the gang was exposed and routed, causing Hank to reflect, "If you give the people the truth, they'll recognize it." Waugh did some interesting drawing on the strip, his layouts were imaginative and he experimented now and then using white lettering in black balloons. Unfortunately, his good intentions were dangerously close to the surface in the writing and there was too much preaching and propaganda and too little narrative force. *Hank* ended on the last day of the year.

Another discharged serviceman, who set up as an adventurer in South America, was the hero of the *Jon Jason* strip. A daily that began on January 14, 1946, it was written and drawn by Elmer Wexler and distributed by the Chicago Sun Syndicate. Jason was a former Marine combat artist, now traveling through South America painting covers for *International Woman* magazine and also pursuing his hobby of collecting jade. The syndicate sales brochure promised editors that the new hero would lead readers "into a maze of events filled with action and intrigue! As a cover artist, beautiful women are his business ... and as a former Marine, Jason knows his way around!"

Recently out of the service, Wexler had been a Marine combat artist and when he was approached by his old *PM* editor and invited to come up with a new adventure strip, he saw it as a great opportunity to make a good living. He'd been taking a writing class in Greenwich Village with Dashiell Hammett and he was eager to try the scripting himself. He drew *Jon Jason* in a slick illustration style, fairly similar to the approach he'd developed for *Vic Jordan*. The new strip was a nicely done, creditable job, even exhibiting some postwar *film noir* touches, but it never managed to build up a sufficient list of newspapers. After he was informed, very politely over lunch, that the strip was being canceled, Wexler moved on to Johnstone & Cushing. He devoted the next several years to drawing advertising comic strips at a better salary.

Late in 1944, Milton Caniff had been invited to meet with Marshall Field in the apartment he maintained on Park Avenue. The publisher of *PM* and the *Chicago Sun* asked him what it would take to get him to leave *Terry and the Pirates* to start a new strip. Caniff, who was then one of the most popular and most publicized artists in the country, replied he'd want ownership and complete editorial control. Field assured him he could have both, plus a handsome weekly guarantee. They shook hands and shortly after Caniff signed to do an unnamed adventure strip for Field's syndicate as soon as his contract with the Trib-News syndicate expired in October 1946. Caniff had long felt that Colonel Patterson and the syndicate were cheapskates, keeping his

Jon Jason, *Elmer Wexler.* ©1946, Newspaper PM, Inc.

guarantee at its pre-war low and never handing out a Christmas bonus. Years later he observed that he might've stayed with *Terry* "if they hadn't been so damned chintzy." Field, a dedicated liberal, had long been actively opposed to Colonel McCormick and his *Chicago Tribune*. He'd started the *Chicago Sun* in 1941 to compete directly with the colonel and was trying to lure away as many of the top Chicago Tribune-New York News Syndicate comic strip artists as he could. In addition to Caniff, Field made offers to Chester Gould, Harold Gray, and Zack Mosley. He was turned down by the others.

Early in 1945, columnist Walter Winchell leaked the news that Caniff was quitting *Terry* to start a new strip for Field. That put him into a sort of lame duck position for the next two years. Still completely wrapped up in *Terry*, Caniff had made up his mind the quality wouldn't suffer as long as he was associated with it. "For one thing, it was kind of a challenge in that everybody was expecting me to let down," he once said. "For that reason alone I was anxious to do it better than I had ever done before. Some of the best things ... some of the best characters didn't appear until after the die was cast."

Caniff did indeed put considerable effort into the final two years of the strip and the postwar period, especially, contains some of his most impressive work. He'd often compared *Terry* to a picaresque

novel and now, in the Dickens tradition, he had many of the characters from earlier years return, sometimes in new guises, for a grand finale. At war's end Terry seemingly left the service to fly for a ramshackle air cargo line run by Chopstick Joe, a con-man and shady operator who'd figured in the strip years earlier. Actually, Terry was still in the service and working for Air Force Intelligence. He summoned Hotshot Charlie back from Boston to the Orient to serve as his copilot and wisecracking sidekick again. From out of the past Caniff also recalled Burma, allowing her to have a romantic fling with the now mature Terry and also hinting that she was no longer wanted for piracy by the British government. April Kane, the Dragon Lady, Captain Blaze, nurse Jane Allen, Nastalhia Symthe-Heatherstone—first encountered as a child in the late 1930s when she was a sort of pint-sized Bette Davis—Baron de Plexis, and Sandhurst all returned. The drawing and staging were exceptional, even by the standards of the Caniff studio.

Caniff took his leave on Sunday, December 29, 1946. Drawn with little dialogue, the final page shows Terry accompanying Jane Allen to a snow-covered airfield. She's leaving for Australia and she starts to walk to the waiting plane, but then turns, comes running back. She and Terry embrace and kiss. After the ship takes off, Terry walks away from the reader toward his waiting jeep. On a building wall in the foreground was a handbill for a New Year's party. It said, "Ring out the old, ring in the new."

Male Call, *Milton Caniff. Caniff was concerned with returning veterans even before war's end. ©1944, Milton Caniff.*

Caniff had had another wartime activity: producing a weekly comic strip called *Male Call*. He was ineligible for military service because of phlebitis contracted from an insect bite in his youth, but "[he] wanted to do some work for the guys who had to fight; something *just* for them." While *Stars and Stripes* and *Yank* could not accept contributions from civilians, the Camp Newspaper service could. Initially, Caniff donated a weekly GI version of *Terry*. Neither Terry Lee nor any of the various pirates showed up in this version. It concentrated on the blond Burma and was basically a gag feature. Burma resided in China and fraternized with enlisted men, and occasional officers, and her amorous meetings with servicemen provided most of the humor. The strip debuted in October 1942, but fairly soon the syndicate informed Caniff that they were not happy with him using these characters for an alternate version. Rather than give up the GI strip, Caniff simply invented a new leading lady named Lace. Somewhat less worldly than Burma, the brunette Lace was "innocent but sexy as hell." *Male Call* ran in about three thousand service newspapers around the world, giving it one of the largest circulations of all time. Caniff kept it going until March 1946, and in the post-war months the gags frequently dealt with the problems of servicemen returning to civilian life. He would return to this

Vic Flint, *Ralph Lane*. Film noire *in the funnies.*
©1946, NEA Service, Inc.

theme, approaching it more seriously, in the new strip he was preparing for Marshall Field.

Mollie Slott, comics editor for the Chicago Tribune-N.Y. News syndicate began looking for a new *Terry* artist in 1945. Among those who applied were Charles Raab, friend, protégé, and onetime assistant to Caniff. According to Paul Norris, who knew him well, Raab came very close to getting the job and at one time actually believed he had been hired. Finally, though, the assignment of writing and drawing *Terry and the Pirates* went to a dark horse. George Wunder had been in the Associated Press bullpen in the 1930s and, with time out for military service, in the 1940s. He did a variety of odd jobs, including political caricatures and illustrations for fiction serials. He had even done a Christmas strip in the 1930s. Despite the fact that they both worked for the Associated Press, Wunder had few artistic affinities to the man he was to succeed. His basic style was unlike the impressionistic approach that Caniff, with considerable help from Noel Sickles, had developed. Wunder's tryout strips, though, managed to capture some of the feel of the strip and, unlike Raab, he had a reputation for dependability. In October 1946, news magazines ran stories announcing that a successor had been picked and the thirty-four-year-old Wunder was the man. A *Newsweek* account claimed that Wunder had enjoyed "a three months' seminar under Caniff himself." That was completely untrue, since Caniff did not even know Wunder at the time and did not meet him until long after the transition. The first Wunder daily, which ran on Monday, December 30, showed

Terry driving his jeep to the Air Cathay offices and gave the impression that a creditable replacement had been chosen.

Steve Canyon was an optimistic strip. Its lean, lanky, blond hero was in the tradition of such movie icons as Gary Cooper and John Wayne. He was a returning Air Force officer, but his main adjustment problem had to do with money and not war injuries or traumas. He, significantly, called the fledgling charter airline he was trying to start Horizons Unlimited. Caniff's new effort was a hit before he named it or even drew a single sample strip. The Field Syndicate, in collaboration with King Features, had sold it to hundreds of papers on the artist's reputation alone. Quite possibly, Caniff was the most popular comic strip artist in America in 1947. Homefront civilians knew and admired him for *Terry and the Pirates*, and millions of former GIs fondly remembered him for *Male Call*. The publicity surrounding the introduction of the new strip was unprecedented. *Time*, for example, gave Caniff the cover on January 13, 1947, the day *Steve Canyon* began.

The first sequence opened with a teaser, and readers didn't get to meet their new hero in person until the seventh day. Canyon was hired by Copper Calhoon, who was described by Canyon's secretary Feeta Feeta as "the big she-wolf of the stock market." The redhaired, slinky Calhoon was also a homegrown simulacrum of the Dragon Lady. She hired Canyon to fly her to Latin America to inspect some holdings there. Though he was reluctant to work for her, he went ahead with the deal because it meant getting a converted Army C-54 plane for Horizons Unlimited. Canyon recruited a crew, many of them ex-servicemen, to help him with the first mission. Eager to get his new strip aloft, Caniff quite obviously overbooked the flight. In one week, he introduced Breck Nazaire, Oily Riley, Bill Rugger, Two-way Touhey, and Mudder McGee, a onetime jockey who looked a good deal like Hotshot Charlie. None of them lasted long. The Latin American settings were rendered as realistically as had been the China locales in *Terry*. They had the advantage of having no unpleasant war associations and no bombed-out cities. At the top of his form, Caniff certainly had another winner. And, for its first years, *Steve Canyon* was just that. Other wars were coming, however, and both Canyon and Caniff were in for rough times. But nobody could foresee that in the euphoric post-war year of 1947.

Mark Trail, an outdoorsy, conservation-minded strip, began in April 1946. It was the work of Ed Dodd, once a disciple of outdoor artist and woodsman Dan Beard, and a rancher and guide before turning professional cartoonist. His new hero was a tall, lean outdoorsman, another former GI looking to make his way in the world. He was a photographer who worked for *Woods & Wildlife* magazine and he had an amiable St. Bernard named Andy for a

sidekick. Most of the stories centered around the Lost Forest, a vast nature preserve owned and operated by Dr. Tom Davis and his daughter Cherry. Cherry Davis soon became Mark's lifelong love interest. Dodd, who drew in a direct, somewhat rustic style and was fond of crosshatching, favored plots that pitted his good people against landgrabbers, poachers, animal killers, and other ecologically incorrect types. The Sunday page never told a story and was used by Dodd for an endless series of illustrated lectures on the wonders of nature.

Ken Stuart featured a hero who was something of a seagoing Mark Trail. Written and drawn by Frank Borth, recently out of military service, it started in the fall of 1947. Stuart, a handsome, dark-haired fellow who always wore a yachting cap, operated a charter boat named the *Barracuda* out of Montauk Point, New York. His outdoor life was full of encounters with pirates, Nazi holdouts, lost jungle tribes, sunken treasure, and sinister women.

One more feature with a South American locale and one of the most unusual adventure strips of the period was *Drago*, created by Burne Hogarth and syndicated by the *New York Post*. A Sunday page, it was set in Argentina and starred a handsome, muscular aristocrat who dressed like a goucho. It was drawn in the frenzied, convoluted style Hogarth had developed on the recently abandoned *Tarzan* strip, a style that has been described as being "full of expressionistic fury." The plots, also fabricated by Hogarth, mixed elements of Zorro, the Cisco Kid, Tarzan, opera, Elizabethan tragedy, and Saturday matinee serials. Drago had a portly sidekick named

Rip Kirby, Alex Raymond. ©1946, King Features Syndicate, Inc.

Tabasco, and his rich-yet-sinister father was in cahoots with a master criminal named Baron Zodiac. There was a femme fatale named Tosca, a nice girl named Darby O'Day, a fiery pampas beauty named Flamingo, and a nasty, knife-throwing thug named Stiletto. Several months of continuity were given over to the competition for the possession of a mysterious little idol. Hogarth has said that he was inspired to cook up *Drago* while contemplating President Roosevelt's Good Neighbor Policy—"I thought to myself, gee, what an interesting idea." Impressively rendered, the page failed to catch on. It lasted from November 1945 to November 1946, running a total of fifty-four Sundays.

Nineteen hundred and forty-six was the year of the private eye. That summer *The Big Sleep*, with Bogart as Raymond Chandler's Philip Marlowe, opened in movie palaces around the country. That autumn, *The Adventures of Sam Spade*, with Howard Duff as Dashiell Hammett's hardboiled sleuth, began its radio run on CBS. Earlier in the year, two private eyes made their debuts on the comics pages. One was tough and hardboiled, the other more cerebral. Both of them were former Marines.

"The whole thing started late one afternoon. I was sitting in my office reading the papers about a killing. And then my door opened." That was how Vic Flint, handsome and blond and with a fondness for herringbone suits and fedoras, began his first daily in January 1946. He was very much the traditional private operative of movies, pulps, and paperbacks—tough, wisecracking, at odds with the cops.

His cases took him to the haunts of the rich and to the flashy nightspots owned by the underworld. Ralph Lane, who had been Roy Crane's assistant on *Buz Sawyer*, was the artist, and NEA syndicate editor Ernest Lynn wrote the hardboiled copy under the name of Michael O'Malley.

When Alex Raymond returned from the Marine Corps in 1945, he expected to resume work on *Flash Gordon*. King Features, however, had signed a long term contract with Austin Briggs that ran until 1948, and they were content with his version of the space opera. Miffed, Raymond let it be known he was ready to listen to offers from other syndicates. Before that happened, King told him they had a new strip idea for him and would pay him a substantial guarantee. *Rip Kirby*, a daily only, started on March 4, 1946. Kirby was a more intellectual private eye, and even wore glasses. He was a Marine hero, who'd served with distinction in the Pacific theater. Rather than a seedy office, Kirby worked out of an expensive New York City apartment and had a colorful English valet named Desmond. His girlfriend was a stunning blonde model type named Honey Dorian. The initial idea for the mystery feature came from editor Ward Greene, who'd written such novels as *Death in the Deep South* and *The Havana Hotel Murders*. Raymond, like Alfred Andriola, was not fond of sharing credit with anyone, and his was the only name that appeared on

Judge Wright, *Bob Fujitani. The judge and his wife spend a quiet evening at home. ©1946, United Feature Syndicate, Inc.*

the strip during his lifetime. After Greene, Fred Dickenson became the writer. Raymond did have a hand in the plotting of the early sequences, and after he left one story session with some of the King staff, Greene remarked, "That so-and-so really thinks he writes this damn thing." Raymond did a fine job of illustrating his strip. His style had matured and moved much closer to realism. There was a sophistication to his work, and he seemed much more at home now in contemporary locations than he ever had been on Mongo.

Norman Marsh, fresh out of the Marines and as brashly inept as he had been back when he was turning out *Dan Dunn* in the 1930s, managed to sell a new detective strip to King Features in 1946 as well. Well, not exactly new. *Hunter Keene*, begun in the spring of the year, was a fairly close approximation of Marsh's earlier crimebuster effort. Police detective Keene had the same profile as Dunn, the same Dick Tracy hat. He even had the same partner, a fat fellow who smoked a cigar and wore a derby. Called Irwin Higgs in the earlier version, he was now

Ben Friday (a.k.a. Bodyguard), John Spranger. A pair of dailies. The odd shaped little fellow in the odd hat is the Bantam Prince. ©1949, New York Herald Tribune, Inc.

known as Blimpy. The strip succumbed a few days shy of its first birthday.

Thirty Paige, a daily detective strip by writer Vic Take and artist Don McCabe, was introduced by the second-string General Features Corporation in October 1946. Paige was a police inspector, affiliated with the district attorney's office in a nameless big city, and his caseload involved him with everything from big-time gangsters to teenage purse-snatchers. Flippant at times—"What role are you playing in this minstrel show, blondie?"—he could also sermonize with the best of them: "Max, J. Edgar Hoover, the Director of the F.B.I., once said, 'Lawlessness isn't inherited—it is acquired; and so is character.' You don't *have* to steal." Paige's steady female companion was Vicki Monohan, a pretty, blond reporter of the *Daily Press*, who thought of him as a "big ol' sweet guy." Writer Take was more

Casey Ruggles, *Warren Tufts. ©1950, United Feature Syndicate, Inc.*

interested in action and dramatic confrontations than in police procedures, and McCabe drew in a spare style that was heavy on black. Trying for sophistication and a certain hardboiled air, the strip came off as a very pale *film noir* and ended after a couple of years.

Another short-lived detective feature, this one from the late 1940s, was *SOLVE IT YOURSELF—with Lance Lawson* by Harry Cherney and Norm Hamilton. A sort of *Minute Mysteries* puzzler in comic strip form, it provided a new and, hopefully, challenging case each day, including Sundays. There was no mystery that handsome and unfoolable police detective Lawson could not solve, usually in no more than four panels. A final panel, run sideways, would explain how he'd figured out today's baffling problem: "A junior officer walks at a senior officer's *left*," or "The 'shooting' supposedly occurred in a muddy alley, yet the victim's shoes were clean."

Judge Wright, introduced in September 1945, was a hybrid, part detective and part soap opera genre. It had a dark, shadowy look and was laden with slinky women in low-cut gowns, sleazy gigolos, brutal thugs, and an ample supply of interpersonal problems. In its first weeks, the new daily showed an attempted strangling, an assault with a poker, a drowning, and an assault with a blunt instrument. There was also considerable kissing, hugging, and domestic squabbling. Subsequent continuities depicted arson, fatal plunges, numerous stabbings, and more kissing and hugging. To a minority of readers at the time, this sort of material would have looked comfortably familiar, since it was the sort of stuff to be found every month in the best-selling

Crime Does Not Pay comic book. The first regular comic book of this kind, it had debuted in 1942, and its sales were still climbing. The *Judge Wright* strip was a collaboration between two contributors to the magazine. Robert Bernstein, who used the pseudonym Bob Brent, was a scriptwriter for several houses. Bob Fujitani, calling himself Bob Fuje then, was a veteran of several years in the funny book field.

The judge was a handsome, dark-haired man with a touch of gray at the temples. His beautiful wife, the former Ann Sage, investigative reporter on a large metropolitan daily, adored him and was delighted to help him in his off-the-bench detective work. Often not satisfied with the verdicts his juries brought in, Jon Wright, usually aided by the lovely Ann, would track down the real killer in order to save an innocent man from walking the last mile.

Somewhat ahead of its time in the handling of sex and violence, the strip never built up an extensive list of client papers. Since the United Feature Syndicate had offered the partners no weekly income guarantee on the strip, the writer and artist had to get along on their share of the profits. Fujitani has recalled that he never earned more than $35 a week, and in the late autumn of 1946 he resigned. The strip went on with another talented comic book recruit, Fred Kida. He only stayed until June of the next year, and until *Judge Wright* stepped down early in 1948, the artist was George Roussos, another comic book regular.

Detective strips showed up in some unusual places during the postwar years. The New York Herald Tribune Syndicate, after decades of bland domestic humor with the likes of *Mr. & Mrs.* and *Clarence* and animal whimsy with *Peter Rabbit*, took a fling with mystery and adventure. In the waning years of the 1940s, under the editorship of Harold Straubing, the syndicate started offering its customers action and intrigue. Straubing, who'd been an editor of *Crime Does Not Pay* in its last days, had acquired the job of comics editor by convincing the sedate old syndicate that its list of strips was in need of revision. He was responsible for the addition of *Bodyguard* and *The Saint*.

Bodyguard, which began as a Sunday feature on May 2, 1948, should have been a hit. The writer was Lawrence Lariar, a gag cartoonist, cartoon editor at *Liberty*, and, in his spare time, a prize-winning mystery novelist. The artist was John Spranger, who had worked his way up through comic books and had assisted and ghosted on Will Eisner's weekly *Spirit* comic book insert since 1946. He had an impressive style of his own, which echoed Eisner's in the use of imaginative angles and lighting. The hero of the strip was Ben Friday, who, like so many other new arrivals to the comic sections, was a returning serviceman. He'd been in the OSS and his onetime commanding officer helped him set up as a private eye who specialized in bodyguard work. The stories took Friday to a Caribbean island, the jungles of India, the streets of Paris, and other colorful locales. There were lovely women, trustworthy and not so trustworthy. The feature changed its name to *Ben Friday* in 1949, and a daily version was added. The next year, a cute little kid with an immense intellect, whom Friday had encountered in India, was given the leading part. The strip became *The Bantam Prince*, and Friday gave up bodyguarding to marry a pretty blonde.

Leslie Charteris was not only an able mystery novelist, he was a whiz at merchandising. His suave, roguish detective, Simon Templar, had first appeared in book form in 1928. Charteris proceeded to sell *The Saint* to the movies, to radio, to comic books, and

in 1948, to the funny papers. The comic strip adventures of the "Robin Hood of Modern Crime" were initially written by Charteris himself. After auditioning several artists, Straubing and Charteris picked Mike Roy for the job. Roy had worked in the Funnies, Inc., shop, providing material for various Marvel comic books in the early 1940s and later had been a contributor to *Crime Does Not Pay*. Basically a penciller, he did the strip with several inkers. The most gifted of them was Jack Davis.

Charteris brought over Hoppy Uniatz, the Saint's lowbrow tough-guy sidekick, from the books and involved them in crimes and intrigues that took place all around the globe. There were, of course, beautiful women and nasty villains. Some of Templar's opponents were after money or jewels, but others sought secret weapons that might destroy the world. In 1951, Roy left the strip and John Spranger took his place. There had never been any agreement as to exactly what the Saint looked like. Both Louis Hayward and George Sanders had portrayed him on the screen. Roy's Templar was a handsome, dark-haired chap, on the lean side. During Spranger's stint, he favored a pointed beard that gave him a rather devilish look.

Another well-known detective was to be seen in the Sunday funnies in these years, but only to sell hair tonic. Sam Spade made his debut in 1929 when the pulp magazine *Black Mask* serialized Hammett's *The Maltese Falcon*. The latest movie version, starring Humphrey Bogart, had appeared in 1941 and, as noted, the Spade radio show had taken to the airwaves in 1946. The sponsor was Wildroot Cream-Oil, a hair preparation whose major ingredient was sheep fat. In the later 1940s, Wildroot advertised by

Cynthia, *Irving Novick*.
©1946, *McClure Syndicate*.

way of a Sam Spade advertising strip that appeared about once a month in the Sunday comic sections. The drawing was by Lou Fine, an excellent artist who left comic books to become the most widely seen advertising strip artist of the period. The cases usually had something to do with hair and hair oil. In one Sam, with the help of his secretary Effie, found the culprit who was sabotaging the airplanes involved in skywriting *Wildroot Cream-Oil* high above the city.

In 1949, a hundred years after the Gold Rush, *Casey Ruggles* began. A meticulously done feature in the tradition of *Prince Valiant* and *Flash Gordon*, it was the work of a young Californian artist named Warren Tufts. Ruggles was an ex-Army sergeant, and his first adventure involved the gold fever of 1849. In later story sequences, he captured a Black Bart-style stage robber, journeyed across the Sierras in the dead of winter, and met such historical personages as Joaquim Murietta, Kit Carson, Jean Lafitte, and Millard Fillmore. He also encountered a great many lovely women, some quite fiery. *Casey Ruggles*, which ran daily and Sunday, was a carefully researched and effectively staged funny paper equivalent of a big-budget technicolor movie. Tufts had gone to school with *The Wild Bunch* director Sam Peckinpah and that may have had some influence on his later career.

Tex Austin, which dealt with a contemporary cowpoke, arrived on March 21, 1949. Syndicated by the *New York Post*, it was the joint effort of writer Sam Robins and artist Tom Fanning. The story commenced in Manhattan, where Tex, "a lad from the Big Bend country in Texas," had come to enter the World's Championship Rodeo. Readers did not see much of the rodeo—beyond Tex being tossed by a Brahma bull—before he and his chubby sidekick, Banjo, were embroiled in an intrigue involving an old Army buddy, a pretty, female magazine illustrator, some tough street kids, and the prize fight racket. Thereafter, Tex and Banjo headed home to his Lazy Y Ranch, which conniving rivals were plotting to take away from him. Rosita O'Brien, crusading

editor of the *Sweetgrass Gazette* and a long-time admirer of Tex, entered the strip at this point. "I wonder if you realize I'm a big girl now," she told him. From then on it was B-movie Western plots, the kind Robins had once scripted. Since this was a modern Western, there were also jeeps and pickup trucks as well as galloping horses. Fanning, a former advertising artist, drew in a simple, illustrative style that was at times a bit cold and slick. The strip lasted less than a year.

The soap opera strip, a genre destined to become increasingly prevalent in the next decade, began to blossom in these years. The earliest entrant was the McClure Syndicate's *Cynthia*, which debuted in late October 1946. A fairly close imitation of *Mary Worth*, it was drawn by Irving Novick and written, for most of its life, by Bert Whitman. Novick, just out of the Army, had been a comic book artist in the early 1940s, working on such superheroes as the Shield and Steel Sterling. For the new strip, he changed his approach, fashioning an acceptable imitation of Ken Ernst's style. Cynthia Blake was an attractive redhead, described as a "career girl, editor of a fashion magazine." Her husband was Jeff Blake, "a struggling lawyer employed by a large law firm." The first continuity involved Jeff's bringing home a client to live with them in the person of Leslie Van Druten Crane, a "beautiful and unscrupulous socialite." Mrs. Crane was going after a divorce, but also managed nearly to sabotage Cynthia's heretofore happy marriage. She caused Jeff to stammer such things to his wife as, "I was ... ah ... really working overtime with ... a ... er ... client!" and eventually provoked Cynthia into accusing her of being a "vicious, rotten little home-breaker." Mrs. Crane finally got her comeuppance and subsequent story lines found Cynthia playing a less personal part in the action. She served as a glamorous busybody, and a caption explained that her "time is divided between putting together the broken pieces of people's lives and editing." Although attractively drawn, *Cynthia* was not an especially inspired soap. That fact, plus increasing competition, put it out of business after a five-year run.

Eventually it occurred to Publishers Syndicate that they themselves could profit by imitating their own *Mary Worth*. The first surrogate was *Rex Morgan, M.D.*, which began in May 1948. Although the scripts were credited to Dal Curtis, the actual author was Nicholas Dallis, himself an M.D. who was practicing psychiatry in Toledo, Ohio. The artist was Marvin Bradley, who'd most recently been Ken Ernst's assistant. His assistant was Frank Edginton, who did backgrounds and shared the art credit. This was to be yet another strip drawn in a variation of the basic Caniff-Sickles style. Indeed, most of the soapers that came along over the next few years paid homage to that realistic, lushly inked way of drawing. Dallis was an acquaintance of Allen Saunders, who helped him sell the strip, and it's likely that Apple Mary's renovator gave the doctor advice and counsel on how to construct this particular sort of story strip.

Readers met Dr. Morgan, a traditionally handsome bachelor in his thirties, as he opened up his practice in the pleasant town of Glenbrook. Beneath the cozy surface of the place, however, was the usual seething ferment of troubles so essential to any respectable soap opera. Almost any medical problem that the young doctor, aided by his pretty nurse June Gale, turned to could lead into a tangle of mystery, violence, romance, and chicanery. Dr. Dallis had his surrogate treat just about every physical disease known to man, with side trips into psychiatric problems, drug addiction, and alcoholism. Rex Morgan was also a crusader against medical quackery, and several plots over the years had him unmasking a charlatan. One of Marvin Bradley's

editors recently recalled how amused he had been by the fact that the artist swore by a homemade root elixir that he cooked up in his kitchen and handed out to friends, obviously something Dr. Morgan would never have approved of.

A new batch of adolescent adventure strip heroes also came along just after the end of the Second World War. William Randolph Hearst's King Features Syndicate became especially interested in boy heroes and introduced no fewer than four of them. Hearst had also become interested in the idea of "incorporating American history of a vivid kind in the adventure strips of the comic section." This probably accounts for the fact that two of the four new boy hero features dealt with American history.

King Features continued to be partial to artists who drew like Alex Raymond. And that's no doubt one reason they bought John Lehti's *Tommy of the Big Top*. "I did, oh, about two weeks of it and went to King Features on a Friday," he once explained. "And on Monday they called me and said they wanted to do it." Lehti had drawn for comic books before the war, his best known character being the Crimson Avenger in Batman's *Detective Comics*. After four years in the service, most of it overseas, he returned to the field as a contributor and art director for a short-lived nonfiction comic book called *Picture News*. Besides being a disciple of Raymond's, Lehti "was a good friend of Alex. He gave me a lot of tips." The new daily began late in October 1946 and dealt with a somewhat naive teenager who took a job with the traveling Bingham Circus. He found romance, adventure, and some unusual complica-

John West, *John J. Olsen. Two panels from a seafaring sequence. ©1949, the* Chicago Tribune.

Miss Cairo Jones, *Bob Oksner. Cairo catches up with her missing husband.*

tions: "Aw, gee, Hamgravy, Sue's mad at me on accounta Madame Olga kissed me for saving her tiger." Although Lehti did a creditable job, *Tommy* never caught on and by the early 1950s was gone.

Hearst, as noted, wanted an American history strip. "Perhaps a title, *Trained By Fate*, would be general enough," he'd suggested to Ward Greene. "Take Paul Revere and show him as a boy, making as much of his boyhood life as possible, and culminate, of course, with his ride." Greene suggested a somewhat less dull method of approaching the idea. "There is another way to do it, which is somewhat fantastic, but which I submit for your consideration," he wrote to the Lord of San Simeon. "That is to devise a new comic…. A 'dream' idea revolving around a boy we might call Dick. Dick, or his equivalent, would go in his dream with Mad Anthony Wayne at the storming of Stony Point or with Decatur at Tripoli." Greene didn't bother to mention that Caniff's *Dickie Dare* had used the exact same premise nearly a decade and a half ago. "The dream idea for the American history series is splendid," pronounced Hearst.

A Sunday page entitled *Dick's Adventures* was introduced in January 1947, the same month Caniff's *Steve Canyon* began running in all the Hearst papers. The writer was Max Trell, who'd scripted *Secret Agent X-9*, and the artist was the seasoned pulp illustrator Neil O'Keeffe, who'd last worked for King on *Inspector Wade of Scotland Yard*. In its earliest days *Dick's Adventures* followed the *Prince Valiant* format, occupying a full page and having its copy let-

tered below the illustrations. Dick was a teenager and, unlike Dickie Dare, had absolutely no sense of humor. His first dream sequence teamed him up with Christopher Columbus, for whom he worked as cabin boy. Since Dick was aware how things were going to turn out, he never refrained from giving advice to the historical characters he popped in on. To Columbus, for example, he urged, "We *must* go to Spain! You will get your ships, my captain! I know! I know!"

More at home with tough detectives up until then, Norman Marsh showed up drawing a daily history strip for King in 1947. *Danny Hale* was the title and it was "the story of a clean-cut American boy who was on hand when great American history was being made." The time was the late eighteenth century and Danny was a frontier scout who dressed in coonskin cap and buckskin suit. Marsh threw in plenty of action and melodrama, but he had obviously done his research and this represents his major accomplishment in the comics. It was also his last and ended within a few years.

Undoubtedly one of the most accomplished pen and ink artists ever to work in comics was Frank Godwin. He could draw anything and was especially good with animals. Both his previous strips, *Roy Powers* and *Connie*, were joys to behold but not much fun to read. Unfortunately, the same was true of *Rusty Riley*, which he began for King in January 1948.

The previous year Godwin had drawn up five complete weeks of a strip he called *Rusty Ryan*. It was about a fifteen-year-old redheaded lad who lived in the state orphanage and was handy with automobile repairs. He almost immediately gets involved with a crooked couple who want to use him in a claimant scheme. The only horses that appear in the entire thirty dailies are on a merry-go-round. *Rusty Riley* stars a similar boy, but now his love is for horses and the continuities center around the world of horse breeding and racing. Rod Reed, an editor and writer for the Fawcett line of comic books, wrote the scripts. The stories were very much in the Horatio Alger, Jr. tradition and had the plucky orphan lad overcoming crooks, scoundrels, and curmudgeons. King kept the strip going, daily and Sunday, until 1959.

Wheaties, the Breakfast of Champions, had brought Jack Armstrong, the All-American Boy, to children's radio in 1933. In his earliest radio days Jack was an athletic hero at Hudson High School, but eventually he was roaming the world in search of adventure. He usually traveled with his teenage chums, Billy and Betty Fairfield, and a deep-voiced mentor named Uncle Jim. In the spring of 1947, the Register and Tribune Syndicate introduced a *Jack Armstrong* comic strip. Bob Schoenke was the artist and his lackluster style matched the rather prosaic plots. The strip never captured the wild and slightly cockeyed feel of the radio show, and it didn't, like the radio show, give away terrific-sounding premiums.

Several women found employment as the stars of adventure strips from war's end to the decade's end. *Miss Cairo Jones* began as a Sunday page in July 1945, after V-E Day but before V-J Day. A pretty blonde, Cairo had no fixed occupation and in her early adventures simply kept getting entangled in international intrigues that were unfolding around her. Her very first adventure had to do with her missing husband, a Nazi war criminal who it turned out was hiding in Mexico. Cairo had had no idea Saber Von Tigron was a Hitler supporter when she'd

married him and, at story's end, she learned they'd never actually been married legally. Steve Racy, a handsome American newspaperman, met Cairo while pursuing the Von Tigron story and they teamed up for the next several months. After considerable globetrotting, Cairo settled down in the United States and took a job as a secretary. The continuities turned satirical, poking fun at such targets as big business, advertising, and Hollywood. The artist on the strip was Bob Oksner, who drew in a style that was a personal blend of the Caniff approach with some more cartoony touches. It was while working on this feature that Oksner first established himself as a master of the then acceptable profession of drawing pretty women. He'd started his career working for Marvel comics in the early 1940s and it was while holding down a job at the B. W. Sangor shop, an outfit that packaged various comic books, that he decided he wanted to try a newspaper strip. Jerry Albert, an editor and writer at Sangor, wrote the strip for its first year and then Oksner took over. An appealing strip, *Miss Cairo Jones* lasted for only two years. It was syndicated by Associated Newspapers, a subsidiary of Bell. Looking back some years later, Oksner said he felt the switch from adventure to humor was a mistake, but he had a lot more fun doing it that way. "I really wasn't happy," he admitted, "dealing with a woman character in heavy melodrama."

Mitzi McCoy was definitely a Sunday page dealing with a woman character in heavy melodrama. Handsomely drawn by magazine illustrator Kreigh Collins, it started on November 7, 1948. Mitzi was a pretty blond heiress who resided in "the picturesque little town of Freedom," a quaint New England coastal spot. Her independent spirit and impulsive nature, coupled with the fact that she knew how to fly a plane, got her into assorted troubles. The other main characters were Tim Graham, a good-looking reporter on the local paper, and Stub Goodman, the paper's colorful old editor. Collins, apparently not fond of Mitzi, began ignoring her to deal with other matters, including a sequence going into the colorful history of the Irish wolfhound. In the autumn of 1950 the strip recounted the adventures of one of Mitzi's Irish ancestors, a chap known as Kevin the Bold. Soon the strip changed its title and Mitzi was gone. An even shorter career was enjoyed by *Merrie Chase*. The McNaught Syndicate introduced this strip about an attractive policewoman in the summer of 1949. Renny McEvoy was the writer and Carl Hubbell, who'd drawn for such comic books as the original *Daredevil* and *Crime Does Not Pay*, was the artist. Paul Reinman replaced Hubbell fairly soon and in the second year Merrie switched professions to become a private detective. An uneasy mix of mystery and humor, the strip did not thrive.

A few years earlier, an established adventurous lady had fallen on hard times. *Flyin' Jenny* had ceased in July 1946. The world of flying was not thought of as romantic and exciting after the war. In the first few months of peacetime, Jenny Dare had trouble finding any sort of flying job at all. She discovered, like a great many returning Air Force people, that, as one executive told her, "Pilots are a dime a dozen." She did manage to keep flying, hired by a couple of former GIs to help them find a Nazi treasure hidden on a mysterious island. But eventually she found herself out of work. Russell Keaton had died early in 1945, and Marc Swayze, his former assistant and sometime ghost, had taken over as artist. Glenn

Elmo, *Cecil Jensen. Elmo stands up for Sultry Lebair.*
©1946, The Register and Tribune Syndicate.

Chaffin continued as writer, and the two did an excellent job of carrying on. That did not keep *Flyin' Jenny* from becoming a casualty to changing tastes, however.

Art Huhta's *Wild Rose* was a one-third-page Sunday started for the *Chicago Tribune* in 1946. The idea for the feature had apparently been given to him by his editor, and Huhta, who felt his specialty was "corn and slapstick" was not ever completely happy with a relatively serious creation. "I worked under a kind of stress there. It wasn't what I wanted to do." A straight strip, although drawn in his usual cartoon style, *Wild Rose* took place in mountain country in a small community called Thunder Ridge and combined elements of *Li'l Abner* and *Tobacco Road*. Rose was a longhaired, blond young woman, usually seen wearing cutoff overalls and a white shirt. Goodhearted and naive, she was dedicated to helping her benighted rural town and her ailing Pappy, with time out for a little romance now and then. Huhta dutifully populated his mountaineer country with escaped bank robbers, feuding clans, and an interesting array of bewhiskered old coots. Looking back on *Wild Rose* years later, he observed, "It did not do too well as a syndicated feature because I was doing only the Sunday page. I think something is usually lost when you do only a weekly thing." During this same period, Huhta was ghosting *The Nebbs*, ghosting *Tiny Tim*, and producing a series of original *Dick Tracy* comic books.

The *Chicago Trib* gave a Sunday home to a trio of other adventure features as well. *Surgeon Stone*, a

1946 entry, dealt with the adventures of "the best plastic surgeon in the state." The handsome, dark-haired Stone, who was continually getting entangled with gangsters, lovesick heiresses, and civic scoundrels, led a fast-paced life that would have made any soap opera medic envious. The page was the work of Richard Martin Fletcher, who'd drawn for comic books and assisted on *Dan Dunn* before moving up to a strip of his own. He had an effective, boldly inked style, and *Surgeon Stone* was usually more interesting to look at than it was to read. Bill Perry had been an assistant to Frank King on *Gasoline Alley* since the middle 1920s, and by this time was drawing the Sunday page. His *Ned Handy* was subtitled *Adventures in the Deep South*. Ned was an average-looking youth who wore a high-crowned straw hat and enjoyed mild adventures in rural settings, sometimes getting to do "a little detective job." Perry's version of the Deep South, by the way, contained no blacks. John J. Olson also worked as an assistant and ghost on a *Trib* strip. In his case it was *Brenda Starr*, to which he devoted many years of his life. His *John West* was a well-done adventure page that had dealt at the outset with a clean-cut young man making his way in a typical Midwest small town. Both West and Olson matured as the page evolved, and eventually the young hero, now a husky lad who looked a good deal like movie actor Robert Mitchum, was adventuring on the high seas. He worked as a deep-sea diver and with a whaling crew, and in the last days of the feature, in 1950, spent time in the frozen North. An admirer of illustrator Rockwell Kent, Olson had assimilated many elements of the Kent style into his work, and the whaling sequence was particularly impressive.

Late in 1945, the McNaught Syndicate announced a new strip to be called *Hollywood Merry-Go-Round*. The author was Renny McEvoy, who was both a character actor who appeared in such movies as *Miss Susie Slagle's*, *The Story of Dr. Wassell*, and *Wing and A Prayer* and the long-time script ghost for his father's *Dixie Dugan* strip. The artist was Jim Pabian, who'd previously drawn characters like

Andy Panda in comic books. When the strip actually started appearing that December, it was initially titled *Hollywood* and then, within a few weeks, it became *Hollywood Johnnie*. The protagonist was a brash, red-haired talent agent named Johnnie Wolfe. The daily dealt with rather mild show business continuities, and the Sunday page went in for gags. Real film stars, mostly from the Paramount Pictures roster—Bob Hope, William Bendix, Bing Crosby, and Sonny Tufts—made cameo appearances. After a two-year run there was another title change, this time to *Screen Girl*. One of Johnnie's clients, Joan Gray, took over the lead and he became better looking and less brash. The changes didn't keep it alive for long.

Christianity came to the funny papers in 1947, when the Chicago Sun and Times Co. started syndicating *Jack and Judy in Bibleland*. Produced by Robert Adcomb and drawn by William E. Fay, it was a non-denominational daily and Sunday feature centered around a preteen brother and sister, blond Jack and brown-haired, pigtailed Judy. The two were able to move into a rather pious fantasy world to witness and often participate in Bible stories. They had access to both the Old and New Testaments, dropping in, for example, on Joshua when he went after the walls of Jericho, visiting Noah while the ark was under construction—Jack asked Shem, "What kind of animals are you bringing into the ark?"—and witnessing the birth of Christ. Most strips suggested what verse of the Bible to consult: "Read 'The Rainbow' in Genesis," "Read 'The Book' in Jeremiah." Although it may have seemed somewhat out of place rubbing shoulders with the likes of *Mark Trail*, *Donald Duck*, and *Rip Kirby*, the strip lasted for five years.

Bumpkin strips, no doubt inspired by the continuing success of *Li'l Abner*, also surfaced in the middle and late 1940s. Don Dean, former ghost artist on *Chief Wahoo & Steve Roper*, got a strip of his own with *Cranberry Boggs*. It was syndicated by McNaught and began January 1945. Cranberry was a blond, well-meaning Abner type who dwelt in the

New England fishing village of Cod Cliffs. He and his aggressively quaint, peglegged grandfather, Cap'n Gramps, worked as lobster fishermen. But the majority of Cranberry's time was taken up with humorous adventures that involved him with jewel thieves, kidnappers, bank robbers, and an assortment of attractive, and not always trustworthy, females. His loyal sidekick was a pudgy, bucktoothed lad called Woodchuck, and his more or less steady sweetheart was Kandy Kane. Nowhere near as satirical or slapstick as Al Capp, Dean increasingly came to favor melodrama over comedy.

Begun in 1946, *Elmo*, by the well known, liberal Chicago political cartoonist Cecil Jensen, chronicled the adventures of a blond young rube who somewhat resembled Danny Kaye and was a shade more naive and optimistic than Candide. An urban Li'l Abner, he inherited the Popnut Skrummies breakfast food company and came to the big city. There, a true innocent, he encountered unscrupulous business moguls and exotic and untrustworthy women. Fortunately, his hometown sweetheart, Emmaline, followed him to the metropolis and was able to keep him from serious harm. Jensen's work was an idiosyncratic stew of satire, farce, and baggy-pants burlesque. His gags were apt to produce pained winces as often as they provoked real laughs. Much closer to Al Capp and the Dogpatch style was *Jasper Jooks* by Baldy Benton, which was brought forth by the New York Post Syndicate in April 1946. Set in Appleknock Territory, a New England locale where everything

was still as it had been in colonial days, it followed Jasper, a blond Abner imitation in Revolutionary-era togs. Benton had the Capp studio manner of drawing down, but he never got, try as he might, the comedy quite right.

A whole slew of other humor strips attempted to brighten the post-war period. The majority of them faltered and fell by the wayside. Burne Hogarth, noted for his serious work on *Tarzan* and *Drago*, made a try at comedy with his 1948 *Miracle Jones* Sunday page. It was a muscle-bound variation on the Walter Mitty theme, with its henpecked little central character indulging in faintly amusing flights of fancy each week. Jay Irving had a lifelong fascination with the police. His *Willie Doodle*, introduced in 1946, was one of the features he drew about an amiable but dumb beat cop. In 1947 Clyde Lewis began a Sunday page called *Fatso*. This was the companion piece to his daily gag panel about a little fellow called Buck—*Private Buck* during the war—and Buck appeared in it with his large, redheaded buddy Fatso. Charles Kuhn was fifty-five when his *Grandma* got going in 1947. He'd been a political cartoonist since before the First World War and had also done gag panels. After a little more than a year with a small syndicate, *Grandma* was picked up by King Features. It was a folksy feature about a feisty old widow who got a kick out of hanging around with a bunch of clean-cut little boys. Kuhn aimed his simple humor at kids, and his Sunday page always included a black-and-white panel with an invitation for his readers to get out their crayons and color it in. A longtime resident of the King bullpen, Bob Naylor had ghosted or taken over a number of strips, most notably *Barney Baxter*. He had also ghosted Walter Hoban's *Jerry on the Job* for a series of advertising strips in the late thirties. His fondness for the smallfry office boy persisted, and in 1946 he was able to talk the syndicate into taking the unprecedented step of reviving a long dead feature. While his version was a reasonable

The Wolf, *Leonard Sansone. A promotion drawing done to promote the Wolf's debut in a civilian panel.*

Pogo, *Walt Kelly. Most of the major characters are in residence in the swamp in this January 1949 daily from the New York Star. ©1949, Walt Kelly.*

facsimile of Hoban's, it was a couple of decades too late to find a receptive audience. In 1946, sports cartoonist Lou Darvas, back from the Air Force, started a strip about a former wrestler turned cab driver. *Haff Nelson*, a broadly satirical work, lasted just a year.

The domestication of the comic page continued as several new families moved in. Bernard Segal, under the penname Seeg, began doing *Honey and Hank* early in September 1946. It was a gentler, quieter version of *Blondie*, with a gag-a-day format and focused on a pleasant young married couple and their likable toddler son. The blond little boy, named Ellsworth, gradually upstaged his parents, and in 1949 the feature's title was changed to *Ellsworth*. In 1947 *The Orbits*, a humorous continuity, began. The work of William Juhre, it was syndicated by John F. Dille. A low-key series, it was probably at least partially autobiographical, since the plump, bumbling, well-intentioned head of the family was a commercial artist. *The Dailys*, from the Chicago Tribune Syndicate, strongly resembled *The Gumps*. Not surprising, since it was the work of Stanley Link, who had served as Sidney Smith's ghost for many years. An uneasy amalgam of humor and dramatic continuity, *The Dailys* centered around a bickering, middle-aged couple named Doris and Dan, rich and outspoken Aunt Agatha, a plump and outspoken housekeeper, and various argumentative and greedy friends and neighbors.

Three pantomime strips, none exactly new, began national syndication in the middle 1940s. Foxo Reardon, whose nickname derived from the

initials of his first and middle names, Francis Xavier, had been drawing *Bozo* since the middle 1920s. A staff artist on the *Richmond Times Dispatch*, Reardon probably had to wait longer to get picked up by a syndicate than any other cartoonist before or since. It was not until November 1945 that the Chicago Sun Syndicate started distributing it nationwide. Bozo, short in stature and never seen without his jauntily tilted derby, was what then would have been called a bum. The majority of the wordless gags dealt with his making his feisty and iconoclastic way through the world. When Reardon was under the weather, George Sixta ghosted the strip for him.

Another silent strip was Harry Hanan's *Louie*, which centered on the life and times of the small, plump, bald and mustached Louie. The gags dealt, usually cleverly, with domestic life, office work, and other basics of the urban routine. *Louie* was introduced in England in 1947 but was soon being syndicated in this country. Hanan, who drew in a simple, uncluttered style, transplanted himself to the Untied States in the late 1940s and would continue doing his unobtrusive strip for almost the next thirty years. Pantomime is easy to import. In 1947, United Feature brought over Dahl Mikkelsen's *Ferd'nand* from Denmark, where it had originated a decade earlier. Though built along the lines of Louie, Ferd'nand inhabited a much gentler, and cuter, world. Comics historian Dennis Wepman describes the strip's humor as "bland, genial" and explains that it "revolves around the titular hero, an amiable little fellow with an amiable little wife and son, living in an amiable little town, all singularly free of conflict." Mikkelsen, who signed himself Mik, eventually also settled in America and became increasingly occupied with dealing in real estate. From the middle 1950s onward, *Ferd'nand* was ghosted, first by Frank Thomas and then by Al Plastino.

Aggie Mack, a teen strip that was the Trib-News syndicate's answer to *Penny*, started in 1946. Hal Rasmusson, who'd spent years in the greeting card business, was the artist. The most successful teen character of the century also entered newspaper comics in 1946. *Archie* had originated in *Pep Comics* in 1942, a backup feature for such slam-bang heroes as the Shield and the Hangman. Artist Bob Montana was the creator, with some input from writer Vic Bloom. The redheaded Archie, whose creation had been inspired by the likes of Andy Hardy and Henry Aldrich, lived in an idealized town named Riverdale. A likable bumbler, his comic book adventures centered around his fouling up the basic situations of adolescent life—dating, homework, and household chores. The regular cast included Archie's pal Jughead, his rival Reggie, his two girlfriends, the blond Betty and the dark-haired and wealthy Veronica. There were also sufficient parents, teachers, and peers to cause further complications. Montana had relinquished the comic books—a full *Archie* magazine had soon been added—when he went into the service. Upon his return, he started the newspaper strip and was able to come up with a joke a day for the rest of his life.

PM, the newspaper that introduced *Barnaby*, ceased publication in May of 1948. It returned the next month, so to speak, as the *New York Star*. *Barnaby* was found on its comics page, along with *Claire Voyant*, *The Berrys*, and *Buck Ryan*, a British private eye import.

On October 4, 1948, the *Star* added *Pogo*, the work of Walt Kelly, a thirty-five-year-old staff artist

and political cartoonist. The *Star* folded the following January, but Kelly's animal strip began national syndication in May. Born in 1913 in Philadelphia, Walter Crawford Kelly moved to Bridgeport, Connecticut, two years later along with "father, mother, sister, and sixteen teeth, all my own." The impulse to be a cartoonist struck early and while in high school he drew not only for the school paper and the yearbook, but for the local newspaper as well. In the late 1930s, he went to California to work for the Disney studio. While there, Kelly "and 1,500 other worthies" turned out *Snow White*, *Fantasia*, *Pinocchio*, *Dumbo*, and *The Reluctant Dragon*. Attentive watchers of the credits on some of these animated features will notice Kelly's name included in some of the long lists. Finding himself on the wrong side during the strike of 1941—Kelly crossed the picket line—he returned to the East. "Kelly went straight," is how he explained it some years afterwards. "He got a job doing comic books." He was hired by Oskar Lebeck, who was editing the comic books that Whitman and Dell were jointly publishing. With several years of funny animal drawing to his credit, Kelly was perfect for the new kid titles—*Animal Comics*, *Our Gang*, and *Fairy Tale Parade*. It was for *Animal Comics* in 1942 that he invented Pogo, a sort of fuzzy Candide who resided in a southern swamp where all the creatures great and small could talk. Some of them even wore clothes. Even in the funny books, supposedly aimed at children, Kelly indulged his fondness for slapstick and burlesque, puns, plays on words, satire, and rowdy behavior. He carried most of the major swampland characters from the comic book—Albert the Alligator, Churchy LaFemme, Howland Owl—into the newspaper strip. And he became increasingly fond of using *Pogo* as an instrument of political satire. In the decades that followed, this made Kelly the most outspoken cartoonist working in the funny papers.

The end of 1945, saw the advent of two new strips in the uncrowded sports genre. *Ozark Ike*, which commenced in November, was written and drawn by Ray Gotto. He'd been a sports cartoonist, and when he left the Navy he sold his baseball strip to packager-agent Stephen Slesinger, who in turn placed it with King Features. Ike McBatt was a husky blond fellow. A natural ballplayer, he soon made it to the big time. He had a blond girlfriend named Dinah, who was a Daisy Mae surrogate, and when he was not playing ball, he was mixing in a mountain-country feud. A patient man, Gotto drew in a rigid, pen style that made use of numerous kinds of shading and crosshatching. In December 1945, the venerable *Joe Jinks* became *Curly Kayoe*. Joe had been managing Curly for quite awhile by that time. Curly, who bore a striking resemblance to Joe Palooka, also became the heavyweight champ. The Jinks strip had undergone several staff changes during the earlier 1940s and had been drawn by George Storm, Morris Weiss, and Al Leiderman, successively. Sam Leff's name began appearing on the strip in 1944, and he passed himself off as both artist and writer. Actually, his more talented brother, Mo Leff, was pencilling for him. Since Mo Leff was also ghosting *Joe Palooka*, the similarities between Joe and Curly are not difficult to explain.

Besides the addition of new strips, some long-time favorites were renovated during this period. Among them were two pioneering adventure strips, *Buck Rogers* and *Tarzan*. In 1947, Dick Calkins was permanently removed from the strip he'd helped create, and the daily was assigned to Murphy Anderson and writer Robert Williams, using the pen name Bob Barton. Recently out of the Navy, Anderson had drawn for *Planet Comics* and provided illustrations for the *Amazing Stories* and *Planet Stories* pulp magazines. *Buck Rogers* was no longer as popular as it once had been. "I started on the strip for $65 a week," Anderson once said. "Don't ask me why. I was making better money doing comic book work." He did a nice job with the strip, however, upgrading its appearance considerably. But he tired of the chore by 1949 and went back to comic

books. The versatile Leonard Dworkins assumed the daily. During these same years, the Sunday page was still being done by Rick Yager.

Rex Maxon, never a favorite of Edgar Rice Burroughs, was finally bounced from the daily *Tarzan* in August of 1947. Hogarth was back doing the Sunday page by then and for a brief spell his name appeared on the weekday apeman adventures as well. The actual artist, though, was Dan Barry. An impressive young cartoonist, Barry was then one of the stars of the comic book field. Never satisfied with the salary, Barry stayed in the jungle a bit less than two years and never signed the *Tarzan* strip. Several other comic book graduates put in brief stints after his departure, including Nick Cardy and Paul Reinman.

Many of the strips and panels created for such GI publications as *Stars and Stripes* and *Yank* converted to civilian life after the war. George Baker's *Sad Sack* was introduced in a brand new Sunday page by the Bell Syndicate in 1946. Sack was a civilian now, and the humor was toned down considerably. Leonard Sansone's *The Wolf*, about the GI with the lupine head and amorous designs on just about every women on Earth, had been one of the most popular of serviceman features. United Feature had a postwar fling with a *Wolf* daily gag panel. He was still dedicated to pursuing women, but much more sedately now that he was appearing in family newspapers. The most celebrated GI cartoonist was Bill Mauldin, who won a Pulitzer Prize. He did a peacetime version of his Willie and Joe panel, called *Back Home*, but it was not a hit. *Hubert* by Dick Wingert began as a wartime panel for *Stars and Stripes*. Hubert was a squatty, slovenly, perennial private with a tomato-nose. Crude and unlucky, he was the poor man's Sad Sack. King Features took on a civilian version, and *Hubert* continued until the early 1990s. He was the last survivor of the World War II bunch.

Chapter 10

The Frenzied Fifties

The 1950s was to be the first decade in which television played an important part in providing daily entertainment. Soap operas had begun showing up on daytime TV as early as 1949, when radio's popular *One Man's Family* made the transition. *The First Hundred Years*, starring Jimmy Lydon and Anne Sargent and created for the burgeoning medium, came to CBS in 1950. It was followed over the next couple of years by *Love of Life*, *Search for Tomorrow*, and, brought over from radio, *The Guiding Light*. In the early fifties several new soap opera strips began as well.

Dr. Nicholas Dallis, this time calling himself Paul Nichols, made a try at repeating the success of his *Rex Morgan, M.D.* with *Judge Parker*. Dan Heilman, recently the artist on *American Adventure*, had already proven himself fully capable of working in the Caniff-derived style that this sort of enterprise required. Judge Alan B. Parker was a handsome, flawless man in his middle years, the hair at his temples touched with gray. A widower, his household consisted of a pretty daughter who was a student nurse at General Hospital, a son in college, and a kindly housekeeper named Mrs. Benson. An early caption explained that Judge Parker devoted his life to "two interests—his work and his children." The earliest continuities centered on the judge and involved the kidnapping of his daughter to put pres-

sure on him, his brief romance with a woman who turned out to be involved in an adoption racket, and his son's entanglement with a spoiled rich girl who became a murder suspect. The strip caught on and as it progressed, while there were still courtroom scenes, Judge Parker gradually came to take a less active part in the lives of the constantly changing cast of characters.

Another 1952 release from Publishers Syndicate was *Blade Winters*. Written by Lafe Thomas and drawn by Ed Mann, this was set in the glamorous world of New York television. While more and more people were becoming interested in television itself, a sufficient number did not take to the strip, and it was soon gone. NEA's entry in the soap opera derby was *The Story of Martha Wayne*. Initially credited to Wilson Scruggs, it commenced in May 1953. Martha was a pretty, blond, young widow with an eight-year-old son. She lived in a middle-sized city and ran the Odds and Ends Shop in partnership with her pretty, young red-haired friend, Thelma Meeker. Many of the stories revolved around the shop, with Martha intruding in the problems of customers and employees. And every now and then, either Martha or Thelma would fall in love with the wrong sort of man.

Elliot Caplin was especially productive in the 1950s. His major soap opera for the decade was *The*

Heart of Juliet Jones, which he sold to King Features in 1953. Having heard that the syndicate was looking for something that would compete with *Mary Worth*, Caplin came up with a strip that followed the life and times of dark-haired, thirtysomething Juliet, plus her "more impulsive, more emotional" blond, younger sister Eve and their kindly, old, widowed father. The Jones family resided in a small town named Devon, which was rich with the required rogues, rascals, passions, and dark secrets. For the *Juliet Jones* artist Caplin selected, on the recommendation of cartoonist Gill Fox, the talented Stan Drake. A comic book artist while in his teens, when Drake returned from service in World War II he went to work for the Johnstone & Cushing shop and drew many of their Sunday advertising strips. A distinctive artist, he turned out an impressively slick product. In its early years, *The Heart of Juliet Jones* lived up to everyone's expectations and built up a list of over six hundred newspapers.

The small, Cleveland-based Lafave Newspaper Syndicate, whose biggest seller was Clifford McBride's dog strip *Napoleon*, entered soapland in April 1955 with *Dr. Guy Bennett* by Dr. B. C. Douglas. The Douglas pen name covered Dr. Michael A. Petti, a Phi Beta Kappa graduate of Dartmouth, a teacher at Western Reserve Medical School, and a practicing physician in Cleveland. For good measure, his wife was also an M.D. According to syndicate publicity, the handsome gray at the temples Dr. Bennett

Judge Parker, *Dan Heilman. The judge is about to find out that you can't trust a woman who tells you that you dance divinely. ©1953, Publishers Syndicate.*

was modeled after Dr. Petti's office partner. Unlike Rex Morgan, Bennett was married and the father of a daughter and two sons. His secretary, though, was a dead ringer for Dr. Morgan's adoring nurse. The first man to draw the medical soap was Jim Seed, a competent Cleveland commercial artist. When Seed left in 1957 to take over *Jane Arden* and help turn it into a soap opera, he was replaced by Frank Thorne. It was while working on *Dr. Guy Bennett* that Thorne decided there was more to life than drawing like Alex Raymond. Working diligently, he developed a new style of his own and turned the strip into one of the most imaginatively drawn features of the decade. While the layouts and the characterizations improved, the continuities remained pretty much standard soap fare. If anything, Dr. Petti was even more of a stickler for medical detail than his rival scripter Dr. Dallis. Stories would often stop dead while the graying physician explained a point. "Jaundice is a yellowish discoloration due to bile in the pigment of the skin," he would say. Or, on another occasion, "It's commonly called dumb cane, and this is truly descriptive. It resembles a sugar cane plant, but if you nibble on it, it strikes you dumb." Petti, who also created a daily feature called *Health Capsules*, which was drawn by Jud Hurd, quit writing the strip in 1961. Thorne took over that chore and commenced phasing Dr. Bennett out and replacing him with a younger, more dynamic medic named Dr. Duncan. It was under the title *Dr. Duncan* that the strip ended in 1962.

Mixing soap and religion, Ed Dodd came up with *David Crane* in 1956. He sold it to the Hall

Dr. Guy Bennett, *Frank Thorne. The doctor explains jaundice.*

Syndicate, which was handling his successful *Mark Trail*. Dodd only wrote this "story of a small town minister whose warmth and wisdom extends from his church into the hearts and lives of his neighbors." Canadian-born artist Winslow Mortimer, who'd drawn both Superman and Batman in comic books, was picked to draw the strip. He worked in a mild-mannered illustrative style. The initial story found handsome, blond Crane as he graduated, married his college sweetheart against the objections of her wealthy parents, and took up his first parish in the small town of Boulder Bluff. One of his chief allies in town was a crotchety middle-aged banker and church official named Frank Dabney. Their relationship was somewhat like that of Big Crosby and Barry Fitzgerald in *Going My Way*. In fact, the strip was a sort of Protestant version of the 1943 Oscar-winning movie. Once Reverend Crane and his pretty bride got settled, a round of soap-opera problems began swirling around them. When Mortimer left the parson in 1960, Creig Flessel took over as artist. Although *David Crane* was milder and less heavy than most of its soap strip competitors, it was not overly pious, and readers were never told exactly what the young priest's denomination was. Crane, however, was occasionally to be seen praying.

Leonard Starr, like Stan Drake, had worked in comic books in the 1940s and then taken a job with Johnstone & Cushing. In 1956, deciding it was time to try a comic strip, he began working up samples. After taking nearly a half dozen different proposed

strips to Sylvan Byck at King Features and getting nothing beyond encouragement to try again with something else, Starr bundled all his previous samples up and took them over to Moe Riley, a vice president at the Chicago Tribune Syndicate. There were two ideas that Riley liked, one about a medical missionary who worked in foreign countries and one about a young woman who comes to New York in hopes of becoming an actress. Since *Terry and the Pirates* was still flourishing and had foreign locales, the syndicate decided to go with the Broadway strip. That developed into *On Stage*. At that point, Starr was not a theater buff, but he thought the theater would be a good milieu for a story strip and he did considerable research. After *On Stage* was launched and became a hit, he went on to read several hundred theatrical memoirs and biographies, and he even invested in a few Broadway shows.

On Stage began in February 1957 as Mary Perkins, a pretty, small-town girl, arrived in the big city to try to become an actress. Starr followed her career as she made her way from cigarette girl in a night club to roles on the stage. After the strip had been running for a while, Starr changed the title of the Sunday page to *Mary Perkins On Stage*. His friend Milton Caniff had suggested that people like to see the name of the character in the title. Caniff was one of the major influences on Starr's drawing style, the other was Alex Raymond. "The artwork is excellent," comics historian Bob Bindig has said of the strip. "Starr … likes to draw and it shows in his work. Each panel is a well developed planned illustration." Starr wrote the strip as well, mixing romance with adventure and mystery and often using characters who were recognizable variations on show business celebrities of the day. "*On Stage* transcended the

On Stage, *Leonard Starr.* ©*1958, the* Chicago Tribune. *Reprinted by permission of Tribune Media Servces*

The final soap of the decade was *Adam Ames*. A daily effort written by the prolific Elliot Caplin and drawn by Lou Fine, it started in the summer of 1959. Fine, still an exceptional artist, had become increasingly slick and there is a certain coldness in his work of this period. Ames, the handsome, graying protagonist, was an artist, a painter who was reluctant to tackle any subject that did not interest him aesthetically. Readers first met the widowed Ames as he and his three children—a teenage son, a preteen daughter, and a small son—arrived in a commuter town and took up residence in a large, old Victorian house. They hired a no-nonsense housekeeper named Bessie and proceeded to get into one emotional mess after another. If Adam Ames got a commission to do a portrait of a wealthy and beautiful matron, you could be sure she'd be throwing herself at him before the paint was dry. If his son met an older woman—someone, say, in her late twenties—he'd soon be lured into a potentially dangerous relationship. Like all towns in soap opera country, the one where the Ames family settled seethed with untold problems that were always ready to erupt.

conventions of the sentimental romance and tear-jerker," Dennis Wepman has commented, "incorporating elements of high comedy and often gripping adventure and suspense. It was written with considerable polish and presented the glamour of the Broadway theater world with neither sensationalism nor cynicism." Starr continued with the strip until 1979, when he began drawing the revived *Annie*.

The influence of *Mark Trail* was again felt in the early 1950s, when three new outdoorsy adventure strips emerged. *Glen Forrest* was a Sunday by William Ferguson, who'd put in over twenty years on a non-fiction natural history panel called *This Curious World*. It began in 1952, and advance ads invited readers to "seek adventure with young Glen Forrest thru the rugged terrain of the west!" There would be plenty of opportunities to "see wildlife pictured in the primitive beauty of its natural surroundings." There was plenty of nature in the page, but the young Glen was not an especially appealing fellow and did not stay around long. The Chicago Sun Times Syndicate started *Nick Haliday* by Keats Petrie in 1953 and, since adventure strips continued to be perfectly salable, touted it as "adventure at its best." Set in the Florida Keys, the strip starred dark, handsome Nick, the skipper of a charter boat named the *Lark*. The Sunday pages, in true *Mark Trail* tradition, were individual nature sermons, about undersea life for the most part. Nick was in business for roughly three years. Even less successful was the seagoing *Marlin Keel*, introduced in the autumn of 1954. Its handsome, blond hero resided in a New England harbor town named Seaford and wore his skipper's cap at a jaunty angle. His stodgy father wanted Marlin to join him at his bank, but his mother realized he was like her brother: "The sea is in his blood!" There was action in the strip, including underwater battles with sharks and devilfish, and a sufficient amount of pretty women. For a soap opera touch, Marlin's girlfriend Wendy was blind and, at the story's start, also seemingly an orphan. George Shedd, who drew like a somewhat less talented Wally Wood, was the artist on the strip. It ended the following year.

The decade of the 1950s has been commemorated in many ways. Sometimes as an era filled with nothing but hoody-looking yet terrifically

Adam Ames, *Lou Fine.*

decent teenagers who lived out their entire lives at drive-ins and proms, sometimes as ten bleak years of Eisenhower dullness, McCarthy witch-hunting, and Asian entanglements. The fifties was also the time of the Cold War and Sputnik and an incredible competition between the West and Russia. One of the side effects of this competition was an increased interest in the sciences in this country, extending even to a boom in science fiction. SF films proliferated, new magazines blossomed on the newsstands, and several new comic strips showed up. The Second World War had, in a very unsettling way, made many of the earlier wild notions of science fiction come true. In the frenzied fifties rockets and atomic weapons were no longer the exclusive property of Buck and Flash and their four-color cronies.

That increasingly popular technological wonder, television, provided the first big new science fictions trip. *Tom Corbett, Space Cadet*, starring Frankie Thomas, Jr., had come to television in 1950. The doings of Tom, Astro, Roger, and the gang from the Space Academy fascinated the youth of the day and led to considerable merchandising. The comic strip, like the toys, costumes, and lunch boxes, was one of the results of the extensive licensing of the show. It began in September 1951. Ray Bailey was the artist and got the sole credit. Paul S. Newman wrote the scripts for the first year or so and Willy Ley, the noted science writer and rocket expert, was the technical advisor. Ley served the same function on the show. While *Tom Corbett* was space opera, it did try to impart some scientific information. As with his previous *Bruce Gentry*, Ray Bailey drew this strip in his boldly inked version of the Milton Caniff style. *Tom Corbett* lasted for only two years and obviously

could have used more of what Tom and Astro were always wishing everybody, "Spaceman's luck!"

Quite a few syndicates entered the SF sweepstakes in the early 1950s. NEA came up with *Chris Welkin, Planeteer* a couple months after Tom and his fellow students hit the comic sections. Although Chris called himself a planeteer, he was close to being what would later be known as an astronaut and the strip often emphasized the technological and training aspects of his profession. The author was Russ Winterbotham, an NEA staff man but with considerable credits in the science fiction field. He'd sold his first story to *Astounding* in 1935, written for other pulps, and turned out several SF novels. A prosaic scriptwriter, he at least managed to bring some knowledge of real science fiction to his job. The drawing was by Art Sansom, later of *The Born Loser*, trying not quite successfully to join the Caniff school.

Lee Elias did a much better job of assimilating the Milton Caniff approach to drawing. He collaborated with veteran science fiction writer Jack Williamson to produce *Beyond Mars* from February 17, 1952, to May 13, 1955. This was a handsome Sunday page that appeared in exactly one newspaper. "This was when TV had just begun to hurt the circulation of Sunday papers," Williamson once explained. "Somebody at the *News*

noticed that all the competing papers had much the same comics and decided that the *News* might gain a competitive edge by developing some original strips of its own." The editors of the *New York Daily News* had approached Williamson after an unflattering review in the *New York Times* had said of his novel *Seetee Ship* that "the quality of the writing is such that this 'space opera' ranks only slightly above that of a comic strip." Adapting his novels about Seetee (CT stood for contraterrene, now known as antimatter) to comic strip format, Williamson added a hero named Mike Flint and based him on Brooklyn Rock in the asteroid belt. The strip was lively and good-looking, but the *News* dropped it after three years. During that time, by the way, the *News* had not added any other exclusive strips.

United Feature's science fiction entry was *Twin Earths*. Convincing in detail and a touch wacky in content, the strip was the joint effort of writer Oskar Lebeck and artist Alden McWilliams. Lebeck, who'd been a set designer for Max Reinhardt in Berlin, fled to America in the 1930s. An artist as well as a writer, he eventually became an editor at Western Publishing's New York offices and was responsible for such comic books as *The Funnies*, *Walt Disney's Comics & Stories*, *Crackajack Funnies*, and *Animal Comics*, for which he bought Walt Kelly's *Pogo*. McWilliams started off in comic books in the late thirties and did several features for Lebeck, using the editor's scripts. He developed a style that had its roots in the work of Alex Raymond and

Tom Corbett, Space Cadet, Ray Bailey. ©1951, Field Enterprises, Inc.

became especially adept at drawing planes, boats, and just about anything mechanical. When Lebeck came up with the idea for *Twin Earths*, he invited McWilliams to do the drawing. The strip was accepted by United Feature and started as a daily on May 15, 1952.

Twin Earths was built around the premise, a familiar one in pulp science fiction, that the Earth had a twin planet hiding on the other side of the sun. It had several other things to offer, among the most important being flying saucers and pretty women. In Lebeck's version of the story, the planet Terra was ruled by women and they made up 90 percent of the population. Scores of years ahead of Earth technically, the Terrans developed space travel in the nineteenth century. Once they discovered a weightless metal, they built flying saucers and began to make surveillance trips to Earth. They have also built an orbiting space station from which they launch the saucers. As the strip began, a young woman named Vana called on Garry Verth at FBI headquarters and succeeded in convincing him she was a Terran agent who wanted to defect. A lengthy continuity now unfolded, mixing action and adventure with lectures and diagrams. While interesting, Lebeck's narrative unfolded at an exceedingly slow pace and it's likely that it was McWilliam's drawing and skill at rendering all the gadgets and hardware, as well as the numerous pretty women, that had readers coming back every day. It wasn't until the second year that Garry was able to accompany Vana and a pretty blond lady colonel to Terra.

Sky Masters, Jack Kirby–Wally Wood.

The strip managed to link the interest in and speculation about flying saucers with Cold War paranoia, much in the way several science fiction films of the day did. The notion that agents of an alien power are moving among us unnoticed had a special appeal in a period when many suspected that Russian agents and Communist sympathizers were everywhere. A *Twin Earths* Sunday page was added on December 27, 1953. Subscribing to the theory that the Sunday funnies were mostly for kids, it focused on Punch and Torro, two Terran lads who flew around their planet in their futuristic plane in search of adventure.

The George Matthew Adams Syndicate entered the space race in the spring of 1958. The new strip was *Sky Masters* and was signed Kirby-Wood. Jack Kirby, a comic book veteran, penciled the feature and Wally Wood, who'd made a reputation in the innovative EC comic books, provided inking. The two had just collaborated on the *Challengers of the Unknown* comic book for DC Comics. Two other Woods, Dave and Dick—brothers but no relation to Wally—did the writing. The syndicate publicity labeled the feature as "a great new comic strip that is modern, exciting, believable and authentic." The setting was the near future and Sky Masters, a typically sturdy and handsome Kirby hero, was a major in the Space Force. This military outfit ran America's space program and the daily continuity was about the space program and the launching of

Beyond Mars, *Lee Elias. The Caniff style in outer space.*
©1952, the News Syndicate Co., Inc.

a manned spacecraft called the Bird of Tomorrow. On Sundays there was a different story, involving Sky in adventures on The Wheel, "Earth's first manned station." *Sky Masters* was an expertly drawn high-tech strip, filled with convincing hardware. But there was little of the eccentricity and oddball characterizations that Kirby would bring to his 1960s Marvel Comics work and none of Wally Wood's humor.

While some syndicates were blasting off with new SF strips, others were equally diligent at reviving or refurbishing old properties. King Features dusted off the idea of a *Flash Gordon* daily and introduced a new version in November 1951. This was a more serious, realistic Flash than was seen in the swashbuckling Sunday page. The opening continuity dealt with a prison break on an orbiting prison satellite and all the hardware looked as though they were functional and not just props. Dan Barry, who'd previously done the *Tarzan* daily, was the artist. Another comic book alumnus, he'd developed and perfected his own, somewhat earthier, version of the Alex Raymond style. There was melodrama and a bit of hokum, yet the strip had the feel of being real science fiction. Barry had help from writers like Harry Harrison and artists such as Frank Frazetta, Harvey Kurtzman, Jack Davis, Fred Kida, Emil Gershwin, and his brother Sy Barry. Another strip that was undergoing mid-life changes was

Brick Bradford. In the fall of 1952 Paul Norris, after several spells of ghosting, officially took over the writing and drawing of the daily from the ailing Clarence Gray. When Gray died in 1957, Norris assumed the Sunday as well. His *Brick Bradford* was slicker and he avoided the lost civilization and mad scientist stories of the past and concentrated on space opera and planet adventure. The Associated Press' *Scorchy Smith* flirted with science fiction in the fifties. Rodlow Willard was in charge of the strip then and he converted the venerable aviator into a planet-hopping hero for a while.

King Features had brought Erle Stanley Gardner's flamboyant lawyer-sleuth, Perry Mason, to newspapers briefly in 1944 in a month-long adaption of *The Case of the Crooked Candle*. These were in the *Tarzan* mode, with text set beneath the illustrations. In 1946 there were two Perry Mason comic books, published by Hearst affiliate David McKay. *The Case of the Lucky Legs* was drawn by Vernon Greene, and *The Case of the Shoplifter's Shoe* by Paul Norris. When a regular comic strip finally started in May 1950, however, it was initially distributed by the much smaller Universal Syndicate. The original artist was Mel Keefer, a Navy veteran and a student of the Jefferson Machamer cartoon school in southern California. Gardner apparently had nothing to do with the scripts, which were provided by his publisher William Morrow in New York and not based on his best-selling novels. The strip did not replicate the punch and pace of the books, nor the effective dialogue and touches of humor. There was not even much of the celebrated Mason courtroom pyrotechnics, and the episodes bore names that did not match Gardner's book titles—*The Case of the Missing Cricket*, and *The Case of the Innocent Thief*. After some months, Keefer was replaced by Charles Lojgren, whose bland, wispy style was even less well-suited to illustrating the hardboiled lawyer's adventures. During his tenure, King Features took over the distribution of the strip.

The final Mason artist was Frank Thorne, who got the job by chance. A youth in his twenties at the time, he was in the office of comics editor Sylvan Byck, when a phone call came in to inform Byck that Lojgren had suffered a serious heart attack and wouldn't be able to continue. At the time Thorne was very much under the influence of Alex Raymond, which the samples he was showing clearly indicated. The Raymond look was Byck's favorite for adventure strips and he hired Thorne on the spot at a handsome salary. Thorne dealt from then on with Thayer Hobson, president of Morrow. He got the scripts from him, never learning who wrote them, and turned in his artwork each week to the publishing house. His version was the best looking by far, even though in later years it was considered a roadshow *Rip Kirby* at best. Despite a new look, the strip only managed to hang on until midway through 1952. Gardner would have much better luck with the television version of his Perry Mason character, which began in 1957.

The world's best-selling fictional private eye came barging into the funny papers in the spring of 1953. Mike Hammer, the hardboiled misogynist, had first appeared in Mickey Spillane's *I, The Jury* in 1947. A onetime comic book scriptwriter, Spillane hit the jackpot with his violent, sexy sleuth. Radio, movie, and television adaptations eventually followed. Spillane chose to license the comic strip rights to Jerry Iger's tacky Phoenix Features syndicate. The artist was Ed Robbins, who'd worked with Spillane years before at Funnies, Inc., a shop that packaged such comic books as *Blue Bolt* and *Marvel Mystery Comics*. For the Hammer strip Robbins drew in a scratchy style that suggested a punch-drunk Alex

Raymond. He modeled the tough, crewcut cop after Spillane himself. The continuities, written by Joe Gill, Robbins and, occasionally Spillane, were, like the novels, narrated in the first person, "I grinned at her—the kind of grin that called her a liar—a beautiful half-blonde liar" and "I didn't want to crash the party, but I had two good reasons—both of them cooling off in the morgue." There was violence in the strip, but little on-stage bloodshed and absolutely no nudity. In its early phase the strip, whose official title was *From The Files of ... Mike Hammer*, picked up enough papers, including the *New York Mirror* and the *San Francisco Chronicle*, to assure its success. Gradually, however, the list dwindled. In a January 1954 Sunday page, a panel depicted a blond young woman, her lingerie showing, tied to a bed in a cheap hotel room and about to have her naked foot burned by a hood's cigarette. For good measure, the same panel was repeated the following week. "I attempted to capture the flavor of Hammer as Spillane had created him," Robbins explained in an interview with mystery writer Max Allen Collins. "The panel of the girl on the bed brought screams of protest from some readers, and cancellations by some papers, notably the *New York Mirror*. This single page, and panel, resulted in the discontinuing of the strip." *Mike Hammer* ended that March.

A much gentler and more cerebral detective returned to the comics in March 1954. The Herald

Jet Scott, Jerry Robinson. The man from Scientifact is investigating the dumping of toxic waste. ©1953, New York Herald Tribune, Inc.

Tribune Syndicate, still adding story strips to its list, introduced a new *Sherlock Holmes*. A Holmes television show, starring Ronald Howard, also began in 1954 and the syndicate may have wanted to get in on what might prove to be a Holmes boom. It was written by Edith Meiser and Frank Giacoia got the credit as artist. Meiser, both a writer and a Broadway actress, had scripted a Holmes radio show in the 1930s. She adapted some Arthur Conan Doyle stories and invented new adventures of her own, including one in which the evil mastermind Professor Moriarty plots to unleash the Black Plague on Edinburgh. Giacoia had spent a decade or more as an inker in comic books. The drawing was by Mike Sekowsky, also recruited from comic books. Comparing the new version with the Holmes strip of the thirties, one critic observed that this one was "more dramatically staged, more concerned with Victorian atmosphere and more given to action and movement." It lasted until 1956.

Jack Webb first played Sgt. Joe Friday on the radio. The downbeat, gritty *Dragnet* came to NBC television in December 1951. The following year The L. A. Mirror Syndicate started a daily newspaper strip based on the popular show. The theme of *Dragnet*, with it's dum-da-dum-dum opening, and Webb's low-key delivery—"Just the facts, ma'am."— were already being parodied and parroted all across the country. For a while the newspaper strip used type-written copy in the captions to approximate Webb's voice over narrative techniques: "It was 7:23 A.M. and we were working out of Bunco." Several artists drew the strip, including Mel Keefer and Bill Ziegler.

Jed Cooper, American Scout, *Richard Fletcher. A portion of a Sunday page.* ©1954, the Chicago Tribune.

Webb changed artists because he had trouble finding one who could draw him as good looking as he thought he ought to be.

Jet Scott, from the rejuvenated *Herald Tribune*, combined science fiction and detection. Scott was a dark, lanky man who worked for a Pentagon branch known as the Office of Scientifact. In policing such problems as the theft of plutonium, the illegal dumping of toxic waste, and the development of strange new sonic weaponry, Scott also encountered mystery, murder, and a parade of lovely young women with such exotic names as Safron, Topaz, Feather, and Tawny. Jerry Robinson, an excellent comic book artist since his teens and a ghost for Bob Kane on *Batman*, did a lively job of illustrating Jet Scott. The scripts were by Sheldon Stark, who'd written the radio show *Straight Arrow* and before that the 1930s detective strip *Inspector Wade*. Perhaps too much of a hybrid, *Jet Scott* was shut down in 1955.

By the time Rex Stout's elephantine armchair detective Nero Wolfe appeared in a comic strip, the successful mystery novels in which he first appeared had been adapted to the screen—with Edward Arnold as the first Wolfe, Lionel Stander as his Boswell, and legman Archie Goodwin—and the radio, where he was portrayed by both Francis X. Bushman and Sydney Greenstreet. The *Nero Wolfe*

strip, syndicated by the second-string Columbia Features, got underway in November 1956. Stout received the writing credit, but France Herron actually provided the scripts. Herron was a comic book writer and editor who had worked on such characters as Captain Marvel, Batman, and Captain America. Among the artists who drew the strip, which ran daily and Sunday, were Mike Roy, former artist on *The Saint*, and Fran Matera, former artist on *Dickie Dare*.

The first new adventure strip inspired by the Cold War was *Wade Cabot*, introduced in the spring of 1953. A joint effort of Bob Robertson and Pat Sammon, with some help from Leonard Dworkins, the strip was set in the Middle East. "Here the forces of the Free World engage in a mighty undercover struggle against Communist powers ... with untold wealth of black gold, hidden beneath the sands ... with vital military positions as the prize to the victor.... All humanity watches—and waits!" Cabot was handsome and looked a bit like Burt Lancaster, the gray at his temples attesting that he was experienced. He was a former OSS agent, but his current affiliation was never made clear. His first assignment took him to Istanbul. "Nothing's changed since the war," he observed upon arrival. "Same sounds ... same smells ... and, I suppose, the same intrigues." The opening intrigue involved an archeological dig, a professor and his lovely daughter, a bald Russian villain named Lukov, a native dancer known as Tamara, and a cache of uranium. Such words as "Commie," "Red," and "Roosky" were frequently spoken. Although not badly drawn, *Wade Cabot* didn't especially shine in the script department. Even though it espoused an increasingly popular view of how to deal with Russia, it expired before year's end.

Frank Frazetta moved from comic books to comic strips in early 1952 with a feature that began as *Johnny Comet*. Its handsome, muscular hero lived a self-described life "wrapped up in racing cars and speedways." The scripts, although attributed to Pete DePaolo, a real-life racing driver who'd won at

Indianapolis a quarter of a century earlier, were actually the work of Earl Baldwin. His continuities offered racing thrills, romance, and mystery, including an early sequence with a slick villain named Al Gore. Frazetta, in his middle twenties at the time and still very much under the influence of his idol Hal Foster, did an ambitious job on the strip, frequently over-rendering panels. At the end of the year the title was changed to *Ace McCoy*, and Baldwin began to get a writing credit. The name change came as part of the storyline, occurring when a movie producer suggested Johnny needed "a good actor's name." All the other regulars remained unmodified, including the hero's blond girlfriend Jean and his bald mentor Pop Bottle. Frazetta has said that he had continually complained that the strip was stupid and that it ought to be changed. Changing Johnny to Ace was the only change anyone made. The McNaught Syndicate canceled the strip when it was just a week beyond a year old. A much healthier adventure strip proved to be Pete Hoffman's *Jeff Cobb*, a newspaperman saga drawn in the same style he'd used while ghosting *Steve Roper*. It began in 1954 and lasted into the middle 1970s.

Perhaps it was a portent of what lay ahead for story strips, but many of the continuity features that were introduced in the 1950s did not do especially well and relatively few of them got through the decade alive. The prolific Jack Sparling managed to achieve two flops in that ten-year span. They were *Mr. Rumbles* in 1955, which had the handicap of a leprechaun as the title character, and *Sam Hill* in 1957. And in 1960 the soap opera, *Honor Eden*, came and went. Sparling had probably tempted fate when he stated in the *Album of the National Cartoonists Society of America* that with this new strip "I *finally* bid farewell to the Losers Club."

The enormous popularity of *Hopalong Cassidy* on television had inspired, as noted earlier, a great wave of merchandising that included a Hoppy comic strip. Other established Western heroes were prompted to follow the silver-haired cowboy into TV and the funny papers. The enterprising Roy

Beetle Bailey, *Mort Walker. The first daily, when Beetle was a college boy.* ©1950, King Features Syndicate, Inc.

Rogers didn't make his television debut until 1951, but his King Features strip started in December, 1949. It was another product of Western Publishing, whose southern California office was turning out the Roy Rogers comic books. Tom and Chuck McKimson, graduates of the animated cartoon field, headed the strip packaging operation and they signed the pen name Al McKimson to the strip. It had several artists during its twelve year run, including Hy Mankin and Mike Arens. Gene Autry, the singing business tycoon, entered television in 1950 and the comic sections in 1952. The new strip was distributed by General Features and presented a modern Autry who flew his own plane as often as he rode Champion. Several artists worked on this as well, among them Tom Cooke.

The Cisco Kid television show and the comic strip both began in 1951. Duncan Renaldo as Cisco and his plump sidekick, Pancho, played by Leo Carillo, repeated their roles on the syndicated television series *Cisco Kid*. King Features introduced the strip, a daily only, in January. Argentine artist José Luis Salinas drew the feature. He was an excellent artist with a style that suggested both Alex Raymond and Frank Godwin. "He was a whiz at drawing both horses and pretty women," as one comics historian has noted, "both essential ingredients to the saga." The writer was Rod Reed, writer-editor with the Fawcett comic books. He was also the scriptwriter on Godwin's *Rusty Riley*. In explaining how the strip was done between such far-flung cities Reed said, "The Salinas-Reed collaboration may have been one

of the longest distance ones ever. It is 5,297 air miles from Buenos Aires to New York City. Another oddity is that, although we worked together smoothly (at least I thought so) for eighteen years we never met, conversed on the phone or exchanged correspondence. But my esteem for the artist never flagged and I looked forward each week to seeing a new set of proofs of Jose's live, vigorous drawing." Together they managed to capture some of the flavor of the movies and the television show and the expected mix of Western action and Cisco's habitual flirtations with just about every woman who stepped into a scene.

From radio came *Straight Arrow* in 1950. The half-hour kid's show had first aired on the Mutual network in 1949 and was written by Sheldon Stark. The hero was another fellow who had been raised by Indians. The show's opening monologue introduced the hero: "Steve Adams appeared to be nothing more than the young owner of the Broken Bow cattle spread. But when danger threatened innocent people and when evil-doers plotted against justice, then Steve Adams, rancher, disappeared. And in his place came a mysterious, stalwart Indian, wearing the dress and warpaint of a Commanche, riding the great golden palomino Fury!" The strip was syndicated by Bell and among its artists were John Belfi and Joe Certa, two comic book veterans. A real-life, more or less, Western hero showed up in July 1950 in the *Buffalo Bill* strip. Drawn by Fred Meagher, who was also doing *Straight Arrow* comic books at the time, it replaced *Broncho Bill* on the United Feature list. The original title of Harry O'Neill's strip had been, back in 1928, *Young Buffalo Bill*, so in a way the strip had come full circle.

Warren Tufts had abandoned *Casey Ruggles* in 1954. But like his friend Sam Peckinpah, he could not shake his interest in the Old West. In 1955, Tufts started a new feature called *Lance*, which he syndicated himself. It dealt with a Cavalry officer stationed in the Missouri and Kansas area in the 1840s, who was caught up, at the onset, in battles with the Sioux. Never especially successful, *Lance* ended in 1960. The drawing was exceptional, as was the color work on the Sunday page, and it was one of the most authentic Western strips ever attempted. Stan Lynde, a Westerner himself, began *Rick O'Shay* in 1958. An adventure strip with humor and drawn in a light style, it was set in the imaginary town of Conniption. Its title character was a lawman and the time period was post Civil War. Lynde left the strip in 1977, but *Rick O'Shay* continued until 1981.

Among the other Western strips was *Bronc Sadler*, drawn by Herb Rayburn. It started in January 1951 with a contemporary cowboy hero who traveled the rodeo circuit, winning prizes and getting entangled with pretty women and assorted crooks. *Bat Masterson*, based on the television version of the lawman's life, began in 1959. That was the same year the Gene Barry show started. France Herron wrote it and both Bob Powell and Howard Nostrand, who was working for Powell then, took a turn at drawing it. Lighter in tone was *Buck O'Rue*, a Western burlesque written by animation veteran Dick Huemer and drawn by Paul Murry.

The *Chicago Tribune* offered a pair of Sunday pages about American history, drawn by two different artists named Richard Fletcher. *Jed Cooper, Indian Scout* began at the very end of 1949 and then ran through the 1950s and into the 1960s. It was illustrated by Richard Martin Fletcher, who'd been

drawing the *Surgeon Stone* page for the *Trib*. Cooper was a handsome, young man in buckskins and coonskin cap. Fletcher drew in a bold, illustrative style that suited this account of the American colonies in revolutionary times. The writing was by Lloyd Wendt, a longtime newspaper reporter, who had signed on with the *Chicago Tribune* in 1934 and worked his way up to the position of Sunday editor. He also wrote several historical works. *Jed Cooper* was an appealing feature and was fairly evenhanded in its treatment of all the groups involved, colonists, British, and Indians. It ran, however, in only a few other papers. Rick Fletcher, a longtime assistant on *Dick Tracy* and the man who would take over the drawing of that strip when Chester Gould retired, was the artist on *The Old Glory Story*. Written by Athena Robbins, it took an historical approach to the American Revolution. Rick Fletcher used a more realistic style in the illustrations than he did on *Dick Tracy*.

The New York Herald Tribune Syndicate dealt with a different conflict, the Civil War, in *Johnny Reb and Billy Yank* (later shortened to *Johnny Reb*), a Sunday page that focused on two young soldiers, one in the Confederate Army and the other on the Union side. Though Frank Giacoia received sole credit, editor Ben Martin had a hand in the writing. And as usual, Giacoia had to rely on others to do the penciling. One of those who did the drawing on *Johnny Reb* was Jack Kirby.

Publishers Syndicate turned to the Bible for inspiration for their 1954 Sunday page, *Tales from the Great Book*. "Old Testament Bible stories spring to life—ever new," promised a promotion piece, "under the dramatic pen of John Lehti." This was pretty much a funny paper version of the *Picture Stories from the Bible* comic books of a decade earlier, with Bible episodes chopped up and given week-to-week continuity. Each Sunday ended with a teaser: "Next Week—Retribution!," "Next Week—Moses' strategy!," "Next Week—Four Barrels of Water!"

It was still possible to sell a serious sports strip, and several of them began in the 1950s. Elliot Caplin

Pogo, *Walt Kelly. One of the Bunny Rabbit strips.*

teamed with magazine illustrator John Cullen Murphy in 1950 to produce *Big Ben Bolt* for King Features. It was about a young man who came to America from an unnamed Communist country in Europe and became a successful boxer. Ray Gotto stepped up to the plate again in the summer of 1955 to take another crack at a baseball strip. *Cotton Woods* was more serious that his earlier *Ozark Ike*, which was still in business and constituted his chief competition. The new strip was drawn in his usual stiff, patient style, with hardly a square inch of surface free of crosshatching or some other time-consuming pen and ink technique. The opening daily introduced handsome blond Cotton, who was from the Carolina mountain village of Lonesome Gap and was "destined to rise from obscurity." His best girl was Candie Lane, "daughter of the wealthiest family in the community." Cotton, by contrast, lived in a "humble home on the edge of town" with his impoverished mother and crippled little brother. In need of money for an operation on little Willie, Cotton agreed to try out for a big-league team known as the Ducks. Derided as a runt and a half-pint, Cotton nevertheless proved to be a natural all-around baseball whiz and, after an impressive stretch with a farm team called the Fleas, became a star of the Ducks. The strip continued for three years, syndicated by General Features. During its run, Gotto did all the writing, but a couple of other artists helped out. Don Sherwood did a stretch, and the final cartoonist was Bob Sherry, who had tried a very short-lived baseball strip of his own, *Hook Slider*, in 1955.

Jack Berrill's *Gil Thorp*, distributed by the Chicago Tribune-New York News Syndicate, started in September 1958 and, unlike its 1950s competitors, is still running. It dealt with a high school coach and the teams he worked with. The setting was a suburban town, and the strip was concerned with the young jocks' lives on and off the playing field. Berrill had worked with Martin Branner on *Winnie Winkle*, but his drawing on his own strip showed the influence of one of his idols, Milton Caniff. *Mac Divot*, as the title indicates, was a strip about a golfer. It started in 1955, written by Jordan Lansky and drawn by Mel Keefer.

In 1956, after spending over fourteen years in California working on such Disney strips as *Mickey Mouse* and *Brer Rabbit*, Dick Moores relocated to Florida. He went to work for Frank King and gradually took over the drawing and writing of *Gasoline Alley*. The time spent with the Disney outfit had loosened Moores's style and broadened his range. With both his drawing and writing, he brought an extra folksiness and warmth to the long-running strip and enlivened it considerably. He was another of those artists who quite obviously enjoyed what he was doing and conveyed that in every panel. In the 1950s *Terry and the Pirates* continued to be drawn by George Wunder. But he had by now shed all traces of the Caniff approach. Wunder's work in this decade is his most impressive, for all its quirks and idiosyncrasies. He put an enormous amount of effort into *Terry*, and there's an energy to his drawing that few of his colleagues equaled. He kept Terry in the Air Force and now and then set a continuity in what was still French Indo-China. While that sort of thing was still perfectly acceptable, it would eventually topple the strip.

Walt Kelly increasingly used his *Pogo* strip for political satire and criticism in the 1950s. His most controversial character was Simple J. Malarkey, a shotgun-toting wildcat who bore more than a passing resemblance to the Communist-hunting Senator Joseph R. McCarthy. Malarkey first entered the swamp in May 1953 and proceeded to trample on the other animals' civil rights. He was also not above donning a KKK-type sheet and threatening to tar and feather his opponents. While political points of view had been expressed, usually somewhat obliquely, in comic strips before, Kelly was the first strip cartoonist to use the medium as a political cartoon. A liberal, he went after several conservative targets, including the John Birch Society. Not all the newspapers who carried *Pogo* shared Kelly's view that people like McCarthy were dangerous buffoons. Eventually, rather than quit poking fun at political figures and fools, Kelly came up

with his bunny rabbit strips. These were innocuous alternate dailies, featuring two rabbits doing mild and pleasant gag material. Whenever a Kelly strip that was sure to offend conservative editors and readers came up, the syndicate sent out the substitute strips along with it.

Humor, perhaps as a perceived antidote to the Cold War jitters, made a strong comeback in this decade. It was a simple, direct humor for the most

Hi and Lois, *Dik Browne.*
©1957, King Features
Syndicate, Inc.

part, not critical or satirical. The earlier funny paper staples—kids, pretty women, family life, pets—prevailed. The most auspicious kid strip of the century began unobtrusively on Monday, October 2, 1950. When it commenced, *Peanuts* by Charles M. Schulz appeared in only seven newspapers. It was a tiny strip, about half the size of most of the others, and it usually appeared on a page by itself somewhere in the newspaper. United Feature touted it as "the GREATEST *little* Sensation Since TOM THUMB!" On that first day, as Richard Marschall notes,

> *Shermy and Patty issued history's first recorded put-down of Charlie Brown.... The early list of characters was rounded out by Snoopy, and at the beginning Schulz himself had not yet decided upon a lead. The large cast of strong characters that populates* Peanuts *today was not present in the strip's early years. Characters were added slowly but with regularity; the strip's famous tone—children speaking as adults—was not present from the start; there was a definite evolution toward Schulz' singular modes. All of which confirms the cartoonist's genius; his contributions have been arrived at instinctively rather than clinically.*

The Schulz genius and his simple, appealing drawing took a while to capture a sizable audience. It took *Peanuts* over two years to achieve a list of at least fifty papers. The rise continued, accelerating, and fairly soon the strip was in hundreds of papers and later in thousands. The licensing and merchandising of the *Peanuts* characters, particularly Snoopy, brought in millions for both Schulz and United Feature.

Schulz had been a magazine gag cartoonist before Charlie Brown, Snoopy, Lucy, and the rest allowed him to leave magazine

Betsy & Me, *Jack Cole. The first daily. ©1958, Field Enterprises, Inc.*

work, but he had not been notably successful. Mort Walker, on the other hand, was doing very well, selling to numerous magazines ranging from the *Saturday Evening Post* to *1000 Jokes* when he began *Beetle Bailey* for King Features. Kansas-born and a dropout of the Landon course, Walker was determined to become a cartoonist since boyhood. At the University of Missouri he worked on the humor magazine *Showme*. After college, many of his magazine cartoons were devoted to college life, and he developed a character named Spider, who closely resembled the later Beetle. Using the Spider character, Walker developed a college life strip and submitted it to Sylvan Byck at King Features. Byck bought it, Walker changed the name to *Beetle Bailey*, and it began running in September 1950. Walker was somewhat wordier in his balloons than he would later be, and his drawing was more detailed, but he already showed a strong ability to stage a gag and deliver a punchline. *Beetle*, however, was far from being a hit. "We began and it was terrible," Walker once said, "a dismal failure. Started in about twelve papers. At the end of six months we were in twenty-five. I found out later they considered dropping it when the year's contract was up. But then, I went to Sylvan Byck and I said the Korean War's going on, maybe I ought to put Beetle in the Army." At first Byck was against the notion, but when an editor from their biggest client paper at the time, the *Philadelphia Inquirer*, called the syndicate and made a similar suggestion, he decided to go ahead with it. The Army made a man of Beetle and turned him into one of the most popular comic strip characters in the country. "*Beetle* took off after that," said Walker, "and immediately sold to about a hundred

Terr'ble Thompson, *Gene Deitch*. ©1955, United Feature Syndicate, Inc.

more papers." It has been successful ever since for the men of Camp Swampy.

In 1954, Walker created his second strip and brought in Dik Browne as its artist. "*Hi and Lois* was started because someone had asked me to write gags for a family strip for another syndicate and I called Sylvan Byck and I asked, 'Can I write gags for another syndicate?' He said, 'No, but if you want to write a family strip, write one for us.' And it was as easy as that.... I found myself in the midst of writing another strip and looking for an artist, and found Dik Browne. Turned over a rock and there he was." No stranger to the funnies, Browne had for several years been drawing advertising strips for Johnstone & Cushing. He had also created the Chiquita Banana advertising character and updated the Campbell Soup Kids. An inventive and talented man, Browne made *Hi and Lois* one of the most visually interesting strips on the comic page. A gentler and more sentimental variation of the basic *Blondie* setup, it became a hit. Lois is Beetle's sister, and he now and then drops in on her and her family.

The new artists of the fifties came chiefly from two areas. Adventure strip men were recruited mostly from comic books and, following in the wake of Mort Walker, gag cartoonists found themselves increasingly welcome by syndicate editors looking for humor strips and panels. Hank Ketcham had put in time as an animator with Walt Disney

Productions. After Navy service in World War II, he became a frequent contributor of gag cartoons to slick magazines. Adapting a kid he'd used in the magazines to a daily panel, Ketcham sold *Dennis the Menace* to the Post-Hall Syndicate (until recently it had been the New York Post Syndicate). It started in March 1951. Named after Ketcham's own son, the freckled Dennis was, as one historian has noted, "a menace only occasionally and always by accident."

Dick Cavelli was also an established gag cartoonist, selling to many of the same markets as Ketcham, when he began *Morty Meekle* for NEA in 1955. Morty was a nondescript, white-collar office worker. Cavelli seemed more interested in the oddball little kids he used in the strip and, finally, in 1966 Morty was vanquished and the kids took over. Under the name *Winthrop* the strip continued into the 1990s. It was simply drawn, funny, and given to fantasy. At times it looked like a surreal version of *Peanuts*.

Jack Cole's ambition since childhood was to be a magazine cartoonist. An exceptional artist, he was inventive and had a quirky sense of humor. Coming to New York from the Midwest in the late 1930s, he'd been unable to make a living as a gag cartoonist. The comic book industry was starting up and Cole found work there, eventually becoming one of the major artists in the field. He created the popular, and not completely serious, superhero Plastic Man. Never completely content in comic books, Cole made frequent attempts to crack the cartoon markets. In the early 1950s he began to sell beautifully drawn, if rather obvious, girlie cartoons to *Playboy*. He soon established himself as a top contributor and, at the suggestion of Hugh Hefner, he and his wife moved to the Chicago area where the magazine was then located. In 1958, Cole fulfilled another longtime ambition when he sold a comic strip to the Chicago Sun-Times Syndicate. Dorothy Portugais was an editor at the syndicate and she later recalled that Cole had simply walked in off the street one day, after a visit to *Playboy*, with about five or six weeks of penciled strips and two or three finished ones. The syndicate loved the strip, titled *Betsy and Me*, and offered Cole a contract within a few days of his submission. Nobody up there had ever heard of him and they didn't find out until after he was signed up that he was a veteran of nearly twenty years in comic books and one of *Playboy*'s favorite cartoonists.

Betsy and Me was in the young married couple category, yet unlike anything else in that genre. Cole adapted a simplified style, reminiscent of the drawing approach in the UPA animated cartoons, featuring Mr. Magoo and Gerald McBoing Boing, of a few years earlier. His focal character was Chester B. Tibbit, a young man with an eggshaped head who worked as a department store floor-walker. Chester would begin many of the strips sitting in his living room and talking directly to the reader: "It all began a few years ago. I'll never forget the day I met Betsy. Let's see ... was it June or August?" Chester had a tendency to romanticize or spruce up the past, and many times the gag was built on the contrast between what he was telling the reader in his voice-over narration and what was actually going on in the panel. Chester talked about his wife Betsy and their little genius son Farley, how he'd met his wife, their wedding, the birth of their son, his job at the department store, about their friends, their new car, and leaving their apartment and moving to a suburban home. The strip began in May, and by August, Cole brought the family up to date and was ready to continue the story in the present. According to Dorothy Portugais, the new strip was successful from the start and continued to pick up papers. She saw Cole every week and had lunch with him on several occasions. She was fond of him and thought of him as a pleasant, easygoing sort of man. On the morning of August 15 that year, Cole went to a store in the town of Cary and bought a .22

pistol. Getting back in the car, he drove for awhile. Then he stopped and shot himself in the head.

The dumb blonde made a substantial comeback in the 1950s. Anita Loos's prototypical Lorelei Lee, played by Carol Channing, captivated Broadway in the musical version of *Gentlemen Prefer Blondes* that debuted in December 1949 and ran for 740 performances. When the show became a movie in 1953, Marilyn Monroe, the worldwide epitome of the beautiful but dumb stereotype, starred as Lorelei. Among the several pretty scatterbrains who entered the comics was Mamie, who appeared in a Sunday page of the same name that started in 1950. It was drawn by the erstwhile glorifier of the flapper, Russell Patterson. A cartoonist named Yar Yarbrough, who was one of the *Superman* ghosts in comic books, started *Tallulah* in 1950. He later changed the title, probably after complaints from Tallulah Bankhead, to *Jezabelle Jones*. The *My Friend Irma* show, starring the noted flighty blond Marie Wilson, started out on radio and branched out into television in 1952. It also inspired a short-lived comic strip in 1950. *It's Me, Dilly!* began in 1957 and was credited to Alfred James and Mel Casson. James was actually Alfred Andriola and he and Casson provided the gags. The actual artist was Sururi Gumen, who'd been ghosting Andriola's *Kerry Drake* for several years. This is one of the few instances in comics history where a cartoonist used a pen name for work someone else was ghosting for him. Dilly was a blond model who looked a good deal like Marilyn Monroe.

One of the most unusual strips of the decade was *Terr'ble Thompson*, begun by animator Gene

Deitch in 1955. It was about a very odd little boy who had his "World Hedd Quarters" in a tree house and was regarded far and wide as "the bravest, fiercest, most-best hero of all time." Deitch had worked for the innovative UPA studios, and his strip was drawn in a simple, effective version of their house style. This approach to drawing, the antithesis of the Disney look, had already spread into advertising and could be seen regularly in both the print medium and in animated television commercials. Deitch was the first to apply this modernist style to a syndicated strip. *Terr'ble Thompson* was visually a great deal of fun but the continuities, involving the little hero with historical figures like Columbus, were not especially funny. The strip folded after six months, but Deitch did not give up on the idea. In 1956, he was hired as a supervisor by Terrytoons. For the very popular live-action kid show *Captain Kangaroo*, Deitch created a daily five-minute cartoon serial. Its central character was an invincible boy champion of justice, and he shared the same initials as his comic strip predecessor. Tom Terrific, aided by Mighty Manfred the Wonder Dog, had a much longer career than poor Terr'ble.

Mort Walker came up with a third comic strip in 1957. Drawn by his former assistant Frank Roberge, it was titled *Mrs. Fitz' Flats* and dealt with the goings on in a boarding house that was full of such eccentric characters that even Major Hoople might have balked at staying there. Ralston "Bud" Jones had been a magazine cartoonist and he also worked for Walker, specializing in thinking up gags. In 1957 he and fellow gag cartoonist Frank Ridgeway invented *Mr. Abernathy*, which was about an aging little millionaire who divided his time among such rich men's leisure activities as golf and pursuing beautiful women. Mell Lazarus's *Miss Peach*, which has been described as "a droll strip about a gang of improbably bright children whose private clubs, squads and committees virtually con-

King Aroo, *Jack Kent. The king and Yupyop have just returned from a bit of time traveling. ©1954, McClure Syndicate.*

trol their school," started in February, 1957. Miss Peach was the teacher at Kelly School and she tried to bring some order to the chaos. Lazarus worked in a simple style, suggesting the work of one of Miss Peach's more gifted pupils. The strip was originally syndicated by the *New York Herald Tribune*. Several canine characters also emerged in the fifties. These included *Rivets* by George Sixta, *Marmaduke* by Brad Anderson, and *Scamp*, another Disney property drawn anonymously by cartoonists such as Roger Armstrong over its run.

Johnny Hart, after serving in the Air Force in Korea, sold a smattering of gag cartoons to *Collier's* and the *Saturday Evening Post*. In 1958 the *Herald Tribune* took on his *B.C.* Though it has a prehistoric setting, it bears no resemblance to *Alley Oop* and is used by Hart as a vehicle to indulge in his fondness for word play, puns, and non sequitur humor. He was an early practitioner of the less-is-more school of cartooning and the gags in *B.C.* are essentially verbal in nature. The strip, as Dennis Wepman has pointed out, "features a well-defined cast of cave men, women and animals (no children appear, as sex has apparently not been discovered yet)."

Remembered today chiefly for the many award-winning children's books he wrote and illustrated from the late 1960s onward, Jack Kent also created one of the most unusual strips of the 1950s. When he was a teenager in the thirties, Kent had corresponded with several cartoonists, including Tom McNamara and George Herriman. Although his strip bore some similarities to *Krazy Kat* and to the more recent *Pogo*, it was at the same time a highly individual work. *King Aroo* got going in November 1950 with an introductory strip that began, "Once upon a time (for this is *that* sort of story) there lived a king whose name was HIS IMPERIAL REGALITY KING AROO—but everybody just called him 'Your Royalty' for short. His kingdom was called MYOPIA—and it covered almost an entire acre." Kent also introduced the other regular human character, the King's Royal Retinue, the mustached yesman Yupyop. Most of the other residents of

Myopia were talking animals, such as Mr. Pennipost the kangaroo mailman, Professor Yorgle, an erudite dog, Mr. Elephant, who was absent-minded, and Drexel Dragon. Some of them looked and behaved like animals, others walked on their hind legs and wore clothes. There was also a variety of talking birds, notably the gifted poet Dipody Distich. All sorts of other characters wandered through Myopia, including Cupid, Diogenes, and Bo Beep. When Yupyop asked Bo Beep how she'd lost her sheep, she explained it was in a poker game with the wolf—"I had four of a kind but the wolf had a royal flush." From time to time the King and Yupyop ventured into neighboring kingdoms. One such was Hebefrenia, which was divided—by a dotted line down the middle—into West Hebefrenia and East Hebefrenia and resembled a Salvador Dali landscape. King Aroo was also fond of visiting the Kingdom Next Door, since he had a crush on the Princess who resided there. Yupyop fared better in the kingdom of Antimacassar. It had a population of two, pretty twin sisters named Selma and Velma. For awhile Yupyop filled in as king.

King Aroo has been described as "an engaging blend of childlike fantasy and literate wordplay." Kent was indeed fascinated with words, with puns, rhymes, asides, and out-and-out nonsense. But unlike some strips that dealt in verbal humor, Kent's was also visually gratifying. He had an easy, attractive style that was less spare than the one he developed for his kids' books. The pace of the strip was leisurely and Kent's amiable, naive little king would often go off on a tangent while on one of his quests with Yupyop. He might stop along the roadway for a few days to chat with a perplexed caterpillar or wander over to the edge of his kingdom to take a look at the infinity that loomed beyond it. The McClure Syndicate handled *King Aroo* in the beginning, placing it in about one hundred newspapers, including the *San Francisco Chronicle* and the *New York Mirror*. When the list began to dwindle, McClure dropped it. In the final years of the Myopia saga, the loyal *Chronicle* paid Kent to draw it and managed to place it with a happy few other papers.

Some of the other oddities were *Short Ribs* by Frank O'Neal, which NEA introduced in 1958. The strip alternated characters and locales, moving from a medieval setting with a king, knights, and a jester, one day to the Old West with lawmen, owlhoots, and the like. O'Neal was one more former magazine cartoonist. Al Jaffee was a comic book artist in the 1940s and then became a *Mad* regular. His *Tall Tales* was a long, thin panel that delivered a pantomime gag each day. Arnold Roth, an early disciple of Ronald Searle, was an established magazine illustrator and had been a contributor to Harvey Kurtzman's briefly seen *Humbug* magazine. From 1959 to 1961 he drew a Sunday page, *Poor Arnold's Almanac*, for the Herald Tribune Syndicate. It was a lively potpourri of funny bits and pieces. The versatile Gill Fox, a veteran of comic books and advertising strips, teamed up with Selma Diamond, writer, television personality, and later actress on *Night Court*, to produce *Jeanie*. It was a humorous Sunday page about another young woman who came to Manhattan to succeed in show business. Early in the next decade Fox took over the longrunning suburban panel *Side Glances*.

Chapter 11

A Funny Thing Happened on the Way to Nixon

The 1960s was an uneasy decade, a time of division, protest, and violence. American society was, depending on what pundits you followed, being fragmented or brought together, polarized, or healed. The sixties witnessed the rise of a political and cultural underground and the growth of what came to be called the counterculture. For the most part, the comics reflected little of what was going on in the country. The civil rights movement did inspire a few new strips, the escalating war in Vietnam was fought in some of the established military-based features, and Walt Kelly became even more political. Most of the new comic strips that were born in these years, however, avoided controversy or commitment, and the majority of them were in the humor category. It was not an especially good time for heroes or heroics. The number of adventure strips dropped, and, with one exception, none of the new straight strips survived. The recruitment of gag cartoonists continued as more magazine veterans started newspaper strips. For good measure, the Mort Walker group generated a couple of new ones, too.

By the early 1960s, over 90 percent of the homes in America had television sets. The availability of large quantities of free entertainment had several effects on the funnies. It gave rise among editors to the theory that with complete dramas available every night, the popularity of adventure strip continuities that stretched over weeks and weeks would diminish. Syndicates also came to believe that a public brainwashed by television was developing an increasingly short attention span. Terser, simpler strips with easy to understand jokes were what this restless audience required. In addition, the syndicates continued to adapt popular TV shows to the comics format and to appropriate some of television's themes and techniques.

The Hanna-Barbera cartoon factory had begun to turn out television shows in the late 1950s, all done in the limited animation style they'd perfected. Early hits were the kid series *Huckleberry Hound* and *Yogi Bear*. *The Flintstones*, a Stone Age knockoff of Jackie Gleason's *The Honeymooners*, was first telecast in the fall of 1960. Aimed at adults as well as children, the new animated series aired on ABC in the evening and proved an almost immediate hit. A *Flintstones* comic strip followed in October 1961. At the same time, a *Yogi Bear* strip began. Gene Hazelton, a former gag cartoonist and animator, drew both. Jay Ward's *The Bullwinkle Show*, another animated show aimed at young and old alike, came to NBC in September 1961. A comic strip, drawn by Al Kilgore, started soon after. "For three years,"

ICE CREAM

"I'm out of cones."

Big George, *Virgil Partch.* ©1976, Field Enterprises, Inc.

Kilgore once explained, "it appeared in the most obscure towns in the U.S." As it was, the comic strip ran longer than the show.

Rowan & Martin's Laugh-In began its weekly run in January 1968 and very soon was the top-rated show in America. In addition to comedians Dan Rowan and Dick Martin, many of its other regulars, such as Ruth Buzzi, Goldie Hawn, Arte Johnson, and Henry Gibson, became instant celebrities and the show's catch phrases—"Sock it to me," "Beautiful downtown Burbank," "You bet your bippy"—spread across the country. Even President Richard M. Nixon popped up on the show to intone dourly, "Sock it to me." In September of the year the Chicago Tribune-New York News Syndicate introduced a *Laugh In* (no hyphen in their version) comic strip that tried to capture the hot show's frantic pace, shifting locales, outrageous one-liners, and borderline bawdy tone. The artist picked for the strip was Roy Doty, a veteran commercial artist and cartoon illustrator with a concise and simple deco-

rative style. Doty shared the writing with the prolific Paul S. Newman. The strip and the show both continued until May 1973.

The practice of having magazine cartoonists draw newspaper features continued into the 1960s. Virgil Partch, better known as Vip, drew in a style that blended his early training as a Disney animator with his fascination with such artists as Picasso. He had a screwball sense of humor and a near obsession with wordplay. From the 1940s on he'd been a very successful gag cartoonist. In the early 1960s he undertook *Big George*, a gag panel on weekdays and a traditional Sunday page on the weekend. The feature got off to a splendid start, with over three hundred papers, but eventually slipped considerably. As Dennis Wepman has pointed out, it was "something of a disappointment to his fans. The barroom and the desert island—two cartoon settings Partch had made peculiarly his own—were abandoned for the suburban town; and the voluptuous girls, heavy drinkers, and soldiers of his magazine cartoons had to make way for a middle-class married couple."

Jerry Dumas went to work for Mort Walker as an assistant and gagman on *Beetle Bailey* in the middle 1950s. In his spare time he sold cartoons to such magazines as *The Saturday Evening Post* and *The New Yorker*. His *Sam's Strip* ran from 1961 to 1963 and was about a fat fellow who, with the help of a thin associate, ran his own comic strip. The gags, which Walker and Dumas both provided, made fun of the conventions of comic strips. Sam, for example, had a closet full of sound effect words like "bong," "pow," and "bop," and he once consulted a realtor about getting a small desert island to use in his desert island jokes. Sam would often directly address his readers, he'd sometimes interview new characters for jobs in his strip, and noted comics stars, ranging from Blondie and Popeye to Happy Hooligan and Krazy Kat, would frequently drop in. It was an amusing and brightly drawn strip, but, as Dumas later noted, "too far out for too many editors."

King Features and its comics editor Sylvan Byck continued to be receptive to magazine cartoonists. Jerry Marcus had been a successful gag artist since the late 1940s, appearing in *The Saturday Evening Post, The New Yorker, Collier's,* and dozens of other top markets. His *Trudy* panel was introduced by King in March 1963. It was about a young married couple who lived a middle class life in

the suburbs. Marcus has an exceptional ear for the speech cadences of suburban life and a keen eye for its props. Bob Weber was also an established magazine cartoonist when he sold *Moose Miller* to King in 1965. Moose, an overweight layabout who lives to freeload and avoid gainful employment, was the antithesis of the conventional suburban head-of-the-household. He and his wife Molly and their kids have hung on for three decades, studiously avoiding upward mobility. Weber draws in a broad, lively style and is a great fan of clutter. There is a generous

Trudy, Jerry Marcus. ©1995, King Features Syndicate, Inc.

"How come you always make a crunching sound when you eat soft-boiled eggs?"

Sam's Strip, Jerry Dumas. ©1962, King Features Syndicate, Inc.

supply of it indoors and out at the Moose and Molly homestead. Other syndicates also welcomed gag cartoonists. *Eek & Meek* was in the tradition of *B.C.* The drawing was minimal, the humor usually entirely verbal. Rather than cave folk, though, it was staffed with talking mice. Howie Schneider, who contributed to such magazines as *Playboy, The New Yorker,* and *Esquire,* sold the strip to NEA in 1965.

The Born Loser, a simply drawn strip about the frustrations and setbacks of a bland, middle-class family, began in 1965. It was the work of Art Sansom, a longtime resident of the NEA art bullpen. At the high point of its circulation, the strip appeared in over one thousand papers worldwide. *Tiger,* a nicely drawn and rather quiet kids strip by Bud Blake, was another 1965 entrant. *Redeye,* begun in 1967, was a throwback to the ethnic strips of decades before. It offered a cast of Indians delivering a joke a day. Gordon Bess, a former art director for a greeting card company, was the creator. Introduced in 1968, *The Dropouts* was drawn by Howard Post, erstwhile comic book artist and animator. It dealt with a bunch of disparate characters marooned on a desert island and was in the vein of the earlier television hit *Gilligan's Island.*

Bil Keane's *The Family Circus,* originally called *The Family Circle,* was introduced by the Register and Tribune Syndicate early in 1960. Without doubt one of the gentlest and most heartwarming panels in comics history, Keane's feature became enormously successful. In 1964, Johnny Hart added a second

strip to his list. *The Wizard of Id*, set in a mythical kingdom in a time period that might be the Middle Ages, was illustrated by Brant Parker with jokes provided by Hart and his two gagmen. Drawn in what has been described as a "loose, slapdash style of broad caricature befitting its less-than-subtle humor," the strip rapidly climbed to a circulation of over one thousand papers. Mort Walker took on another strip in 1968. *Boner's Ark* was about Captain Boner, a human, and a boatload of talking animals. Walker signed it Addison, using his first name as a pen name. He was assisted by Dumas and Ralston Jones on gags and by Frank Johnson on the drawing. Never as successful as *Beetle Bailey* or *Hi & Lois*, the strip has managed to stay afloat. It is another example of a strip with a restricted setting.

Wee Pals, begun in 1974 by Morrie Turner, was something of a landmark. Turner was, as Dennis Wepman points out, "one of the first black cartoonists to use race relations as a major theme for humor in a nationally syndicated strip." A feature that probably could not have gotten going in an earlier period, *Wee Pals* centered on an integrated group of kids and stressed racial diversity. Ted Shearer was a Jamaican-born black cartoonist. His *Quincy*, begun in 1970 for King Features, also focused on an integrated group of street kids. Shearer had worked for the *Amsterdam News* and sold magazine cartoons. At the time he sold *Quincy*, he'd been an art director with the BBD&O ad agency for fifteen years. His strip was subtler than Turner's and more slickly drawn. Shearer felt he should not preach in his strip, even though "I've been hurt so many times—being a so-called 'Black-

American,' but I always have to catch myself and realize I'm doing a humor strip and not an editorial cartoon. It goes back to the time I was in the army—a segregated army—and after, and I can remember so many bitter things which have happened to my kids—my brother—the hurt which a lot of people aren't aware of—even when they're dealing it out." His approach involved letting readers "see the conditions under which these individuals live. In other words, I'm making it possible for the reader to come to his *own* conclusion."

Dateline: Danger began in November 1968 and was promoted by the Field Enterprises Syndicate as an integrated adventure strip. Black characters had been in adventure strips before, but in this one the black and the white characters were on an equal footing, and there was not a white hero and black sidekick setup. Written by John Saunders and drawn by Alden McWilliams, *Dateline: Danger* owed something to the *I Spy* television show that ran on NBC from 1965 to 1968. The show had starred Robert Culp and Bill Cosby as a pair of world-traveling secret agents. As *The Complete Directory to Prime Time*

Quincy, *Ted Shearer. The punchline panel from a daily strip.* ©1970, King Features Syndicate, Inc.

Network TV Shows notes, Cosby was "the first black performer to have a starring role in a regular dramatic series on American television." McWilliams had drawn the comic book version of *I Spy*, and when Bob Hall, head of the syndicate, decided he wanted a strip with a similar feel, McWilliams was one of the artists he approached. *Dateline: Danger* focused on two investigative reporters for the Global News Service, the black Danny Raven and the white Troy Young. In addition to action and adventure, the strip also dealt with the family life of both its protagonists.

While *Dateline: Danger* was moderately successful, the integrated adventure strip never managed to come a popular category. In January 1970, the *Chicago Tribune* gave it a try with *Friday Foster*. Written by Jim Lawrence and drawn by Spain-based artist Jorge Longaron, it was about a young black woman who became the assistant to a highly successful white magazine photographer. The settings ranged from the streets of Harlem to the haunts of the rich and famous. Friday, who looked a good deal like Diana Ross, soon found herself traveling all over the world and mingling with the Jet Set as her handsome boss, blond Shawn North, covered assignments for various slick periodicals. *Friday Foster* combined soap opera situations with spy movie intrigues. When the strip ended in 1975, the dependable Gray Morrow was doing the drawing.

Despite social upheavals, soap opera remained popular in the sixties. In 1961, Nicholas Dallis invented his third soaper, *Apartment 3-G*. Rather than come up with another pen name, he let artist Alex Kotzky take sole credit. An exceptional cartoonist, Kotzky began in comic books in the early 1940s. He assisted Will Eisner on *The Spirit* and later ghosted *Steve Canyon*. The three girls in 3-G were, as syndicate promotion copy introduced them, "Tommie, dedicated, big-hearted nurse; Margo, smart, stylish ad agency secretary; LuAnn, wealthy young widow with a weakness for underdogs." Night time television soaps, both medical dramas, inspired two strips. *Dr. Kildare*, based on the popular movie series, which was based on the stories of Max Brand, became a television show in September 1961. Richard Chamberlain starred. The ever enterprising Elliot Caplin, whose earlier *Dr. Bobbs* had been inspired in part by the Kildare movies, put together a comic strip version of the television show and sold it to King Features in 1963. Ken Bald was the artist. *Ben Casey*, a similar though somewhat gutsier show, went on the air a few days after *Dr. Kildare*. It starred Vince Edwards and was produced by Bing Crosby. In October 1962, NEA introduced a *Ben Casey* strip. The artist was twenty-one-year-old Neal Adams, who was influenced by magazine illustrators Austin Briggs and Bernie Fuchs, and comic strip artists Lou Fine and Stan Drake.

When NEA originally contemplated adding *Robin Malone* to their package of strips, what they had in mind was a traditional soap opera. They approached Bob Lubbers, provided him with a sample script, and asked him to sign on as the artist. He thought the theme was much too trite, but rather than turn it down, he persuaded the syndicate to let him do a different kind of *Robin Malone*. He brought in Paul S. Newman, who wrote the first six months

Friday Foster, *Jorge Longaron. Soap opera and street lingo meet in this sample from a Sunday page. ©1970, The* Chicago Tribune.

of continuity. Romance was still in the strip, but it was mixed with adventure and international intrigue. Robin, a blonde of the sort Alfred Hitchcock was fond of starring in his later films, was a young widow and the richest woman in the world. After a few months, Lubbers decided that the continuities should be lighter and more satirical, closer to what had been done on *Long Sam*. He had Stu Hample take over writing the scripts, and the tone of *Robin Malone* changed, and the look became more cartoony. The strip held on for three years, but did not manage to become a hit. Aware that the strip was going to end and ticked off with the syndicate for not renewing the contract, Lubbers and Hample came up with a downbeat finish for the strip. The final panel of the final day was a long shot of a figure, that might or might not be Robin, plunging from a penthouse parapet. Some of the tiny cars on the street far below formed the message "RIP RM."

Batman, in a campy version that spoofed the idea of costumed crime-fighting, came to ABC television in January 1966. An immediate hit, the show inspired an enormous wave of merchandising. One of the innumerable byproducts was a new comic strip, packaged by DC Comics and distributed by the Ledger Syndicate. Whit Ellsworth, former editor-in-chief at DC and supervisor of the earlier *Superman* television show, wrote the first scripts. Among the several pencillers and inkers were Sheldon Moldoff, Carmine Infantino, Joe Giella, Al Plastino, and Nick Cardy. Not as campy as the

Adam West show nor anywhere near as much fun, the strip did toss in an occasional sound effect, and Robin would occasionally exclaim something like "Holy explosives!" It managed to outlast the show, but in 1972 underwent some strange changes. "As of January 3, 1972, and in mid-story, the Ledger Syndicate replaced the previous creative staff with another group," reports Batman historian Joe Desris. "Within a few months, Batman and Robin had disappeared from the strip bearing their names. The recurring characters consisted of Bruce Wayne, Dick Grayson, and a superhero named Galexo. Ledger carried the feature into 1974."

Between July 1965 and December 1966, the number of U.S. combat troops taking part in the war in Vietnam grew from 23,000 to 385,000. As reports of casualties and atrocities increased, so did the protest movement in America. In retrospect, April 1966 does not seem an auspicious time to launch a pro-military adventure strip. Nevertheless, the Chicago Tribune Syndicate introduced *Tales of the Green Beret*. The writer credit went to Robin Moore, whose 1965 novel *The Green Berets* was the inspiration. Joe Kubert, an excellent artist who'd been in comics since his early teens, was chosen to do the drawing. Though warfare was not his favorite subject, he had recently been editing and drawing for such DC Comics war titles as *Our Fighting Forces* and

Star Spangled War Stories, and his most popular character then was the tough World War II hero Sgt. Rock. The central character in the new strip was Chis Tower, a surrogate for Moore, who was a handsome, roving reporter for his father's news syndicate. Tower covered several Green Beret counter-insurgency operations around the world. First in Vietnam, then in Latin America, and after that in Berlin. In the first week, the copy explained exactly who the Green Berets were: "The U. S. Army Special Forces— fighting men who proudly wear the GREEN BERET—were formed in 1952. Special Forces guerrilla teams first fought behind enemy lines in Korea.... Every GREEN BERET speaks at LEAST two languages fluently ...

Robin Malone, *Bob Lubbers. A typical business day for the Widow Malone.* ©1969, NEA, Inc.

and some speak as many as TEN. All the languages of an area are studied ... including the DIALECT and IDIOM of the ENEMY." The enemies that Tower watched, and sometimes helped the Green Berets combat, were all described as being ruthless Reds of one sort or other. A sufficient number of readers did not like the strip. Kubert pulled out in 1967 and was replaced by John Celardo.

King Features took a chance on a historical adventure strip in 1967. *Captain Kate* was by Jerry and Hale Skelly, a husband and wife team. Jerry Skelly, an advertising agency art director, drew the strip, and Hale Skelly wrote it initially. Jerry worked in a competent but not especially illustrative style. Fairly soon, Archie Goodwin came aboard as the new scriptwriter. He was already writing *Secret Agent Corrigan* for King. This was the updated version of *Secret Agent X-9* and was drawn by Al Williamson. Goodwin never got a credit on *Captain Kate*. The strip was set in what looked to be the eighteenth century and centered around a dark-haired young woman who inherited a sailing ship named *Wind Song*. This allowed her to have an assortment of adventures on the high seas. Although Captain Kate was certainly a liberated woman, the strip never became very popular. Interest in adventure strips of any kind was beginning to wane, and it is doubtful that even a livelier historical saga could have survived beyond the early 1970s.

Chapter 12

No More Heroes

The 1970s saw the decline and fall of a number of the major adventure strips and, a mild resurgence at the decade's end not withstanding, pretty much marked the end of the whole genre. A humor strip offering a joke a day, in as few words as possible, again became the standard. Several of the long-time continuity strips ended in the early years of the decade. There was a new flurry in the late 1970s, but more than half of those were adaptions of material from other media—movies, television, and comic books. Only one of them survived for more than a few years. Over a dozen of the more than thirty new humor strips that began in this same period are still appearing in newspapers and some of them are among the most popular in the world. The soap opera strips have managed to hold on, but heroes and action have yet to make a noticeable comeback.

The New York News-Chicago Tribune Syndicate thinned their list of adventurers considerably. Within two months in early 1973 they dumped both *Terry and the Pirates* and *Smilin' Jack*. Zack Mosely's daredevil aviator managed to hold out longer than any of the other pilot heroes who took to the air back in the thirties. He outlasted Tailspin Tommy, Scorchy Smith, and Barney Baxter. When his strip ended in April 1973, Jack was a gray-haired old codger with a grown son who'd been handling most of the action and romancing the de-icers. When *Terry and the Pirates* was discontinued at the end of February 1973, the event received considerable attention throughout the country. The *New York Times* speculated that the once popular strip was "perhaps a victim of the war in Vietnam, perhaps a casualty of shifting tastes." *Terry* had been in decline for several years and had dropped appreciably from its circulation of nearly 450 newspapers during its peak in the days of the Korean War. It was only earning its artist a few hundred dollars a week. George Wunder, even with the help of assistants George Evans and Frank Springer, was still putting in sixty- to seventy-hour weeks at his drawing board. Ailing as well and dissatisfied with what he was now earning, Wunder decided to quit. The New York News Syndicate did not bother to continue with *Terry*, especially after being unable to find another artist who'd work for the small weekly salary guarantee they were willing to offer.

Terry Lee had remained a career Air Force officer and Wunder, who also wrote the strip, had set several continuities in Vietnam over the years. This served to make the strip popular with the gung-ho set, but it increasingly alienated many readers. Wunder told the *New York Times* he felt the strip's popularity was declining because of two factors. One was television. "They get an average of three to four complete stories a night off the boob tube. There's no reason why they should hang around anywhere from eight to twelve weeks to find out how one story came out." He also acknowledged that anti-Vietnam War feeling had "a lot to do with the end of Terry." Air Force flying heroes "once had the image of square-jawed young men on a new frontier. The image has changed to that of droppers of napalm on women and children." Wunder later revealed to another interviewer that he regretted having kept Terry in the service and that many of the things done in Vietnam had appalled him.

Though *Steve Canyon* managed to hold on during the 1970s, it kept losing papers with increasing frequency. The descent had begun in the middle 1960s and continued throughout the next decade. To the end of his life, Milton Caniff believed that the same factors that killed *Terry* were responsible for the sharp decline in his strip's fortunes. There was, however, a third factor that he chose to overlook. The look of his work had deteriorated sadly, and the confident impressionist drawing that had impressed both readers and critics in the thirties and forties was gone. Back in 1953, Caniff had turned most of the penciling of *Steve Canyon* over to a journeyman comic book artist named Dick Rockwell. Using Caniff's thumbnail sketches, Rockwell tried to emulate the slick cinematic staging that was one of the trademarks of the earlier work. He never quite achieved his goal, and the Caniff inking, which grew increasingly sloppy and unsteady over the years, did not help the end product.

Canyon, too, was a career Air Force man and Caniff had sent him to Vietnam several times in the sixties. Caniff's attitude at that time was summed up by his biographer R. C. Harvey: "Milton Caniff stood for the mainstream view, reasonably confident that there was no other serious view worth troubling about." He quotes some Caniff dialogue in which a general in a 1964 Vietnam sequence explains things to Canyon. "The Russian Reds hate the Chinese Reds, but they hate *us* more. They'd gang up on us, come a showdown. If all Asia goes Commie, we'll be frozen out, just as Hitler tried to raus us out of Europe. Our business people can't compete with slave labor, so there would go our world trade." As the protests against U.S. involvement in the Vietnam War grew, Caniff began to realize that he was in trouble. "By the winter of 1966-1967, Caniff knew he could no longer do a story in Vietnam without offending some of his readers," reports Harvey. "There was no longer a mainstream of opinion for him to represent." Stubborn and loyal to his beliefs, however, Caniff "took his hero back to Vietnam again, this time to say a word or two for those who were fighting the war." More newspapers dropped the strip. Caniff devoted more and more time to trying to get back the newspapers he'd lost and to hold on to those on his dwindling list. He flew around the country attempting to cajole editors. He urged his many friends in the mil-

Johnny Hazard, *Frank Robbins. ©1973, King Features Syndicate, Inc.*

Annie, Leonard Starr. ©1981, Chicago Tribune—New York News Syndicate, Inc.

itary to put pressure on papers and he enlisted his show business friends to write letters and make phone calls. He became something of a Willy Loman, trying to sell an inferior product and doomed to defeat. "Sometimes Caniff won his fights," reports Harvey. "But increasingly as the 1970s rolled on, he lost. And often even his victories were short-lived." Years later, toward the end of his life, Caniff told Harvey, "The flag-waving label caused a lot of problems for me. I lost a lot of papers. All of the Canadian papers. And I never got them back."

Frank Robbins had been shrewder about Johnny Hazard and avoided letting him fall into the trap that caught Terry Lee and Steve Canyon. He got his hero out of the service as soon as the Second World War ended and kept him out. Although Hazard became an international freelance adventurer and remained one, he did get involved in many of the standard conflicts of Cold War thrillers. He frequently went up against Russian and other Communist villains. *Johnny Hazard*, still an impressively drawn and scripted feature, continued until 1977. Robbins decided then that the revenue from

his strip was not sufficient reward for the effort and retired his hero. He was also aware that the work he'd done for so many years was not especially popular in the funnies anymore. In the final daily strip, he had Hazard observe, "Guess the day of the he-man is finally *over!*" After spending a few years drawing for comic books, working on such characters as Batman, Robbins moved to Mexico and devoted the rest of his life to painting. He died there late in 1994.

Other adventure and continuity strips that ended in the 1970s included *Jeff Cobb*, *Abbie an' Slats*, *On Stage*, *Mickey Finn*, *The Jackson Twins*, *Dateline: Danger*, and *Big Ben Bolt*. This last one was drawn by the ubiquitous Gray Morrow in its final months. For its last two weeks, the strip title was altered to *Bolt*. Neal Adams provided the artwork, and Big Ben became a James Bond-style hero. This odd innovation was not enough apparently to save the strip.

Little Orphan Annie made an unusual transition in 1974, when the New York News-Chicago Tribune Syndicate went into reruns and began to distribute Harold Gray strips from the 1930s in place of new material. This practice continued until 1979. Then because of the Broadway musical *Annie*, Leonard Starr was asked to do an updated version of the adventurous waif's life. The new, improved strip was also called *Annie*. Several venerable humor strips also bit the dust. Among them were *Smitty*, *Freckles and his Friends*, *Smokey Stover*, and *The Teenie Weenies*. In 1979, United Feature canceled *The Captain and the Kids*, which was being drawn by the creator's son, John Dirks.

The Vietnam War, in a way, also did in Al Capp and *Li'l Abner*. Capp's admixture of broad burlesque, satire, and lowbrow gags, which caused one comics historian to call him the "outhouse Voltaire," had been declining in popularity for several years, and Li'l Abner, Daisy Mae, and the other denizens of Dogpatch were vanishing from a growing number of newspapers. Like his friend Milton Caniff, Capp had considered himself a liberal in the 1930s and 1940s. As he grew older, he underwent the classic transition, turning into a conservative

Hagar the Horrible, *Dik Browne*. ©1978, King Features Syndicate, Inc.

and a curmudgeon as well. He shifted his targets and took to kidding anti-war protesters, student rebels, and assorted bleeding hearts. Even though there was often material for satire in many of the groups he made fun of, Capp did it in such a way that earned him scorn rather than laughs with far too many readers and editors. Capp had never been politically correct, but at this time increasing numbers of readers felt they could not tolerate his views. Capp had also long been a notorious sexual harasser—his targets included Grace Kelly and Goldie Hawn, among many others—and charges caught up with him and found their way into the newspapers. His reputation, his popularity, and his health failing, Capp chose to retire. He terminated *Li'l Abner* late in 1977. Capp, chain-smoking until the end, died less than two years later.

In 1973, Dik Browne, a fat, bearded cartoonist, launched a strip about a fat, bearded Viking. At that point in his career, even after years of association with master minimalist Mort Walker on *Hi & Lois*, Browne was still a compulsive cartoonist and his new *Hagar the Horrible* was clearly the work of someone who enjoyed drawing. He crowded dozens of figures into the mock battle scenes, put extra little details into the landscapes. In interviews, Browne claimed he wanted simplicity in art and ideas, that he was a dedicated disciple of Ernie Bushmiller and believed in "dumbing down" the gags and keeping the drawing sparse. Even so, *Hagar* initially was a very individual work and one that displayed Browne's sometimes contradictory personality in every panel. Browne's Viking saga, which had little to do with actual Vikings or real history, was one of the biggest comic strip hits in years, and before the decade was over *Hagar the Horrible* was appearing in well over a thousand newspapers worldwide, which put it in the same league with such established hits

as *Peanuts*, *Blondie*, and *Beetle Bailey*. For all its success, however, *Hagar* did not do especially well in the merchandising department, and the extra millions of dollars that Charles Schulz took in from *Peanuts* products eluded Browne.

The 1970s strip destined to give Charlie Brown and his gang some serious competition began in June 1978. There have always been cartoonists with rather modest attainments who achieved enormous success in the comic strip field. Bud Fisher of *Mutt & Jeff* and Sidney Smith of *The Gumps* are but two examples. This decade established for good and all that great technical skill in cartooning no longer was a requirement for a hit strip. When Jim Davis sold *Garfield* to United Feature in 1978, he'd already been a professional cartoonist for quite awhile. He'd worked as an assistant to Tom K. Ryan on *Tumbleweeds*, a simply drawn gag strip about the Old West, for nearly ten years. Drawing in a manner even less detailed than that of his former boss, Davis presented the public a fat, bug-eyed creature that vaguely resembled a cat. *Garfield* quickly turned into one of the biggest successes of the century. By the middle 1980s, it was appearing in over two thousand newspapers. Better still, Garfield was bringing in millions of dollars in merchandising money to the syndicate and Davis. The cat became an icon, a talisman, to multitudes of people around the world and they bought up toys, greeting cards, lunch boxes, cat food—anything with the image of Garfield on it. In analyzing the phenomenal rise of Davis' "fat, lazy, sardonic feline," Dennis Wepman has said that "both cat lovers and cat haters respond to the indolent, self-indulgent Garfield, whose life revolves around naps, lasagna, and his ongoing battles with his rivals. Garfield's effortless manipulation of his owner, Jon Arbuckle, strikes a familiar note for anyone who has ever known a cat."

Lynn Johnston's *For Better or for Worse*, a low-key, contemporary sitcom, began in the late summer of 1979. Reality-based and fairly autobiographical, the strip's quiet humor grew out of household relationships and the problems of married life and child rearing, avoiding many of the stock setups of earlier efforts such as *Blondie*. As in many of the gentler family comedies on television, there was a good deal of communicating, talking things over, amateur group therapy, and hugging. A genuinely humorous woman, Johnston had done animation and medical illustrating as well as three humor books on family life before the unconventional Universal Press folks took on her strip. In an interview in *Hogan's Alley* magazine, when asked about the fact that, unlike some of her contemporaries, she went in for subtler things, she replied, "I think maybe it's because I'm a girl. There are so many men in the business who are good at the comedy part, but the subtle, gentle, nuance part, you don't see that much." She was in favor of artists who "make you say, 'Yes, I know how that feels.' It's not necessarily funny, but it's real." Johnston's instincts about comics served her well, and by the time *For Better or for Worse* had been in business for ten years, it was appearing in over eight hundred newspapers.

While it is probably the opinion of every campus cartoonist that the work he or she is doing for the college paper is good enough to be syndicated nationally, relatively few young cartoonists move directly from local notoriety to national recognition. Garry Trudeau was an exception. In 1970, the fledgling Universal Press Syndicate sold his *Doonesbury*, based on a strip he'd been drawing for the campus daily while a student at Yale, to something under three dozen newspapers. Five years later, Trudeau's simply drawn, static, and satirical strip was appearing in nearly five hundred papers, and he won a Pulitzer Prize. Since the Pulitzer committee has yet to recognize the comic strip as a legitimate category, *Doonesbury* copped the award as an editorial cartoon. Trudeau, with considerable help on the drawing, has continued to satirize all the obvious targets in American life, and most especially the country's politicians. In the opinion of *The Encyclopedia of American Comics*, the fact that Trudeau's skewering of political figures is so often quoted and noted around the country has made him into "probably the most influential comic strip artist in history."

Cathy Guisewite lived out another fantasy that many aspiring cartoonists have. At the suggestion of her mother, she developed the self-caricatures she'd included in her letters home into a comic strip. That became *Cathy*, and the Universal Press Syndicate added it to their growing list of strips late in 1976. Decidedly unslick, *Cathy* had a spontaneous, homemade look and its beleaguered, twenty-something

Broom-Hilda, *Russell Myers. ©1973, The* Chicago Tribune. *Reprinted by permission of Tribune Media Services.*

heroine sparked a shock of recognition in large numbers of readers. "The gags in the strip," as Dennis Wepman observes, "revolve around Cathy's problems with food, love, mother, and career—what Guisewite calls 'the four basic guilt groups.'" Quietly funny, the strip expressed the sort of truths that people like to tape to the refrigerator and to the office bulletin board.

Several other strips that would prove to have considerable longevity were first seen in the seventies. The indefatigable Elliot Caplin continued to mastermind new strips. Sometime in the late 1960s he began kicking around the idea for a humor strip about a witch. After working with an assortment of artists and writers, Caplin got together with Russell Myers, who was working as an artist and idea man with the Hallmark card company in Kansas City. The resulting strip was *Broom-Hilda*, distributed by the New York News-Chicago Tribune Syndicate. In a 1972 interview in *Cartoonist PROfiles*, Myers gave an account of the development of the strip without once mentioning Caplin's name. "About all I got

from the writer in question was the name—Broom-Hilda. They let me take it from there. Everything that's ever been done on the strip I've done—I've written and drawn it all. The famous writer I spoke of owns the title to the strip and is called 'the manager' in the contractual arrangements. He handles all the extra details." Myers drew in a direct contemporary style, one that reflected his greeting card background. The squat and licentious little Broom-Hilda moved easily between an approximation of the contemporary world and the realms of fantasy. The strip has been called one "that respects neither the unities of time and place nor the laws of logic." At its high point it was appearing in over three hundred papers.

Bob Thaves's *Frank and Ernest* was added to the NEA list in 1972. Although occupying the same space as a regular comic strip, it consists of one panel and a hand-lettered caption. In appearance and spirit it is closer to a gag cartoon or an offbeat greeting card. While unlike *Mutt and Jeff* in most ways, the team also consists of one short guy and one tall one, and they do not stick to any one job. They are bankers one day, traveling salesmen the next, unemployed the day after that. Some days they do not show up in their strip at all, and somebody else does the gag. Thaves was a

Sam and Silo, Jerry Dumas. The Sunday pages are frequently filled with foliage. ©1981, King Features Syndicate, Inc.

Sunday Comics, *Gahan Wilson*. ©1974, *The Register and Tribune Syndicate*.

magazine cartoonist and an industrial psychologist—something syndicate publicity has made much of—before he added *Frank and Ernest* to his workload. His style is up-to-date, with affinities to what advertising artists once called "decorative cartooning."

Jeff McNelly had already won a Pulitzer Prize before branching out into the comic strip business. A political cartoonist since 1970, he won his first Pulitzer in 1972 and began his *Shoe* newspaper strip in 1977. The feature is inhabited by a bunch of humanized birds who are in the newspaper business or on its fringes in one way or another. It is attractively drawn and quite probably its theme appealed to editors. *Shoe* eventually picked up over one thousand newspapers. When *Momma* by Mel Lazarus started in 1970, the artist already had several features to his credit, including a tiny one titled *Wee Women* and the larger and more successful *Miss Peach*. In addition, under the pen name Fulton, he'd also scripted *Pauline McPeril*, a short-lived mock adventure strip illustrated by *Mad* artist Jack Rickard. *Momma*, about the quintessential nagging mother, proved to be Lazarus's most popular effort.

Bill Hoest, whose shorthand style of cartooning made even the work of Mort Walker and his disciples look cluttered, moved officially into strips in October 1977 with *Agatha Crumm*. It was, in Hoest's words, about "a zany seventy-seven-year-old, the head of a giant conglomerate, who is ruthless in her dealings with her empire, with her employees and with her son who's a bumbling type." *Crock*, which is a *Wizard of Id* in the French Foreign Legion sort of strip, was started in 1975. Brant Parker came up with the idea and recruited Don Wilder to do the writing and Bill Rechin to draw it in a style very sim-

ilar to his. The titular character's full name is Vermin P. Crock, and he commands a ragtag group of Legionnaires.

The simple, direct Brant Parker-Johnny Hart approach to cartooning, first seen in *B.C.*, was becoming increasingly popular and influenced several later comic strips. *Motley's Crew* by writer Tom Forman and artist Ben Templeton started in September 1976. It dealt with blue-collar characters and was, as Forman put it, "simply a look at middle-class life in America today." Templeton, a former advertising artist, drew in a style that fell somewhere between that of the Mort Walker and the Parker-Hart school of cartooning.

The uncrowded genre of sports strips added a new member in 1974, when *Tank McNamara* commenced. The title character in the gag strip was a former pro football player who became "the third worst sports reporter on TV." Jeff Millar wrote *Tank McNamara*, Bill Hinds drew it. According to promotional material, both men were 6 feet 3 inches and both worked for the *Houston Chronicle*.

King Features introduced *Sam and Silo* in 1977. Supervised by Mort Walker and drawn by Jerry Dumas, it revived the two leading characters from their earlier and much odder *Sam's Strip*. NEA had approached Walker about reviving the original strip and doing it for them, but then King, who'd done it originally, decided they wanted it. What was not wanted, however, was the screwball approach, the inside jokes, and Sam's awareness that he was a character in a comic strip. *Sam and Silo* concentrated on life in the small town of Upper Duckwater and had Sam and Silo as members of the local constabulary. It proved more viable than the earlier version and is still appearing in a modest list of newspapers.

This was also a period that had room for more than one popular cat. George Gately's Heathcliff was as sly and manipulative as Garfield, but he led a richer, fuller life. He raised havoc not only at home but throughout the city and had an agenda that always had room for one more odd project. Gately's full name was George Gately Gallagher, and he and his brother John Gallagher were both magazine gag cartoonists. His *Heathcliff* panel, originally distributed by the McNaught Syndicate, started in September 1973, almost five years before Garfield debuted.

Larry Wright's *Wright Angles* became a syndicated strip in August 1976. He started it while a political cartoonist on the *Detroit Free-Press* and continued it when he moved to the *Detroit News*. By the time United Feature picked it up, *Wright Angles* was a family strip. Wright had a knack for drawing cats, and the family cat in his strip, Motley, another cunning and self-centered feline, soon became the undisputed star. In 1980, Wright started a panel, *Kit 'n' Carlyle*, about a single young woman and her cat.

Among the other humor strips that arrived in the 1970s were *Funky Winkerbean*, initially about high school life, by Tom Batiuk, and *Drabble*, originally about college life, by Kevin Fagan. Less successful were *Doctor Smock*, by George Lemont; *Half Hitch*, Hank Ketcham's attempt to do a Navy version of *Beetle Bailey* and ghosted by Dick Hodgins; *The Badge Guys*, an attempt to do a police version of *Beetle Bailey*, by cartoonist Chuck Bowen and writer Ted Schwarz; *The Circus of P. T. Bimbo* by Howie Schneider; *Mixed Singles* (later *Boomer*), a strip about unmarried yuppies by cartoonists Mel Casson and William F. Brown; *Koky*, a married life feature by writer Richard O'Brien and gag cartoonist Mort Gerberg.

In 1973, the NEA introduced a strip that was definitely a throwback to an earlier era. *Benjy* was, as the publicity releases at the time were not ashamed to state, about a bum. That a strip like this could appear in a period when homelessness was already rising in America seems odd when looking back from our politically correct time. Cartoonist Jim Berry, whose *Berry's World* panel was already an NEA hit, wrote the strip, and Bill Yates, who was already drawing a strip called *Prof. Phumble* under contract to King Features, drew it. Because of his commitment, Yates signed *Benjy* in lower case type with the name "yale." If he ever wanted to use his real name, he had only to cross the l and add an s. The public did not take to the amiable little bum, and *Benjy* ended in 1975.

Roger Bradfield's *Dooley's World* was a rather gentle strip about a seven-year-old boy. No other kids and no grownups shared Dooley's world, and all the other characters were toys from his collection. They included a pompous wind-up toy named Professor, a pushy ragdoll named Thelma and a sensible wind-up knight named Norman. There was also a real mouse named Max. The King Features strip ran from 1972 to 1978. Gahan Wilson is, with Charles Addams in first place, the second-best-known macabre gag cartoonist in America. In 1974 the formerly fairly staid Register & Tribune Syndicate of Des Moines, Iowa, offered *Gahan Wilson's Sunday Comics*. In the format, though certainly not the mood, of such pages as *Grin and Bear It*, Wilson's page consisted of five gag cartoons each week. These were populated with his usual monsters, ghosts, freaks, bizarre human beings, and an occasional talking vegetable. All were rendered in Wilson's distinctive and slightly askew manner. In those days before Gary Larson and similar eccentrics, *Sunday Comics* failed to find an audience and was soon gone from the Sunday comics. King Features added one more Walt Disney strip in June, 1978. *Winnie the Pooh*, like the animated cartoons it derived from, was heavy on Disney touches and light on A. A. Milne.

Inside Woody Allen was introduced by King in 1976. The central character was a kvetching, neurotic misfit who behaved like the Woody Allen of his early comedy films. Stu Hample took credit for the writing and drawing. This was another project cooked up by the enterprising Elliot Caplin. Henny Youngman, veteran standup comedian, violinist, and master of the one-liner, followed Allen into the funny papers later that same year. His tiny strip, distributed by the Field Newspaper Syndicate, consisted of two panels with a setup and a punchline each day: "My wife wanted to go somewhere she had never been before—I said try the kitchen," or "I just solved the parking problem—I bought a parked car." *Henny* was drawn in a no-frills style by Art Cummings. Youngman didn't feel that Allen would siphon off any of his potential audience. "I think his is going to be for the intelligent," he told an interviewer. "Mine is going to be for the masses." The masses felt otherwise.

While the *New York Times* had no intention of ever running comic strips in its own pages, it was not adverse to trying to syndicate them to other less fastidious newspapers. The *Times'* Special Features syndicate offered its first strip in September, 1975. David Gantz' *Don Q* had Don Quixote and Sancho as its central characters and the setting suggested the Spanish locales of Cervantes' seventeenth century picaresque novel. Most of the people Gantz' pair encountered, however, looked a good deal like the political and show business celebrities of the seventies— Gerald Ford, John Wayne, and Henry Kissinger. Gantz' drawing was suitable for a

strip blending satire, burlesque, and political commentary, but he wasn't able to match the effects of his model, Walt Kelly's *Pogo*. *Don Q* seemed ill at ease and conveyed a lack of confidence. For its later strips the *Times* turned to properties that were already established. In 1979, after *Buck Rogers* had been revived in a movie and then a televisions series, they syndicated a new strip. The original writer on *Buck Rogers in the 25th Century* was Jim Lawrence, the artist Gray Morrow.

Shortly before putting some of its veteran adventure strips out to pasture, the N.Y. News-Chicago Tribune Syndicate experimented with a brand new straight continuity feature. *Ambler*, which started in 1972, was by Doug Wildey. The blond young Ambler was a successful singer-musician whose major preoccupation was roaming the country on foot with his guitar strapped to his back. Like the wandering heroes of such popular sixties television shows as *Route 66* and *The Fugitive*, his peregrinations brought him into contact with all sorts of crimes, intrigues, and human dilemmas. Never forming close ties with any person or place, Ambler usually served as a catalyst, savior, or mentor. Wildey, not a first rate illustrator, relied heavily on photo swipes for many of his panels. His

Star Hawks, Gil Kane. Demonstrating the layout possibilities of the two-tier format. ©1976, NEA, Inc.

far from masterly inking gave *Ambler* a muddy, blurred appearance. The strip ended before its second birthday.

Elliot Caplin, while continuing to package new humor strips, didn't lose faith in serious continuity. In 1971 he produced a comic strip version of television's fleetingly popular gothic soap opera, *Dark Shadows*. The drawing was by Ken Bald hiding behind the pen name Ken Bruce. The strip didn't last. 1977 found Caplin persuading John McMeel of the Universal Press Syndicate, an unlikely home for a straight adventure strip, to take a chance with *Best Seller Showcase*. The promotion pieces promised "TOP books translated into the comic strip genre." The first two titles, running eight weeks each, were Clive Cussler's *Raise the Titanic* and Jack Higgins' *Storm Warning*. Caplin had been involved with a similar project, *Famous Fiction*, more than thirty years earlier. On the new strip he used a rotating group of artists that included Frank Bolle and Gray Morrow. *Showcase* started with an impressive list of papers, but eventually faltered. In 1979 it gave way to *Encyclopedia Brown*, which was based on the kids' whodunits by Donald Sobol. Bolle was the artist.

Stan Lynde, who'd left *Rick O'Shay* in 1977, still had faith in both cowboys and continuity. In June of 1979 he started a more serious and realistic strip titled *Latigo*. What Lynde was after, he said at the time, was a strip about "the less spectacular 'common' people—the homesteader, the miner, the underpaid frontier horseman, the American Indian." Though well drawn, with considerable help from Russ Heath at one stage, and well researched, *Latigo* met the fate of just about every adventure strip begun in this decade and expired after a relatively short run.

I was contacted in 1976 by John "Flash" Fairfield, who was then the comics editor of the NEA syndicate. I'd met him once and he had read some of my science fiction novels. He thought I might be able to create a new strip, a space adventure with action and some humor. I later found out that NEA had tried to get the rights to do a comic

strip version of *Star Trek*, but had decided the licensing fee was far too high. Fairfield also wanted to try a fairly audacious experiment. To showcase the artwork on the strip, he wanted it to be two-tiered, that is, twice the size of any other daily strip. To offer an adventure strip in the period when they were falling left and right and to insist that it take up the space usually given to two strips in a time when most strips were shrinking was courageous, although probably not good business. Ignoring all that, I went ahead and wrote up some ideas, using the Barnum System of planets that I'd initially concocted for my novels and short stories. I recall being impressed at the time with the pace and characterizations of the *Starsky & Hutch* television show and I tried to get some of that feeling into my proposed space opera. Originally I called the strip *Star Cops*, but was talked out of that.

In the middle and late 1970s Gil Kane was one of the most popular comic book artists in the country. He'd drawn every sort of superhero, including Green Lantern, Batman, and Spider-Man and was also Marvel Comics' premier cover artist. Since we were friends and neighbors, I invited him to come aboard as an artist. The eventual strip we produced was called *Star Hawks* and was one of the most impressively drawn to come along in many a year. It debuted in the fall of 1977 and the following year Kane won the National Cartoonists Society's award for best adventure strip. The fact that *Star Hawks* was handsome didn't help in the long run and the strip ended within a few years. I left it in 1979 and was replaced by Archie Goodwin.

The advent of George Lucas' *Star Wars* movie in the spring of 1977 inspired a science fiction boom. Eventually there was a *Star Wars* strip, initially written and drawn by Russ Manning. It knocked *Star Hawks* out of several papers, including the *New York Post*. Later on Archie Goodwin became the writer on the *Star Wars* strip and Al Williamson did the drawing. For a time there was even a *Star Trek* comic strip. In addition to the brief upswing in science fiction adventure strips, there was a wave of new superhero strips at about the same time. Marvel Comics was in one of its periodic popularity highs and several of the company's top characters broke into the comic sections. Among them were *The Amazing Spider-Man*, credited to writer-editor Stan Lee and artist John Romita, and *Conan the Barbarian*, written by Roy Thomas and drawn by John Buscema. There was also, briefly, an *Incredible Hulk* strip and, even more briefly, *Howard the Duck*. Also emergent in this peri-od was *The World's Greatest Superheroes*, peopled with an assortment of DC Comics characters, including the Flash, Superman, Wonder Woman, and Batman. George Tuska penciled the strip, sharing a credit with a fluctuating group of inkers and writers. Only Spider-Man survived in the newspapers and his strip is still appearing, after numerous changes in artists, today.

Chapter 13

Truth, Justice, and the Comics

Hordes of humor strips continued to descend on the comic sections in the 1980s and 1990s. The size of individual strips has been dwindling over the years, due in part to the crowding necessitated by the shrinking of advertising revenue and the escalating cost of newsprint. The size of the average newspaper page has reduced several inches. The dimensions of most strips are now 6 inches wide and $1 \frac{3}{4}$ inches high. A daily strip in 1920, by way of comparison, measured 12 inches by $3 \frac{1}{2}$ and in 1950 $7 \frac{1}{2}$ by $2 \frac{1}{4}$. A Sunday strip is usually $8 \frac{1}{2}$ inches wide and 4 inches high, compared with a maximum of 15 inches by 21 inches some fifty years ago. This means that newspapers can now squeeze at least twenty strips, as well as four or five panels and a puzzle, onto a single page every day, and as many as five features per page in the Sunday sections. Simply drawn humor strips, with a minimum of panels and words, are much easier to assimilate in the tinier format, and this is one of several reasons for their continually increasing popularity.

The panel cartoon, which can often be scrunched into an even smaller space than a strip, became increasingly popular. Gary Larson's *The Far Side*, initially under the title *Nature's Way* and then *Garyland*, got going in the late 1970s and came into its own, under its new name, in the early 1980s. Syndicated by Universal Press, it began adding hun-

dreds of papers to its list and branching out into books, calendars, and other forms of merchandising. Larson was one of the first cartoonists to bring the outlook and attitudes found in B. Kliban's popular mid-1970s books—*Cats, Never Eat Anything Bigger Than Your Head*—into newspaper comic sections. He broadened the range of gag panels from the domestic to the cosmic and took as subject matter the entire animal and vegetable kingdom, dealing as well with nostalgia, popular culture, politics, and sundry other topics. Like Kliban, he pioneered in replacing the caption with the descriptive phrase— "Professor Wainwright's painstaking field research to decode the language of bears comes to a sudden and horrific end," "Sheep that pass in the night," or "Environmental disasters in a flea's world." After taking a series of vacations, during which the syndicate went into reruns, Larson retired *The Far Side* early in 1995. The event inspired editorial cartoons and op-ed pieces all across the land. The merchandising, however, will continue.

Several artists chose to follow the trail blazed by Gary Larson. Among them were Dan Piraro, who draws the calmly outré *Bizarro*, Buddy Hickerson, who's responsible for *The Quigmans*, and Jerry Van Amerongen, the creator of *The Neighborhood*. King Features invented a daily panel called *The New Breed*, which showcased a variety of different bizarre cartoonists. Charlie Rodrigues, a longtime master of the macabre gag cartoon, entered the competition in 1991 with *Charlie*, a small panel blending autobiography and fantasy. There are also strips that venture into *The Far Side* territory.

Among these single panel strips are *Non Sequitor* by political cartoonist Wiley (pen name for David Wiley Miller), *Mixed Media* by political cartoonist Jack Ohman, which limits itself to show business and entertainment, and *Bound and Gagged* by Dana Summers. Another strayed editorial cartoonist, Summers also collaborates with cartoonist Ralph Dunagin on a conventional family strip titled *The Middletons*.

In earlier decades many comic strip artists were recruited from the ranks of magazine cartoonists, but in the eighties and nineties political cartoonists were much more likely to make the move into the funnies. Mike Peters is another editorial cartoonist who's won the Pulitzer Prize. His *Mother Goose & Grimm*, begun in the middle 1980s, is technically an animal strip, since it stars a bird and her dog. A practical joker in real life, Peters draws with force and vigor and has been at the forefront of the movement to broaden the definition of good taste in comic strips. Urination, a topic that earlier funny paper dogs like Napoleon and Officer Pupp never got around to dealing with, serves as the basis for many of the Grimm gags. Brian Basset, an editorial

Charlie, Charlie Rodrigues. ©1991, Tribune Media Service, Inc. Reprinted by permission of Tribune Media Service.

Bizarro, Dan Piraro. ©1991, Chronicle Features.

cartoonist based at the *Seattle Times*, began his strip *Adam* in 1984. The strip is about a young married couple but with a switch; Adam is "a particularly lethargic house-husband, father of three, whose wife, Laura, brings home the pay check." His style is in the Mike Peters tradition, with a touch of Bill Watterson.

Mark Cullum, editorial cartoonist for the *Birmingham News*, weighed in with a suburban comedy strip titled *Walnut Grove* in June 1991. Tom Toles, one of the relatively few editorial cartoonists who wasn't influenced by either Ronald Searle or Pat Oliphant, branched out into strips in the early 1990s with *Curious Avenue*. Syndicated by Universal Press, the strip deals with an assortment of little kids. A blurb for Toles's strip said that it "reveals the human condition as seen from the perspective of a group of children." Yet another Pulitzer Prize winner who added a daily and Sunday comic strip to his chores was Doug Marlette. The North Carolina-born artist started the satirical *Kudzu* in 1981. His strip is set in the small town of Bypass, North Carolina, and centers on its young hero, who is named "for the rank weed spreading uncontrollably throughout the South." One of the most popular, albeit controversial, characters is the sly, venal Rev. Will B. Dunn, a television evangelist whom Marlette has considerable fun with.

One of the most popular and successful contemporary strips is also the work of a political cartoonist. Actually, Bill Watterson failed

Unfortunately, Charlie is only able to serve as an "honorary" pallbearer.

at that profession and was let go after only a few months on the staff of the *Cincinnati Post*. He did better with his comic

strip *Calvin and Hobbes*, which began appearing in November 1985. In the tradition of both *Barnaby*, which Watterson has said he had never heard of when he started his feature, and *Pogo*, *Calvin and Hobbes* mixes fantasy, social comment, slapstick, and satire. Like Barnaby, Calvin has what most take to be an imaginary playmate. But to the hyperactive, imaginative, and opportunistic little Calvin, as well as to the readers, his toy tiger seems alive. Not only alive but clever and perceptive, a cross between Bertie Wooster's Jeeves and Pogo's Albert the Alligator. In spite of an unfortunate tendency to revert to his true animal nature and pounce on Calvin, Hobbes makes an admirable companion. Calvin is an abrasive little fellow, but there is a sad quality to him as well. He is certainly the most likable brat to grace the funnies in decades and certainly the most thoughtful. Calvin often speculates on such profound topics as the meaning of life, the nature of the universe, and the inevitability of death, even more so than Percy Crosby's Skippy. An exemplary strip in both drawing and writing, *Calvin and Hobbes* displays an energy and enthusiasm that is lacking in many current strips. Watterson's strip has become a major success and, if he didn't restrict the merchandising chiefly to reprint books, it would be competing with *Peanuts* and *Garfield* in earning capacity. Like some of his colleagues, Watterson has found it necessary to take leave of his strip now and then. Old *Calvin and Hobbes* strips were reprinted while he was away

Kudzu, *Doug Marlette. The Reverend Will B. Dunn in the pulpit. ©1992, Doug Marlette.*

from the drawing board.

Another popular strip that started in the eighties was *Bloom County*. The work of Berke Breathed, it was first a college paper strip that moved into syndication. Very much in the *Doonesbury* tradition, it began its national run in December 1980. The most popular character was a penguin named Opus. Breathed shut down the strip in 1989, having won himself a Pulitzer along the way. He returned with a Sunday page titled *Outland* and eventually, by popular request, added Opus to the cast. Restless apparently, Breathed abandoned *Outland* in 1995.

A very quiet domestic strip, *Sally Forth*, began in 1982. Distributed then by the North America Syndicate (formerly Publishers Syndicate and today assimilated by King Features), it was the work of a midwestern lawyer named Greg Howard. A self-admitted contender for the title "one of the worst cartoonists in America," Howard nonetheless managed to capture an increasingly large and loyal audience. In 1991, hoping to upgrade the looks of his strip, he hired commercial artist Craig McIntosh to take over the drawing. Apparently the fans of *Sally Forth* didn't know much about art but they knew what they liked. Thousands of complaints came in protesting the fact that the strip now looked too good. Howard ordered McIntosh to give Sally and family back some of their old clumsy, badly drawn

Dilbert, *Scott Adams. Dilbert and Dogbert at home. ©1989, United Feature Syndicate, Inc. Reprinted with permission.*

look and eventually the furor abated. The *Sally Forth* incident substantiates the theory that cartooning ability is no longer a prerequisite for success in the funnies. It might even prove a handicap.

One of the most appealing examples of what might be called the Grandma Moses School of Comic Strips is *Dilbert*. The strip, distributed by United Feature, is the work of Scott Adams and began in 1989. It is about, as Andy Meisler recently put it in the *New York Times*, "a mouthless and hapless techno-nerd shaped vaguely like a shaving brush who performs an unspecified task at an unnamed company." Dilbert lives with a small and non-supportive hound named Dogbert. Adams himself is something of a techno-nerd and occupies a cubicle

in a Northern California office complex. Thus far he's been turning out the strip in his spare time. Funny in a way that appeals to people who view modern life as bleak and hopeless but essentially hilarious, *Dilbert* has been climbing rapidly toward five hundred papers. Adams draws in the manner of someone who's doodling during business meetings and is definitely the minimalist's minimalist.

The parade of eccentric strips has been a long one. It includes *Overboard* by Chip Dunham, dealing, according to syndicate ads, with "a wacky crew of modern-day pirates ... mixing together eighteenth-century piracy and twentieth-century humor for a shipload of laughs;" *Mr. Boffo* by Joe Martin, about a hapless everyman who has no fixed temporal abode and pops up in various times, climes, and occupations to deliver one-liners, often in the company of his pet, Wonder-Dog Weederman; *The Nutheads*, begun in 1989, by Don Martin, longtime resident screwball at *Mad* and more recently on the staff of *Cracked*. Another oddball strip is Bud Grace's *Ernie*. His scraggly-looking effort centers around a group of scruffy characters who are meanminded, thick-witted, and unattractive. King Features ads for the strip used the headline "Atomic physicist-turned cartoonist creates a Big Bang on world's comic pages!"

In 1984 Jerry Dumas, serving as writer this time, formed an uneasy alliance with *Mad* cartoonist and ace caricaturist Mort Drucker to produce *Benchley*, about a low-level Washington bureaucrat. It ended two years later. Rex May, gag cartoonist and prolific supplier of gag ideas to other cartoonists, had a brief fling in 1993 with a working class family strip called *Lunchbucket*.

Mister Boffo, *Joe Martin.* ©1989, *Tribune Media Services, Inc.*

Betty is a collaboration by cartoonists Gerry Rasmussen and Gary Delainey. A family strip of sorts, it focuses on the Slug Family, Betty, Bob, and Junior. Betty is the star of the enterprise and most of the attention is paid to her, especially to her time at the office, where she can often be seen sitting at the computer. United Feature introduced the strip in December, 1991. Another family strip, closer to *Sally Forth* in looks and content, is *One Big Happy* by Rick Detorie and distributed by Creators Syndicate. Somewhat in the *Dilbert* tradition, though much less strange and sharp-edged, is David Miller's *Dave*.

The abundant crop of humor strips also includes kid strips *Marvin* by Tom Armstrong and *Big Nate* by Lincoln Peirce, family strips *Fox Trot* by Bill Amend, *The Buckets* by Scott Stantis, and *Rose Is Rose* by Pat Brady. Other recent arrivals are *Crankshaft* by Tom Batiuk and Chuck Ayers, *What a Guy!* begun by the late Bill Hoest and carried on by Bunny Hoest and John Reiner, *Mallard Fillmore*, about a conservative duck, by Bruce Tingley, and *Chris Browne's Comic Strip*. This latter, drawn by the artist who is carrying on *Hagar the Horrible*, came and went in a matter of weeks in 1994.

The number of race-based strips grew some, too. *Jump Start*, by Robb Armstrong, started in October 1989. United Feature publicity releases explained that Armstrong is "one of the very few African American cartoonists syndicated in the United States." The central characters in his strip are a young married couple consisting of Joe, a cop, and Marcy, a nurse. *Curtis*, syndicated by King and drawn by Ray Billingsley, is another black family strip, this one concentrating on a grade school kid. Tribune Media introduced *Herb & Jamaal* in 1989. The work of Stephen Bentley, it was promoted as "blending good-natured humor with the social and historical experiences of black culture." The short Herb and the tall Jamaal are partners in a small lunch counter, and the majority of the gags take place there, though the home lives of both of them are also touched on.

Barbara Brandon is a second generation cartoonist. Her father, Brumsic Brandon, Jr. drew the kid strip *Luther* for nearly two decades. Her own *Where I'm Coming From* began in the *Detroit Free Press* and was picked up for syndication by Universal Press in 1991. Brandon is, as she points out, "the first black female cartoonist to become nationally syndicated into the mainstream press and I'm proud of it!" Her two-tier strip is laid out in the manner invented by Jules Feiffer for his *Village Voice* strip many years ago. It consists of monologues and dialogues, often over the phone, involving a rotating cast of black women.

In January 1989, the Los Angeles Times Syndicate made an attempt to revive the dead. With the blessings of the Walt Kelly Estate, they brought *Pogo* back into syndication. Rather than recycle old material, they offered brand new stuff. Neal Sternecky was the artist and Larry Doyle was the writer. The two men had been friends since college and worked together on other projects. The new strip, officially titled *Walt Kelly's Pogo*, looked and talked like the original, yet there was something missing. Like a zombie who's been summoned back from the grave, it simply was not alive. The strip was a noble, if misguided, effort and managed to pick up a fair list of papers at the start. The material was all passed on by Selby Kelly, Walt's widow. After several months, Doyle moved on and Sternecky continued alone. In March 1992, he, too, left the faltering

Dave, *David Miller. ©1992, David Miller.*

strip. It was then assumed by two of Kelly's children. His daughter Carolyn did the drawing and his son Peter supervised the writing. *Pogo* continued its downward slide and was soon gone once again, proving that genius rarely strikes twice in the same place—or in the same swamp.

King Features turned to television for inspiration in 1981 when it started *The Muppets*. Licensing the Jim Henson characters, who became known to millions of tots by way of their participation in the *Sesame Street* show, they hired Guy Gilchrist, a disciple of Walt Kelly, to do the drawing and his brother, Brad Gilchrist, to help with the writing. The strip offered Kermit the Frog, Miss Piggy, and the rest of the regulars and was aimed at a wider, more sophisticated audience than the *Sesame Street* crowd. Even so, it was not a long-term success. More directly aimed at children, and much more successful, is *Comics for Kids* by Bob Weber, Jr. A second generation cartoonist, he's the son of the Bob Weber, who draws *Moose Miller*. Begun as a Sunday page in 1987, his feature offered a mixture of puzzles, comic strips, and cartooning lessons. The most popular character proved to be Slylock Fox, a Sherlockian type who figures in a mystery puzzler each week. The page proved popular and is now appearing in several hundred papers. A daily version was eventually added and the title currently is *Slylock Fox*.

During these years the story strips continued to decline. With the exception of *The Lone Ranger* strip by artist Russ Heath and writer Cary Bates that ran from 1981 to 1984 and a short-running *Bruce Lee* by Fran Matera, very little new adventure material emerged in the eighties. The soap opera strips, such as *Mary Worth*, *Dr. Morgan*, and *Apartment 3-G* still appear in a sizable number of papers. *Mark Trail*, *Gil Thorp*, and *Gasoline Alley* continue to do moderately well. *Dick Tracy*, *Annie*, *The Phantom*, and *Steve Roper* continue to slip. The Tracy strip, for example, according to statistics assembled by comics researcher Jeffrey Lindenblatt, now appears in only eleven of the top one hundred newspapers, ranked by circulation, in America. *Flash Gordon* appears in but one of the top one hundred, and *Mandrake* in none. Late in 1994 Tribune Media Services took out trade ads announcing "Action and Adventure Return to the Comics." A new version of *Terry and the Pirates* was in the works and "America's legendary adventure strip returns with fantastic art, terrific characters, and stories ripped from today's headlines." This new *Terry*, which made its debut in March 1995, is written by Michael Uslan and drawn by Greg and Tim Hildebrandt. Part of a promotion plan to launch a television series, the strip updates the Caniff concept, turning Terry Lee into a punk-rock type with an earring and Pat Ryan into a stubble-faced young fellow who resembles Kurt

Slylock Fox, Bob Weber, Jr. ©1994, King Features Syndicate, Inc.

SLYLOCK FOX

Slylock Fox captured Harry Ape under a tree as the crook was counting money he robbed from a bank. The forest floor was covered with dry, fallen leaves, yet Slylock was able to sneak up on Harry without making a sound. How was that possible?

Solution – The forest floor was covered with leaves shaped like needles (called pine needles). These needle-shaped leaves do not make noise when walked on.

Herb & Jamal, *Stephen Bentley. The two partners on the job. ©1990, Tribune Media Service, Inc.*

Russell in one of his macho roles. The locale in the opening sequence is Hong Kong, referred to as "the Casablanca of the 1990s." Excellent book illustrators, the Hildebrandt Brothers draw the strip in a manner reminiscent of the Marvel Comics house style. It seems unlikely, however, that the return of *Terry* will inspire a revival of adventure strips.

Comic strips have come a long way from Hogan's Alley. They have become a part of our daily lives and, despite competition from dozens of new forms of entertainment over the years, they have managed to survive. While the number of daily newspapers continues to drop, comics are moving into such electronic outlets as the CD-ROM. It seems safe to assume that comic strips will celebrate many birthdays beyond their one hundredth.

Bibliography

Becker, Stephen. *Comic Art in America*. Simon and Schuster, 1959.

Blackbeard, Bill, and Williams Martin, editors. *The Smithsonian Collection of Newspaper Comics*. Smithsonian-Abrams, 1977.

Dunning, John. *Tune in Yesterday*. Prentice-Hall, 1976.

Gifford, Denis. *The International Book of Comics*. Crescent, 1984.

Goulart, Ron. *The Adventurous Decade*. Arlington House, 1975.

——, editor. *The Encyclopedia of American Comics*. Facts-On-File, 1990.

Horn, Maurice. *Comics of the American West*. Stoeger, 1977.

——, editor. *The World Encyclopedia of Comics*. Chelsea House, 1976.

Harvey, Robert C. *The Art of the Funnies*. University Press of Mississippi, 1994.

Inge, M. Thomas. *Comics as Culture*. University Press of Mississippi, 1990.

Jenkins, Henry. *What Made Pistachio Nuts?* Columbia, 1992.

Marschall, Richard. *America's Great Comic-Strip Artists*. Abbeville, 1989.

Robinson, Jerry. *The Comics*. Berkley, 1974.

Seldes, George. *Lords of the Press*. Julian Messner, 1938.

Sheridan, Martin. *Comics and Their Creators*. Hale, Cushman & Flint, 1942.

Steinbrunner, Chris, and Otto Penzler, editors. *Encyclopedia of Mystery & Detection*. McGraw-Hill, 1976.

Waugh, Coulton. *The Comics*. Macmillan, 1947.

Index

Page numbers in *italic* refer to illustrations.